Landscapes of Urban Memory

The Sacred and the Civic in India's High-Tech City

Smriti Srinivas

Globalization and Community / Volume 9
University of Minnesota Press
Minneapolis • London

307.760954
S77L

All photographs reproduced in this book were taken by the author.

Published by the University of Minnesota Press
111 Third Avenue South, Suite 290
Minneapolis, MN 55401-2520
http://www.upress.umn.edu

Library of Congress Cataloging-in-Publication Data

Srinivas, Smriti.
    Landscapes of urban memory : the sacred and the civic in India's high-tech city / Smriti Srinivas.
        p.   cm. — (Globalization and community ; v. 9)
    Includes bibliographical references and index.
    ISBN 0-8166-3615-X (HC : alk. paper) — ISBN 0-8166-3616-8 (PB : alk. paper)
        1. High technology industries—India—Bangalore.   2. Urban beautification—India—Bangalore.   3. Hinduism—Social aspects—India—Bangalore.   I. Title.   II. Series.
    HC440.H53 S65   2001
    307.76'0954—dc21   2001000492

Printed in the United States of America on acid-free paper

The University of Minnesota is an equal-opportunity educator and employer.

12 11 10 09 08 07 06 05 04 03 02 01   10 9 8 7 6 5 4 3 2 1

Contents

Note on Transliteration
and Translation

This book is a translation at many levels: it refers to materials not only from different fields and disciplines, but also from different languages. In the interests of its audience, I have not used a scholarly system of transliteration for Kannada, Sanskrit, Tamil, Telugu, or Urdu words, but rather have chosen the most common and recognizable English forms. This is true for the proper names of individuals, places, deities, communities, and so on, and also for common nouns. I italicize those common nouns derived from an Indian language when used frequently in the text, such as *shakti*, or when first referred to, such as fort *(kote)*, or for texts such as the *Mahabharata*, but not for proper nouns such as "Karaga." I do not italicize those words that have become familiar to an English-speaking audience (such as "guru"). An occasional non-Indian, non-English word or a book title is italicized. I have taken the liberty of creating plural forms of Indian words by adding "s" to the ends of words, such as "Tigalas" from "Tigala." Most of these are proper nouns. I do not use diacritical marks, which are cumbersome for those who are not familiar with South Asian studies or languages.

The translation and transcription of the oral epic in chapter 6 is from a recording I made in 1996 during its recitation. I am deeply indebted to Mrs. Nirmala Sarma, who translated and transcribed the *Karaga Purana*. The epic is presented in the same order as the prose and song sections during the recitation, but in the interests of readability I have not included the transcript of the original Telugu and Tamil.

List of Illustrations

Maps

List of Tables

Abbreviations

BCC   Bangalore City Corporation

BDA   Bangalore Development Authority

BMPB   Bangalore Metropolitan Planning Board

BMRDA   Bangalore Metropolitan Region Development Authority

CDP   Comprehensive Development Plan for Bangalore (approved in 1984; revision approved in 1995)

KUIDFC   Karnataka Urban Infrastructure Development and Finance Corporation

ODP   Outline Development Plan for Bangalore (approved in 1972)

Acknowledgments

This book was written in many cities, in the context of several conversations, and through the generous support of a number of institutions and persons. It is a pleasure to remember them all.

I received a research grant for the project Cults, Charisma, and Modernity from the Institute for Social and Economic Change (ISEC), Bangalore, in 1995, while I worked there as an assistant professor. I would like to thank Dr. P. V. Shenoi and Dr. G. K. Karanth for their support during my years at ISEC. I would also like to acknowledge the financial support of the India Foundation for the Arts, Bangalore, for the project Draupadi's Story: Symbolism and Practice in the Karaga Performance, from 1996 to 1997. In December 1995, I organized a conference, "Religious Imagination and Practices in the City," supported by the Goethe Institute (Max Muller Bhavan) and ISEC in Bangalore. Both of these projects and the conference laid the foundation for the present book. I would also like to thank and remember Professor M. N. Srinivas, who in 1995 suggested to me that the Karaga performance was central to Bangalore and encouraged me to study it. I deeply regret that he did not live to see this book.

The interest and assistance of so many members of the Tigala community in Bangalore in producing this book were truly generous. In particular, I would like to thank M. Abhimanyu, Mr. Adiseshaiah, E. Krishna Narayana, K. Lakshmana, T. M. Manoharan, the family of S. M. Munivenkatappa, L. Narendra Babu, Ramaswamy Naicker, V. Ramaswamy, S. Srinivas, S. Tyagaraja, and Shri Venkataswamappa and his family. I would also like to thank devotees at other shrines in Bangalore: Mr. Dhananjaya, Mr. Khuddus Sahib, Mr. Krishnappa Reddy, Mr. Nissar Ahmed, and Mr. Pilla Krishnappa. Subinspector Indira and my research assistant, Shaji, also assisted me in many ways during my fieldwork in 1996 and 1997. I am very grateful to Mrs. Nirmala Sarma for translating the oral epic for me in 1996. Vinay Baindur at Citizens Voluntary Initiative for the City (CIVIC), Bangalore, was an inexhaustible source of information about the city. Shubha Ramnath not only scoured the newspapers for items about bodies of water and green spaces in the city, but is a wonderful friend.

During 1997–98, I was awarded a Rockefeller Humanities Fellowship by the International Center for Advanced Studies (ICAS), Project on Cities and Urban Knowledges, New York University, for my research project Cities of the Past and Cities of the Future: Modeling Community and Space in the Metropolis of Bangalore, India. The year spent in New York City was a very stimulating one: I benefited greatly from the Friday seminars and other conversations at ICAS as well as from the excitement of life in Greenwich Village. I am very grateful to Thomas Bender, Michael Gilsenan, and Barbara Kirshenblatt-Gimblett for reading, sharing information for, and encouraging the writing of this book. I was fortunate to meet Farha Ghannem, Robin Hicks, Meskerem Brhane, and Geoffrey Rogers in New York and to have their companionship during my years there.

A Mellon Fellowship at the Department of Sociology, University of Maryland, College Park, supported not only a project for analyzing my data on family genealogies in the Himalayan region of Ladakh, but also the extensive rewriting of this book during 1998–99. I am grateful to Sonalde Desai for the time, space, and friendship to work on this project during that year. In Washington, D.C., Stefan Bauschmid, Pat Edwards, Kalpana Prakash, and Anand Venkaswamy made life while writing less lonely. Alf Hiltebeitel at George Washington University carefully read parts of my book, made many key suggestions, and deeply enriched my study with his own work on the Draupadi cult. I would also like to thank Fred Smith at the University of Iowa for reading and commenting on various chapters of this book.

My friends and family have lovingly supported me all these years. I have been inspired by the conversations, intellectual projects, and courage of May Joseph, Srilata Raman, Shiv Visvanathan, and V. Geetha. I want to especially thank Sudha Menon for her encouragement of this work during its formative stages and for her presence in my life. This book could not have been completed without James Heitzman, whose scholarship, criticism, companionship, and labor fed into this work in innumerable ways. Animal lovers will understand the sentiment with which I remember the companionship of my dog Gosh, who died in 1998. My parents and sister have sustained, endured, and encouraged me in so many ways, and their own paths have been an inspiration and example to me. To all of them I dedicate this book.

Introduction

Moving through the City under a Full Moon

It was the middle of April 1995. The night was balmy, compared to the oppressive heat of the day, because the monsoons had not yet begun to lash Bangalore City. Outside the Dharmaraja Temple in the older portion of the city, there was neither a seat to be found nor place to stand as crowds of people jostled and pushed to get a view of the "Karaga" procession as it emerged from the temple.[1] Leaning against a tree facing the temple, I tried desperately to keep awake, for now it was almost 2:00 A.M. The sky was thick with people perched on balconies, walls of compounds, and roofs of houses and stores. Once in a while, a murmur of excitement would pass through the crowd: "The Karaga will leave the temple in an hour!" While minutes and hours went by with agonizing slowness, some people vacated their seats near me to walk down the streets of the area and visit other temples or simply the numerous hotels catering to the thousands milling around.

Suddenly, there was a flurry of movement as the spectators parted to let the chief guest, the minister of home affairs, P. G. R. Scindia, move through the throng to sit on a special chair directly in front of the temple entrance. His presence rapidly ceased to be a focus of interest. Within half an hour, gunshots were fired and the temple doors opened to let the sword-bearing Virakumaras—the "hero-sons"—rush through the spectators. These hero-sons, protectors of the goddess Draupadi, pounded down the main road. In their midst, barely visible to those sitting or standing at street level, was a male priest dressed in a turmeric-colored sari carrying a huge floral arrangement made of jasmine on his head under which sat the "Karaga," the symbol of the goddess's power. He held a curved dagger in his right hand and a sacred staff in his left. A cheer went up as people jostled, some to get closer to the Karaga and others to move away, partly in awe and partly in fear of the goddess. Within moments, the procession of the priest and his protectors had moved down the temple road on its tour of the old city, visiting houses, shrines, and stores, the priest-as-goddess granting benediction in his wake and the hero-sons creating a powerful, mobile ring of protection around him.

Bangalore, the capital of Karnataka state, with a population of about six million, is today regarded as a center for high-technology research and production, the new "Silicon Valley" of India (see Map 1). The Karaga performance occurs in Bangalore annually over nine days in the month of March or April. The festival takes place in the older portion of the city, newer suburbs, and surrounding towns of the metropolis, attracting about 200,000 people on the final day alone. All the ritual players are "Vahnikula Kshatriyas," traditionally gardeners by occupation, who now also hold other occupational niches in Bangalore. Some of them are factory workers, some workers in the informal sector of the economy, whereas other members of the community ply a number of trades and include government servants and professionals. The key players, the hero-sons and the priest, undergo several rituals, penance, and a separation from the roles and positions of everyday life that allow them to transcend their persons in the drama of Draupadi and her protectors. The apex of the performance is the incarnation of Draupadi, the polyandrous wife of the five Pandava brothers of the *Mahabharata* epic, for a few days in the city.

According to two writers associated with the Vahnikula Kshatriya community, in the seventeenth century the king of the Mysore region (in which Bangalore is situated) called a convention of scholars to establish the scriptural basis of the performance.[2] One scholar stated that the word "Karaga" referred to two terms: "kara," meaning "hand," and "ga," meaning "that which is held." Since the Karaga—which refers to a water pot in Kannada, the official language of Karnataka state—is carried in the left hand of the priest on the day of its "birth," the festival is called the "Karaga." Another opined, perhaps in deference to the king, that the Karaga was the female principle of divinity *(shakti)* and indeed a form of the tutelary deity of the royal family. Today, it is commonly believed by many of Bangalore's citizens that the Karaga *shakti,* which is invoked after secret rituals in the form of an earthen pot, is Draupadi, seen in this performance as a goddess. In consequence of a promise made by Draupadi to the Vahnikula Kshatriya community, she manifests herself every year. On the final day of the festivities, Draupadi is married to Arjuna, one of the Pandava brothers, and the idols of the two are taken in a procession through the city's streets in a

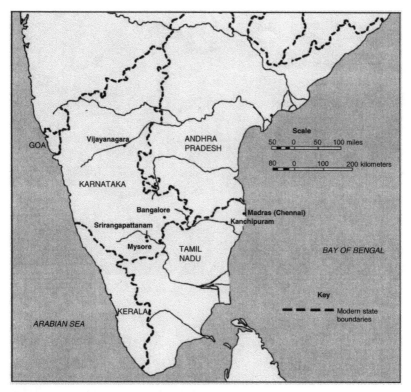

Map 1. The south Indian region and Bangalore.

chariot (see Figure 1). The priest, now carrying the Karaga on his head, is clothed in a wedding sari and also wears expensive jewelry, bracelets, and flowers. The priest and Draupadi *shakti* become a conjoint unit and are both referred to as the "Karaga." Quite often, the performance itself is called the Karaga because it is centered on the earthen pot. In order, therefore, to avoid confusion of these various meanings of the term, the word "Karaga" is used in this book to refer to the sacred pot embodying the goddess's power and to the priest when he is carrying the pot and is identified with it. The performance as a whole is referred to as the Karaga *jatre*, meaning, in Kannada, a periodic festival in honor of a deity—usually associated with the movement of a chariot carrying the image of the deity—and the people gathered for this purpose.[3] The man designated to be the bearer of the Karaga is called the Karaga priest *(pujari)*.[4]

When this study was first conceived, images of the festival were vivid in my mind: the vibrant public spectacle of the procession; the crowds gathered under the full moon; the city, awake through the night, transformed

Figure 1. The chariot carrying images of Draupadi and Arjuna moves through the streets.

into a sea of sparkling lights; and chariots from different temples moving through the streets. Although considered a sacred event because of the long-awaited appearance of the goddess, the festival also bore a carnivalesque spirit, and certain kinds of inversions were visible: the goddess was a man dressed in women's clothing, and the city, a bustling industrial and software metropolis, became a fairground. The performance itself created a cultural space within which many kinds of genres were narrated, performed, and practiced. It was only with time that it became clear to me that the performance as a whole bears a complex relationship to urban form in Bangalore. Not only is space in the city symbolic in the performance in several ways, but the symbolic is also spatialized in various formations. Within this context, I began to ask how communities construct the realm of the urban and the city as normative worlds.

Constructing a Language for the Metropolis

Many of the concerns expressed in this book stem from the realization that it is necessary to go beyond the existing work on religious traditions and practices in cities, both in India and elsewhere. There has been a theoretical neglect of the myriad forms and practices that are embedded in the processes of urbanization, not all of which have resulted in the creation of communal identities or violence, which are the themes of much academic discourse about cities today. Urban sociology in (and of) India is still a field reconstituting itself. In part, this is because much of the early energy of Indian sociology had been directed to rural India, especially in the years after independence, when concerns about the economic and cultural transformation of the rural and tribal landscape permeated social science research. There is also a definitional problem that haunted some scholars, which is not merely one of chronological separation or of overlap between "modern," "colonial," and other layers of Indian cities. D. F. Pocock (1960) alluded to this in an early paper in which he claimed that the distinction between urban and rural sociologies was superfluous, because the city and the village in India demonstrated a continuity of form. Sociologists studying the urban in India have struggled with this issue as well as the interaction between supralocal institutions and the urban milieu.[5] Most urban research up until the latter half of the 1980s, in the shadow of the developmental state, concerned itself with the now-familiar themes. These included demographic and socioecological parameters of cities, provision of services, industrialization, migration and caste, and the "three Ps"—planning, political change, and poverty in the postcolonial dispensation.[6] Other lenses for viewing the urban have slowly begun to emerge since the end of the 1980s—gender, popular culture, cinema, aging, urban disaster, colonialism, science, sustainability, selfhood, archaeology, and architecture.[7] Works dealing directly with single cities, focusing on state capitals (Chandigarh), colonial cities (Bombay [Mumbai]), older "walled" cities (Hyderabad), and medieval and ancient centers (Banaras, Vijayanagara) and their transformations have also grown in number.[8] These add to the compass of earlier academic literature that saw the urban as a template of religious cosmology or focused on temple cities or ritual sites (Banaras).[9] Some of the most interesting writing on cities and their networks is fictional and includes novels exploring family history, medical mysteries, and the taut relationships between sexuality and politics, to mention a few themes.[10]

There is reason to take urban sociology forward, if only because of the sheer significance of urban centers in India today. Although fifteen years ago less than a third of the gross domestic product of the country was produced in cities, today this figure is almost 60 percent. And whereas at the beginning of the twentieth century India's urban population was less than 11 percent of its total population, by 1951 this figure had increased to about 18 percent, and by 1991 the Census of India indicated that it was about 26 percent. According to estimates, by the year 2001, when India's population is likely to be over one billion, the proportion of the population living in urban areas will be about 35 percent. In 1901, according to the

Census of India, there were 1,811 urban areas in India, and only one city had a population of over one million (Calcutta, which was also the second-largest city in the British Empire after London). In 1951, there were 2,795 urban centers and five "metro" cities with over a million people; in 1991, the Census of India enumerated 3,609 urban centers and twenty-four metro cities. The projection is that by 2001 there will be about forty metro cities with a population of one million or more.[11]

Faced with the scale and richness of India's urban experience today, there are a number of directions in which the study of the city may proceed. Given the transformation of many contemporary urban locations and the growing mobility of persons and resources, there has emerged a heightened sense of affirmation of religious sites for different communities and a reenchantment of the world of the city. Again, the language of the modern polis has become a tool for the refashioning of a sense of the self and the community, religious or otherwise. In certain situations, the city and encounters within the city have made some traditions more exclusive and narrowly "religious." In other contexts, the appropriations of concepts and practices from other spaces and traditions have created new and more inclusive cultural forms. All this means, among other things, that the realm of the urban has a content that is not merely amenable to a language of individual rights, liberal philosophy, urban planning, economics, or demography. Whichever line of research we may pursue, it is important to recognize that the city in India and the multilayeredness of urban experience are legitimate and urgent objects of theoretical inquiry.

Bangalore, where I did fieldwork and research for this book, chiefly in 1994–97, is a city in which I had previously lived for a year or so at a time. The first period was in 1977–78, when the Congress Party's rule in the central government in the mid-1970s and a period of repression ("the Emergency") had ended and the Janata Party had formed the government for the first time in India's history. My father, after a career as a diplomat, had moved our family to Bangalore from Beijing, ending a three-year stay there and the peripatetic life that I had led as a child in various other Asian metropolises, including Kuala Lumpur. Bangalore was very cosmopolitan even then, known primarily as a science city, and had come to be home to numerous expatriate Indians from East Africa, Malaysia, and Hong Kong, who saw it as a place for relocating business opportunities or fresh endeavors. By this time, it had long shaken off the sleepy, somewhat provincial feel that Mysore, a neighboring city, still has in spite of being the capital of a regional kingdom in the past. The second period that I lived in Bangalore was in 1982–83, some years before the city was launched as the new "Silicon

Valley" of India and came to be dotted with software firms. I was an under-graduate at that time, and Bangalore's colleges were filled with a number of Iranian students, as well as Jordanians, Palestinians, and other West Asians (chiefly men), fleeing repressive regimes in their own countries or seeking moments of respite from military duty, war, or marriage. This was also a time when a number of Indians working in the Persian Gulf area were be-ginning to remit money home to families in the city, who came to own all kinds of electronic appliances, from sophisticated music systems to wash-ing machines and televisions, which were still novelties in many homes.

In retrospect, it seems as if most of my time was spent in the newer parts of the city and in the Cantonment area on its northeastern side, where these types of transnational networks were more apparent. What I remember about these two periods, however, was that despite the pres-ence of multiple life-worlds in the city, they intersected in some types of public spaces—for instance, in the main shopping districts, cinema halls, colleges, offices, parks, and cricket stadiums, many of them creations of the developmental state. Even my mother's family, who had lived in the older sections of Bangalore since about the early part of the twentieth cen-tury and moved in somewhat different circles from the groups that I have mentioned, converged with other communities within these arenas.

It was only when I was doing the fieldwork for this book, while I was beginning work as a faculty member at the Institute for Social and Eco-nomic Change in 1994, that I came to understand better the nature of the various social arenas of the city and their spatial conjunction and disjunc-tion. The research institute where I worked was set up in the early 1970s on land that was on the outermost western periphery of the city, although it drew many of its personnel from within the city limits. I had never even traveled to that area until I joined the faculty of the institute, by which time urban sprawl had overtaken this region known as "Nagarbhavi," or Snake Well. Houses and apartment buildings, many of them unauthorized, stood crowded on various hillocks encircling older villages in that area and were characterized by poor road, water, and sewage connections. En route to the institute on a bus that ran on a somewhat irregular schedule, besides houses, I would pass an entire dental college crowded into two floors of a rather small building, a local village market, and a well-known law univer-sity, and would see, on a distant hillock beyond my institute, an agricul-tural college. This kind of patchwork suburban growth was characteristic of other parts of the city as well.

Between 1994 and 1995, with a grant from the institute, I began field-work on the nature of urban religiosity in Bangalore with a project entitled

"Cults, Charisma, and Modernity: The Constituency of Faith in South India."[12] This was really my first "urban" research engagement. My previous
fieldwork had been done in Ladakh, a Himalayan frontier region in the
Jammu and Kashmir state among Muslim and Buddhist communities.[13] I
had also briefly done some fieldwork in coastal and dryland areas of Karnataka as part of a large collaborative project looking at the impact of economic liberalization processes among the rural poor. The urban religiosity
project examined three popular cults in Bangalore: the Infant Jesus cult in
a poor suburb of the city, a cult based at a Sufi Muslim shrine in the Cantonment area, and the cult of Sai Baba in a middle- and upper-class suburb
of the metropolis. These cults used public spaces that were quite different
from the cinema halls or the parks that I had frequented and provided realms
of convergence between other constituencies in the city. The shrines themselves often attracted overlapping groups, or, more interestingly, had symbols that bore a family resemblance.

A year after I witnessed my first Karaga procession, I received a grant
from the India Foundation for the Arts, Bangalore, to study the Karaga *jatre*. In January 1996, I began my more sustained documentation of the performance, first by conducting interviews with temple officials, and then
through participant-observation of the performance between March and
May 1996 in Bangalore and other sites. After the end of the performance
cycle in 1996, I carried out detailed interviews with other members of the
Vahnikula Kshatriya community and collected secondary materials about
the performance. I also documented the Karaga *jatre* in 1997 and completed
more fieldwork until August 1997. The report submitted to the foundation
was framed as an "ethnography of performance."[14] Even at first glance, it
was clear that the Karaga *jatre* was an event that included elements that
were not merely those of "dramatic art," but also those of spring festivals,
street parades, and sacred theaters. I paid detailed attention to the ritual
process itself, trying to bridge the divide between sociology, anthropology,
and performance studies by focusing on the relationship between cultural
forms and social history.

On a Rockefeller Fellowship to New York University in 1997–98 at the
Project on Cities and Urban Knowledges located at the International Center for Advanced Studies, I began to connect my earlier fieldwork on the
charismatic cults with the Karaga *jatre* and to situate them both spatially
and temporally within the metropolis. Some of Bangalore's historical connections stretch backward into the last great empire in south India in the
sixteenth century, whereas others intersect more contemporaneously with
British colonial rule, migrations from neighboring regions, and the city's

place within a transnational economy. Cult events, performances, and practices of the body related to them weave in and out of these numerous histories. Memories of place, like my own of the city, also follow these cultural pathways. These recollections of place, which I term "landscapes of urban memory," are not static even if they are locally marked and are modes of cultural self–invention intimately tied to historical, spatial, somatic, and ritual practices.[15] These landscapes are a means of accessing how various strata of society and different communities construct the metropolitan world. Processions by different strata in the city dedicated to deities, rallies, marches, parades, or royal visits create maps, narratives, and other kinetic and oral constructions of movements and migrations within the city that are symptomatic of these landscapes. This book examines the landscape of urban memory that emerges from the Karaga *jatre* dedicated to the goddess Draupadi, a performance that today is one of the largest civic rituals in Bangalore.

Landscapes of urban memory are tied to a triadic geography of the city that includes public realms of the sacred, markets, and the marketing of icons of the city.[16] Different urban strata, mercantile groups, factory workers, bureaucrats, and scientists in Bangalore produce collective maps and readings of the city, different landscapes that center on specific shrines and their arenas. For the gardeners who have become workers in the informal sector of the economy and members of the petite bourgeoisie, who are the subjects of this book, the landscape is tied to a horticultural, bazaar, and informal economy within the city centered on the Dharmaraja Temple in the old marketplace. For the managerial, scientific, and administrative strata that form the main constituencies of the cult of Sathya Sai Baba, which revolves around the main ashram of Sathya Sai Baba in the neighboring state of Andhra Pradesh as well as another ashram situated on the outskirts of Bangalore, the landscape is tied to a formal economy and bureaucratic apparatus as well as to constructs of a pan-Indian civilization and international networks. There is also a larger context for both these types of flows: the marketing of various symbols of the city. The city constantly signals its emergence and the new forms of creativity that arise in its space by the circulation of various images of and discourses about it and its communities, such as those of the "garden city" or the "science city."

The postulation of a landscape of memory questions the assumption that oral, somatic, and kinetic traditions of relating to urban places have been replaced or dominated by sites for the artificial production of regional and national memories—museums, political and religious monuments, nature parks, and recreation sites.[17] It is not that the former type is historically prior to the latter or that there is an essence "behind" things, but rather that if we construct a genealogy for representations of either sort, we find a diversity of sources. In other words, the formation process cannot be seen in terms of a historical telos, as if there was some kind of true memory to access beyond more recent layers of the civic unconscious. In the process of constructing the urban, older sites are forgotten, their representations censored or recombined with nascent ones through political action, ritual, collective desire, or fantasy to produce different configurations of meaning. The "past" and the "present" are both contemporaneous, and memory is dependent on current social practices. Whether landscapes of urban memory emerge from the annals of city planning, the workings of capital, or the practices of different communities within the city, they require control, classification, and naturalization of representations of space; memory, concerned with time, is intimately tied to space.[18]

What Is the Civic?

Although cities such as Bangalore, Dar es Salaam, Cairo, Kuwait, and Bangkok have become sites of global flows of capital and labor in the last few decades, these were, for many decades and centuries before that, embedded in several transnational circuits and were destinations for various populations. This is particularly apparent in the case of port cities, but can be demonstrated for inland cities as well.[19] Socialism was one such circuit, as was trade with the Persian Gulf and the Southeast Asian and African coasts. The roles that London, Tokyo, and New York play on the world stage and the sometimes economistic arguments about the globalization process seem to have obscured these connections and several temporal layers of global circuits.[20] Further, for many theorists of the twentieth-century urban experience the "first-world city" holds a special place, and along with others is read as representing a stage of late capitalism, with culture serving the processes of capital accumulation.[21] At the other end of the spectrum from these global theories of urbanization that tend to "empty" space are studies that emerge from many postcolonial perspectives. These employ a spatialized language that is deeply sensitive to heterogeneity, but they tend not to focus so much on the "lived" urban spaces of postcolonials, concentrating instead on texts, colonial discourses, master narratives, and their imaginaries.[22] Studies by some other scholars have shown instead that constructions of both locality and globality have emerged from existing cultural milieus and older histories and demonstrate the continuing agency of communities in this process.[23] In many cases, the assertions of new legitimacies and the delegitimations of earlier constructs have signaled the emergence of new manifestos about the civic. The issue for many cities is not so much whether the scale and the flow of persons, media commodities, and capital have accelerated in recent decades, but whether there are cultural aesthetics and ethics related to movements, migrations, and other protocols that can be adequately theorized.

One of the ways in which teleological and economistic arguments can be put aside and we can begin to examine the diversity of modes of constructing the urban is to reexamine formulations of the civic. This term actually includes a range of sometimes separate and sometimes overlapping ideas of the nature of the polis, publics, the public sphere, and civil society and does not always emerge from discussions of an urban location. In some arguments, civic virtue is defined on the basis of the classical European republican tradition that separates the private realm of necessity and the public realm of freedom; this bifurcation serves to exclude most persons in the polis.[24] Other definitions are rooted essentially in an eighteenth-century understanding of the Greek polis and in post–Enlightenment constructions in which the sacred becomes increasingly part of the intimate sphere, whereas the public sphere and the secular realm become conjoint.[25] In related discussions, most forcefully formulated by Habermas, the idea of the bourgeois public sphere (examples of which seem to be drawn chiefly from European capital cities) is linked to that of civil society. Civil society, an arena of organization and practice that is outside the state, somewhat separate from the private realm of the family, and not equivalent to the private market, can include a range of institutions, literary, educational, and economic. It creates the ground for a public sphere of private people who assemble to engage in a rational-critical discourse about matters of public concern and common interest. Perspectives and practices of public life and political participation are realized, ideally, not through status or hierarchy, but through a degree of universality and dialogue.[26] Although this inclusivity is the theoretical norm, in reality the distinction between civil society and the state, the private and the public, is difficult to make.

The formulation of the public sphere in terms outlined earlier has not been particularly sensitive to the gendered character of the public sphere, identity politics, the proletariat, social movements, and the role of religion in creating or transforming the public sphere. As some scholars argue, not only do we need to accept that there are multiple public spheres, but we also need to clearly articulate their limits and internal dynamics and the communicative relationships within and beyond them to other arenas, especially under late capitalism.[27] There are also sophisticated "immanent" critiques of the idea of rationality rooted in the historical experience of Western Europe and liberal philosophies.[28] This idea also bears interrogation by recent developments in historiography, whether they question scientific reason or posit multiple rationalities or rewrite narratives about modernity, reflected only in part in many sites in Western Europe and elsewhere.[29]

My own objection rests on the understanding that public discourse and being "public" need not be premised on the model of speech or the printed word, but can also be performative, rooted in different geographies of urban space. In this book I ask, What are the constituents of discourses about being citizens? How are political communities and publics in the late-twentieth-century city constructed? What are the kinds of public spaces and practices that support or exclude such discourses and communities? The answers to these questions will point us to formulations of the civic and being citizens that are deeply embedded in local, ritual, oral, somatic, and spatial practices of groups within the city. Urban memory, the body, performative modalities, cultural identities, the ritual terrain, aesthetics, and topography are as much part of constructions of political community and of claims to and debates about public rights as are the relationships between the state, transnational institutions, and civil society. These formulations are not necessarily parochial or tied only to the life-world of a single group, but can also become the vehicle of civic communication for others. It is possible to demonstrate, first, that sacred arenas offer models of the civic through articulations of landscapes of urban memory, and second, that the secular, in many cases, is a staging of deeply ritualized actions. The first process is the concern of this book.

Civic Rituals in the New "Silicon Valley"

The Many Cities of Bangalore

Kempe Gowda, a local military chief who owed allegiance to the Vijayana-gar Empire, founded Bangalore, then called "Bengaluru," in 1537.[1] At that time, the urban center consisted of a mud fort with a settlement inside or alongside it, quadrisected by two main streets. Inside the fort and settle-ment were areas apportioned to different communities and social strata. Surrounding the fort was a moat, as well as separate farming and trading communities, and interwoven with these were shrines, forests, and bodies of water that gradually came to be linked to the fort and the new settle-ment through a variety of relationships. The presence of a single central temple at the core does not seem to be characteristic of this urban pattern, although a number of shrines were patronized or built by Kempe Gowda.[2] Instead, a fort surrounding or abutting a settlement, with various gates—perhaps seven or eight in the case of Kempe Gowda's fort—and bodies of water around it, seems to be the usual mode of urban planning during this historical period.

A type of urban organization with some of these elements seems to have been in existence in other parts of south India even before Bangalore's founding. It was the result of a slow process of consolidation between the fourteenth and sixteenth centuries linked to military strongholds and tied to trading centers that began to cluster and situate themselves in these new urban environments.[3] These market and fort towns were a sign of ac-tive inland trade routes and the circulation of vast numbers of products. These towns stood as new formations in addition to sites such as Kanchipu-ram, which were also linked to coastal trade (see Map 1). It is possible that the ruler was supported both by taxes on these goods and by revenue derived from farmers in the countryside in which these fortified centers grew up. These urban sites were ruled by authorities variously called "Dandanayakas" (under the Chalukya and Hoysala Dynasties in the Kannada country), "Nayakas" (under the Kakatiyas in the Telugu country and under the rulers of the Tamil country), or "Palaiyakkarars" (Tamil) and "Palegaras" (Kannada) when they were in charge of a single fortress. When the Vijayanagar Empire with its capital, Vijayanagara (see Map 1), became dominant between the fourteenth and the sixteenth century and penetrated much of south India, it incorporated many of these regional kingdoms, fortresses, and polities. The local rulers (more or less powerful), such as Palegara Kempe Gowda, tended to have their own power bases and juridical functions, as well as the control of rather cosmopolitan armies, and they were tied in a variety of relationships to the royal court. These martial heroes appear to have been an adventurous, mobile elite with accumulated wealth who developed a quasi-autonomous state by invoking loyalties and linkages to a distant king even while developing horizontal autonomy. It was believed that a deity or deities had authorized the formation of the state or had significant symbolic roles to play in it.[4] Kempe Gowda's faith in the deity Gangadhareswara is often cited, especially after he invoked the wrath of the Vijayanagar ruler who withdrew his blessings from Kempe Gowda's endeavors after the local ruler established a mint of his own, obviously a sign of mobile resources. The Palegara was apparently thrown into prison for five years, whereas earlier he had received a number of villages from the emperor.[5] He eventually bought his way out of imprisonment by offering a huge sum to the emperor in exchange for freedom when the empire was confronted with the threat of a Muslim sultanate alliance from the middle Deccan.

After the fall of the Vijayanagar Empire in 1564, a number of Palegaras and other rulers in the south asserted their sovereignty, although the empire's control of vast regions had not been total by any means. Kempe Gowda II was soon involved in several military campaigns against his neighbors. The old settlement, the "City" as it is called today and as it is referred to in this book, was eventually besieged and conquered by military powers from the north. The Deccan Bijapur army attacked the City of Bangalore in 1637. In 1687, the armies of Aurangazeb, the Mughal ruler from Delhi, invaded it and occupied it for three years. Thereafter, it was sold to the local ally of the Mughals, Chikka Deva Raja Wodeyar of Mysore (see Map 1), in 1690. There were some architectural changes: although the mud fort with the moat built by Kempe Gowda still existed, a new fort separated from the settlement grew up on its south side. This was built by the Mysore king's governor of Bangalore, Doddayya, and had a temple within. The shifts in the fortunes of the City also led to the in-migration of various cultural groups—for instance, speakers of Tamil and Marathi from neighboring regions and new Muslim communities. There was also a clearer demarcation of zones within the settlement for trade by specific communities in various goods, such as rice (today, Akkipet) and ornaments (today, Nagarthapet), as well as for general trade (in Chickpet) and petty merchandizing (in Dodpet). It is estimated that the settlement had 10,000 to 15,000 inhabitants.[6]

Chikka Deva Raja's successors were generally weak, and a commander of the army, Haider Ali (1722–82), captured power and received Bangalore as his personal endowment from the king in 1759. The political scenario had also altered by this time. Haider Ali, and later his son, Tippu Sultan (1753–99), engaged in four major battles with the British East India Company, along with other allies and powers such as the French. In 1799, after the final Anglo-Mysore war with Lord Cornwallis, the British governor general who came to India after his somewhat ignominious losses in North America, Tippu Sultan fell and the City was handed over to the Wodeyar kings. In 1809, the British moved to Bangalore from Srirangapattanam (see Map 1) and set up the "Cantonment" near Halsur, about four miles northeast of the City. The modern expansion of Bangalore relates to this decision to move a regiment each of European cavalry and infantry to the Cantonment, with some administrative offices within the fort and some in the City. The new center, which grew by absorbing several villages in the area, had its own municipal and administrative apparatus, although it was technically a British enclave within the territory of the Wodeyar kings. The British were largely centered at the port city of Madras (Chennai) (see Map 1).

"Bangalore" is, therefore, a term that has varied connotations today. Although from the sixteenth to the early nineteenth centuries it referred to the fort-settlement built by Kempe Gowda and embellished by his successors, after 1809 there existed a twin township. The dual political and legal nature of the area was recognized by the creation of separate municipal boards for Bangalore Town and Bangalore Cantonment in 1862.[7] Toward the end of the nineteenth century, the area of the City also began to expand. A number of "extensions" based on a grid plan were laid out, in part because of the growth of the population of the City, the problems of water and sanitation in it, and the plague epidemic of 1899–1900. About twenty-six surrounding villages were engulfed in this expansion.[8] In 1901, Bangalore (both the City and the Cantonment) covered an area of 74.72 square kilometers.[9] In 1949, the City and the Cantonment came together to form the Bangalore City Corporation, with fifty territorial divisions. In 1956, with the reorganization of state boundaries in India, it became the capital of the enlarged Mysore state, now called Karnataka. In 1991, the area of the Bangalore City Corporation was 200 square kilometers.[10] A more recent figure for the area of the Bangalore City Corporation, given in 1998, was 241 square kilometers.[11] The small towns and villages outside the City Corporation area have lost their independent status and, along with the City Corporation, are part of the "Bangalore Urban Agglomeration," which covers an area of about 357 square kilometers.[12] The "Bangalore Metropolitan Area" is the planning area designated under the Karnataka Town and Country Planning Act of 1961, covering 1,279 square kilometers.[13] In terms of territorial location, the Bangalore Metropolitan Area is part of the new Bangalore Urban District formed in 1986, which covers an area of 2,190 square kilometers.[14]

In addition to these different spatial entities, there are also a number of administrative and planning agencies in Bangalore that have somewhat separate jurisdictions (see Map 2). The City Improvement Trust had been formed in 1945 with its own City Planning Board prior to the founding of the Bangalore City Corporation in 1949. The state government constituted the Bangalore Development Authority (BDA) in 1976 to coordinate the activities of these two bodies. The BDA's jurisdiction covers the Bangalore Metropolitan Area. By the 1980s, however, it was clear that urbanization had spilled over these boundaries, and in 1986 the Bangalore Metropolitan Region Development Authority (BMRDA) was formed to coordinate the development of the entire region as a single unit, an area of about 8,662 square kilometers.[15] Heitzman (1999a, PE9–10) argues that the proliferation of agencies has created a complex planning scenario in the city. Not only are there several planning bodies (although the BMRDA is technically the highest in the hierarchy), but the state government has also established a number of agencies for the provision of services such as water and electricity, as well as industrial parks and estates. In 1992, the passage of the seventy-fourth Amendment to the Indian Constitution—the Nagarpalika Act—required the government of Karnataka to amend its own laws in order to create, among other things, district and metropolitan planning committees. According to Heitzman (1999a), from 1994 onward the government has been engaged in a process of redrawing the boundaries of electoral constituencies at the local level and defining the powers of local ward committees:

During this period the future of the BDA and the BMRDA and their relationship with either the service agencies or industrial development corporations remain uncertain, for their roles within the projected metropolitan council remained unknown and virtually undebated. BDA has accumulated a large staff and considerable power over its own planning area, but had a poor reputation and did not officially operate at the "metropolitan" level. In the immediate aftermath of the 74th Amendment's passage, BMRDA expected its own demise, but as time went on there were indications that the state government might rework it into some new form of metropolitan council. Meanwhile, there were three chief ministers of the state within a three-year period, resulting in a discontinuity of leadership (PE10).

After 1949, Bangalore witnessed a phenomenal increase in population that was a result of the migration of a number of new social groups into the city. In 1951, the population of the Bangalore Metropolitan Area was 991,000. By 1991, it had increased to 4,086,000, whereas the urban population of the district as a whole was only slightly greater than this figure. The Revised Comprehensive Development Plan of the city foresees a population of 5,800,000 by 2001 (see Table 1).[16] The composition of this population is extremely diverse. Already in the sixteenth century, Bangalore had speakers of Marathi, Telugu, and Tamil besides those who spoke Kannada. Bangalore's location in the central part of south India between four linguistic regions is a contributing factor to this speech diversity, and multilingualism is extremely common in the city. One of the central features of Bangalore district is that even though Kannada is the state language, according to the 1981 Census speakers of Kannada were only about a third of the population (35.45 percent). Speakers of Tamil (22.22 percent), Telugu (17.73 percent), and Urdu (12.50 percent) contributed to the varied linguistic profile of the district and the city.[17] The district also comprises a number of religious groups: according to the 1981 Census, Christians (6.35 percent), Muslims (13.27 percent), and a variety of Hindu sectarian groups (79.26 percent) create a highly diverse cultural situation.[18] Although there are residential clusters of certain religious or linguistic groups—for instance, a large number of Christian households in the Cantonment and a number of Muslim households near the old fort—it is difficult to distinguish areas in Bangalore purely on the basis of religion or caste. The older spatial twinning of the City and the Cantonment has disappeared. Much of the urban sprawl of the city occurred after the 1960s with the establishment of many

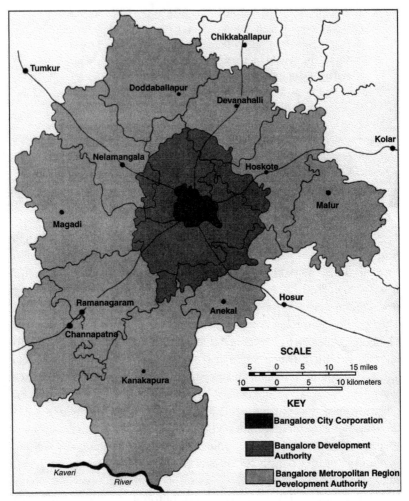

Map 2. The administrative jurisdictions within the Bangalore Metropolitan Region.

industrial estates and residential suburbs. The liberalization process of the Indian economy in the 1980s and 1990s, along with the establishment of a number of software companies, information-based industries, and multinational corporations, further altered the space of the city.

Before and after the New Silicon Valley

One must ask, therefore, What consequences have ensued from changes in the political economy of Bangalore for various spatial arenas and social

Table 1.
Decadal growth of population in Bangalore, 1901–2001

Year	Metropolitan area	Percentage increase	Corporation area	Percentage increase
1901	228,000	15.5	161,000	—
1911	260,000	14.5	192,000	19.2
1921	311,000	19.2	240,000	25.4
1931	396,000	27.5	308,000	29.1
1941	510,000	28.9	407,000	32.6
1951	991,000	94.0	779,000	91.6
1961	1,207,000	21.4	906,000	16.7
1971	1,664,000	37.0	1,422,000	56.9
1981	2,913,000	76.72	2,482,000	74.57
1991	4,086,000	40.27	2,650,000	6.77
2001	5,800,000	41.95	4,500,000	69.81

Source: Bangalore Development Authority 1995, 16.

strata? What are the factors that have contributed to its status today as a high-technology center? Two factors must be recognized immediately for even a partial understanding of the effects of Bangalore's position in the global economy, its external linkages, and its internal political and cultural networks. First, the penetration of global capital occurs in particular fields and has an uneven effect in various sites or sectors of the economy of a city. For example, it may exploit cheap labor pools (as in Bangkok), high-technology fields (as in Bangalore), or finance (as in Tokyo). Second, occupational strata and cultural groups in the city do not face such shifts, passively, but at different points in time and in different modes are implicated in networks, contests, and accommodations with local and national governments as well as multinational corporations. Bangalore, the "Silicon Valley" of India today, could be seen as partaking of the "informational mode of development" described by Manuel Castells.[19] Castells (1985 and 1989) describes New York and Los Angeles as characterized by a polarized growth accompanied by distinct social spheres that are primarily linked economically within the same functional unit. In Bangalore, however, the situation does not lend itself to this opaque generalization. The formal sector of the economy with the largest number of workers is probably still textiles; next in importance are the inducstries of the public sector and central and state government institutions.[20] Although the information industry is significant in Bangalore, to ignore other aspects of the city's economic history would result in a failure to understand the nature of various urban strata that have emerged from shifts in its production base in the last five decades or so. These shifts have included the decline of old industries and the growth of a surplus in the semiskilled labor force, the dynamism of high-technology industries that employ both professionals and low-paid workers with fewer skills, and the slower growth of the manufacturing sector, a large part of which is either small in scale or in the public sector. In addition, an expansion of contractual and semiformal service activities has been triggered by the economic dynamism of the city, particularly in consumer services, and the persistence of a large informal sector of the economy.

We may trace three major shifts in the political economy of Bangalore in the twentieth century.[21]

The Period of Textile Hegemony (1900–50)

The older production base of the city was comprised of trade in grains, fruits, vegetables, spices, and other products, because the area immediately around the city was agricultural or horticultural in nature. There were also household industries such as carpet manufacturing, basket making, pottery making, furniture production, metal work, printing, and saw, flour, and oil milling. Some large factories existed in the City and the Cantonment, although most of the early factories were located on the western outskirts of the City. The Mysore Chrome Tanning Company (established in 1908) and the Government Soap Factory (1918) were two of the factories built earliest. Most were established in the 1930s. The Mysore Industrial and Testing Laboratory (1931), the Government Porcelain Factory (1932), the Government Electric Factory (1934), Amco, Ltd. (1934), the Mysore Lamp Works (1936), the Mysore Tobacco Company (1937), Firebricks and Potteries, Ltd. (1937), Mysore Vegetable Oil Products (1938), and the Mysore Glass and Enamel Works (1939) were some of the major companies. All these industries and companies together employed about 3,932 persons around 1950.[22]

Up until the end of the 1940s, however, the economy of the city relied heavily on the textile industry. Textiles were produced in mills that came into existence in the late nineteenth and early twentieth centuries and included state-owned and private plants producing cotton, woolen, and silk goods. The first textile mill was the Bangalore Woolen, Cotton, and Silk Mills Company, Ltd., which was established in 1884 and employed about 7,486 people in 1950. The Mysore Spinning and Manufacturing Company, Ltd., established in 1894, employed 3,700 people, and the Minerva Mills, established in 1919, employed 3,100 persons about the same time.[23] In addition, thousands of smaller looms were owned by individuals and households, and an entire range of castes was associated with different stages of the production and marketing of textiles. This was the industry in which large proportions of the population of the city had varying degrees of financial and labor involvement. Weaving alone employed 12,990 persons, and there were nearly 8,000 looms in the city.[24]

By the end of the 1940s, spurred in part by the Second World War and government encouragement, a few other scientific and industrial organizations were set up—for instance, the Indian Institute of Science (1909), Hindustan Aircraft, Ltd. (1940), and the Radio and Electrical Manufacturing Company (1946). This type of industrial base was established easily because Bangalore was the first city in India to be electrified, because of British investment, and because the enlightened policies of the "diwans" (ministers who administered the city for the Wodeyar rulers) resulted in an early pattern of state sponsorship of projects. Technical education had also been sponsored by the state: a mechanical engineering, agricultural, and commercial school was established in 1913 in Hebbal on the city's outskirts. The University of Mysore also established a college in Bangalore in 1916. By 1950, there were nine colleges for general education, three engineering colleges, one medical college, one technological institute, and one agricultural college.[25]

Banking grew alongside industry and education: the Bank of Mysore (established 1913), the largest in the state, had an authorized capital of 2 million rupees about 1950, but there were many other cooperative banks serving particular merchant groups. Most of the banks clustered in the central business districts of the City area and the Cantonment. All this activity caused enormous growth in the population of the city, particularly through in-migration from surrounding states, one of the two major increases in that century. It also resulted in the spatial expansion of the city as workers in various factories began settling in their neighborhoods.

The Dominance of the Public Sector (1950–80)

In the 1950s and 1960s, the national government set up a number of public-sector institutions for research and production in Bangalore. What is significant about this period is the high level of government commitment to industry, research, funding, and infrastructure and the high level of labor participation from the city in these efforts in terms of permanent employment. This period also saw the intensification of employment in government bureaucracy, the administrations of state-run enterprises, and a number of educational institutions that had been created by the state government—for instance, Bangalore University and a number of technical, agricultural, and vocational colleges.

The establishment of engineering and electrical works set the tone of development for nearly three decades. These included public-sector giants such as Indian Telephone Industries (1950), Hindustan Machine Tools (1953), Bharat Electronic, Ltd. (1954), and the New Government Electric Factory (1961), as well as private concerns such as Kirloskar Systems (1962). By 1994, there were thirty-one medium- and large-scale electrical industries in Bangalore district, all established between 1948 and 1981; nine medium- and large-scale machine tools industries, all set up between 1953 and 1983; eleven industrial machinery plants that had come into being between 1953 and 1983; and seventeen metallurgical industries established between 1946 and 1984.[26]

The creation of a number of industrial estates where power and other infrastructural inputs such as land were provided by the state led to the location of production in compact areas on the periphery of the city, such as Peenya. Much of the labor force was drawn from the city, and these workers and managers traveled daily to their places of work. The number of research institutions, many of them controlled by the national government, also grew. Hindustan Aircraft, Ltd., was a precursor of many other institutions that were established in the next three decades, including the Indian Space Research Organization, the Defense Research and Development Organization, the Central Power Research Institute, and others. Although these institutions were, more often than not, located on the periphery of the existing metropolis, subsidiary construction, subcontracting, and service activities related to these primary nodes grew both within the city and on its outskirts. In small homes and workshops in the City and the Cantonment, where the hum of machines can be still heard, and near many industrial estates, were a range of two- to twenty-person outfits that produced screws, machine tools, plastic goods, and other products. For instance, the number of small-scale industries registered in 1983 was 9,959 in Bangalore Urban District.[27]

The textile industry continued to be important to the city in spite of these developments: between 1947 and 1983, fourteen medium- and large-scale textile mills and related companies such as garment-making companies were added to Bangalore district, of which many were located at Bangalore.[28] Further, it must not be forgotten that the informal economy of the city—including people working as hawkers, carpenters, petty shopkeepers, drivers, construction workers, and weavers—employed more people than all the formal sectors combined.

Due in part to these processes, the second major spurt in Bangalore's population growth in that century occurred during the 1970s. The city witnessed the burgeoning of the middle classes associated with the formal-sector industries, national research organizations, scientific establishments, and state bureaucracy. Even in 1991, the five largest public-sector industries officially employed more than 81,000 persons in Bangalore plants.[29] The Indian army is a major and stable presence in Bangalore, where it not only has an important southern military base, but also owns a large amount of prime land within the city for its officers, troops, and activities. Although the defense strata are drawn primarily from outside the city, they are a fairly permanent aspect of the city's population. These various occupational groups had an impact on the space of the city after 1950. A few large residential neighborhoods, mainly middle-class in constituency, had been inaugurated about 1948—for instance, Jayanagar and Rajajinagar. These grew rapidly in the decades that followed, and additional neighborhoods such as Indiranagar (which adjoined the new "Defense Colony") also developed from the late 1960s onward.

The Emergence of a Vibrant Private Sector (1980 to the Present)

Even before the 1980s, Bangalore had a pool of technical, educational, and research skills that led to its characterization as India's premier science city. By the 1980s, although the stage was set for global linkages on an extensive scale, it was also set for the establishment and development of local microelectronics, information-based, and software industries in Bangalore, such as Infosys Consultants and Informatics. By the end of the decade, with the liberalization of the Indian economy and the removal of certain restrictions to imports and licensing, the microcomputer revolution occurred in Bangalore. The concept of Bangalore as the new Silicon Valley developed in part through these changes as well as through the concessions to technology parks announced by the government in 1985. The establishment of symbiotic relationships became more frequent, with the high-technology private sector providing software outsourcing for multinational companies. One of the first such multinationals to set up a base in Bangalore was Texas Instruments, which chose the city in 1985–86 "because of the ability of technical personnel to work with English and to absorb training, a potential labour pool emerging from the Indian Institute of Science and other educational institutions, the already installed base of electronics industries and subcontractors, the attractive climate, and the relatively cheap real estate" (Heitzman 1999a, PE7).

It is important to recognize that even previous to this influx, multinationals had been present in Bangalore, although on a somewhat restrained scale, in such fields as finance (Grindlays Bank) and engineering (Siemens). Although the banking industry saw the entrance of new multinationals such as the Hong Kong and Shanghai Banking Corporation and Citibank, what was particularly significant about the 1990s was the emergence of multinationals that built on a local, vibrant, high-technology sector as well as the older, largely public, engineering-electronic base. Initially, the offices of many high-technology companies were located in the central business district (see Figure 2). Toward the end of this decade, however, these concerns began moving to the fringes of the city (for instance, the Electronic City and the Information Technology Park), because of inexpensive land and government encouragement. In fact, Bangalore today has an "information technology corridor" that stretches all the way from Whitefield on the east side of the city to J. P. Nagar on the south side, where about four hundred information technology and telecommunicatons companies are located, sending the land prices in these new suburbs upward.[30] The biggest problem experienced by all these companies is the need for basic infrastructure that the government has not been able to provide effectively. Many companies faced with the growing costs of inexpensive outsourcing have begun looking for new sites in other countries or in other cities in India, such as Hyderabad.[31] It appears from a number of public announcements made in 1999, however, that the government is showing signs of renewed commitment to developing the roads and providing other amenities in these areas, especially because the software exports from Bangalore alone were expected to exceed 34 billion rupees in 1999.[32]

Whether or not the information revolution in Bangalore turns out to be a fragile event, there does seem to be the growth of a "cyber culture," particularly among young people, and the number of "cyber cafes" and salons where Internet services can be obtained cheaply has mushroomed since 1997. Accompanying the process of liberalization has also been the growth of consumer industries, both local and international, looking for middle-class and upper-middle-class markets—for example, Levi Jeans, Kentucky Fried Chicken, Pizza Hut, and Coca-Cola. Star TV, CNN, and other cable channels provide American and British serials and news easily and cheaply. No one who has visited Bangalore can fail to be startled by the numbers of pubs that have grown up in the 1990s in the city, which is home

Figure 2. The central business district in Bangalore.

to the beer prince of India, Vittal Mallaya, who runs United Breweries. Bowling alleys, which are patronized by teenagers and youth, seem to be the latest import to the city.

Although these industries exploit new desires and create new consumerist fantasies in the city, the stratum of society chiefly associated with them is but a small percentage of the city's population, though a visible and vocal one. The city is still dominated by occupational groups that form part of the workforce in the state-induced and small-scale sectors of the economy, as well as the enormous informal economy. For instance, the number of small-scale industries in 1993 was 26,534 in Bangalore Urban District.[33] The Bangalore Development Authority has calculated that in 1991 the workforce in the metropolitan area of Bangalore was about 1,267,000 persons, constituting 29.13 percent of the total population of 4,086,000 persons. Some 20 percent of the workforce in basic employment were state and central government employees (105,000 persons), 45 percent were industrial workers (236,000 persons), and commercial workers (those engaged in trade and commerce) comprised about 35 percent of the workforce (184,000 persons).[34]

According to the same document, the workforce in "service employment" was about 742,000 persons. The ratio of basic to service employment was about 1:1.4. Official estimates exclude large numbers of people.[35] Some estimates of the informal economy have been made by other authors. Thippaiah (1993) points out that according to the 1971 Census of India, the percentage of workers in the informal sector of the Bangalore Urban District (of which the metropolis is a large part) was 55.25 percent. This figure increased to 60.93 percent in 1981 and to 69.16 percent in 1991. His estimate is that in the Bangalore Urban Agglomeration the share of the informal sector in 1971 was between 50 percent and 60 percent of the workforce. In 1991, the share was between 65 percent and 72 percent, and therefore greater than that of the formal sector workforce. The job histories of informal workers suggest that there is little mobility between the formal and informal sectors. There is a high level of household participation in the informal sector, with the major portion in self-employment activities.[36]

The Vahnikula Kshatriyas connected with the Karaga *jatre* stand, on the one hand, at the intersection between the lower end of the formal sector and the developmental state's activities and, on the other hand, in the informal sector of the city, with most of them part of the latter. A survey was conducted for this book in 1997 in three areas of the city. It covered one hundred Vahnikula Kshatriya households with 534 persons, 287 males and 247 females (see appendix). There were a number of different occupational groups among the adult working men; all adult working women except two were engaged in housework. The occupational groups included "government employees"; those who worked for various departments in the city's bureaucracy, at the Government Press, or as accounts officers; all those surveyed in all three areas of the city (thirteen persons) fell in low-income categories. "Professionals'" included doctors, engineers, lawyers, and insurance agents, of which there were only four persons in all three areas of the city. "Factory workers" included twelve persons who worked for public-sector factories, such as Hindustan Aeronautics, Ltd., or Bharat Electronics, or in the private sector. The majority of the men (82 persons) worked in "petty self-employment," such as in limestone stores, vegetable shops, printing and binding works, or small engineering works as electricians, carpenters, mechanics, and so on. Others (forty-eight) had no businesses of their own and worked for others as "petty laborers" for a small wage; these included gardeners, drivers, and others. In reality, an enormous number of persons stood outside the formal economy.

Most of the Vahnikula Kshatriya households had earlier been engaged in horticulture, an activity that, along with other primary ones, has shown a steady decline in the Bangalore Urban Agglomeration. The share in the occupational structure of agriculture and allied activities declined from 7.81 percent in 1961 to 2.04 percent in 1971 and was about 2.66 percent in 1981, the last figure showing a mild increase from the previous decade because between 1971 and 1981 forty-six villages were added to the metropolitan area and urbanized.[37] The Bangalore Development Authority did not even include agriculture in its calculations in its 1995 Comprehensive Development Plan. To a large extent, as the case of the Vahnikula Kshatriyas demonstrates, many of these agriculturists had long been displaced by the growing metropolis and had had to compete with a workforce in work that was industrial, commercial, or service oriented. Most of them were eventually absorbed into such activities. A few of them found employment in the state or the central bureaucracy. Although they are not part of the high-technology, global landscape in the way that the software engineers are, the Vahnikula Kshatriyas participate in an urban arena that is interwoven with the global milieu and regional networks in several ways. How can we begin to conceive of these relationships of intersection and separation and of the cultural claims made on the city's space and history by this group? The next few sections posit some answers to this question.

Urban Sacrality

Studies that are sensitive to the roles of ritual centers, markets, and urbanism within a "world systems" framework in South Asia provide a fruitful methodology for examining the interaction between cultural formations and urban economies today while deepening the historical frame of our understanding. As various world-systems theories have shown, global economic and cultural movements in the past have included flows of mercantile or diasporic populations, religious ideologies, ideas of city planning and civic culture, and items of material culture such as food, medicine, and so on.[38] The four hundred years of Chola rule in south India, from the ninth to the thirteenth centuries, was a time when links with Southeast Asia were forged, especially through trade by Tamil merchants, according to Heitzman (1997a, 9–10). There were two tiers of this activity, made up of groups of traders who operated at the local level through mercantile assemblies and long-distance traders who operated through a variety of associations with regions as far away as Borneo, Sumatra, and China. Abu-Lughod (1989, 261–90) describes the thirteenth and fourteenth centuries as a period when Old World trade in various sections—Southwest, South, Southeast, and East Asia and the Mediterranean—became integrated into a world system. The Indian subcontinent was the link between different parts of the system. The prominence of the city of Calicut on the western coast of India in the mid-thirteenth century was linked to the lucrative trading terms offered by the rulers of the city to Muslim merchants coming from the Red Sea. Local Jewish and Gujurati merchants also shared in the wealth of this transit trade. On the eastern coast, trade was more closely integrated with the agrarian economy, and the textile production associated with cotton, such as in the weaving center of Kanchipuram, gave cities an industrial character. Although primary products such as spices were an important part of this system, manufactured ones such as textiles were just as central.

This commercial and industrial expansion was related to ritual centers in many ways: many traders founded temples and patronized existing ones, and in certain periods, temples stood at the centers of networks of urbanism and redistributive flows.[39] Focusing on a different type of world system, Waghorne (1999) studied the growth of temples in Madras city from 1640 to 1800, the period when the British founded this colonial port. She argues that in the new trading cities temples were not founded by kings, but were shaped by Indian merchants who moved into the settlement from other regions or by local mercantile interests. She identifies three types of temples in the city that were born of a dialogue between communities, the marketplace, and sacred sites in the new world system. The first were the eclectic or generic temples that were all-community temples. These celebrated the shared mercantile nature of the new settlement, including the British settlers. The second type were the temples of different castes, or community-only temples. The rivalries between them were often played out in performative ways with processions, flags, or the rights to use certain streets. The third type were the "duplicated" temples, which were "branch offices" of more impressive or older shrines. At a time when the port cities were gaining dominance as well as traders and persons of the professional classes, the three types of temples spoke of various issues: How could "foreigners" be accorded a place in the world? How could difference and similarity be constructed in religious vocabulary and in community?

Bangalore, unlike Madras, was not a colonial port city, but an inland site born in the interregnum between the Chola period and the development of the English presence in South Asia. The city bears the marks of many urban models and many kinds of ritual centers that emerged from its various histories and communities, a theme taken up in detail in the next chapter. Today, two kinds of spatial arenas can be delineated in Bangalore alongside the shifts in its political economy in the last hundred years. On the one hand, there is a high population density and spatial concentration in the older portions of the metropolis, such as the Cantonment and the City. These areas are often very highly priced in terms of land and building value, and the residential areas are dotted with markets, private production centers with textile looms or small machine tools, older factories, schools, and private businesses. On the other hand, suburbanization has occurred on the periphery of the city (the boundaries of which keep shifting), creating areas that are industrial, commercial, defense, or residential zones. These are surrounded or interwoven with slums and old villages. The effects of the transformations in the production base can also be seen in the cultural capital deployed in these arenas, whether the production of particular lifestyles or the holding of religious celebrations or public events. At least three types of ritual centers associated with these spatial arenas can be identified in the city today, two of which represent the different spatial arenas of the city—the sites of concentration and suburbanization— whereas the third type represents both spatial zones. This is not to say that other shrines based on a different principle of classification cannot be identified. Each of these types, however, creates specific mediations of the space of the city and its markets, and constructs memories of older places and the sacred.[40]

The first type of center is associated with cults of old village deities, Christian or Muslim saints, and holy personages. Such centers tend to be controlled by a single community but attract a multidenominational following. They are usually located in the areas of spatial concentration of the city. Goddess shrines, such as that dedicated to Patalamma in Jayanagar on the south side of the city, often display an autochthonous relationship to the land. The goddess is believed to have appeared suddenly or manifested herself to traders at the time of the founding of the city, often in the midst of forests, and in time gained popularity chiefly because of her powers to heal afflictions. Although her shrine may be tended by members of a specific caste today, she attracts devotees across communities. The Basilica of Our Lady of Health in the Cantonment market is patronized by Tamil Christians, but also by persons from a host of other religious denominations. Although the Christian presence in Karnataka is probably as old as the fourteenth century, when Dominican friars began to preach on the west coast of the state, it was Abbe Dubois, the famous French missionary and author of *Hindu Manners, Customs, and Ceremonies,* who founded the shrine in 1811. Our Lady of Health is petitioned for healing individual afflictions, and her mediation at the level of the larger neighborhood is also sought—for instance, when Bangalore faced a famine in 1876–78 and the plague in 1899.

Memories of beneficence such as this are important in the construction of the local role of such figures. For instance, the tomb in the Cantonment of Haider Shah Jilani, a Sufi of the Qadiriya tradition, is revered by Kutchi Memon merchants who migrated to Bangalore from Gujarat, on the western coast of India, during Pax Britannica.[41] The Memons are important retailers in the Commercial Street of the Cantonment, and, in contrast to some of the older Muslim groups in Bangalore, have moved out of the market area to live in other residential neighborhoods. However, the tomb of the holy man provides a locus for the gathering of the community that identifies its fortunes closely with his blessings and the lineage to which he belonged. In these cults, what I shall term sites of "locational sacrality," it is the association of the deity or saint with a locality and the history of a community in that place that provides the key symbolic markers and ritual idiom of spatial practice. Many of these centers attract traders, factory workers, those who compose the lower end of the state sector, and workers in the informal economy or petty businesses. Very few of them are professionals.

The second type of ritual center emerges from the "sacrality of urban sprawl." The years since 1950 have witnessed the emergence of two kinds of suburban cults in Bangalore. One kind features high-income, public-sector employees or those who provide professional services (accountants, lawyers, doctors, or engineers) as its constituency. These persons have linkages with both the state apparatus and the private sector, but not a large number seem to be connected with high-technology, information-based industries. An example of this kind is the cult dedicated to Shirdi Sai Baba, temples to whom are found in new and upper-class suburbs of the city. The cult of Sai Baba, a saint who lived in a village in the state of Maharashtra until his death in 1918 and is revered widely by Muslims and Hindus, appears to have found its way into Bangalore in the 1940s and 1950s. In Bangalore, devotees responsible for the founding of one of the first temples dedicated to Sai Baba were retired defense personnel and traders. Not only is he revered today in Bangalore by a largely upper- and middle-class constituency in the temples, but he is also, and primarily, worshiped as a Hindu guru.[42] The other kind of sacrality of urban sprawl attracts an overwhelming number of minimally skilled, low-income workers from the public and private sectors as well as the informal sector of the economy. An instance of this type of sacrality is the cult dedicated to the Infant Jesus of Prague, which is found in a lower-income slum area of Bangalore called Viveknagar.[43] This neighborhood was on the periphery of the city in the 1970s, but is now fairly central given the recent expansion of the metropolis. The cult attracts a wide range of devotees, although the core constituency is comprised of Tamil Christians, chiefly from the working class. What is particular about each of these suburban cults is the way in which memories of previous places and regional affiliations are transposed and displaced within the architecture and ritual practices of the cult. One "global" aspect of these sites is the way in which they participate in narratives and circuits that serve to link shrines across political boundaries. For instance, at the Infant Jesus shrine there is a circular building with painted panels that link Christ's birth in Nazareth to the Infant Jesus cult in Prague and to the church in Viveknagar.

The "Karaga" performance dedicated to the goddess Draupadi is an instance of the third type of ritual center. The main locus of the Karaga in Bangalore is the Dharmaraja Temple in the City belonging to the Vahnikula Kshatriyas, who were traditionally horticulturists, as mentioned earlier. The performance is attended by persons enormous numbers from social strata and communities from surrounding villages, as well as those involved in the city's informal economy, mercantile people, factory workers, employees of state-run enterprises, government officials, and some professionals in the private sector; the high-technology sector does not seem to be represented widely, if at all. Historically, this perfomance was primarily a center of locational sacrality, but in the last few decades has spread to some of the suburban arenas of the metropolis as well, in addition to other urban centers in the vicinity, where it has occurred for a longer time. The meshing of old and new centers in the city, towns, and suburbs is characteristic of what is treated by many as the primary civic ritual in Bangalore.

A Theater of the Civic

"Yakshagana" dominates traditional theater forms in Karnataka. The earliest documentation of this form is said to be about 1480, when a play about two dynasties in Karnataka was written by Kempanagowda of Mandya.[44] Yakshagana has come to connote different practices in various parts of the state, but in general refers to free performances on an open stage that could be a field or an area in front of a temple. Many of the performances are based on mythological or historical themes, including the *Mahabharata* and *Ramayana* epics, heroic deeds, or other legends. They can include some dance forms and musical instruments (such as drums), and many are performed on religious occasions throughout the night. Troupes continue to perform Yakshagana in the state: in 1992, there were 30 full-time troupes that performed between November and June every year, and about 250 amateur groups.[45] In Bangalore, these performances are less common than in rural areas, and their popularity has been overtaken by that of professional drama companies, and, of course, the cinema.[46]

The second half of the nineteenth century in Karnataka saw the emergence of several Kannada drama companies both in the northern part of the state and in princely Mysore. Music and song were important features of these plays, as were male and female actors, whereas the older theater forms had been largely performed by male players. By the 1940s, theater companies such as that of Gubbi Veeranna, graduating from gaslights to electricity and from touring shows to permanent stages, had become very popular. The Kannada theater movement also consolidated itself in the next three decades, and groups such as Samudaya brought about innovations in form and content, including the use of translations from other Indian languages and foreign ones.[47] The city today has a vibrant theater culture, both in Kannada and in other languages, including English, and includes many professional theater companies and auditoriums.

Although these theater forms may be compared to the Karaga festival, there is a Kannada term that more accurately describes its performance genre—the "*jatre*." The *jatre* is an interlocal festival that regulates the relationships between settlements. It has been described as having a role to play in conflict management at the intervillage level.[48] Many festivals are associated with local deities, male and female. In parts of Karnataka, a *jatre* links not only rural sites, but also urban ones, to each other. Indeed, given the pattern of urban organization described at the beginning of this chapter, public arenas such as the *jatre* and the market were and are important mechanisms of economic and cultural linkage between disparate sites that compose the urban realm. A concept comparable to the idea of the festival in the *jatre* is the idea of pilgrimage *(yatre)*, although the *jatre* can refer to both, suggesting sacred arenas and movements and transformations of the body in space and time. In early Kannada literature, there are many descriptions of the *jatre*. In the work of Pampa (tenth century), we find mention of the deity's chariot, the movement of which was an integral part of the *jatre*, as it continues to be today. Again, the twelfth-century work called *Samaya Parikse*, by Brahmasiva, mentions the *jatre*.[49]

In most parts of the Karnataka region, the *jatre* is connected with trade in a variety of goods, from groundnut to cattle. It is estimated that in Karnataka there are more than 1,000 annual *jatre*.[50] The *Karnataka State Gazetteer Bangalore District* (1990) mentions twenty-eight important *jatre* that are held in the district, the largest among them being the Karaga *jatre* and the St. Mary's festival, both in Bangalore, drawing over 100,000 people.[51] In 1930, there were thirty-four major *jatre* in Bangalore district, and at eighteen of them cattle shows were also held; at eight of them over 5,000 people assembled. The Karaga *jatre* in Bangalore at that time drew 20,000 persons.[52] Therefore, the *jatre* involves a range of activities, from a religious celebration to an aesthetic experience and increased economic activity.

The Karaga *jatre* is primarily associated with two kinds of ritual players from the Vahnikula Kshatriya community, although many other groups attend it. First, there are the Virakumaras, or "hero-sons," who consider themselves to be in the mold of mythic heroes, embodying qualities of martial heroism and performing difficult feats for the goddess. Second, there are the Karaga priests, who bear the sacred icon. Virakumaras have on their persons two symbols: a wristband *(kankana* or *kappu)* tied around the root of a turmeric plant and around the wrist, and a sword *(katti)* (see Figure 3). The former is held to be a sign of purity, whereas the latter is considered a sign of their warrior status. These explanations are, however, not unproblematic. Virakumaras undergo a period of fasting and separation from their womenfolk, a time to "contain their strength" rather than simply achieving a state of ritual purity. Their "heat" seems to be constantly in a process of spilling over, because the Virakumaras were born of the goddess to fight a demon, and this heat has to be restrained through the consumption of "cooling" foods and other practices. Similarly, the sword is not simply a symbol of the warrior caste, but is related to an older cult of heroes and the deification of male protectors found in much of south India. A number of "hero-stones" have been identified in many areas of Andhra Pradesh, Karnataka,

Figure 3. A Virakumara holding a sword and wearing a wristband.

and Tamil Nadu and refer to an old tradition of revering a hero who died defending the village, cattle, the chief, or fighting a duel through a memorial stone.[53]

The support of performances by such martial and hero cults has been widely documented. These performances include such forms as "Teyyam" in Kerala, ghost *(bhuta)* worship and the recitation of their histories in coastal Karnataka, and the "Terukkuttu" in Tamil Nadu.[54] Although all these bear a generic resemblance, it is the Terukkuttu in Tamil Nadu (the core areas of which are the North and South Arcot districts) that has the closest affinity to the Karaga *jatre.* The Terukkuttu is a Tamil theater form in which plays largely based on the Tamil versions of the *Mahabharata* are performed. The principal contexts of these plays are festivals dedicated to Draupadi.[55] The Karaga *jatre* has in common with the Terukkuttu the fact that it is centered on the cult of Draupadi and on mythic and ritual aspects connected to her cult, although plays are not performed during the Karaga festival at all. However, unlike a large part of the literature and ethnography of the cult and related performances in Tamil Nadu, the Karaga *jatre* is completely urban, and in Karnataka is not found outside of Bangalore and a few urban centers in its vicinity.

The Karaga *jatre* also shares the features of other goddess cults in that it includes the worship of local goddesses such as Mariamma, Muthyallamma, and Yellamma, with whom Draupadi is considered to have a sibling relationship. In the case of the Karaga *jatre,* the hero cult and the worship of the goddess are intertwined: the Virakumaras have a special relationship of kinship to the goddess as "sons." The ritual player who complements the Virakumaras is the Karaga priest, who is transformed through his role as the bearer of the icon into the "Karaga" itself. Not only does he undergo penance and training in preparation for the performance, but also during the Karaga *jatre* his body is marked in certain specific ways—for instance, through elaborate headdresses and changes in clothing. The epic story of the *Mahabharata,* in particular, provides themes for elaboration of this relationship, although, as we shall see, there are many *Mahabharata* narratives and stories involved that belong to other narrative traditions.

There is one additional feature that singles out the Karaga *jatre:* its association in Bangalore with a Sufi, Hazrat Tawakkul Mastan Baba, a figure eighteenth century in the city, but representing aspects of popular Islam in the region from a period even before the founding of Bangalore. The presence of this saint in other Karaga *jatre* in the Bangalore region also suggests the significance of the connection between the goddess and the Sufi, which will be discussed further in chapter 3.[56] It is the constellation of the Draupadi cult with hero-sons, goddess worship, frame narrative(s) of the *Mahabharata,* the Sufi, and its urban nature that gives the Karaga *jatre* its specificity.

This discursive repertoire transcends mere representations of divine and demonic warriors who are the agents of mythological battles. Instead,

the Karaga *jatre* can be understood as radically reconfiguring and opening
up an arena of possibilities about the city and the body, both the individual
and the social.[57] This can be seen with respect to the ritual players: not
only is the goddess a man, but the hero-sons are said to make the goddess
perform a "dance" *(kunita)* with their fervor. They are said to make the
Karaga "play" *(ata adisu),* occasions that are perceived as spontaneous. The
dance of the Karaga in the city choreographs a pattern of urban space and
sense of the body-in-the-urban that relies on a different concept of the city
and the body. It breaks up the map of the city constructed by technology,
planning models, caste, and neighborhood and converts it into a performative space at the same time that the body is also transformed through
rituals, representations, and kinetic, oral, and somatic practices.

In trying to understand the *jatre,* its discursive complex, and its relationship to the metropolis, we might go in three possible directions. A "func-
tionalist" argument views the Karaga *jatre* as a purely symbolic activity
achieving societal consensus within a culturally heterogeneous city. Unlike
the chain of events in the Sanskrit *Mahabharata,* the birth of the goddess
every year in the *jatre* ends the sequence of performance before the depiction of the Kurukshetra battle. It suggests that the goddess's manifestation
and the penance of the Virakumaras stave off such a battle and uphold
order.[58] The goddess, substituting for the various incarnations of the god
Vishnu, the Preserver, appears as a defender of sociocosmic order.[59] The
space of the city parallels the space of the cosmos and vice versa. This function of maintaining cosmic order can also sometimes include the maintenance of social order, especially communal harmony. This is the type of argument that appears in newspaper articles on the Karaga every year:

> The Karaga, a symbol of communal amity and nightlong pomp
> and pageantry, is celebrated at the Dharmaraja temple in the old
> city area. The festival . . . draws over a few lakh [100,000] people
> with 1,000 strong posse of policemen keeping vigil throughout
> the night. The Karaga, after being placed before the deity in the
> temple, is taken around the old city with the traditional stop at
> the Hazrat Tawakkul Mastan dargah [a Sufi Muslim shrine] sym-
> bolizing the secular traditions of the city and the festival. The stop
> over at the dargah has its own two century-old legend. It is said
> that the Karaga while passing the dargah came to an abrupt end
> and all attempts to move it proved futile. It could continue on its
> journey only when Mastan Baba, the patron saint of the Hazrat
> Tawakkul Mastan dargah, tied a thread on the foot of the man

carrying the Karaga and pulled him forward ("Devotees celebrate Karaga," *Indian Express,* April 16, 1995).

The second type of argument is the "historical atrophy" argument. The historian D. D. Kosambi (1956) saw this festival as essentially a non-Aryan fertility rite that absorbed elements of local cults and was transformed in the new areas to which the festival migrated. Referring to Bangalore, Kosambi stated that the main cult object of this festival—an earthen pot to which in an earlier time animal sacrifices were performed—contains a gold fetish. In the last 150 years or so, these practices have disappeared, and the gold fetish has come to represent Draupadi today.

The third type of argument is a "mechanical materialist" one. The thesis here is that the Karaga *jatre* is related directly to the changing economy of Bangalore city. If Bangalore has become a "theater" of capital accumulation and a center for the diffusion of consumerist lifestyles and modernization, the persistence of the theater of the Karaga side by side with these elements reflects these economic shifts. Processes of capital accumulation and urbanization do not necessarily undermine noncapitalist cultural belief systems even if they do undercut the production base on which these beliefs rest.[60] For instance, in the 1970s and 1980s the Karaga priest was an employee of the public-sector Hindustan Aeronautics, Ltd. In the last few years, a carpenter has been the Karaga bearer. The shift in the status of the Karaga bearer from public-sector employee to informal-sector worker may signal the end of the dominance of the public sector in the city.[61]

This last argument is a compelling one, but it does not adequately represent all the contests and alliances that are being engaged in at the levels of both culture and economy in the city, or between different groups and institutions. The Karaga performance in Bangalore is not merely a parallel reality of the city, but relates to urban form in a far more complex manner. Before we can discus this relationship in the next section, the concepts of "theater" and "performance" have to be understood differently.

Until recently, a sometimes rigid distinction has operated in the study of performances between text and context, structure and expression, the content of the performance or story and its form, symbols, and social history. Many of these distinctions are based on a particular theory of language and meaning that separates structure from process, langue from parole, society from the individual, and in essence dehistoricizes the nature of meaning. However, a focus on the ethnography of performance inspired largely by sociolinguistic works from the 1970s led to an examination of the contexts of performance rather than simply its textual basis.[62] The influence from sociology and anthropology of the works of Victor Turner and Erving Goffman also stimulated a movement in the study of performance away from the emphasis on models inherited from general linguistics toward the construction of social meaning in performance.[63] The separation between text and context has thus been partially resolved, but at the other end of the spectrum are studies that have merged categories between cultures with the effect of essentializing meaning.[64] Here, the term "performance" is indiscriminately applied to events and spectacles that in their own cultural contexts are embedded within specific constructs of theatricality (or not), what Fabian (1990, 13) calls the danger of "misplaced concreteness."

The definition of the Karaga as performance in this book avoids misplaced concreteness by retaining the cultural associations evoked by the term *jatre*. I also see the "text," including an oral one, and the event as constituting parts, phases, or modalities of the same performance. Although the focus is on experience, symbols, and interpretation (rather than merely text, speech events, and rules), I do not agree that in moving toward a performative anthropology or sociology we should not separate performance from its embeddedness in "real" time by synchronic analysis.[65] There is a spatial recursivity that occurs over time that is not only important for analytical purposes, but also important to ritual players and spectators themselves. For instance, the Karaga procession charts routes through the city that over time have come to be marked as significant. Certain stops are made at key shrines and homes that are awaited and prepared for, such as the visit to the Sufi shrine in the City. Departures from these are equally crucial: it is a matter of debate every year how many circumambulations of the temple the Karaga will complete on the night of the performance when there is a full moon. While flexibility is thus built into the larger recursive process, the process is also self-reflexive for actors. It is important to remember that the Karaga *jatre* shares features with religious drama in other parts of India. Haberman (1988) argues, for instance, that the religious practices of the Gaudiya Vaisnava community in north India are based on classical Indian aesthetic theory, but the roles assumed during devotional practices are roles in a cosmic drama. He writes, "Salvation, to the Gaudiya Vaisnavas, is unending participation in the cosmic drama, and the skills of the actor are employed in pursuit of the true identity which allows such participation" (4). Exemplars, whom Haberman calls "paradigmatic individuals," are important in the process of entering this other reality because they serve as guides for various roles; scriptures, myths, and sacred biographies present these exemplars to the community, providing scripts for religious life. The ritual players in the Karaga *jatre* are like these holy actors, whereas the characters and roles of the *Mahabharata* and other narratives provide paradigmatic individuals for self-transformation. However, although their peregrinations through the city might be read as stations on a sacred journey rooted in mythic narratives, it is important to emphasize that these actions do not merely create a stage for salvation, but also stage their sense of the civic.

The Performance as a Mnemonic

Although many aspects of the performance may be studied, my specific interest in this book is to understand the Karaga *jatre* in its function as a mnemonic, its relationship to urban form and the body and to constructions of the civic. In moving toward a conceptualization of the Karaga performance as a mnemonic, we might refer to a textual distinction that is made between what is culturally termed *shruti* and *smriti* in classical Sanskrit literature. *Shruti* ("that which is heard") refers to a class of texts, primarily the *Veda*, that are held to have been divinely inspired and revealed to sages. *Smriti* ("that which is remembered") includes other texts, such as the *Dharmasastra* (legal codes), epics, philosophical systems, and mythological narrations, which are seen as historical and social products and can be assigned authorship. Although the boundaries between them can be a bit fluid, the categories themselves are widely accepted. In most languages in India, as in Kannada, the word *smriti* is commonly deployed as "memory," "remembering," or "reminiscence." In the *Bhagavadgita* text, one of the manifestations by which the divine pervades the world is memory, a feminine form that displays divine excellence. However, there is another word closely related to this one that is less rooted in the association with classical texts. This word is *smarana*, which means, in Kannada, recollection and memory. The practice of *smarana*, more than *smriti*, is embedded in many regions in recitations, oral narratives, and musical, mimetic, devotional, and performative practices where one individually or collectively remembers and invokes the name or form of the divine, a historical narrative, or the deeds of ancestors, deities, paradigmatic individuals, or mythic heroes. The nine stages of devotion described by the *Bhagavata* text, for instance, include remembering the divine, the name, qualities, powers, form, and acts of God.[66] This emphasis on recalling the divine accompanied by musical and oral praxis is also of central importance to the veneration of numerous saints and to their cults in India.

Approaching the matter from another angle, we might recall that in many performance arts in India memory has a primary function for participants in learning, transmitting, embodying, and improvising the performance. Performers and teachers of this knowledge sustain memory, in this context, whether they are saints, dancers, or musicians. Kersenboom (1995) argues that by the sixth century the Tamil language had been defined as being threefold *(muttamil)*, comprising word, music, and mimetic dance. The significance of this definition for the understanding of language is that praxis is always the condition of theory, that the experience of the text is "sensuous, performative" (15) and "living a reality of performance" (16). Manuscripts, musical scores, or choreography acquire meaning only when they are practiced; therefore, they have to be acquired and committed to memory for the purpose of performance. This type of memory "presupposes physical commitment, as the recall is largely somatic. To remember means to make the body work out the memory, speaking it, sounding it, dancing or miming it out to the world" (47).[67] To the extent that *smarana* has these associations and is embedded in kinetic, mimetic, oral, and musical practices, the Karaga *jatre* suggests memory-as-*smarana*. What is remembered, how is it remembered, and what are the features of the Karaga *jatre* as a mnemonic?

It is obvious that as many social memories are possible as there are groups, whether these are religious collectives, social strata, families, or other types of institutions. The conditions of existence of collectives and their conventions provide what Maurice Halbwachs (1992) has called "frameworks" of collective memory. As he wrote, "No memory is possible outside frameworks used by people living in society to determine and retrieve their recollections" (43). The past, as Halbwachs pointed out, is reconstructed on the basis of the present; and collective frameworks are "instruments" used by communities to remember. In the case of religious memories, these instruments may include commemorative cults, rites, texts, their scholastic elaboration, and material traces. In an intriguing formulation, he argues that frameworks of memory exist both within the passage of time and outside it: "while following them we can pass as easily from one notion to the other, both of which are general and outside of time, through a series of reflections and arguments, as we can go up and down the course of time from one recollection to another" (182). This suggests a fundamental feature of social memory. Frameworks of memory are constituted of relations between ideas and propositions (about behavior, society, the individual, religion, and so on), and in this sense they stand "outside time" because they are of a cognitive order. But they also refer to activities in the present, to locality, to the localization of memory, to commemorative events, to the need to attach the group and memory to terrain.

Memory, in the context of this book, is formulated as an active mode whereby cultural material (events, persons, or places) are "re-collected" or gathered up into a configuration. It is not an object that is brought back into consciousness, but a set of relations. It consists of devices that rework the relations between historical and cultural materials in various locales through several processes. Halbwachs (1992, 219–22) states that new communities take up the traditions of older ones, but also appropriate them through what he calls "laws governing the memory of groups." They rewrite them by changing their positions in time and space; they renew them by unusual parallels, by unexpected oppositions, and by combinations; there can be a concentration of events in a single place and a duality of locations across regions. If one may extrapolate Volosinov's ([1927] 1987) formulation of the unconscious as a social product and the language that represents it to the workings of memory, we might say that at least four other processes can be seen in operation: displacement, inversion, substitution, and condensation. This does not mean, however, that the logic of memory follows the rules of grammar and syntax, for language is understood by Volosinov as inherently fragile and part of the changing forms of history, praxis, and sociality rather than as a strictly formalized system.

These processes are also embodied. Memory is part of material reality, and it operates through forms that share the nature of other parts of a locality, such as physical bodies, buildings, or instruments of production. Imagine a city: buildings, parks, neighborhoods, and burial sites are added and replaced, grow and decay; certain sites achieve a heightened sense of meaning, such as memorials, churches, gardens, or stadiums; exits and entrances to the city change over time, as do its boundaries. Places within the cityscape, such as parks, markets, temples, or streets, and the networks between them allow memory to be activated or brought into the open. Roach (1996, 25–28) defines these sites as "vortices of behavior." In his study of circum-Atlantic performances in New Orleans and London, he highlights places such as the grand boulevard, the theater district, the marketplace, and the burial ground as sites where a "kinesthetic imagination" comes into play. In other words, the relationship between landmarks in the city and the acts and constructs of urban memory is crucial, although neither the cityscape nor the landscape of memory is reducible to the other.

Further, the landscapes of urban memory that ensue through these operations and processes are not only conceptual constructs, but also experiential moments and collective activities. In other words, it is the activity of communities in the city that sustains landscapes of urban memory. In this book I wish to argue that memory is constructed through two main modes: performances (including their musical, kinetic, mimetic, oral, devotional, and ritual aspects) and practices of the body that are linked to these performances. Cultural resources are sedimented on and stored in the bodies of citizens through particular gestures and practices. Memory is transmitted and transformed through movement, music, rituals, words, and other practices of the body. As Connerton (1989, 6–13) shows, in Paris during the French Revolution, the ceremonial trial and execution of Louis XVI and the assumption of certain styles of clothing marked two ways in which memory and society were altered. The first pointed to a public rejection of dynastic succession, the second to bodily deportment under the ancient regime. The "historical deposit" that was confronted in these acts also included the emotions, habits, and practices tied up with kingship and social hierarchy as represented, among other things, through costume.[68]

There is a range of studies that demonstrates how urban memory is constructed. Favro (1996) shows how in Republican Rome each place had its own *genius loci* and there existed a diversity of styles of architecture and patrons. Rome lacked a focused image as a city until the reign of Augustus Caesar. After 29 BCE, Augustus created the image of an imperial city through the "orchestration" of urban experience. He did this not by means of a comprehensive master plan for the city (as did Baron Haussman for Paris, Mussolini for Rome, or Le Corbusier for Chandigarh), but by imprinting new narratives through various paths in the city and reorienting these paths around newly placed landmarks. The reorientation was emphasized through processions in which citizens walked, prayed, and participated, tying them to their environment and their recollections of it in new ways.[69] Again, as Halbwachs (1992, 193–235) pointed out in his essay "The Legendary Topography of the Gospels," in pilgrimages through Jerusalem sacred sites were embedded in the narratives of the Gospels, a truth that was settled in pilgrims' memories through localization of the mythic drama. However, this framework also provided a new way of moving in physical space. Jerusalem was the city chosen for this sacred theater, but it was a city where places were already commemorated and associated with ancient memories of Jewish history as told in the Old Testament. This feature was also true of many other Christian pilgrimages that made use of places already part of collective memorabilia, endowing them with a different meaning and situating them within new narratives or ritual actions.

Closer to home in south India, Fritz, Michell, and Rao (1984, 146–54) show that the spatial organization of Vijayanagara, as an imperial capital, was linked to medieval concepts of kingship in which the king was seen as an upholder of traditional law, an agent of material prosperity, and embedded in a system of order where there were cycles of good and evil. This rhythm was reflected in the pattern of the ruler's life that would alternate annually between a period of rest (when the court, army, and king resided at the capital) and a period of movement (which included war, pilgrimage, or peaceful missions in the empire and beyond). The transition between the two periods was the celebration of the Mahanavami festival, which was meant to commemorate the propitiation of the goddess Durga by the epic hero-king Rama before he marched against his enemy Ravana. In these celebrations at the capital, the display of the king's military strength, the wealth of his household, and his marital alliances was crucial. Yet this festival was part of the reorganization of space in the capital that occurred as the kings' relationships to an older sacrality and memories of place changed. In the first period, they were primarily local rulers who had obtained the support of Pampa, a local goddess associated with a sacred center on the south bank of the Tungabhadra River. The first seat of power may have been located close to a hill near that spot. In the second period, this sacred power was incorporated into the male deity, Virupaksha, who was adopted by the kings as their dynastic emblem. A temple for this god—which also marked the site of the "marriage" of Pampa with the male deity, an incarnation of Shiva—was constructed west of a newly laid-out royal zone that was somewhat south of the old seat of power. In the third period, when Vijayanagara became the capital of an empire, the city came to manifest cosmic significance. The city was associated with the kingdom of Rama, and the king was linked with this divine epic hero. The newly constructed Rama Temple at the center of the royal core signified this association at the same time that it divided the "zone of performance" to the east from the "zone of residence" to the west, splitting the king's two bodies, as it were. The former was the region where the display of the king's office and the festivals occurred. The latter was associated with the private aspects of the royal household, and, significantly, in this direction lay the old temple dedicated to Shiva, who had become the protective deity of the household rather than the kingdom. The many roads constructed in this new center oriented the royal core toward a mythic landscape in which Rama, rather than Shiva or the goddess Pampa, had a role to play. The cults and temples of various members of the court and other communities also allied themselves with this new orientation, and many were located on the main road that led out of the Rama Temple.

Studying Suchindram, near the tip of peninsular India, whose main features were completed in a slightly later period than that of Vijayanagara, probably the period of Tirumala Nayaka of Madurai (1623–59), Pieper (1980, 65–80) shows that the central elements of urban space are related to older memories. Therefore, the east-west axis of the town, which creates a haptic experience of moving toward the town, also connects it with the collective memory of the town's foundation on the east. Then again, the body of water beside the temple creates a polarity and a duality between the upper, "male," town located around the temple of Shiva and the lower, "female," town located near the body of water and the goddess shrine. This goddess shrine is part of a system of shrines that includes four other goddess shrines on the periphery of the urban center and possibly belongs to an alternative scheme of urban space, if not an older one. Pieper analyzes how the collective stagings of the experience of space through festivals also record these various urban memories.

Madras, founded by the British when they gained the right to use the southern part of the present city as a trading post in 1639, replicated the fort settlement pattern that was in existence elsewhere in south India, such as Bangalore, although it was created by a different kind of polity. "Fort St. George," as it was called, stands next to the settlement of George Town, and as Mines (1994, 88) remarks, the organization of the settlement reflects the social character of the surrounding region. The number of East India Company servants and soldiers was small, and Indian traders largely carried out trade and production. The most prominent among these were the Beeri Chettiar merchants, who were largely Tamil-speaking Shaivas, and their rivals, the Komati Chettiars and Balijas, who were Telugu-speaking Vaishnava merchants. Their economic competition led to a number of community conflicts and riots, especially in the eighteenth and nineteenth centuries, and also to the division of the town into a western part occupied by the Komatis and an eastern part occupied by the Beeris. In each division stood temples associated with one of these communities that came to be linked to its display of prestige, wealth, and status. Spatial zones of influence and institutional networks were created by various civic leaders who, Mines argues, were crucial in shaping not only the boundaries of "community," but also the forms in which authority within it functioned. Today, processions such as the annual one of the Kandasami Temple from Park Town, considered a "satellite" area of residence of the Beeri Chettiar community, to the older "center," where the community no longer has houses, businesses, or control over the main community temple, reflect earlier memories of place. The route itself, extensions of it into new areas, and the patronage of the festival have also become means whereby the sphere of influence of the leaders can be demonstrated as they rework their memories of George Town in the post-1950s metropolis. In a period when the relationship between the neighborhood and the caste has been lost, Mines shows how new leaders seek to integrate members of the caste, now a citywide community, on a new basis through the newer temple that was once spatially peripheral and ritually subordinate.

Dominant landscapes of urban memory represent Bangalore as a "garden city," a "science city," a "Silicon Valley," or the "state capital." In contrast to these, the Karaga *jatre* produces and celebrates another landscape, the "gardeners' city" or the "city of the children of fire." The performance recovers architectural fragments, spatially peripheral tracts, and older axes of the city from a zone of urban amnesia and also uses contemporaneous axes and institutional sites in other patterns of meaning. The protocol of urban memory activated in the Karaga *jatre*, unlike the archives of a library or a museum, is a protocol of enactment and embodiment. The *jatre* achieves this through two compositional devices that are embedded in different practices and norms of the body and enhanced by musical accompaniments and rhythms. The first are kinetic devices that include movement in time and space in the city carried out through ritual events on the days of the *jatre* and the routes taken by the Karaga priest, the sacred icon, his retinue, and citizens. The space of the city is dense, and the ritual players have to move through "actual" space, through certain streets, across parks, through milling crowds, between buildings. Certain temporal constraints are imposed by the itinerary and ritual events; for instance, the priest and his retinue cannot be at different places at one time. But within these spatial and temporal constraints, there are also "virtual" spaces and times that are activated by the procession. These are indicated by different stages of the procession and the places where rituals occur, charging some sites with greater significance than others.

The second device, an oral one, is the recitation of a narrative about the origins of community and the *jatre*. This oral epic, called the *Vahni Purana* or the *Karaga Purana*, links locality with the tradition of the classical *Mahabharata*, other historical sites, and paradigmatic individuals. It depicts the city and the forest as part of the same landscape of memory. The oral epic rewrites the social memory of the community by connecting it to other spaces, but also by allowing a new kind of temporality to emerge. This occurs because the time of the epic is not connected directly to the time of the itinerary of the procession, and in fact its recitation occurs after all these events are over. Slippages of various kinds also take place in the oral epic: it reverses the sequence of events of the classical *Mahabharata*; many of the characters are disguised allusions to other characters from different narrative traditions; and metonymic substitutions take place in the oral epic.

The Karaga *jatre* as a mnemonic is not only a store of images and motifs about the city that unfolds in time and space in various combinations; it also has a certain intentionality with reference to the present. Early studies of performances saw them as carnival spaces, ritual rebellions at the end of which normal social order was restored, but the study of the Karaga *jatre* reveals a much more complex process. It is imbued with a dialogue of contexts, both past and present. One kind of intentionality relates to political mobilization and community formation. Throughout the year, not only are there preparations of various kinds for the performance itself, but the performance acts as a kind of "newspaper," gathering up events of the past year(s) and staging them.[70]

This has repercussions for events the rest of the year: the festival requires mobilization, and mobilization proceeds from it. It is related to the existing and previous regimes of place and the implications of these for community formation. For instance, the main object of cult devotion, Draupadi, is represented in the performance as a "hot" (angry, reproductive, fiery) goddess who is relatively independent of her male consorts, who have a smaller role to play in this festival. Her chief relationship is to the Virakumaras. The Karaga *jatre* relies on the icon of the wild goddess surrounded by a group of male offspring who are her protectors and who roam a region between the forest/exile and the city/battlefield. The martial, maternal imagery of the performance is shot through by elements of sexual reproduction and nonreproduction. These include the goddess's marriage on the final day, the relations of kinship established through sister-exchange between the epic heroes and local kings, the valorized celibacy of the hero-sons, and the virginity and chastity of various other female deities. However, it must be recalled that the Karaga performance first began to receive explicit state patronage and public legitimation in 1811, when the ruler of Mysore, Krishnarajendra Wodeyar, donated a large amount of land to the temple.[71] This occurred when the rulers of Mysore were politically somewhat impotent and de facto vassals of the British, who had established the Cantonment in Bangalore in 1809. Today, the performance is presented in a context in which, for all the martial representations, the ritual players and strata associated with the *jatre* face increasing contests within the city's production base and its politics, particularly those over space.[72] The Karaga *jatre* is thus what Bakhtin (1981) would call a "double-voiced" discourse: a cultural form that simultaneously expresses at least two axiologies and draws its ambivalence from social struggle.[73] Faced with a certain kind of impasse, the community that performs the Karaga *jatre* has been consolidating itself through a wider political alliance of different groups in the city, many of them part of the informal economy or the lower end of the formal sector. This alliance, which draws from the performative terrain, has a complex relationship to the economic policies of the state, other elites, and power brokers.

The second kind of intentionality is with reference to public space. In cities such as Bangalore, old elites, the state, and other groups struggle over cultural and economic resources within the city due to the effects of globalization processes, regional hegemonic aspirations, and the impact of state policies. These contests occur in various public domains and have specific spatial manifestations. In the context of the Karaga *jatre,* two kinds of spaces that are sites of public debate and conflict today are bodies of water and garden land. To illustrate, the bed of a large body of water where the Karaga is "revealed" every year is now the site of a huge sports stadium. This process of converting extensive bodies of water in the city into sports complexes, housing colonies, or bus terminals has aroused a great deal of discussion about the direction of planning in the city and definitions of public space. The Karaga *jatre* is thus located in a discursive arena that is occupied by other groups, multinational capital, and the state, all of which struggle with conceptualizations of the city, whether as "city of the past" or "city of the future." By creating a landscape of memory, the Karaga *jatre* draws attention to social, narrative, and discursive asymmetries in dominant models and stages alternative possibilities for the construction of political community and public space in the city.

Models of the Garden City

Unmasking the Urban: A Precolonial South Indian Model

The Karaga *jatre* is broadcast every year on the state television network as well as on some private cable channels. It achieves this popularity because politicians and ministers often attend and because it is historically a key event in Bangalore. The sustained cultural importance of the Karaga *jatre* for communities in the City as well as its increasing relevance in new suburbs of the metropolis testifies to a public sphere that has grown in the city alongside others created by television, film, or literacy. Over a period of two months, a number of locales of the metropolis, the city, and the Cantonment, bodies of water, temples, communities, and cults, are brought into the cycle of performance. The festival connects caste and local identities, cults, and the state authorities; fosters a rich civic culture; and supports a vibrant milieu for business and elite interests. It is a commentary on the city, its internal dynamics, and its relationship with a wider polity, and it provides a medium of discourse for various groups.

Topological and institutional inputs create a specific aesthetic for the performance. These filter through oral accounts and narratives of citizens as they speak about their neighborhoods and discuss historical events or changes that have taken place in the city. Paths along which citizens customarily move, such as streets and railroads, central nodes, landmarks, and crossroads, as well as material traces of institutional forms, also suggest these inputs.[1] Rather than the present metropolitan agglomeration, these narrations, practices, and traces reveal different contours for Bangalore, including bodies of water, gardens, markets, villages, and open lands linked to the original fort and settlement areas. Although the creation of the Cantonment began to change some of these features, this urban complex still seeped through the new pattern.[2] It was the years after 1950, when Bangalore became the capital of Karnataka state and was recognized as India's science city, that the process of creating an urban armature with consciously designed landmarks, technological centers, and a bureaucratic apparatus accelerated. Instead of civic activities being dispersed, new public institutions emerged that were set up by the law and the state, such as the Bangalore City Corporation, bodies that were strongly influenced by industrial and scientific production within the city.[3] An urban model consisting of a grid plan and a radial pattern of roads emerging from a central core overlay the older network. The transformation of the cityscape from gardens, fort, small settlements, and bodies of water to a built-up environment consisting of residential neighborhoods and housing colonies, high-rise buildings, roads, factories, petty businesses, hotels, city corporation offices, and stadiums is visible on land previously cultivated or inhabited by the Vahnikula Kshatriya community. Interviews conducted with various members of the community, a survey undertaken in three study areas (see appendix), and city maps also reveal the transformations of older spatial conceptions of Bangalore.

Three elements were central to the spatial order of Bangalore from the middle of the sixteenth century until about 1800. The organization of Bangalore as a complex of a fort *(kote)*, settlement-market *(pete)*, and a large artificially constructed body of water, or tank *(kere)* can be described as one type of precolonial south Indian urban model. Although natural lakes existed in the region, these manmade "tanks," as they are commonly called in south India, were used for multiple purposes, including bathing and the provision of drinking water and water for agriculture and horticulture. Since it is difficult to say which bodies of water were natural and which manmade, I use the word "tank" to designate any such body in the Bangalore region. Other variations are possible, as seen in examples elsewhere in south India; for instance, a river instead of a tank, a central temple instead of a fort, and trade activity of the settlement-market oriented toward the coast instead of a network of interior trade routes.[4] The realm of urban activity in Bangalore was widely dispersed in a variety of public arenas and spatial locations tied together through relations of trade, military functions, agriculture, kinship, and religiosity. Even temple construction and patronage does not seem to have been the exclusive prerogative of the ruler, for a number of smaller shrines, especially those dedicated to local goddesses, were supported by mercantile and producing communities. The tighter stitching together of zones such as tanks, horticultural land, centers of craft, and various settlements and the creation of a more concrete and extensive urban settlement characterized the growth of the city of Bangalore in the four hundred years after its founding.

Archaeological evidence shows that the capital of the Vijayanagar Empire, too, could be defined similarly: in the narrowest sense, the city of Vijayanagara lay inside a walled core containing the palace, markets, and residences. There were also settlements outside this core and within the outer walls of the city, along with a zone of temples. The settlements maintained discrete identities and names, although linked to the core. Finally, there was a greater metropolitan region that comprised dispersed settlements and agricultural zones connected to the core in numerous kinds of relationships.[5] Many of the sultanates in the middle Deccan who emerged after 1300 (and eventually destroyed Vijayanagar in the sixteenth century) also had a similar urban culture, although many of their specific innovations came to be followed by other polities—for instance, the use of cavalry by the rulers of Vijayanagar or Islamic-styled forms of urban architecture.

A bird's-eye view of Bangalore in the period after the founding of the settlement would have revealed a mud fort and a residential-cum-market area surrounded by tanks, forests, and other farming communities. What was significant about the fort was that it formed a ring of defense around the urban settlement, as did the forts in a thirty-mile radius on the periphery of Bangalore. Bangalore stands in a somewhat rocky region of the Deccan Plateau, and each of these forts commanded a panorama of the surrounding area with its villages and agricultural lands.[6] Within the political milieu of the post-Vijayanagar period, these forts and their control were crucial for the protection of thriving urban communities and trade.

From the time of its founding in 1537 until the middle of the seventeenth century, the fort had a number of gates.[7] The fort itself was surrounded by a moat, and around the fort walls were plots of gardens or open land surrounding the settlement and a number of tanks. In the period between Kempe Gowda's rule and the end of the eighteenth century, a mosque—the Jumma Masjid in Taramandalapet—came into existence about 1687, a second oval fort was built to the south of the old fort about 1691, and a palace was completed about 1791. The oval fort was later rebuilt in stone and got two new gates, the Delhi Gate in the north and the Mysore Gate in the south, along with a foundry for the manufacture of brass cannons and other military equipment. From 1759 to 1799, Bangalore was the scene of great military activity and the locus of four Anglo-Mysore wars. During Haider Ali's Second Anglo-Mysore War (1780–83) with the British, his army of about 83,000 strong camped close to the settlement on its southeast side.[8] The construction of the oval fort linked the settlement and

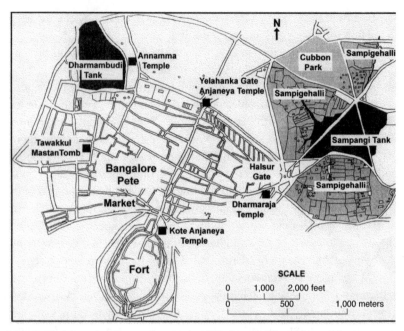

Map 3. The fort, the City, and tanks in 1870. Source: Directorate of Survey Settlement and Land Records, Bangalore, map of the Cantonment of Bangalore, 1870.

the fort together into a joint unit, albeit with definable parts that were still visible in a similar form nearly a hundred years later (see Map 3). The fort was extensively damaged after the battle for Bangalore in the last Anglo-Mysore war in 1799; the moat existed up until the 1860s, when it was closed up and, in place of the old fort, a compound wall was built.[9] Today, only a small fragment of the fort stands (see Figure 4).

The settlement-market, which today is referred to as the City, was surrounded by a deep ditch after the oval fort was built. This existed until the 1880s, when it slowly began to be filled with houses, public gardens, and stores. The City had two principal paths: running east-west from the Halsur Gate to the Sondekoppa Gate was Chickpet Road, and running north-south from the Yelahanka Gate to the Anekal Gate was Dodpet Road. Neither the western nor the southern gate is marked today by architectural remains or a ritual site, nor is either labeled on Map 3. Different caste and community groups, still recognizable today from the names of the localities and streets in the City, occupied distinct parts of the settlement. Many of these were artisan and merchant groups that were devoted to a variety of trades and products. Bangalore was an important entrepot, with an ex-

Figure 4. Remains of the Bangalore fort.

port trade in betel, pepper, and sandalwood. Although much of the manufacturing activity centered on textile production, different areas of the City had come to be associated with other products and castes as well. There were weaving castes (such as the Devangas and the Pattegaras) and independent trading castes dependent on textiles (the Komatigas, the Nagarits, and the Banajigas). There were also horticulturists (the Tigalas), specialized dyers (the Niligas), oil producers (the Ganigas), and tanners (the Madigas).

Temples functioned as significant nodes in the City; for instance, the Dharmaraja Temple, which stood near the Halsur Gate on the eastern side of the City, was probably already in existence by 1800.[10] This temple was the site of the annual Karaga *jatre*, for which thousands would congregate. The Karaga procession itself went down a number of important paths in the City. These were routes connecting several nodes along which were ritual sites: one such path led from the Dharmaraja Temple to the western edge of the City, where there stood a Sufi shrine, the tomb of Hazrat Tawakkul Mastan. Another path led from south to north to the Annamma Temple, near the Dharmambudi Tank (see Map 3). Annamma, a "pox goddess" believed to both cause poxes of various kinds and heal them, stood at the northern boundary of the City. She is sometimes spoken of as the "goddess of Bangalore," but was probably one of several boundary goddesses of the City. Other paths led to two gates of the settlement and to the fort, where temples dedicated to the warrior god Anjaneya stand today. As citizens walked along these paths, they encountered a dense maze of streets, markets for specialized products, settlements of various communities, and activities ranging from trading to conversations with neighbors and kin to worship.

Markets, either permanent or temporary, were also important nodes. The market to the south of the City and north of the oval fort was one. Here goods were traded; small temples existed along with shrines of Sufis and a mosque and, a little distance away, the entrance to the fort. This market (today called the Krishnarajendra Market, or K. R. Market) emerged after an esplanade was created near the Siddikatte Tank connecting the City with the fort in the last decade of the seventeenth century. Another was the market area that converged along the two main roads of the City. This market was more or less permanent, with rows of shops lined up on the edges of the road. Within Bangalore and outside of the City were also periodic fairs where produce from the city and the farming communities were traded. Many of these fairs coincided with a *jatre* of a deity or saint. For instance, the Nandi Bull Temple near the Kempambudi Tank, with an idol of the animal mount of the deity Shiva that was ten feet high and fifteen feet long, was the site of an annual groundnut fair, where heaps of fresh nuts brought directly from the fields were sold. This temple stood close to the village of Sunkenahalli, where groundnuts were the main produce. One author mentions that Kempe Gowda built the Nandi Temple and that it was probably a custom for villagers from Sunkenahalli and other villages to offer groundnuts grown by them to Nandi before selling them in Bangalore. Or, unwilling to enter the tollgate of Bangalore, they may have started their own fair.[11]

Tanks were perhaps one of the most crucial elements of the spatial order and had in their vicinity several temples. Situating a settlement generally near a large manmade body of water such as a tank *(kere)* appears to have been the form of urban organization in this area.[12] Tanks are the most important water-harvesting structures in the state of Karnataka (there are more than 40,000 today), but there are other types of bodies of water as well; these include an artificially created receptacle for storing water *(katte, kunte)*, a natural pond for the provision of drinking water and for washing *(kola)*, a well *(bhavi)*, and an artificial reservoir near a temple *(kalyani)*.[13] Since much of Karnataka is in the rain-shadow region of the Deccan Plateau, tanks and natural lakes were historically the primary sources of water for drinking and irrigation. Most of these tanks were built in pre-British days. Around 1830, the Mysore region, of which Bangalore was a part, had 19,800 tanks and 16,371 wells.[14] A linked chain of such tanks was created in each region; the surplus water from one tank would flow into another situated below it or at a lower level in the same catchment area.[15]

Kempe Gowda himself built a number of tanks after he founded the city in 1537, including the Kempambudi, Dharmambudi, Sampangi, and Siddikatte Tanks (two of which are shown in Map 3). The tanks fed the needs of horticultural land and provided water for the populations within and outside of the settlement area, for the well water within the town was mostly brackish.[16] Some of the tanks had special functions. The Dharmambudi Tank, to the west of the City, fed its moat, whereas the Karanji Tank, to the south, fed the fort's moat.[17] Of the total number of water bodies, five—the Dharmambudi (on the northwestern side of the fort area), the Sampangi (on the eastern side), the Kempambudi (on the southwestern side), the Korapollayam (on the southern side), and the Lalbagh Tanks (on the southeastern side)—formed an interconnected ring around the City and the fort about 1870.

The tanks also had ritual and recreational roles. The Sampangi Tank, on the eastern edge of the City near the Dharmaraja Temple, was associated with the "birth" and manifestation of the Karaga icon every year. The Lalbagh tank, on the south side of the city, lay next to a pleasure garden by the same name laid out by Haider Ali and his son, Tippu Sultan, in the second half of the eighteenth century, and it was used to water the garden. One author attributes the impulse to build the garden to Haider Ali's visit to the French colony of Pondicherry and the model of the garden to the plans of gardens in Sira that were built on Mughal lines.[18] Haider Ali named the garden "Lalbagh," meaning Red Garden, due to its profusion of roses and other red flowers.[19] It was built in a classic Mughal four-part, cross-axial pattern rather like that of the gardens built by the emperor Shah Jahan in north India in the previous century. Shah Jahan's gardens, adapted from gardens in other parts of the Islamic world, such as Persia and Syria, channeled water in two main modalities. The emperor's gardens were either built near a river on the plains of north India (as at the Taj Mahal in Agra), with a waterfall running through, or in terraces with a central water channel (as in the Shalimar Gardens in Kashmir) collecting the water of mountain springs. Another version of this four-part garden could be seen in the funeral gardens of the Mughal kings, where the center of the cross was occupied by a pavilion, tomb, or waterpool.[20] In the case of Haider Ali's Lalbagh, a large tank watered the garden. Each plot of land was allocated for a separate plant, and the walks were lined by various trees and plants imported from Delhi, Lahore, and Multan. Tippu Sultan supplemented this garden with flora from Kabul, Persia, Mauritius, and Turkey, and his portion of the garden was watered by three wells.[21]

Gardens, Parks, and Parades

The British took over Lalbagh in 1799 after the last Anglo-Mysore war, which ended with the defeat of Haider Ali's son, Tippu Sultan, by the English governor general Lord Cornwallis. It remained in the possession of Major Waugh, a military botanist, up until 1819, when it was given to the British governor general Warren Hastings. Until 1831, it was a branch of the Royal Botanical Gardens in Calcutta. It passed thereafter into the hands of Sir Mark Cubbon, who founded the Agri-Horticultural Society of India in 1839 and handed over the gardens to the Society. In 1856, the gardens became the Government Botanical Gardens for the "improvement of indigenous plants and for the introduction of exotic plants of economic importance" (*Karnataka State Gazetteer Bangalore District* 1990, 237), a horticultural norm that was somewhat different from that underlying the pleasure gardens of Haider Ali and Tippu Sultan. Until 1874, zoo animals were also collected, but these were eventually transferred to the zoo in Mysore. Although in Haider Ali's time Lalbagh had covered an area of about sixteen hectares, by the end of the nineteenth century it stood at forty hectares.[22]

In the interim, the British created the Cantonment in the area of Halsur village (later known as Ulsoor) near a tank by the same name in 1809 (see Map 4). There was no fort near Halsur; the main landmark there was the Someshwara Temple, which had been rebuilt in stone by Kempe Gowda II in the seventeenth century and crowned with a tall spire. Around the temple, which stood in the central part of the settlement, were markets and shops for different goods, houses, and several smaller shrines. The annual chariot procession of the Someshwara Temple traced the main path through the settlement, running southwest to northeast. It attracted hundreds of persons from the area and villages close by, such as Damlur and Dukanhalli. After the British settled in the area, Halsur and other settlements came to be increasingly filled with Tamil-speaking households, many of them having migrated from the Madras Presidency, which was under British rule. Soon, large and small churches could also be seen in the vicinity, such as Trinity Church outside the southwest end of Halsur.

The separation of the City and the Cantonment took a new form under the British Commission (1831–81), which changed the axes of administration. During the years of the commission, the British ruled the city di-

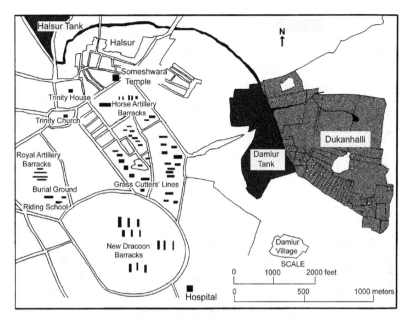

Map 4. The Cantonment, Halsur, and Dukanhalli in 1870. Source: Directorate of Survey Settlement and Land Records, Bangalore, map of the Cantonment of Bangalore, 1870.

rectly after divesting the king of Mysore, Krishna Raja Wodeyar III, of his authority after peasant riots broke out in the kingdom. This shift in authority became perceptible in the landscape. One of the first acts of the commission was to shift the government offices from Mysore to the palace in the Bangalore fort. In those days, this was the only building with sufficient space for accommodating officials. The period of the first sole commissioner, Sir Mark Cubbon, from 1834 to 1861, is associated with this location as well as with the opening of the first railway line in Bangalore and the laying of a large number of roads and telegraph lines. All these enhanced the trade links of the city. The city's orientation shifted further to the northeast a few decades later with the creation of Cubbon Park during the time of the next two commissioners, Lewis Bowring (commissioner from 1862 to 1870) and Col. Meade (whose tenure was from 1870 to 1875).

According to oral accounts of the gardener community, Cubbon Park was laid out between the City and the Cantonment in 1864 on land owned or previously cultivated by the Vahnikula Kshatriya community. As Map 3 shows, Cubbon Park occupies a tract of land north of the Sampangi Tank.

The park (now covering an area of about 320 acres) was an irregular polygon of grass and trees and a few key government buildings. The creation of Cubbon Park and the construction of the Public Offices (1864–66) in it altered the cityscape of Bangalore radically. The Public Offices building, which later housed the High Court of the state, was a new landmark. In front of it was an equestrian statue of Sir Mark Cubbon that was unveiled in 1866.[23] Paths now led out of the City through Cubbon Park, linking the Cantonment and the City on a regular basis. As these paths came to be frequented more and more and as horticultural gardens were eaten up by the park, which was transformed into a large, groomed, green space, Cubbon Park became a node for leisure and business for the residents of the Cantonment.

The Cantonment itself, initially conceived of as a location for troops near Halsur Tank, also spread westward toward Cubbon Park. There was now not only a new market located near the tank, called Russell Market, but a number of Muslim and Christian households, and speakers of Tamil and Urdu had begun to settle in the market area, carrying on a variety of mercantile and service activities. A number of English migrants also began to settle in the expanded Cantonment, where new parks, boulevards, and promenades were laid out. Here suburbs began to develop—for instance, Richmond Town, Langford Gardens, and Cole's Park, with bungalow-type houses for the richer families.[24] The presence of the English in the Bangalore Cantonment also generated exurban expansion. Anglo-Indian families began to settle twelve miles to the east in an area that came to be known as "Whitefield." In 1879, an association was formed to assist these settlers (it was named after the founder of a similar association in Madras, Mr. D. S. White), and the government lent about 4,000 acres of land to them.[25]

The Parade Ground, which measured two miles from east to west and was surrounded by a riding path or mall, was the center of military activity. The mall, called the Parade Road, was bisected by Brigade Road and was lined with various stores, bakeries, and theaters that were used especially by the local elite, both Indian and English. At the western end of the Parade Ground stood the bungalow of the commissioner; to the north were barracks for the native regiments, to the northeast the barracks for the British infantrymen, and toward the east (shown on Map 4) were the Royal Artillery Barracks and Trinity Church. In fact, the route from the Trinity Church at one end of the mall to St. Mark's Church and Queen Victoria's statue near the boundary of Cubbon Park at the other end of the mall formed an important path by the turn of the century.

Cubbon Park mediated the separation between the City and the Cantonment, in essence softening the boundaries between the two and indicating that they were now connected to a larger political and civic body dominated by the Cantonment. In fact, in 1891 the population of the Cantonment was 100,081 persons in comparison to the population of 80,285 in the City.[26] This new experience was dramatically portrayed two decades after Cubbon Park was created, when Prince Albert Victor Christian Edward of Wales, the son of Queen Victoria, paid a visit to Bangalore in 1889. The royal party got down from the train at the City Railway Station, and a procession of horse-drawn coaches took them toward the City. A grand display greeted them at the corner. The Dharmambudi Tank, a broad sheet of clear water, carried a float with a party of dancers in colorful clothes. The procession then moved toward the Cantonment. Later in the afternoon, a huge reception was held for the prince in Lalbagh at the newly constructed "Glass House," a modern engineering feat constructed of cast iron and sheet glass.[27] The Glass House was an addition to the four-part garden of Haider Ali and Tippu Sultan, later the site of countless flower and horticultural exhibitions held by the Mysore Horticultural Society, which was registered in 1912.

Up until 1949, when the City and the Cantonment came to be unified under the Bangalore City Corporation, there were at least two models of urban planning visible in Bangalore: the fort-settlement and market-tank model and the English parks and gardens model. The elements of these two models were different, as I have tried to show in these sections. The Public Offices and the commissioner's bungalow replaced the fort in the first model. Two vibrant markets existed in the two settlements of the City and the Cantonment. Tanks, however, continued to be central in both models. Even after the establishment of the Cantonment, the British and the Wodeyar rulers of Mysore constructed many tanks.[28] Tanks, with wells and canals linked to them, supported gardens in both models. However, each had its own version of what the "garden" meant. In the first model, gardens were essentially horticultural lands where a variety of fruits, flowers, and vegetables were produced for the urban centers. The addition to this model was the pleasure garden of Haider Ali and Tippu Sultan that stood on the fringe of the City. In the second model, with the exception of the Lalbagh Botanical Gardens where "indigenous" and "exotic" species were cultivated, gardens built by the British were large or small grassy parks with trees and flowers and surrounded by suburban bungalow houses with their own green spaces. Later, they came to include the many recreation grounds created by Wodeyar kings for the beautification of the City after the British reinstalled them in 1881.

From Gardens to a Grid Plan

It was the displacement of horticultural gardens and bodies of water after the 1950s in the new capital of the state that marked a definitive shift in land-use patterns and created a new spatial model in Bangalore. Today, control over the gardens and tanks in Bangalore is effected through land zoning regulations, through reports and laws passed by the central and state governments rather than through a monolithic urban policy.[29] The Constitution of India vests the state government with the power to enact laws relating to land. Acquisition and requisition of property, however, are powers jointly enjoyed by both the center and the state government, and the latter also has the right to place restrictions on individual property rights in the public interest.[30] For the classification of land use and a land use plan that applies to Bangalore, the key governing documents are the development plans.

The Bangalore Development Committee was formed in 1952 to work out a development plan for the city. It prepared a report indicating the city's growth and development, and in 1961 the Bangalore Metropolitan Planning Board (BMPB) was constituted and prepared the Outline Development Plan (ODP) for Bangalore in 1963. In 1966, the state government declared Bangalore a "Local Planning Area" under the Town and Country Planning Act (1961), an area of the same dimensions as the area under the purview of the BMPB. A City Planning Authority was constituted in 1967 for this region. It modified the ODP prepared by the board, and the government approved this in 1972. The planning area of the ODP was 500 square kilometers, of which 220 square kilometers was the "conurbation area" proposed for development. The remaining area of 280 square kilometers was earmarked as a "green belt." In 1976, the Bangalore Development Authority (BDA) was constituted and prepared a Comprehensive Development Plan (CDP) covering a period up to 2001. The government approved this in 1984. The planning area was extended from 500 square kilometers to 1,279 square kilometers. The conurbation area covered 449 square kilometers and extended into the green belt of the ODP; the plan envisaged a new green belt of about 830 square kilometers beyond the urbanized area. However, the calculations of the 1984 CDP had to be revised, mainly because population growth fell between 1981 and 1991, from 76 percent in the previous decade to 40 percent. Today, a Revised Comprehensive Development Plan approved by the government in 1995 covers the period up to

2011. The planning area has remained the same, but the conurbation area has increased to 597 square kilometers. The proposed green belt is 682 square kilometers, a decrease from 64.89 percent of the area covered in the 1984 CDP to 53.32 percent of that covered in the 1995 CDP.

The planning area in the documents is thus divided into two categories. It includes the conurbation area, which is the area delineated for the purpose of urbanization, and the green belt (sometimes called the "rural tract" or "agricultural land"), which is supposed to retain its green character without any development. The BDA acknowledges in the plans that the green belt concept is derived from the ideas of the British urbanist and planner Ebenezer Howard and that the green belt is meant to consist of land around the city that is predominantly agricultural in use. The plans are therefore hybrids between Howard's "garden city" model with its ring of green on the outskirts and a modernist grid model within the conurbation area. The two models are linked by a pattern of radial roads (the Madras Road, the Mysore Road, and others) along which industrial and residential activities have come to be located.

Although land use has not always been regulated by the considerations outlined in these development plans, the plans themselves give data about land use at different points of time in the city. Land use is classified in the following categories: residential; commercial; industrial; public and semipublic use; open spaces, parks, playgrounds, or recreational areas; agricultural land; defense or unclassified land; and transport. The area of land in use in the different categories in 1963, 1972, 1983, and 1990, available from the plans, is given in Table 2. Table 2 also gives the proposed land use by the year 2011.

The area in residential and commercial use expanded between 1963 and 1990, but declined in terms of the percentage of the total area. The land in industrial use showed a declining percentage, even though the area increased, which appears to mirror the changes in the city's economic base. The percentage and area of land in public and semipublic use showed an increase in the period under consideration, whereas the percentage of land in use as parks and open spaces remained approximately the same even though the area increased. The land in use for defense has shown a declining percentage over the years, although the total amount of land held is more or less the same. The area in use as agricultural land (including horticultural land) decreased in percentage between the 1960s and the 1970s. The figures for agricultural land are not available in the later plans, although the proposed green belt figures are available in the CDPs as discussed earlier. However, a study by the Indian Space Research Organization that was

Table 2

Land use in Bangalore, 1963–2011

Classification	1963 (area in acres)	1972 (area in acres)	1983 (area in hectares)	1990 (area in hectares)	2011 (proposed) (area in hectares)
Residential	10528 (37.5)	14537 (41.34)	5777.65 (28.48)	9877.65 (34.78)	24369.21 (43.16)
Commercial	683 (2.55)	958 (2.73)	634.07 (3.13)	675.07 (2.38)	1643.68 (2.91)
Industrial	3069 (10.57)	3069 (8.74)	1956.61 (9.65)	2038.61 (7.18)	3844.07 (6.81)
Public and semipublic	2100 (7.6)	2596 (7.4)	2533.64 (12.49)	2615.64 (9.21)	4908.91 (8.69)
Parks and open spaces	2206 (7.98)	2485 (7.08)	2050.16 (10.11)	2132.16 (7.51)	7788.15 (13.79)
Agricultural	2940 (10.6)	2940 (8.37)	—	—	—
Defense or unclassified	6474 (23.2)	7179 (20.43)	2114.24 (10.42)	2114.24 (7.45)	2213.94 (3.92)
Transport	—	1356 (3.86)	5216.81 (25.72)	8946.63 (31.49)	11697.04 (20.72)
Total	28000 (100)	35120 (100)	20283.18 (100)	28400 (100)	56465 (100)

Source: Government of Mysore 1968, 8 (for 1963); Ravindra 1996, 95 (for 1972); Bangalore Development Authority 1984, 24 (for 1983); Bangalore Development Authority 1995, 74, 80 (for 1990 and 2011).

Note: Numbers in parentheses indicate ratio of annual total. A hectare is 2.471 acres.

reported in 1985 showed that in 1912, 69.3 percent of the study area (652 square kilometers) was in use as agricultural land and that this area decreased to 32.6 percent in 1985. At the same time, the built-up area increased from 6.1 percent to 48.7 percent.[31]

The plan data, however, do not show how land use has actually changed within Bangalore from one category to another. This can be seen dramatically with respect to bodies of water and green areas in Bangalore, the fates of which have hung together. In 1985, the government of Karnataka set up a committee called the Lakshman Rau Committee after its chairman to make recommendations with respect to the tanks in the city area.[32] On the basis of its recommendations, submitted in 1987, the government passed an order in 1988 that required that attention be paid to tanks that could be saved and ordered that those that could not be restored instead be converted into parks. The Lakshman Rau Committee report stated that there were about 390 tanks within the jurisdiction of the BDA. Of these, 262 lay between the conurbation boundary and the metropolitan area. Within the conurbation limits (which came under the jurisdiction of the committee for making recommendations), there were two kinds of tanks:

1. Disused tanks (forty-six tanks) that had been breached to become sites for buildings that were leased to the Horticulture Department, the Bangalore Development Authority, and other institutions.
2. Live tanks (eighty-one tanks, thirteen of which received specific recommendations).

Many of the concerns of the report about saving existing tanks have been echoed by newspaper reports and citizens' organizations.[33]

Realising the folly of reclaiming wetlands, most European nations in the early sixties under the auspices of the International Biological Programme decided to preserve and not reclaim their wetlands. They realised that these liquid assets had to be saved even at high immediate cost for their long term economic and ecological advantages. Here in Bangalore, it is a different story. Several tanks which could have remained productive and beautiful are vanishing before our eyes. Those which are not being deliberately destroyed, like the one at Kacharanahalli beyond Lingarajapuram, will die unnatural deaths, their inflow channels being clogged with rubbish dumped by residents and municipal authorities, or by a drastic change of land use patterns in the catchment and periphery of the tank. The Survey of India maps of a few decades ago marked with great precision the several tanks of Bangalore and also indicated their inflow channels. Many tanks which were classified as perennial in these maps two decades ago, are shown as seasonal in the later maps, confirming the degradation which has occurred. (Zafar Futehally, "Bangalore's Dying Tanks," *Deccan Herald*, Bangalore, August 21, 1988)

Other reports have expressed a concern for the fauna of these tanks:

> In less than a week, tens of thousands of fish have perished in two lakes because of high toxic levels resulting from seepage of sewage. The first disaster was witnessed in a lake inside the famed Lal Bagh botanical garden. Civic officials have admitted that severe contamination of the tank by the inflow of sewage led to the disaster. The second was reported at Sankey tank on Friday where over 40,000 fish, including varieties such as Catla, Rohu, Mrugal and Silver Carp perished. ("Sewage in Bangalore Lakes Kills Fish," *The Asian Age*, 26, Bangalore, June 1995)

A report published in 1993 by the Centre for Science and Technology, a nongovernmental organization in Bangalore, can be considered a follow-up to the document produced by the Lakshman Rau Committee. It points out that of the 127 tanks under the purview of the Lakshman Rau Committee, 3 tanks were excluded from the government order of 1988 because the BDA had already converted them into residential layouts. The Centre, working together with the Urban Division of the Karnataka Forest Department, could not trace a further 7 tanks. Of the other tanks, 8 had had their use completely changed to residential and commercial use and could no longer be recognized as tank beds. Eighteen tanks had been converted to slums and housing for poorer strata, some of them under government schemes. Seven tank beds had been leased to various parties, private and governmental, for the purpose of building housing colonies, bus depots, schools, hospitals, and colleges. The BDA had encroached on 27 tank beds for the creation of housing layouts. In addition, 23 tanks were threatened because of indiscriminate mudlifting and brickmaking, and there was solid waste dumping in 25 tanks, domestic waste flows in 56 tanks, and industrial effluents in 14 tanks.[34]

Reports published by leading newspapers and nongovernmental organizations have also discussed the inadequate water supply of the city, most of which today is from the Kaveri River project, and the role that traditional water-harvesting systems have played.[35] In previous years, tanks in the vicinity of the city had supplied water to citizens, but with the construction of various dams in the state, of which the Krishnarajasagar Dam (initiated in 1911 and completed in 1937) was the most prestigious, this picture changed completely. This dam, built across the Kaveri River near Mysore with the Brindavan Gardens (terrace gardens of over twenty acres started in 1927) at its base, was the fulfilment of the engineering utopia of Sir M. Visvesvaraya, one of the Diwans of Mysore. The dam was built to irrigate a vast agricultural belt in the state, and the complex of the dam and the pleasure garden represents a type of garden and wetland environment that emerges from a commercial-agricultural landscape rather than an urban vision.

In 1993, the government set up another committee with the same chairman as the Lakshman Rau Committee.[36] The 1993 Expert Committee inspected several of the tanks identified by the Lakshman Rau Committee and found that the state of Kempambudi Tank, along with many others, had not improved. It also noted that except for Lalbagh, laid out in the late eighteenth century, and Cubbon Park, laid out in the mid-nineteenth century, no new big parks had been added to the city. It recommended that a number of "regional parks" be developed, along with parks at fifty-five other sites (some of them tank beds) in different parts of the city. In a significant departure from many other similar discussions, the committee included places of worship, burial grounds, and crematoriums as potential sites for the development of green spaces. Although it mentioned six temples, the Dharmaraja Temple, the locus of the Karaga *jatre*, was not one of them, indicating that by this time all green spaces near the City had long been swallowed up.

The threats faced by bodies of water and gardens in Bangalore are enormous: landfilling, sewage, encroachment, the collusion of property developers and corporation authorities, and population pressures.[37] Part of the problem is that the grid models of urban planners fit uneasily with the model of the rural regions of the state represented so graphically by Visvesvaraya's dam. It is outside the scope of this book to discuss the tensions and contradictions between the urban and the rural areas and groups in this part of the state. The other part of the problem is that the displacement and disappearance of these sites in the city is based on an official discourse and categories—represented by the CDPs and the ODP—that tend to separate elements of an urban model that were historically linked, such as bodies of water and gardens. Gardens and bodies of water had multiple roles in everyday and ritual processes of communities, and their connections to each other were material and symbolic. For instance, *Kere Haadu* (Tank Song), a Kannada documentary made by the filmmaker L. V. Sharada that premiered in 1997, reminds us of the loss of tanks and their ritual and ideological associations as well as their economic role.

There are, however, four specific issues within the models advocated by the ODP and the CDPs with respect to bodies of water and gardens that need to be emphasized. The first issue is that of jurisdiction. Almost all of the eighty-one tanks designated by the 1987 Lakshman Rau Committee report within the conurbation area fall under the jurisdiction of the Forest Department. A few of these, such as the Yediyur, Kempambudi, Mattikere, and Madivala Tanks, fall under the Bangalore City Corporation. It appears that in the case of some—for instance, the Bellandur Tank—a transfer to the Forest Department is under way. In the case of gardens, the Horticultural Department of the corporation maintained 416 parks and gardens covering an area of 760 acres in 1998. These included 12 museums in the city, 110 ornamental parks, and a miniature forest; 300 more places earmarked for parks and gardens by the 1995 CDP are meant to come under the corporation's control.[38] The BDA looks after 8 parks in four housing colonies east of the city. The 2 oldest parks in the city, Cubbon Park and Lalbagh, fall under the control of the Government of Karnataka Horticultural Department. This incredibly complex jurisdictional crisscrossing creates not only confusion, but also loopholes that allow for corrupt practices and legal evasion.

The second issue is that of the green belt. The formation of new extensions on the outskirts of Bangalore affecting the green belt was one of the factors that led the authorities to draw up the development plans. However, the government failed to move fast enough, and Bangalore exploded with authorized and unauthorized construction.[39] The 1995 CDP acknowledges that "spotted development" has already occurred within the green belt, including the high-technology Electronic City on Hosur Road, an export-processing zone on Whitefield Road, and industrial pockets along other radial roads. It states that these developments were "wrongly classified" under the green belt in the 1984 CDP, and in many cases it reclassifies them; for instance, the University of Agricultural Science was reclassified by the 1995 CDP for public and semipublic use.[40] In reality, the green belt includes a range of establishments that are permissible within its limits: brick kilns, quarries, highway amenities such as filling stations, hospitals and educational institutions, nurseries, orchards, urban villages, and so on. These render meaningless the concept of the green belt as an area protected from constant urbanization. As the twentieth century has drawn to a close, there has been no indication that the government means to seriously pursue the idea of the green belt for much longer.

The third issue is that of the reclassification of many tanks and lakes from public and semipublic use to use as parks and open spaces or from parks and open spaces to other uses. For instance, in the 1984 CDP, the ambiguous language of the document notwithstanding, the Bellandur Tank was not listed under parks and open spaces, but was cited as one of the two large tanks in the area.[41] The 1995 CDP explicitly stated that existing "tank beds," such as that of the Bellandur Tanks, should be classified under major recreational facilities, such as parks and open spaces.[42] The tank faces other threats as well. It lies a few kilometers from Bangalore Airport and covers an area of about 950 acres. A major part of the sewage of the city is released into the tank, and although efforts have been made by a number of civic groups and the High Court has also intervened, further action with respect to the tank is yet to be taken.[43] By the time that the 1984 CDP itself had come into existence, other tanks had long disappeared from the city, their area consumed by transport facilities such as a bus terminal (Dharmambudi; see Figure 5) and a stadium complex (Sampangi), and they were thus effectively assigned to new categories. As recently as 1997, Koramangala Tank on the southeast side of the city was converted into multistoried flats for athletes attending the Indian National Games. This conversion was facilitated by an order of the government, despite public protest, changing the status of the site from a park and recreation area into a residential one.[44]

Even a key source of water for the city has come under threat. In 1991, the Government of Karnataka and the Bangalore Metropolitan Region Development Authority gave permission to a Delhi-based firm called DLF, Ltd., to construct 270 luxury villas on the Arkavati River feeding the Thippagondanahalli Reservoir on the west side of the city, the source of 25 percent of Bangalore's water supply. This constituted an obvious pollution hazard, and although a public-interest lawsuit was filed against this construction and supported by the High Court, in 1991 the Supreme Court of India upheld the decision of the Government of Karnataka. Eventually through public pressure and even involvement from the Bangalore Water Supply and Sewage Board, the government withdrew their permission in June 1999.[45]

The fourth issue is that of the parks and open spaces themselves. Some of the new parks are managed badly, and attempts have been made to change the face of old ones such as Cubbon Park. On the one hand, there are serious environmental concerns; ornithologists claimed that the vegetation in Cubbon Park was withering due to the increase in traffic through the park, posing a threat to sixty species of birds and fifty-five

Figure 5. The central bus terminal created in the Dharmambudi Tank bed.

species of butterflies in the park.[46] On the other hand, there is the threat of enroachment. Although Cubbon Park fell under the category of parks and open spaces in both the 1984 and the 1995 CDPs, the government de-notified a portion of the area, claiming that it was now classified for public and semipublic use. Subsequently, a hostel extension for legislators began to be constructed within Cubbon Park. From 1998 onward, protests by a number of nongovernmental organizations—especially Sanmati, the Environment Support Group, the Citizens Voluntary Initiative for the City, and others—led the court to stay the denotification, but not the construction. Therefore, the conflict about Cubbon Park continues. Although an attempt has been made by some private companies and civic organizations to assist in the maintenance of several small parks and traffic islands in Bangalore, these efforts are woefully inadequate.

Gardeners and the City

By the time the Lakshman Rau Committee made its recommendations, of the three tanks of importance to the Karaga *jatre*, the Sampangi, the Dharmambudi, and the Kempambudi, only the last remained, albeit in a some-what threatened state.[47] Not only these tanks, but also the site of the Karaga icon's "birth"—the "Upnirinakunte" (Saltwater Pond)—have been affected over the decades; now the pond can barely be recognized as a body of water at all. Once a large receptacle for storing water, now it is little more than a puddle. A large portion of the land under construction sites, parks, and streets in Bangalore today was once garden land connected to these bodies of water and once belonged to the Vahnikula Kshatriya community. This land was severely affected by the building activity of both private developers and the BDA. The Siddapura Nursery, for instance, which had been protected because of the creation of a "horticulture zone," is being sold to builders. Of the twenty acres that once constituted the nursery, eight acres had already been sold by 1997. The nursery, which before 1949 encompassed five hundred acres, has been reduced to a small area near Lalbagh Road. Although forty families run the forty nurseries in the horticultural zone, more than 1,500 workers depended on the nurseries and related activities for their livelihood in 1997.[48]

Before the various zones of the city were cemented together by concrete, the urban area could still be seen as a patchwork of settlements (villages, suburbs, the City, and the Cantonment) linked together by horticultural land, parks, and tanks. The Vahnikula Kshatriya gardeners were an integral part of this patchwork. They were important in landscaping efforts in the city, and, in fact, the gardeners claim that they built Lalbagh and other important parks. The gardeners maintained the city's many gardens, nurseries, and parks using water from wells and tanks and supplied perishable horticultural produce to the urban center. Horticultural products are usually classified as fruit crops, vegetables, flowers, and plantation and spice crops in this part of Karnataka state. In Bangalore District as a whole, the total area planted in fruit crops in 1990–91 was 214,164 hectares, whereas vegetables covered 187,275 hectares, flowers 11,540 hectares, and plantation and spice crops 821,531 hectares.[49] Writing in the 1950s, Venkatarayappa stated that many small nurseries in Bangalore were cultivated using wells twenty feet deep to supply water. Besides these nurseries, in the surrounding areas of the city large quantities of vegetables, fruits, and flowers were grown to meet the needs of the city's markets. Seeds, fruits, and flowers were even exported to England. Gardens seemed to have largely occupied the western, northern, and southern edges of the Bangalore City Corporation area in the 1950s. The eastern part of the corporation area was largely agricultural, and paddy, pulses, and other crops were grown.[50]

About 1870, the Sampangi Tank (see Map 3) on the eastern edge of the City was also part of a horticultural zone. Around it were gardens that the Vahnikula Kshatriyas cultivated on both the north and the south sides of the tank—for instance, in the area of Sampangihalli. This cultivation was done chiefly using water from wells that had water most of the year due to the rainwater stored in the Sampangi and other tanks that increased the water table in the region. The Vahnikula Kshatriyas supplied vegetables to the City Market for sale, and after the British Cantonment was established, they began to grow a number of "English" vegetables, such as cauliflower. The area south of the tank was also known for the growth of certain fruits, such as grapes. In other areas outside the City, the Dharmaraja Temple of the Vahnikula Kshatriya community owned a great deal of land donated by the ruler Krishnarajendra Wodeyar in 1811. These plots were used for the maintenance of the temple and performance of the Karaga *jatre;* gardeners with small gardens cultivated many of them. According to T. M. Manoharan, a headman of the community, up until the 1950s, temple lands included tracts in three main villages (shown in Table 3), Wangasandra, Neelasandra, and Doopanahalli, all on the peripheries of the City.

Vahnikula Kshatriya households also owned land in villages close to Halsur, where the British had established their Cantonment. About 1870, a number of Vahnikula Kshatriyas who cultivated gardens along the fringes of the Damlur Tank lived in Dukanhalli village (see Map 4), although most of this area was largely agricultural. Their produce was supplied to the Halsur market, which, after the Cantonment grew up, was surrounded by army barracks. Dukanhalli itself was a small village with a few temples. It is not clear whether the temple of the goddess Muthyallamma, in the center of the village area, was as large a structure as it is today; certainly, a sacred

Table 3.

Land ownership by the Dharmaraja Temple in 1950

Land survey no.	Land in Neelasandra, in acres	Land survey no.	Land in Doopanahalli, in acres	Land survey no.	Land in Wangasandra, in acres
27/5	0.70	4	21.25	26	5.18
57	2.17	5	22.05	33	16.20
58	1.34	7	20.09	34	0.13
74	2.1	8	5.28	35	2.22
79	17.15	50	17.06	36	1.16
98	1.29			37	2.36
99	1.5			58	2.26
				60	2.15

Source: Interview with and survey records obtained from T. M. Manoharan, July 17, 1997.

area for the village goddess existed, though probably as a small shrine. Before the establishment of the Cantonment, only open land and the Damlur Tank lay between Halsur settlement and Dukanhalli. Therefore, two large tanks—Damlur and Halsur—framed Halsur village.

By 1940, when the government prepared village survey maps, the two areas where Vahnikula Kshatriya families had fairly large amounts of land, Sampangihalli and Dukanhalli, had changed in subtle ways. Sampangihalli (see Map 5) had shrunk to the area south of the Sampangi Tank, and the portion of the tank to the west also seemed to have disappeared from the landscape. A study from 1957 mentions that cattle fairs were generally held in the Sampangi Tank, which indicates that the tank had probably gone dry in the interim.[51] Cubbon Park occupied a larger area than before, right up to the road near the tank's edge. There were a few more houses in the village, although most of the key houses in the Vahnikula Kshatriya community—for instance, that of the headman—were still clustered at the northern end of the village. Garden plots existed in the central and southern portions of the village, where a large number of wells stood. Most of the grapes grown there were still supplied to the Bangalore palace. In Dukanhalli (see Map 6), too, the area of the Damlur Tank had shrunk, and there were more houses in the center of the settlement area and on the plots of garden land to its south.

The most startling changes came in the decades after 1950. Of temple land itself, very little remained. According to T. M. Manoharan, between 1950 and 1990 the Dharmaraja Temple lost nearly all its land, which was either acquired by the city authorities or simply disposed of by individual tenants; only a few plots remained of those shown in Table 3.[52] In Sampangihalli, now called Sampangiramnagar locality (see Map 7), all lands were transformed into housing sites or acquired by the City Corporation for its housing projects. Gardens had been totally transformed into a huge number of tiny housing plots and occupied the central and western parts of the area; toward the southern edge, there were City Corporation quarters, the office of Bharat Earth Movers, Ltd., and the telephone exchange.[53] The northern edge came to be filled with a number of buildings lining a main road that ran between the tank and the locality, such as the Vokkaliga Association building, the Pallavi theater, the Woodlands hotel, and shopping complexes. The tank itself bore no resemblance to that of an earlier period. The Kanteerava Stadium, a new and impressive engineering landmark, was built on the tank area that was filled in, and all that remained of the huge tank was a small enclosure of water that was walled in with

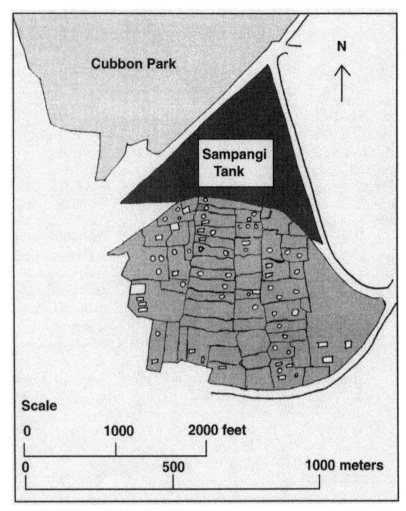

Map 5. Sampangihalli circa 1940. Source: Directorate of Survey Settlement and Land Records, Bangalore, Village Survey Map of Sampangihalli, circa 1940.

concrete. Near the tank, a small pillared hall was constructed as the site to which the Karaga priest is brought annually after his rituals at the pond in Cubbon Park on the night of the Karaga's birth (see Figure 6). Just outside the enclosure, a triangular piece of temple land had become a petrol station. The fate of the Sampangi Tank was similar to that of the Dharmambudi Tank, which was converted into an important node, the city's central bus terminal, after being drained and filled.

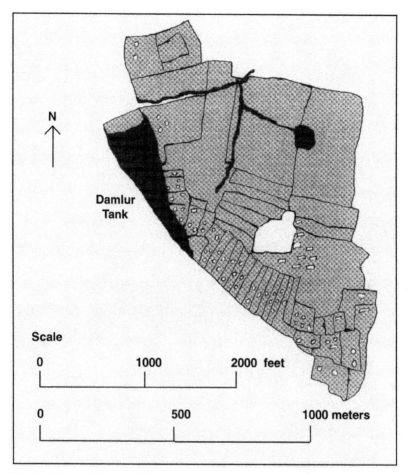

Map 6. Dukanhalli circa 1940. Source: Directorate of Survey Settlement and Land Records, Bangalore, Village Survey Map of Dukanhalli, circa 1940.

Dukanhalli, now called Doopanahalli, also turned to concrete (see Map 8). The settlement expanded, with a large number of houses built on tiny plots. As shown in Map 8, the kind of development that grew up toward the north of Doopanahalli—symmetrical housing plots on a grid plan—dominated the entire area, which still had somewhat villagelike characteristics. The village actually formed an island within the grid. Professionals, members of the armed services, bureaucrats, and businessmen occupied the housing extensions around it. The area of the Damlur Tank had also been converted into plots, such as quarters for the Indian Space Research Orga-

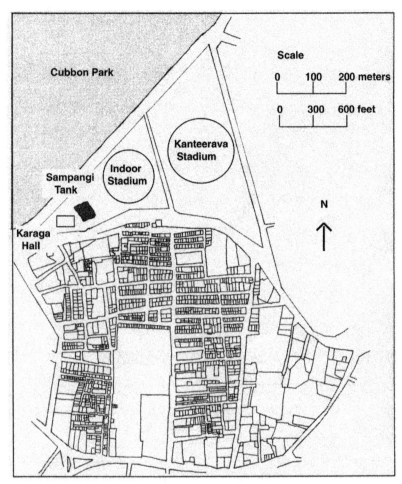

Map 7. Sampangiramnagar circa 1996. Source: Directorate of Survey Settlement and Land Records, Bangalore, Survey Map of Sampangiramnagar, circa 1996.

nization. In the area around Doopanahalli, there are few landmarks; parallel roads with houses lining them follow other such roads. Once in a while, a small park or a religious center such as the Chinmaya Mission Temple or the Methodist Church forms a soft wedge between roads and houses. Only in the area of the old village can one identify a central cultural junction: around the Muthyallamma Temple are other temples, a market, and a small clearing that can be recognized easily as a sort of public square. Today the procession of the goddess in Doopanahalli begins at this site, where residents and the temple chariots of various deities and saints in Doopanahalli

Figure 6. The Karaga hall dwarfed by the sports complex.

congregate along with those of other "villages." The procession also visits the sites of a number of water bodies, although they are now extinct.[54]

The temple, the public square, the market and bodies of water, and the ritual linkages created by the festival of the goddess in Doopanahalli connote a construction of the civic that is also visible in the City, where the Karaga *jatre* occurs. This is the idea that the public sphere is dispersed in many sites—in temples and shrines dedicated to various deities and sacred personages, crossroads, markets—and that urban activity is similarly disaggregated. In part, this rests on a model of a spatial order that can be traced to the period between the mid-sixteenth century and 1800, the fort-settlement and market-tank model. In a sense, even after the British Cantonment was set up, and up until 1950, elements of this model continued under the new dispensation, with markets, bodies of water, and dispersed settlements providing realms of urban activity that were plural and multi-centered. However, this construction of the civic by the Karaga *jatre* and the festival in honor of the goddess is not merely an invoking of previous regimes of space. What, then, is the relationship between older spatial orders, new urban models, and ritual and performative activities?

After 1950, in all three areas of the City, Sampangihalli (or Sampangiramnagar) and Dukanhalli (or Doopanahalli), bodies of water and gardens disappeared as new landmarks and nodes grew up and paths were redrawn.

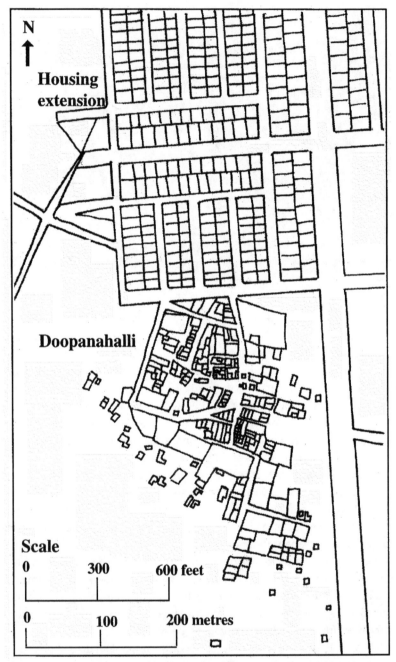

N

Housing
extension

Doopanahalli

Scale

| 0 | 300 | 600 feet |

| 0 | 100 | 200 metres |

Map 8. Doopanahalli circa 1996. Source: Directorate of Survey Settlement and Land Records, Bangalore, Survey Map of Doopanahalli, circa 1996.

The numbers in the working class, petty bourgeoisie, and informal economy swelled with members of communities such as the Vahnikula Kshatriya community as they lost their horticultural land (see appendix). In each of the three areas, the Karaga *jatre* has either continued or gained symbolic importance. For the inhabitants of the City, the Dharmaraja Temple is the site where the Karaga *jatre* has been celebrated for centuries; for those in what is now called Sampangiramnagar, the Karaga is born in a small nearby pond that once was part of a huge tank adjoining Sampangihalli. Those in Doopanahalli began to perform the festival in the years after 1950; the exact year is not known, although villagers claim that it was about thirty years ago. Notwithstanding the fact that tanks and gardens have disappeared, they have become more central to dramaturgical rites and representations than they were in earlier periods.[55] The Karaga *jatre* has come to be perceived today as the primary civic ritual of the city by large numbers of its inhabitants.

As the next few chapters will demonstrate, the older urban models and the contemporary city are reconnected in the performance through various kinetic and oral devices. As we follow the Karaga through the streets of Bangalore today, what we encounter is a recollection of encrypted space, with the materiality of older cities achieving symbolic form in the context of the present cityscape. Also played out is the connectivity of bodies of water and garden land, as ritual and economic units, in a manner different from what is suggested by the land-use categories of various plans that have been worked out for the city since 1950. The *jatre* creates a civic terrain in which the zoning of public space into housing colonies, parks, streets, and public buildings breaks down. In the same way, the civic roles of the gardeners who are the players in the *jatre* are refashioned. No more are the gardeners simply factory workers, shopkeepers, or carpenters; these prosaic identities are merged into the identities of warriors protecting the goddess or becoming identified with her. Through this ritual terrain, the gardeners have also begun to create more expansive political solidarities in Bangalore, an alliance that links them to different social strata in the metropolis. The resulting new community is part of a process of laying spatial, economic, and political claims to the contemporary city of Bangalore.

The Urban Performative Complex

Cults and Performances

Cult centers and their performances, one of which is the Dharmaraja Temple's Karaga *jatre*, reflect the changing histories of Bangalore. Their activities, like the other paths, narrations, traces, and maps described in the previous chapter, also suggest topological inputs and spatial models of the city, constructing and connecting past regimes and contemporary ones. The oral, ritual, and kinetic devices of reconnection differ from one to the other, and the Karaga *jatre* studied in this book is a specific case. However, seen together spatially and temporally, the cults and their performances produce the "urban performative complex," within which the Karaga *jatre* is embedded. The urban performative complex may be defined as a multicentered network of sites of locational sacrality and the sacrality of urban sprawl that links spatial arenas, social constituencies, and civic history on a number of axes through the performance and mediation of sacred power.

Symbols of and beliefs about the possible mediation between living persons and sacred power—embodied in the goddess, saint, guru, or deity to which a cult is dedicated—provide the basic context for this behavior. These do not derive their legitimacy from the same source, but belong to a fund of concepts and practices related to magical intercession (termed *chamatkar, lila,* or *karamat* depending on the linguistic and social identity of the speaker) prevalent in many parts of India. Within the appeals to such an intercessor for redress reside a number of concerns that relate directly to the construction of reality by the city dweller, whether she or he is a government employee, a shopkeeper, or a laborer. Temples and the shrines of deities and holy persons are visited by people bearing petitons regarding various afflictions. For instance, during the summer months, many goddesses receive milk, yogurt, lemons, and other "cooling" substances to ward off skin ailments of children; sometimes chickens are sacrificed for more serious illnesses. In the shrines of Muslim holy men, incense, flowers, and sometimes a cover for the tomb of the Sufi are offered and talismans are procured for safeguarding health. Trees near shrines also become stationary repositories of people's desires. Magical threads (symbolizing wishes for a marriage, children, a good daughter-in-law, or a job), figurines, and garlands are tied to them, and healing, sexuality, and dreams become part of the interface between the interiors of bodies, the bodies of deities and saints, and the exterior surfaces of sacred sites.

The flows between the constructs of sacred power, the body, social groups, and the city are particularly visible, however, at festival time, creating a map of the city for the citizen that is unlike the grid of the urban planner. Points that often have no place within the dominant system of production and political power in Bangalore achieve a significance that is derived from the accumulation of meaning wrought by various processes. It is as if these points, sometimes shrines, public squares, or streets, have gathered value to themselves by accruing cross sections of history and social memories. These spaces provide cultural repositories for the complex of festivals, and through the performances various spatial arenas—the City and the Cantonment, the City and the suburbs, the fort-City-tank—and the transactions between different communities in Bangalore become apparent.

Models derived from cities that were sites of royal power have dominated the discussion of the relationship between the city and its cults. Instead, as the sections of this chapter demonstrate, the Karaga *jatre* is embedded in an urban performative complex that emerges from the cults of "boundary" goddesses.[1] Remarking on the contrast between a boundary goddess and a royal one, Biardeau (1989a, 131–34) states that, as a protector of a territory (usually a village), the goddess is invariably found on the limits of the populated area. In this role, she is usually a virgin goddess (rather than a consort of a god), and if a buffalo sacrifice is made to her, she also evokes images of a warrior. At the level of the kingdom, she is less a territorial goddess and more a goddess associated with a royal lineage. Her shrine is usually in the center of the capital or in the palace, although sometimes she has a "double" on the boundary that may receive a sacrifice. To this one needs to add that the boundary goddess tends to appear with "Backward Class" or "Scheduled Caste" groups that are marginal to the system of power, whereas the goddess of the center appears with ruling groups. The difference is not so much the contrast between a "spouse" goddess and a "virgin-warrior" goddess, but their linkages to political authority and society. An urban performative complex emerges in Bangalore from boundary goddesses who are patronized by social groups that are generally peripheral to the system of power, economy, and culture and from a variety of other sacred personages—Sufi holy men, warrior deities, and Christian goddesses—who are linked to the goddesses on several spatial and symbolic axes. Draupadi, the focus of the Karaga *jatre,* is one of these goddesses.

It is possible to trace the layering of these axes to the period before the founding of the fort and the City by Kempe Gowda in the mid-sixteenth century. Between the fourth and the tenth centuries, the Bangalore region was ruled by the Ganga Dynasty, the first dynasty to set up effective control over the area. Although it seems clear that the area of Bangalore was in-habited for far longer, the earliest reference to Bangalore as "Benguluru" is, in fact, in a Ganga inscription dated about 890 CE that was found at Begur near Bangalore.[2] At the end of the tenth century, the Chola Empire from Tamil Nadu began to penetrate areas east of Bangalore; it later extended its control over parts of present-day Bangalore—for instance, Damlur on the eastern side of the city.[3] Chola power extended over the Andhra and Kar-nataka regions in the eleventh century, and there is evidence that there was constant movement of troops and other personnel into these areas from that period onward.[4]

During this period, the Bangalore region witnessed the migration of many mobile groups—warriors, administrators, traders, artisans, pastoral-ists, cultivators, and religious personnel—from the Tamil country and from other Kannada-speaking regions. With the collapse of the Cholas, espe-cially after 1250, migrations from the Telugu country began to take place into northern Tamil Nadu and into Karnataka. At the end of the thirteenth century, the Pandyas from southern Tamil Nadu and the Hoysalas from western Karnataka disputed control over southern India; during this time, cultivating groups from the Tamil country were also still migrating into the Bangalore region. These events received an additional twist when Turkish armies from Delhi began to make forays into the Andhra and Tamil coun-try, especially in 1311 and 1327–30, more or less undermining these powers and creating more movement of social groups. The next large empire in this region emerged from the Telugu country as the Vijayanagar Empire, the origins of which can be traced to the mid-fourteenth century. This em-pire was finally destroyed two centuries later at the time that Kempe Gowda reconstituted Bangalore as a fort-settlement.

Through these shifts of fortune, there were several settlements, small polities, and administrative units controlled by petty rulers or administrators in the Bangalore region. As Bayly (1989) points out, the tendency of many of these warrior groups and chieftains—Palegaras, Nayakas, and others—was to patronize divinities of "blood and power." The period, especially from the twelfth to the eighteenth centuries, saw the spread of south Indian goddess worship in urban sites such as Bangalore. Various chieftains, warlords, traders, and upwardly mobile groups selected goddesses as the chief deities of new cults or newly patronized cult centers. Some of these were older village deities or lineage deities of particular communities that later came to be associated with more Sanskritized consorts or gods and also with each other. Further, the goddesses tended to be patronized by groups who were speakers of Telugu, Tamil, or Kannada and had a socially diverse following. In Bangalore's urban performative complex today, the first layer—the quadrilateral goddess pattern—invokes these processes, to which subsequent layers were added.

The Quadrilateral Goddess Pattern

From the precolonial period of Bangalore's urban organization, one kind of pattern visible was a quadrilateral set of festivals centered on four female deities whose temples are located within the vicinity of tanks (see Map 9). These occur today in the hot months between March and June and are centered around the goddesses Annamma, Patalamma, Gadagamma, and Muthyallamma. All four are petitioned chiefly for the healing of "poxes" in various forms. The goddess temples today, as in the past, have a heterogeneous patronage drawn from different castes and religious groupings.

The Patalamma Temple lies on the south side of Bangalore in the region of the Lalbagh Tank. It is not visible from afar because it lies at a busy crossroads near various public buildings, including a public library, and the temple area is surrounded by a wall. Once inside the wall, however, one can see that the area consists of three buildings situated in an open field with some large trees shading portions of it. Beneath one tree is a platform on which stand snake-stones *(nagakallu)*, which are stones in the forms of particular snake deities, usually in groups of three. Women hoping for the gift of a child or for the amelioration of reproductive disorders chiefly worship these deities. Nearby stands a platform with representations of the nine celestial beings *(navagraha)* that are believed to influence a person's destiny and must be regularly petitioned. One of the buildings is a temple dedicated to the deity Ganesha (usually identified as the remover of obstacles); the other is a large room in which materials are stored, which also acts as a site for rehearsals by a local drama group. In between these two buildings stands the goddess temple, consisting of a sanctum that

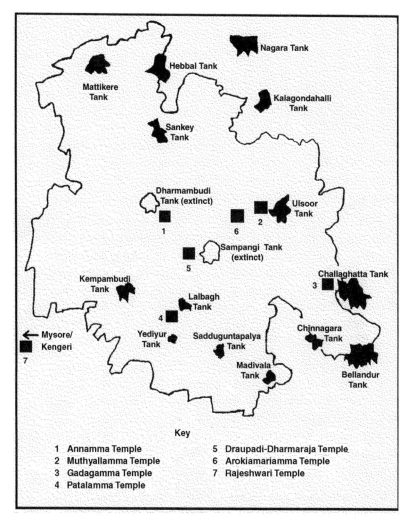

Map 9. Goddess temples and central tanks in Bangalore in the 1990s.

contains a metal image of the goddess and a form that is believed to be her "manifested form" *(udbhavamurti)*. In this temple, favors are sought by lighting wicks placed inside sliced lemons on specific days as votive offerings.

Along one wall are a couple of houses belonging to the priest and his brother, who perform the rites at the temple. They traditionally belong to the oil-presser community (Ganigas) and consider themselves a branch of the family that acts as priests for the other boundary goddess temple on the northwest side of the City, the Annamma Temple. The priest, Pilla Krishnappa, recounted the encounter between Patalamma and citizens of the area:

> The coming of the Amma [literally, "Mother," but refers to the goddess] here goes back about four hundred or five hundred years from the time of Kempe Gowda. The Amma had got ready to have her bath. A group of wayfarers came by after selling their pearls. They did not know that she was there. They wanted to rest and cook their food and looked all around them. They saw two stones standing—this was the manifested form—and with the support of the stones lit a fire and ate their food. At this time, Amma had come from the nether regions *(patala)* and hence was known as "Patalamma." All of the persons who had eaten, except for an old man who was so infirm that he had not partaken of the food, fell unconscious on the ground. The Amma entered the body of a boy [that is, possessed him] and spoke to the old man: "You have lit a fire on me, and I am going to destroy your lineage!" The old man pleaded that they had not known this and would repair the damage by doing whatever they could for the development of the temple if she forgave them. So having given his word, he called the elders from the City, and those who were unconscious also rose. They said to Amma: "How are we to worship you in the form of fire?" She said: "Take this incense with your right hand and throw it over your left side into the fire." That was done and rituals performed. The pearl-sellers gifted this temple to my family as revenue land.
>
> At this time, the temple was in the midst of thick forest, but gradually people began to come here attracted by the Amma. Then, fourteen villages were associated with the temple; now, there are only five villages: Yediyuru, Siddapura, Kanakanapalya, Byalsandra, and Nagasandra. A huge festival goes on for three days every year in these villages on a day which the elders decide, sometime in May or June. There is a fire-walking ceremony, and women and children come with lights, and those who have taken a vow enter the fire after the priest and the man who carries the goddess. The villagers of Yediyuru take the processional idol of the goddess to the Karaga *jatre*, though all the other villagers also join. In 1960, the old structure fell down, and the temple was rebuilt by one Kaverappa, a Adi-Karnataka [Scheduled Caste] man with others' help (interview with Pilla Krishnappa, priest of the Patalamma Temple, June 13, 1997).

Pearls are usually an allusion to pox, and this account suggests that these people had just been cured of pox or were perhaps fleeing from some epidemic in the City to this region. They could, however, also simply have been traders returning from sales in the City. The "pearl-sellers" encountered the goddess, but the first contact resulted in punishment due to nonrecognition of the goddess's true form. This had to be atoned for once the nature of the goddess was revealed, in this case through spirit possession. The narrative moved from the act of endowment of this temple to the family of oil-pressers to the creation of a dense settlement. The clearing of forest land gave way to human settlement. Although this was described as an event that occurred after the creation of the City, it was a process that had been occurring in the Bangalore region even in earlier centuries, a process that had been overseen by a local goddess. The goddess's ritual territory consists of a number of villages, today diminished in number, and each year a festival occurs there dedicated to the goddess. The chief feature of this festival is the fire-walking ceremony, in which devotees follow the priest into a huge pit covered with burning embers to demonstrate their faith in the goddess or in fulfillment of a vow. In fact, the Patalamma Temple has a large pit in front of it. This boundary goddess is also linked to the City, primarily through participation in the Karaga *jatre.*

As suggested by this account, each boundary goddess has ritual jurisdiction over groups of "villages," once outside the old locus of the City and today part of the suburbs of the metropolis. Their temples are associated with an older form of organization of independent but connected settlements. The Gadagamma Temple, for instance, located in Damlur on the east side of Bangalore (see Map 9), lies close to the Challaghatta Tank. Today the temple stands in a busy market area just off the main road leading to the city's airport, a major bus terminal, and a golf course. All around the market area are middle-class residences that have eaten into the land of the old village of Damlur. The market area still has the feel of the old settlement and is made up of a set of narrow streets, with shops on either side and dominated by the Chokkanatha Temple at the western edge.

The Gadagamma Temple is part of a complex of four temples in the area, of which the oldest is the Chokkanatha Temple dedicated to the deity Vishnu. Telugu-speaking Reddys (chiefly a peasant caste) patronize it, and the temple adjoins an old tank now filled with buildings. The more recently built temples include a Rama Temple dating from the 1940s, again patronized by the community of Reddys, and an Anjaneya Temple, also Reddy-dominated.[5] The Kurubas (a pastoral caste) own the Gadagamma Temple; Kurubas and Reddys are the two old resident castes in this area.

The Gadagamma Temple is the smallest of the four and consists of a large room with only one entrance surrounded by shops. The central image is a small one, and in fact is not visible at all from the door, because it faces away from the entrance to the sanctum.[6] As the following account suggests, this temple seems to have been shifted from a hill across from the airport road. The deity is petitioned, as is Patalamma, to ameliorate a variety of afflictions associated with women and children. Although the shrine is the least impressive of the four, the goddess Gadagamma is associated in public memory with the other three goddess temples—the Patalamma, the Annamma, and the Muthyallamma Temples—and a specified number of villages are under her ritual authority. Krishnappa Reddy, the chief patron of the Chokkanatha Temple, whose family are extremely old residents of the area, gave the following account:

> Who has built this temple, or how old it is, I do not know. But there are four temples in the four corners of Bangalore. In the north is the Annamma Temple, with twenty or twenty-five villages attached to it; in the south is the Patalamma Temple, associated with about twenty villages; in the west, the Muthyallamma Temple, with fourteen villages; and in the west, the Gadagamma Temple. I have only found records for the Chokkanatha Temple, but not for this one. This area was the district headquarters of the Vijayanagar Empire and called "Adambaluru Jille." After Vijayanagar fell, it passed into the hands of the Tamils for about ninety years, and they renamed it "Devasitamanipatta," stretching over sixty villages till the banks of the Kaveri River. After many years, about 560 years ago, my ancestors came, cleared the thick forest, and settled here.
>
> A soothsayer once gave me a reading. He told me that this spot was one where the sages Kataka and Agastya had done penance, and the latter had built a Vishnu shrine here. Then came an earthquake, and this mountainous area was leveled. Then the Cholas came and built a temple here.
>
> A Harijan [Scheduled Caste], Rama by name, who used to get possessed by Gadagamma, once told my father, Patel Rama Reddy—he used to have jurisdiction over ten villages—this story: When traders used to come here, there was a mountain called Gatatha; this then became "Gadada," and Amma is its form. She came in a dream to one of the traders and ordered him to build her a temple. So he did that on land behind this area, which is

now military land, and seven villages were associated with it: Challaghatta, Ejipura, Nagasandra, Kodihalli, Doopanahalli, Sinagara, and Damlur.

From 1918 to 1925, the festival of the temple ran very well, as I remember. At this time, one Nagappa said to the goddess, "I wish to have your vision," and as we were all watching, a tree close by with very sharp extremities fell down and there was a lightninglike flash. The goddess then spoke through the body of Harijan Rama. She said, "I was the daughter of a Brahmin, but before I was married they left me in the forest. Then the traders came and built me a temple. Now my time is over, and in three years I will be reborn on this earth." During the plague and the cholera epidemic, she also spoke to us and told us to leave the village and return to it after some time. This happened again when there was a fire later one year. In my father's time, the temple was shifted to the village from the military land. (interview with Krishnappa Reddy, patron of the Chokkanatha temple, June 12, 1995)

Krishnappa Reddy's reference to the Vijayanagar Empire, which controlled much of this area between the fourteenth and the sixteenth centuries, is certainly historically correct, and the "Tamils" are probably Nayakas or Palegaras who ruled this area after the breakup of the empire. At least one other detail is clear, that the temple was at first Shaiva, later becoming a Vaishnava temple, perhaps under the Vijayanagar Empire. Reddy mentioned in the interview that the Cholas from Tamil Nadu, who were devotees of Shiva, had influence over this area, and the inscription on the base of the Chokkanatha Temple attributes it to Rajaraja Chola. It was probably built between 1000 and 1150.[7] As in the narrative of the priest of the Patalamma Temple, recounted earlier, in Reddy's memory sacred personages settled in the midst of forest that in time gave way to settlement. The goddess revealed herself to traders—who seem to be highlighted in narratives about the goddess—and demanded social recognition of her presence. The form of the goddess was inanimate. Like Patalamma, who is associated with earth and stone, in this narrative the goddess is linked to a mountain. She also speaks through the body of a low-caste man, just as the goddess in the earlier narrative possessed a young boy. Memories of her presence or intervention are tied intimately to those of place—for instance, the spread of the plague epidemic that occurred in Bangalore at the end of the nineteenth century.

Every year, usually in the hot months between March and June, goddesses such as Patalamma and Gadagamma have their own festivals, with chariots carrying their idols drawn through the city area. In some cases, of course, telephone and electric cables and other obstructions have made use of a large chariot impossible, but each goddess's processional idol still visits households in the area, carried aloft by her devotees. These festivals are not exclusively "religious," but reflect all types of transactions and domains, from the household to the market to a heightened use of public space and an aesthetic and healing experience. The main festival of the Gadagamma Temple occurs during the day when the deity Rama's birth is celebrated (usually in the month of March or April). A large number of chariots from different temples in the area congregate in the old village of which the four temples form a center. In 1997, there were thirty-five chariots carrying processional idols from various sites and old "villages."

The goddess's role in healing is perhaps the most important of her functions, and at the other two shrines as well; people of many communities flock to the temple for cures. In the Muthyallamma Temple on the northeast side of the city near the Ulsoor (formerly Halsur) Tank (see Map 9), not only Hindus, but also Christians and Muslims, can be seen visiting the temple. The goddess's name is derived from the word for pearl *(muttu)* in Kannada and Tamil, suggesting an association with the pox. This temple lies in one of the busiest market areas of Bangalore. Although the entrance is not very imposing and is on a side street, on certain days, such as Fridays, huge numbers can be seen crowding into the temple, which essentially consists of one room, with the house of the priest behind it. The image of the deity is made of red clay, although there is a processional image of metal that is also placed on one side of the room. It is this second image that is taken to the villages over which the goddess has jurisdiction. Near this image sits an astrologer who is a Telugu-speaking Brahmin and is clearly the most important ritual officiant in the temple. According to him, his family was in the employ of the Vijayanagar Empire and over time found their way to this temple. The astrologer is approached by a number of people seeking charms and amulets to ward off the "evil eye" and to remove afflictions. However, many seek him out for forecasts as well, his end of the room forming a crowded niche in the temple.

As in the accounts of the Reddy and Pilla Krishnappa, in the account the astrologer gave one day in 1995, Muthyallamma was at first not recognized, but later she revealed her nature and assumed a form that associated her with earth. She appeared as a little girl to an old, childless couple who belonged to a community of potters (Kumbharas). The couple raised the little one as their own, but one day she disappeared without a trace. The couple was distraught until she appeared in their dreams and revealed her real nature. They were instructed to make an image of red clay, and she agreed to dwell with them in this form forever.

The goddesses are associated with different communities. In the case of the Annamma Temple, for instance, a family of oil-pressers provides the priests of the temple, although numerous other communities patronize the temple. The temple adjoins what used to be the Dharmambudi Tank and is in the frenetic Kempe Gowda market area on the north side of the City. Close by are over fifty theaters screening films in a variety of regional languages in addition to hundreds of retail outlets. The temple is a fairly large one, although once again, it is not visible from the road. On entering its enclosure, we find images of "Bisilu Maramma," consisting of a number of stones that are propitiated as the goddess who wards off diseases connected with excess "heat," such as skin ailments. Annamma herself is in the main sanctum, which is cordoned off from the rest of the large room that is usually filled with dozens of families carrying offerings for the goddess. The "goddess" is a nonpersonified stone image surrounded by images of seven of her "sisters." Many of the devotees coming to this temple bring chickens, fruit, milk, and yogurt as offerings. Often young women are brought to the temple to remove from their cheeks metal spikes that have been inserted in order to find each a suitable groom (invariably after the marriage), but the most common reason for propitiating the goddess is to obtain cures for ailments connected with small children, again chickenpox or mumps. This goddess, perhaps because her temple is closest to the City, is considered by many to be the goddess of the City. It is for this reason that the Karaga procession visits her temple on the last day of the *jatre*.

Just as the City has a quadrilateral ritual complex situated around nodes formed by the tanks, the fort, too, in public memory, has its own quadrilateral pattern of temples dedicated to Anjaneya, who stands as the guardian of the "gates" of the fort. This association of the deity Anjaneya (or Hanuman, as he is called in north India) with the gates of the fort is probably related to a pattern of organization inherited from the Vijayanagar Empire.[8] Anjaneya, the monkey-god, is a brave warrior and an ideal devotee of the god Rama in public imagination. Four temples dedicated to him exist in Bangalore today; some of them have existed since the time of Haider Ali and Tippu Sultan's fort, and others are probably more recent replacements of older shrines, perhaps associated with the mud fort of Kempe Gowda that surrounded the City. These are the Yelahanka Gate Anjaneya Temple (in the north part of the City, now near the neighborhood of Cubbonpet, on Kempe Gowda Road), the Byal Anjaneya Temple (on the south side of the old fort), the Kote Anjaneya Temple (near the eastern wall of

Haider Ali's fort), and the Gali Anjaneya Temple (on the west side of the city, on the Mysore Road).

The Yelahanka Gate Anjaneya Temple (see Map 3 and Figure 7) today stands at a busy intersection and forms an island in the middle of the road. It is a prominent site, although hundreds of pedestrians and vehicles flow past it daily. Like the Kote Anjaneya Temple (see Map 3), this temple is also patronized by a variety of groups, and certain days of the week are considered particularly auspicious for visits. As in the case of the goddesses, devotees seek out Anjaneya for wish fulfillment. There are also periodic festivals at these temples, and two of them, the Yelahanka Gate Anjaneya Temple and the Kote Anjaneya Temple on the north side of the fort and south of the City, appear within the structure of the Karaga *jatre* as well. This is a reminder of the complementarity of the City and the fort, the figures of the goddess and the celibate warrior Anjaneya, a theme treated in greater detail in chapter 5.

The Christian "Goddess" of the Cantonment

At the beginning of the nineteenth century, in the neighboring city of Mysore, the seat of the Wodeyar kings, the cult of Chamundeshwari (which presents the Dassera performance) began to emerge as a heavily patronized royal cult. The Dassera is essentially a festival that occurs at harvest time in Mysore. It is dedicated to the goddess Chamundeshwari, who is believed to have felled the demon Mahisasura, an event that is celebrated on the tenth day of the festivities. Each day for nine days, various manifestations of the goddess are worshiped. The tenth day is also associated with the worship of weapons, and in Mysore, the rites culminated in the past with the victorious march of the king, who was seated on an elephant accompanied by an array of cavalry men, foot soldiers, and an orchestra.[9]

The Chamundeshwari Temple, on the hill next to the city of Mysore, has existed since at least the sixteenth century. The Wodeyars, in effect, inherited the performance of the Dassera from the Vijayanagar Empire after the latter broke up.[10] Public rituals such as the Dassera were important for ideological control and legitimation of the rulers in Vijayanagar, and archaeological excavations have documented that there were many processional routes through the capital.[11] After the fall of Tippu Sultan and the restoration of the kingdom to Krishna Raja Wodeyar III by the British, not only were the temple to Chamundeshwari and the palace refurbished, but the Dassera processions began again with a lot of pageantry.[12] However, we have to contextualize this display of royal allegiance to the family goddess on the hill within the contest during the nineteenth century between the

Figure 7. The Yelahanka Gate Anjaneya Temple.

Wodeyars and the British.[13] The significance and pomp of the Dassera festival from the turn of nineteenth century onward relate to the political in-
security felt by the Wodeyar kings; the festival was an outward assertion of
symbolic power in the context of threatened royal authority.

Although there is an external synchrony between the cities of Bangalore and Mysore and the cults of Chamundeshwari and Draupadi, nothing
approximating a royal cult emerged in Bangalore. Instead, from the early
nineteenth century onward, a nine-day schema of performances at two
sites, the City and the Cantonment, came to be visible. The Cantonment
area had effectively become a separate town, with private houses, businesses,
and markets springing up side by side with military barracks. Troops had
been sequestered to the north of the Parade Ground (for native regiments),
to its northeast (the Baird Barracks for British infantrymen), and the east
(the Artillery and Cavalry Barracks) on the fringes of Ulsoor or Halsur Tank.
New markets—Russell Market and Johnson Market—arose. Many residential suburbs with large bungalows situated amidst private gardens, boulevards, and public parks were also built.[14]

Seen synchronically, the separation between the City and the Cantonment was marked by two kinds of goddesses. In the City stood the temple dedicated to Draupadi. In Blackpally (a name with its variations typically
given to the "native quarter" of a cantonment or city built by the British)
stood St. Mary's Church with its shrine to Our Lady of Health, Arokiamariamma (literally, the "Mother of Health" in Tamil). Today, this area is the

busiest market in the erstwhile Cantonment, with a variety of wholesale and retail outlets. The church stands across from a large bus terminal and a major government hospital, the Lady Curzon and Bowring Hospital. Its tall spire can be instantly located, and the church occupies a sizeable site, because it is the center of one of the largest parishes of the area. The church itself contains the figure of Christ on the cross, but adjacent to it is an altar dedicated to Arokiamariamma, the most active part of the church complex. Our Lady is depicted in the form of a sari-clad statue carrying the figure of the Infant Jesus in her arms. Her sari, like the clothes of many Hindu goddesses, is changed daily. This statue is not accessible to devotees, but nearby are a number of smaller replicas that devotees can touch or place votive candles before. In the enclosure housing the images, devotees can be seen in their seats or on their knees praying. During the day, regular prayers are conducted at this altar and also within the church. Most of the petitioners are Tamil-speaking Christians, although a large number of Hindu and Muslim devotees are also to be found; this church attracts one of the largest inter-religious constituencies in Bangalore.

The Christian presence in Karnataka dates at least to the fourteenth century; the Dominicans were followed by the Franciscans in the middle of the sixteenth century. The Society of Jesus founded the Jesuit Mission (later known as the Karnataka Mission) a century later in 1650. The Diocese of Mysore had a Catholic population of 17,275, with seventeen foreign missionaries and two Indian priests, in 1862. In Bangalore, there were 1,000 European and 5,500 Indian Catholics about that time. The Diocese of Bangalore was created out of the Diocese of Mysore in 1940. Father Jacquemart, the chancellor of the new diocese, wrote in 1942 that there were seven parishes with a total of 35,000 Catholics in Bangalore. In 1982, this figure had risen to 146,275 Catholics in twenty-five parishes.[15] According to the 1981 Census, the total Christian population in the Bangalore Urban Agglomeration was about 196,126, about 6.7 percent of the total population, and this figure included Protestant Christians, Syrian Christians, and members of charismatic churches.[16]

Of the Catholic parishes, the oldest is St. Mary's Parish, begun in 1702; a church was founded later, in 1811. In 1974, Pope Paul VI designated the church a minor basilica. The souvenir booklet released on that occasion states that Abbé Dubois, who founded the church, had adopted the garb of a Hindu mendicant and was known as the Dodda Swami ("Big Master"), an appellation generally given to holy men.[17] The booklet presents an alternative history of Bangalore; in contrast to the accounts associated with the other goddess shrines, in this account settlement began not in the forest, but in a near desert, and was associated with cultivators rather than traders:

> Our story goes back to 1685 when Kempa Paji Gavounden [Kempe Gowda?] abandoned Kodookkoopally situated about 7 miles to the west to begin the city of Bangalore. At that time Blackpally was almost a desert. Some people came from Ginji and built a small village that they gradually surrounded by a mud wall. This village took the name of Biliakkipally [literally, "white bird village"] because it is said that the rice they cultivated was white and also because a number of white birds were found in those rice fields. Till 1830 some parts of the old mud wall still existed. To the west of the wall the Hindus built a small temple to Hanumantharaya which still exists. To the east another temple was built dedicated to Someshwara. Between these two, the Christians built a small chapel with a thatched roof facing the east and called it Kanikaimatha ["kanikai" has a range of meanings in Kannada and Tamil, from a tax to an offering made by a supplicant to a superior for favors received; "matha" means "mother"]. (*Souvenir St. Mary's Basilica* 1974, no page numbers)

In the public memory embodied in the souvenir booklet, an important local figure in the history of Blackpally was the catechist Gnanamuthu. His parents, after being baptized in 1765 near the French colony of Pondicherry, came to Haider Ali's capital in 1775. Haider apparently received the father with great joy and appointed him his army commandant. Gnanamuthu is said to have done much to assist the small Christian community in the state under Abbé Dubois. The booklet states that there were 1,000 Christians in this parish in 1803, most of them Europeans. Mostly local Christian groups patronized the church, although, as oral testimonies claim, all communities, including Hindus and Muslims, solicited the Christian "goddess" for mediation in a variety of afflictions.[18] For instance, she was petitioned by hundreds living in the area during the plague of 1898, when more than 2,000 people are said to have died.

An account by Peter Konar of his miraculous cure is printed in the souvenir and is fairly typical of many stories told about the church:

> I met with a serious accident on 4th April 1950 at the junction of Cubbon Road and Cavalry Road. While I was riding a motor cycle, a military dispatch rider came and dashed his motorbike against mine. The impact threw me out of my vehicle and I could not lift my right leg. When I opened my eyes, the first object that struck my eyes was the cross atop the steeple of St. Mary's Church,

Shivajinagar. The sight of the cross made me think of Our Blessed
Mother and I prayed to her to save me and to cure me completely.
I was praying silently and I made a solemn vow to Our Mother that
my leg should be cured without amputating and that I would visit
the shrine of Our Lady of Health Vailanganni [one of the central
Christian pilgrimage sites in south India, located in Tamil Nadu]
every year during the Novena in September as well as actively
participate in the solemn feast day celebrations at St. Mary's
Church. (*Souvenir St. Mary's Basilica* 1974, no page numbers)

Peter Konar went on to write that he was certain that his prayers were
heard. His fractured leg was cured completely without any amputation.
The reference that he makes to the festival of Mary is to the nine-day celebration held every year in September. Both the Karaga *jatre* and St. Mary's
Church have similar temporal schemas of festivities for their respective
goddesses: The Karaga *jatre* occurs in the month of March or April, whereas
the novena to Mary is in September, with both employing a nine-day time
frame. During the novena, the church is filled with literally hundreds of
devotees dressed in clothes of saffron color *(kavi batte)*. The color, according to one devotee, symbolizes renunciation. The devotees may fast, and
nearly all of them visit the church daily to light candles or make offerings
in return for favors. Most of these are for intercession in matters of health.
However, there are others who pray for assistance from Mary that is not
sanctioned by the church. For instance, one woman I interviewed said that
she had come to pray to be "married" to a man who already had a wife. Another woman came to solemnize her "union" with another woman. The final
day of the festival usually has the bishop leading prayers along with a number of other dignitaries, such as politicians and film stars. The streets are
packed with devotees who accompany a procession of the image of Our
Lady in a chariot through the market area, as is the case in the festivals of
many goddesses. Traffic comes to a standstill in this business area, and policemen can be seen diverting cars and other vehicles. The flag of the
church, which has been raised at the beginning of the novena period, is
lowered after the festivities are over.

The Goddess and the Sufi

The Muslim population in the Bangalore Urban Agglomeration was 422,841
according to the 1981 Census, about 14.5 percent of the total population,
including both Sunni and Shia groups, although the Sunni population
comprises the majority.[19] The major subgroups include local Dakkini Muslims, who usually speak Urdu, Tamil-speaking Labbe Muslims, Malayalam-

speaking Mopla Muslims from the west coast, and Kutchi Memons, also from the west coast. Among the Sunni population, many are followers of various Sufis. The Sufi presence in south India dates back at least to the fourteenth century and a variety of orders, including the Chishti, Suhrawardi, and Qadiriya, have flourished in urban and rural sites in the region since that time. Many of these orders were associated with old Muslim and new migrant strata, traders, peasants, and officials, and they had symbiotic relations with other local groups with their own traditions.[20] In many cases, the goddess's festival and that of a Sufi saint appear together or one has a symbolic role within the structure of the other. In Bangalore, as in other parts of Karnataka, during the period of mourning marking the martydom of Prophet Mohammad's grandson, Hussain, as well as at temple festivals, "tiger dancers" and other performers belonging to Hindu and Muslim (largely Sunni) communities are present during the rituals of the goddess. Of the twenty-eight major festivals celebrated in Bangalore District today, eight are dedicated to goddesses and six to Sufi holy men.[21] Sufi shrines *(dargah)* have, as can be seen, almost as many festivals connected with their holy men as do goddess temples.

As Assayag (1993) points out in his study of a Muslim shrine and a goddess temple near Belgaum in North Karnataka, often the same terminology is used to describe ritual practices within these sacred sites. For instance, the tombs within the Muslim complex *(mazar)* are often described as *samadhi,* a term used in the context of Hindu holy persons, and the power and blessing *(baraka)* of the person is equally described as *shakti.* Assayag points out that this complementarity and convergence is often ignored in studies of cults in south India, because most research focuses on dominant groups associated with temples. He also emphasizes that for both Hindus and Muslims who visit the places of worship of the other group, "cultural duality is respected through barely differentiated behavior" (241). Many of these relationships have been under strain in recent years for a variety of reasons apart from communal tensions. For instance, in 1974, while Dev Raj Urs was chief minister of Karnataka, the government promulgated a law that stipulated that only Hindus could act as priests in charge of Hindu temples. This made the roles performed by Muslim families in Hindu temples, and vice versa, extremely vulnerable.[22]

Many Sufi shrines in Bangalore—for instance, the tombs of Saiyeda Ma and Saiyid Pasha Baba (both of the Chishti order)—lie on the northern side of the fort of Tippu Sultan and near the mosque toward the east. There are also a number of shrines near the Cantonment, some Chishti, and others, like that of Haider Shah Jilani, of the Qadiriya order.[23] The belief in the holy person's blessing by Muslims who come to the tombs is connected to the symbiotic relationship in Sunni Islam in this region between the mosque and the tombs of various spiritual teachers. For women, a tomb provides access to the sacred power from which they are excluded at the mosque, which they do not usually attend. For men, both these sites are available, and on Fridays both the mosque and the shrine are visited. For both groups, the holy person's power, which is seen as an attribute given to him by God, allows various indications of divine power and acts of grace *(karamat)* to occur. On any given day, men and women come, chiefly to the saint's tomb, to pray for relief from various afflictions and for blessings. An officiant may offer Quranic readings *(fatiha)* on their behalf as well; other practices include a resolve to read the Quran for a certain number of days at the tomb, to light lamps near it, or, if the afflictions are removed, to offer flowers or a cover for the tomb.

For many of the Muslims who frequent these shrines, the spiritual transaction is a continuing one between the believer and the holy person. Intercession is constantly sought for a variety of afflictions, and efforts are made to seek the holy person's blessings. For others who are non-Muslims, the contact is sporadic and does not necessarily involve any continuing relationship. This is demonstrated at the shrine of Haider Shah Jilani, which lies next to the Muslim burial grounds on Nandidurg Road in the Cantonment.[24] The circular shrine is painted bright green and is surrounded by land bearing a number of trees and a community hall. The road itself is a busy one, for there is truck traffic and a petrol station next to the shrine area. The saint *(pir)* honored here is considered the twenty-second descendant of Ghauth al-Azam Dastgir, a Sufi of the Qadiriya path of Sufism.[25] The shrine itself houses the tombs of the saint's relatives and his spiritual successor, who passed away in 1994; the saint passed away in the 1950s.[26]

Most of the believers are Dakkini Muslims and Kutchi Memons; there are also members of other faiths, Christian and Hindu, who may come to pray there for intercession or to ask for charms to remove evil or cure afflictions. Most of the latter persons live in the neighborhood of the complex; they are petty shopkeepers, mechanics, domestic servants, and workers in the informal sector, both men and women. The Dakkini Muslims who come here tend to be of middle- and low-income strata (shopkeepers, vendors, schoolteachers, butchers, and those engaged in informal or industrial work), whereas the Kutchi Memons in general are traders and shopowners in the Cantonment. Some of the latter are also employed as lawyers, doctors, and other professionals.[27]

In 1994–95 I collected a sample of stories about the holy person's intercession at the shrine.[28] A Dakkini Muslim male, an electrician by trade, said that during the four-day festival of Dastgir he and his friends traditionally perform a number of acts, such as eating fire or piercing their bodies with sharp instruments. This is done after taking the saint's name, and not a drop of blood is shed. He had fathered a daughter, but had no son. He prayed for a son during the festival in 1994, and the next year a son was born to him.

Another man spoke about his sister. She works in the Printing Department of the Government Press, is thirty-five years old, and had been unmarried for a long time. Every time an alliance had been arranged, it was broken off. Finally, at the anniversary of the death of Arif Shah Bawa (who is associated with the fulfillment of marriages), she applied a decoration *(mehndi)* to her hands after it had been consecrated at the tomb, and within a year she was married.

A woman who does embroidery work in Shivajinagar came to see the ritual officiant. Her husband does welding work, but was out of work. She sold her jewelry to allow him to go to Saudi Arabia, where he found work as a welder. This decision was made on the advice of the officiant, who, in turn, was "advised" by the saint. The husband, however, wished to return, and the wife came to ask for an amulet to give him fresh resolve in his decision to stay.

An Anglo-Indian lady who used to be an acrobat with the Jumbo Circus had experienced repeated falls because her workmates or someone else had put a hex on her. When the circus was put up at the Palace Grounds opposite the shrine, she sought an amulet from the ritual officiant for her protection. This favorably altered her circumstances.

Another lady, a Punjabi whose husband was a soldier stationed in Bangalore, had been unable to conceive for seven or eight years. Her in-laws wanted her husband to divorce her. After obtaining a thread from the priest, she conceived within a year and had twins, a boy and a girl. The officiant had asked her to come to the tomb for eleven Fridays and to break a coconut near the flag and distribute it to small children.

The shrines are intimately linked with the history of the City and the Cantonment.[29] It is recounted, for instance, how Haider Shah Jilani arrived in Bangalore in 1922 and the entire Kutchi Memon community in the Cantonment gathered to receive him at the station and to give their allegiance to him. He became the leader of the Kutchi Memon community and was instrumental in the establishment of an association *(jamath)*. Khuddus

Sahib, a Dakkini Muslim who worked in Hyderabad as a police official and retired in 1950 in Bangalore, remembered two important miracles performed by the saint. In 1935, there was an epidemic of the plague in Bangalore. In each house, four or five persons were carried away by it. The seriousness of the epidemic was such that the locality of Rahmatnagar was called "Plague-Shed." People flocked to Haider Shah Jilani to ask for his intervention. He directed them to print with sandal paste the symbol of Imam Husain *(panja)* on each house in the area, and the epidemic was staved off. About the same time, there was a fierce drought in the area, and many died of starvation. Hindus and Muslims began to flock to their respective shrines praying for rain. Learned Muslims and other elders decided to consult Haider Shah Jilani. He prayed for rain after the Friday prayers at the prayer wall near the Cantonment Railway Station. The heavens opened, rain poured down, and people could be seen dancing in the rain for joy.[30] He also came to play an important role in local politics during the independence struggle, when leaders such as the Ali brothers and Mahatma Gandhi visited Bangalore. It is said that the saint met with the Ali brothers and gave his blessing to the Non-Cooperation Movement against the British. Led by Usman Sait, who controlled the Cash Bazaar in the Cantonment, British goods were burnt on open land near the Cantonment Railway Station by large numbers of Kutchi Memon traders.

The shrine of Haider Shah Jilani is certainly one of the most important in the Cantonment, and memories of the saint are tied to constructions of place and history. But a number of other saints' tombs, dating at least from the time of Tippu Sultan, are to be found in different areas of the City, and one is associated largely with Dakkini Muslims and with the Karaga *jatre.* The shrine of Hazrat Tawakkul Mastan Baba, a Sufi of the Suhrawardi order, appears directly within the structure and mythology of the festival itself. The shrine is located on the western edges of the City, in Cottonpet on O. T. C. Road.[31] The shrine complex is large and visible from the street and lined on either side by stores and houses. Outside it are a variety of vendors selling flowers, incense, food, and pictures of the Sufi's tomb. At any time during the week, the shrine is filled with people who come to pray, collect an amulet, or fulfill some vow. Hindus, especially those which children, who seek amulets for their young ones, are found here in large numbers, just as Muslim women carrying their children are found at the shrines of the pox goddesses. Most of them appear to be lower-middle-class and working-class persons. The priest or some member of his family is usually found sitting near the entrance to the shrine saying prayers for devotees, creating amulets for children, and directing the affairs of the shrine.

According to the priest of the shrine, Hazrat Tawakkul Mastan was said to be one of the nine hundred disciples of a saint who came to India from Turkey (some devotees say Iraq), having brought with him coffee seeds that were sowed in south India for the first time. The shrine is said to be about three hundred years old. Other devotees have stated that Tawakkul Mastan came to Bangalore during the time of Tippu Sultan and Haider Ali and even worked on the new fort of the rulers, which was in progress at that time.[32] A popular story that circulates among the Vahnikula Kshatriyas is that one year the Hazrat was watching the Karaga procession making its way through the City. He was knocked down and injured by the crowd and cursed it. The procession could not move any further because of the saint's wrath. Finally, turmeric paste was brought from the temple and applied to his wounds. His wrath thus "cooled," the procession moved forward. As a mark of respect for the saint, the Karaga troupe visits the tomb on the final day of the festival (see Figure 8). This legend appears to bear a family resemblance to other legends in south India in which Sufi holy men are embedded in temple folklore. Similar stories are told about Hazrat Hamid Shah Auliya, whose tomb is located in Kanchipuram in Tamil Nadu. One of the miracles attributed to this saint is freeing the chariot of the temple, which had been immobilized at the start of the town's great festival.[33]

Another tale about the reciprocal links between the shrine of Hazrat Tawakkul Mastan Baba and the goddess temple is that when the Karaga *jatre* first began, the Karaga priest was not able to bear the power of the goddess and died. Mastan Baba asked the new priest and the Virakumaras to chant, "Din, Din" (which in Arabic means "religion, religion"), and no harm came to the troupe after that event; so the Karaga troupe visits the tomb every year to pay its obeisance. One year, however, the priest bypassed the tomb, but the Karaga "flew" off his head and went to it. Only after the priest's intervention could the procession move forward.

During the Karaga *jatre*, the crowds gathered to watch the Karaga visit the shrine are enormous, and often men and women can be seen going into an ecstatic trance or desperately seeking the touch of the Karaga priest in order to exorcise a spirit or ghost *(djinn* or *bhuta)*. The priest traditionally throws a lemon, considered to have healing properties, into a large basket in the shrine that contains other lemons. These are then sold for a fee to eager devotees by the management, and the funds are used for whitewashing the tomb and its precincts. The procession from the

Figure 8. The Karaga troupe visits the Hazrat Tawakkul Mastan Shrine.

Dharmaraja Temple to the Tawakkul Mastan Shrine occurs on the night of the full moon and in the early hours of the morning, long before dawn.

The Sacrality of Urban Sprawl

The urban performative complex comprises not only part of the City and the Cantonment and sites of locational sacrality within them, but also the urban sprawl of Bangalore. After 1890, a number of new housing "extensions" and "towns" grew up in Bangalore, but particularly after 1950, the creation of housing colonies, usually built on grid plans, accelerated to meet the needs of the growing population of the city. The city was criss-crossed by a radial system of roads such as Bellary Road, Mysore Road, Old Madras Road, and Hosur Road that led out of the city to other urban sites. Complex relationships between the City and the new suburbs have come to be articulated within the urban performative complex. This is visible in two cults that have grown up in Bangalore since the 1960s.

The first is the cult of the Infant Jesus, which is linked in public imagination to the older St. Mary's Church as well as to other local goddesses, for there are many aspects of this cult that parallel practices in the performative complex. Its nine-day festival, for instance, resembles the Karaga *jatre* as well as the St. Mary's Church novena, whereas the chariot festival parallels practices in many Hindu temple festivals and that of the Christian "goddess" of the Cantonment. The final day of the Infant Jesus festival, January 14, coincides with the harvest festival ("Pongal") of Tamil Hindus.

According to local belief, the beginnings of the worship of the Infant Jesus can be traced to an older devotion to the Infant of Prague.[34] The image of the Infant preserved in the Church of Our Lady of Victory in Prague became an important object of popular devotion in the seventeenth century, a synthesis of the idea of the kingship of Christ as well as that of holy childhood.[35] The church of the Infant Jesus in Bangalore is found in the Viveknagar area. In 1972, its parish was carved out of Sacred Heart Parish, which had previously covered areas that lay on the periphery of Bangalore both spatially and socially. Because of the unwieldiness of the large area, it was felt that division of the parish was necessary. This area was largely marshy, but also comprised of flower gardens. At the church a popular tale circulates of how Father Paul Kinatukara, then the parish priest, prayed to the Infant Jesus of Prague on the suggestion of an Anglo-Indian lady. A site of 4.5 acres of agricultural land was then acquired, and the foundation for the new church was laid by the archbishop in 1969. Father L. Peter brought the statue of the Infant Jesus from Sacred Heart Church and installed it in a church improvised from a tent. This "tent church" was used for eight years in the area known as the "Rose Garden." The miraculous intervention of the Infant Jesus is credited with obtaining the approval of the Bangalore Development Authority to build the church in 1979. In 1989, a separate shrine on the left side of the area was constructed to house the statue of the Infant Jesus. The services in the church cater to speakers of Tamil, and Christians among them, although at any point in time those who come to pray in the shrine may also visit the church.[36] The church itself does not hold a separate statue of the Infant Jesus.

At the right side of the church is a nine-paneled structure that pilgrims circle, praying; the various panels must be "read" clockwise and include panels depicting the birth of Jesus, his church in Prague, and the "tent" church in Bangalore.[37] For the unlettered as well as for others, this pictorial representation of the life of the Infant Jesus connects Jerusalem and European cities to Bangalore in a syntagmatic chain of public memory. The very same events are celebrated at the annual festival novena to the Infant Jesus, which is offered on January 4–14 every year. On January 4 a ceremony is held in which a flag depicting the Infant Jesus is hoisted in the large compound of the church, a ceremony that is attended by hundreds, Christians and non-Christians alike. The nine-day period that follows this is considered especially sacred, and many regard it as a special time to pray and seek blessings. On the final day occurs the chariot festival (popularly referred to by the Tamil word *ter*), during which the statue of the Infant Jesus is drawn through the streets of Viveknagar. Crowds gather for this final event, some of them to complete their nine-day novena, others to witness the spectacle, and on the streets are residents of the area, who throw salt at the idol to seek the Infant's blessings. Salt and pepper have a symbolic significance in the magical beliefs that surround the Infant. Pepper is said to represent a pox of any kind (and many will be found throwing pepper at the flag for the removal of such an affliction), and salt stands for the fulfillment of favors of other kinds.

The shrine to the Infant Jesus is the main site of devotion for those seeking favors. The usual practice is for seekers to bring flowers for the statue and light candles in prayer, practices they conduct as individuals, as there is no priest at the shrine. There are prayers that have been formulated by the priests of the church that can be said every hour or for nine days and are available in different languages.[38] Most pilgrims also believe that if one comes to the shrine for nine Thursdays, there will be some relief from one's afflictions, but the system is not structured rigidly. The body of the faithful can be seen most clearly in two sorts of representations. Most of the local newspapers, but primarily the *Times of India*, have a page or two dedicated to advertisements offering "Thanksgiving" to the Infant Jesus for "favors received" on Thursdays. There is even a stall at the shrine where one can pay 315 rupees for such an advertisement.

Another site is the "Infant Jesus Museum," where offerings are received from those whose prayers have been answered. Often these are accompanied by letters that tell of the miracles performed by the Infant in the lives of the persons or families concerned. A Brahmin resident of Viveknagar who has donated a figure of the Infant to the museum writes: "I was able to fight cancer and also got a job thanks to Infant Jesus." A Tamil Christian woman from Kolar Gold Fields states: "My husband was infected by Tetanus. Doctor gave him only 48 hours to live after the attack. We cried and prayed to the Infant Jesus. He extended his life term." Other letters accompanying offerings refer to the granting of children to childless couples or to safe deliveries. A Tamil Christian resident writes that she was childless for twenty-three years and was blessed with a child due to her prayers. There are gifts of wedding chains. The husband or wife of a Christian couple from Madras writes: "My son was friendly with a good girl for nearly seven years. He used to play in a band. The crooner was a female. Her husband was in the Gulf for some time. My son and that woman became friends. . . . I begged Infant Jesus that if their friendship broke up and my son married the previous good girl, I would have my Thanksgiving to Infant Jesus framed so that all may read and know of His Power. . . . My son had a Church wedding to the good girl. . . . They have also left for Australia. Glory be to God. The Miraculous Infant Jesus does make the Impossible, Possible." Offerings are also made for securing employment or obtaining a house. A devotee writes: "I, J. N. D. Jayakumar, B.E. MIE, though an engineering graduate was unemployed for six years. Even clerical job was not given. By fervent devotion to Infant Jesus, secured engineer's job in the government." A Christian family from Madras writes: "We thank and praise Our Heavenly Infant Jesus for curing us of all our ailments and helping us buy our land after coming to this Church in July 1991."

Miniature silver cribs, gold chains, statues, lamps, awards received by students (even a stethoscope given by a homeopathic doctor grateful for passing his examinations), and images of houses, eyes, and limbs crowd the museum. They testify to answered prayers and reflect the concerns of a social stratum that, for the most part, is in petty employment, government and private—Hindus and Christian alike—most of them Tamil speakers. The votive offerings in the museum and the newspaper advertisements that appear every Thursday are an index of their religious imagination.

The second cult that is part of the sacrality of urban sprawl and linked to the Karaga *jatre* within the performative complex is centered at a temple on the western periphery of Bangalore. The Raja Rajeshwari Temple lies on the Mysore Road near Kengeri, a satellite town of Bangalore. This temple forms part of the monastic organization of Tiruchi Swamigal, a religious leader originally from Tamil Nadu, whose base is now this site. According to Rao (1994), the ancestors of the Swamigal were Nayakas who served the Vijayanagar kings, and after the collapse of the empire they settled in Tirunelveli in Tamil Nadu. His mother, having lost one child, had an epiphanic dream in which she saw a trident entering her stomach; this was interpreted as a sign that a great soul would be born to her. She gave birth to a son on March 29, 1929.[39] Even as a young boy, the Swamigal appeared to have been blessed with various skills, and he cultivated the friendship of a number of adepts and saints.[40] All this prepared him to seek out his own spiritual teacher. Through the assistance of a grateful Muslim merchant, he visited Sri Lanka and the famous hill shrine of Adam's Peak at Kandy, revered by Hindus, Muslims, and Buddhists. His visit to Adam's Peak was particularly auspicious, because there he is supposed to have had the vision of the goddess who directed him to work in the Kannada country.[41]

In Kandy, Nattukottai Chettiars, an expatriate Tamil business community who are devotees of Shiva, became his followers. Links with their community directed him to visit their ancestral region in Tamil Nadu where he found temples in a state of disrepair. He resolved to apply himself to the renovation of temple culture, which he did for a number of years. Finally, at the age of twenty-nine, he resolved to travel to Nepal, where he met an aged saint, Sivapuri Baba (1826–1963), whom he recognized as his spiritual teacher and received initiation. In the Himalayas, he is also supposed to have had a vision of his chosen deity, Raja Rajeshwari, on Kailash Mountain.[42]

Returning to south India, he founded his hermitage in 1960 in Bangalore named after the sacred mountain. The area at that time was a small hamlet outside Bangalore surrounded by largely uncultivated fields. The Swamigal founded a traditional Vedic school in 1960, a primary school in 1965, and a high school in 1968. A temple dedicated to Raja Rajeshwari was begun in 1972. Apparently, when the land was being excavated for the temple after preliminary rites, an old metallic image of the goddess and several other images were discovered at the spot. The Swamigal, however, instructed that these be left in the soil, although a black stone image was made in the likeness of the metallic one. In 1975, the Swamigal created two trusts: one to run the hermitage and all the institutions associated with it and the other to administer the temple. He also started a school for instruction in the scriptures of temple worship in 1976.[43] The center includes fifteen acres of agricultural land next to it. It has developed into a large complex and draws thousands of devotees, especially on the Swamigal's birthday, which coincides with the birthday of the deity Rama.[44] The temple now caters chiefly to an expatriate Tamil population, many of them businessmen. The Swamigal's monastic disciples are to be found chiefly in Karnataka, Andhra Pradesh, and Tamil Nadu.[45] The Swamigal himself, however, not only has traveled abroad to Japan, Italy, and other countries where he has a diasporic Indian constituency, but frequently visits temples in other new suburbs of Bangalore.

According to the Swamigal, the large temple complex stands over a very old shrine that was once surrounded by dense forest, a recurring theme we have seen connected with the goddess. He claims that the ruler Rajaraja Chola conquered this area on his way to the Mysore region and had a vision of the goddess; he therefore changed his name and became a devotee of Raja Rajeshwari. For the last thirty-five years or so, he says, the Karaga bearer has been visiting the temple to ask for the blessings of the goddess and the Swamigal before the flag of the festival is hoisted. He says: "This is because this place is the seat of the guru. Draupadi herself did penance and carried a sacred pot *(kalasha)* on her head praying to Raja Rajeshwari, the Supreme Mother, for a husband. Therefore, the Karaga-bearer (the word "kalasha" is the origin of "Karaga") emulates Draupadi and wears the dress of a woman" (interview with Tiruchi Swamigal, June 14, 1997). Not all members of the Vahnikula Kshatriyas, however, accept this relationship; some claim that it was only one of the Karaga bearers, who carried the icon in the 1970s and 1980s, who was particularly attached to the goddess Raja Rajeshwari. However, in recent years it appears that the Swamigal has been making some attempt to create links with the Vahnikula Kshatriya community and has visited their temple. There are also a number of rumors among the community that the Swamigal is also a Vanniyar (as Vahnikula Kshatriyas are commonly known in Tamil Nadu).

Another account of the links between the temple complex of Tiruchi Swamigal and the Vahnikula Kshatriya community relates to a claim about the descent of the Vahnikula Kshatriyas or Vanniyars cited by Hiltebeitel (1988a, 36). He states that in March 1975, the Swamigal said that the Vanniyars are descended from the guardians of the *vanni* ("fire" in Tamil) tree. The Pandava heroes of the *Mahabharata* hid their weapons in the tree upon entering their period of concealment. Thereafter, these guardians and their descendants worshiped Draupadi and migrated to Kanchipuram, where they served the Pallava rulers. Hiltebeitel describes the Swamigal as a "Vanniyar caste swami." Whether the mythic connections and etymologies claimed by the Swamigal are accurate or not, it is quite clear that after the post-1950 growth of the metropolis the City and its suburban populations have become intertwined in a variety of newly forged relationships and claims, of which this cult represents one.

The Axes of the Urban Performative Complex

In the urban performative complex, the flows between various spatial and social arenas do not emanate from a radial map in which certain portions of the city occupy the central node of a hierarchy; nor do they emanate from the grid patterns that apparently democratize space for citizens. Rather, they present a layered mapping, a kind of labyrinth of possibilities that allow one to play with constructs of place through the mediation of sacred power. The centers of sacred power include sites of both locational sacrality and the sacrality of urban sprawl and are centered around deities, goddesses, gurus, and saints. The cults, their social groups and spatial arenas, and different historical moments of the city are connected and reconnected through various axes.

In the case of the urban performative complex in Bangalore, three axes can be identified today, if we conceive of an axis as an imaginary line around which rotates a body or a fixed reference point for the measurement of spatial coordinates. One axis is the network of goddess worship within which the Karaga *jatre* is embedded (see Map 9). This axis consists of four boundary goddesses whose worship is linked in a quadrilateral pattern of festivals; a temporal and performative synchrony between the rites devoted to Arokiamariamma in the Cantonment and those devoted to Draupadi in the City; and an external spatial synchrony between the temple of Draupadi and the temples of the boundary goddesses in Bangalore and Chamundeshwari, the royal goddess in Mysore. The plane surface that results from this axis of goddess worship has accrued over several centuries and is related to topological coordinates such as tanks, the City, and the Cantonment.

The second axis is the constellation of the temples to the goddess and her "others," such as the warrior god Anjaneya and Sufi holy men (see Map 10). These shrines and their festivals are located in between the nodes of the fort, the City, and the tanks. It must be remembered, however, that Sufi shrines are also to be found in the Cantonment and contribute a second level of "pairing" between the City and the Cantonment.

A third axis, the axis of metropolitan sacrality, connects the symbols, practices, and constituencies of sites of locational sacrality with the sacrality of urban sprawl and is an emergent one, constantly being forged as the city grows. Therefore, the Infant Jesus Shrine is linked not only to the church

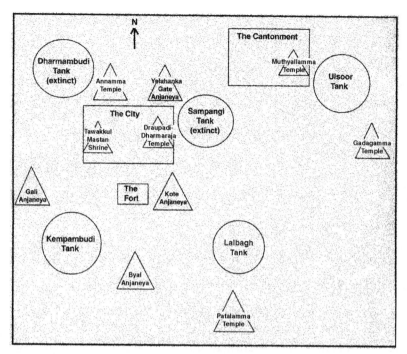

Map 10. The goddess shrines, the Anjaneya temples, and the Sufi shrine.

of Arokiamariamma, but also to goddess temples whose practices closely resemble its own. The Raja Rajeshwari Temple presents the possibility that new suburban claims will emerge in the future. The spread of the Karaga *jatre* to new sites, described in the next few chapters, is also part of this axis. Put together spatially and temporally, the three axes of the urban performative complex create a multiaxial and multiplanar surface of Bangalore, a model wrought by festive practices and belief systems that are located in sacred intercession (see Figure 9).

The three axes analyzed in this chapter present not only another formulation of place, but also ways in which memories of the landscape of the city are created. In the case of sites of locational sacrality such as the goddess temples, a familiar motif is the way in which forests have been replaced by urban settlement, the autochthonous goddess herself represented as mountain, stone, or clay. There is also an alternative visualization, as in the case of Arokiamariamma, in which desert is replaced by agricultural land, signaling different cultural frameworks in which memories of place can be cast. Even in the case of the Infant Jesus, the "tent church" period is compared to the Exodus and wanderings in the desert by

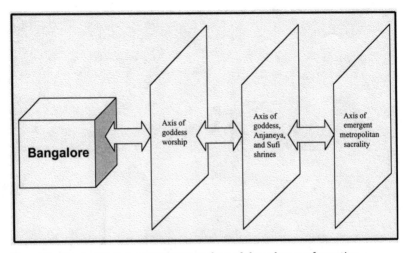

Figure 9. The multiaxial, multiplanar surface of the urban performative complex.

some of the fathers of the church, although the land in Bangalore was marshy or horticultural land at that time. Memories of previous places carry over onto the sites of urban sprawl, as in the case of the Infant Jesus Shrine, where Nazareth, Prague, and the Viveknagar area are part of a single historical frame.

All the sites within the urban performative complex have multicommunity constituencies, although most persons who are part of them belong to lower-middle-class and working-class groups. The shrines are invariably associated with collective local events such as plague epidemics, fires, or droughts during which the intervention of sacred power has been solicited. The role of healing is also central, both at the individual level and at the level of various publics in Bangalore. The festivals at these shrines, above all, represent these publics and embody them through spatial practices such as processions and temporal ones such as the nine-day festivals. The processions carve out a civic territory delineating the linkages of the shrines with the changing history and landscape of the City, the Cantonment, the suburbs, and their social groups.

4°

The Children of Fire

Political Mobilization and Community Formation

The Karaga *jatre* is a commentary about the city's past and present realities and a formulation about being citizens in the late-twentieth-century Indian metropolis. Some of the elements of this will emerge in the next two chapters as we follow the *jatre* in its temporal, spatial, narrative, and kinetic modalities. Elements include the connection of bodies of water and gardens, the breakdown of land zoning in Bangalore in the form presented by the Comprehensive Development Plans, the interpenetration of the city and the forest, and the parallelism of flows between the ritual body and the civic one. Further, as the spatial arenas of Bangalore have changed, the Karaga *jatre* has become significant for several new social strata in the City, has spread to metropolitan suburbs, and has drawn other settlements and their social groups into the cycle of performance. In this chapter, the relationship of the Karaga *jatre* and its ritual terrain to political mobilization and community formation is studied in an attempt to respond to these questions: Who are the main players in the *jatre*? How have their social organization and sense of community unfolded historically within the urban fabric? How is this related to the cultic terrain? What is the relationship between political mobilization and centers of the urban performative complex? How does the community lay claims to Bangalore and its public spaces?

Community formation among the players derives in part from the organizational underpinnings, popularity, and expansion of the Karaga *jatre* and in part from legal and institutional interventions made by the state, such as quotas and reservations for socially and economically weaker castes, communities, and tribal groups in many public arenas. The Constitution of

97

India, which was promulgated in 1950, created specific reservations for "weaker" sections of Indian society, and the Government of India issued instuctions to state governments to create their own commissions to look further into issues of "backwardness." "Scheduled Castes" and "Scheduled Tribes" have been specified and safeguarded under the provision of various constitutional articles; in addition, some state governments have specified other communities as "Other Backward Classes." However, the efforts of the non-Brahmin movement (especially in the early twentieth century), which were inherited by the Backward Classes movement in later years, had already mobilized many such communities and are the backdrop for these shifts.

The main players in the Karaga *jatre* are known as Vahnikula Kshatriyas, who identify themselves as part of a larger group called the "Tigalas." Among them, the Agnikula Kshatriyas speak Kannada and could be indigenous to the Karnataka region. The other two—the Vahnikula and Shambukula Kshatriyas—speak mainly Tamil and are part of a history of migration of various Tamil-speaking groups to the Kannada-speaking region. Not all of them are traditionally gardeners. It is important to describe for the purposes of this chapter the meaning of the term "Tigala," the settlement of various Tamil-speaking groups who were ancestors of the Vahnikula and Shambukula Kshatriyas in Bangalore, and the formation of an alliance of the three groups in the Bangalore region.

The Tigalas, as represented in various censuses, live chiefly in Bangalore, Kolar, and Tumkur districts, with the major concentration in the Bangalore metropolitan area. In 1984, their number in Bangalore District was estimated to be 111,828.[1] There are no official estimates of their population today, but oral estimates give their number as 250,000; a leader of the Vahnikula Kshatriya community, S. M. Munivenkatappa, cited their number in Mysore as 90,000 in 1931 and 1,01,706 in 1941.[2] The estimate of 250,000, as well as those given by Munivenkatappa, probably reflects a larger category than does the government census. It appears that in the state census the term "Tigala" actually meant the Vahnikula Kshatriya group only.

Uncertainty about the exact composition of the Tigala community as a whole is present even in early reports and accounts. Thurston ([1909] 1975) points out that in the Madras Census Report of 1901 "Tigala" was a synonym for a Tamil group called the "Palli," although it is a term also applied to any lower-caste Tamil speaker by Kannada speakers. The original home of the Tigalas was Kanchipuram in the state of Tamil Nadu. The Tigalas, according to Thurston, are mainly kitchen gardeners divided into three units: those associated with garlic and onion produce, those associated with betel nut produce, and the "Tamils." In his description, occupation and linguistic affiliation are brought together in a single category, a conflation that suggests complexity. In addition to this, Thurston states that there are several subdivisions and exogamous groups named after deities or important members of their "caste," introducing yet another category of description. There is also a mythic-historical connection. Thurston claims that Tigalas regard themselves as descended from the fire-born hero Agni Banniraya.[3]

The term "Tigala" is used today by city dwellers to refer to the community of gardeners who celebrate the Karaga *jatre*, whereas the gardeners refer to themselves mainly as "Vahnikula Kshatriyas," "Vahnikuladavaru," "Vanniyars," or "Vanniyans."[4] They belong to the lineage (*kula* in Kannada and Sanskrit) of Draupadi, who was born of fire (*agni* in Sanskrit or *vanni* in Tamil), and Dharmaraja, their patron deities. They include both Vaishnavas and Shaivas (called "Namadara" and "Muljana," respectively), who were apparently endogamous groups earlier in history, but now intermarry. At first glance, it does not appear that any special ritual privileges with respect to the Karaga *jatre* are enjoyed by either group. For instance, the current Karaga priest, Abhimanyu, belongs to the former group, whereas the Karaga bearer in previous years, Shiv Shankar, belonged to the latter. However, T. M. Manoharan, a community leader, has stated that all the ritual players in the Karaga *jatre*, except for the Virakumaras, belong to the Namadara, and the choice of Shiv Shankar as a Karaga priest was historically an exception.[5] Two local scholars claim that the Vahnikula Kshatriyas are descended from the lineage of the mythical sage, Angirasa, who adopted Agni (the god of fire) as his son, or state that the sage, Shambu, conducted a fire sacrifice, and from it emerged the hero Rudra Vahni. The latter's four sons were the ancestors of the four great kingdoms of the south, the Pandyas, the Cheras, the Cholas, and the Pallavas. To these martial and royal lineages belong the Vahnikula Kshatriyas.[6]

The multiplicity of discourses about the meanings of the Vahnikula Kshatriya or the Tigala identity, which range from stressing their mythological origins to their sectarian and linguistic differences, royal linkages, and endogamy, relate to a history of settlement in the Bangalore region when various Tamil-speaking groups migrated to the city. Specifically, this migration is the basis for the two dominant definitions given to the term "Tigala": first, that they represent an alliance of three groups, the Vahnikula, Shambukula, and Agnikula Kshatriyas; and second, that they are the chief players in the Karaga *jatre*—that is, the Vahnikula Kshatriyas. The central

elements in both these definitions are the connection to the cult of Draupadi and the mythical and ritual links to fire, fire-born heroes and heroines,
fire sacrifices, and the heat of fire.

The Settlement of Tamil-Speaking Groups in Bangalore

A fund of conjectures and claims circulates in the city about the origin of
various Tamil-speaking groups in Bangalore. It is sometimes said that the
ancestors of Kempe Gowda hailed from the Kanchipuram area of Tamil
Nadu.[7] Many Vahnikula Kshatriyas believe that Kempe Gowda was "one of
us." It is also claimed that there were aboriginal horticulturists in Karnataka even before Kempe Gowda's time; these are defined by some as the
Agnikula Kshatriyas, to whom the Vahnikula Kshatriyas are generically related. Another common belief is that the Vahnikula Kshatriyas migrated to
Bangalore from the Tamil country in the eighteenth century at the time of
Haider Ali and Tippu Sultan's rule.

The first wave of migration probably occurred in the period after the
tenth century, when the Bangalore region became a frontier zone for Tel-
ugu-, Tamil-, and Kannada-speaking groups.[8] The extension of Chola rule
into Karnataka in the eleventh century led to the migration and movement
of large numbers of personnel into the region. It also encouraged the proliferation of urban settlements that were largely commercial centers that
came to acquire an important role in creating inter-regional linkages.[9] There
were peasants, pastoralists, soldiers, traders, and priests at these centers.
Champakalakshmi (1996, 45–46) points out that, with the spread of Chola
influence in the eleventh century, there are historical references to Tamils
holding ranks as officers, administrators, trustees, and managers of temples besides merchants, artisans, and craftsmen residing in various centers in Karnataka. She states that there were settlements of "Tigulas" as far
north as Belgaum district in the eleventh to the thirteenth centuries. It
seems likely that the figure of Draupadi, today the goddess associated with
the Vahnikula Kshatriyas, existed in the Bangalore region even prior to the
founding of the City in the mid-sixteenth century, and in time came to be
associated with other migrations, rituals, performances, and narrative traditions. According to Sundara Rao (1985, 21), it appears that when Kempe
Gowda founded his mud fort, the gardeners associated with the Karaga *jatre* were already located in the area cultivating their plots of land around
the site earmarked for the fort. He states that Kempe Gowda created a special area within the fort-settlement for the gardeners, who were known as
"Tigalas," to live in, a neighborhood on the east side that came to be
known as Tigalarapet. Therefore, the gardeners became a boundary group

in the new fort-settlement, and the eastward-looking Draupadi Temple formed a niche between the settlement, the gardens around it, and the forest beyond.[10]

The second wave of migration took place during the Vijayanagar period, when there were new pressures on the plains people (basically those who lived in the dryland areas) of Tamil Nadu, who were, until about this time, largely hunters and herdsmen.[11] Karashima (1992) states that the consolidation of Vijayanagar's rule occurred through the creation of power blocs by vesting estates in the hands of the Nayakas. These leaders, in turn, had the collaboration of those who were in control of the means of production, "Tandirimars," who were soldiers, or Pallis, who came down from the western hills before the twelfth century. From inscriptional data, it appears that this latter term referred specifically to leading members of the Vanniya community. They took over the proprietary rights of many villages and rose to be local leaders in the anarchy that prevailed in the fourteenth century. With the advent of the Vijayanagar armies, they seem to have become followers of these invaders.[12] There was large-scale recruitment to the armies of local rulers called the Nayakas or Palegaras, who were spread out in various parts of south India under the Vijayanagar Empire. As the plains economy experienced a shift toward agriculture, there was the growth of a number of cults that centered either on the martial aspects of some Vedic gods or on goddesses and gods of the plains people, who came to be linked through ties of kinship to Vedic deities. There also arose in the plains of south India fort-mart centers that were linked to three sets of groups, sometimes described as castes and sometimes as tribes. North of the Kaveri River were the Palli, Padaiyichi, and the Vanniyan; in the south were the Kallar, Ambalagar, and Agamudaiyan; and in the far south the Maravar.[13] Many of these clan-based groups began to acquire the characteristics associated with caste identities, although not necessarily through the acquisition of Brahmanical codes of purity and pollution. The veneration of deities of blood and power, many of them female, created corporate identity.[14]

The third wave of migration is associated with the continued importance of recruiting these groups in the eighteenth century as the need for militia and trade revenues increased in significance for three powers—the rulers of Mysore, the Nawab of Arcot, and the British East India Company. In the armies of Haider Ali and Tippu Sultan, these groups—the Pallis, Padaiyichis, and Vanniyans/Vanniyars, regarded as Vahnikula Kshatriyas today—also found their way into Bangalore District from earlier settlements.[15] A popular narrative about their origin runs as follows:

When Haider Ali was warring with the Nawab of Arcot, he camped
in some fields near the site of the battle. By day, only some
gardeners were working there, and Haider Ali imagined that his
camp was secure. But by the next morning he found his camp
ransacked. This happened three nights in a row. Finally, he kept
watch one night and found that the lowly gardeners, working
innocuously on the fields by day, carried torches of fire, "ti," by
night, showing them in their dual incarnations as gardeners and
soldiers. He realized the value of these men, carriers of fire ("Tigalas"), and invited them to settle in his dominions. (Interview
with a Vahnikula Kshatriya male, March 3, 1996)

In the course of these migrations, these groups appeared to have acquired garden land in the Bangalore region, large and small tracts managed by families or lineages. They used wells in addition to tanks for irri-
gating their garden land. In Karnataka, however, the Vahnikula Kshatriyas
are considered part of a broader category composed of the Agnikula and
Shambukula Kshatriyas, who are settled in different parts of the state.[16]
What connections do these two groups claim to the earlier migrations and
movements?

The Agnikula and Shambukula Kshatriyas

Although the Vahnikula Kshatriyas are the largest group among the Tigalas,
the Agnikula Kshatriyas may be the oldest group among them; it is claimed
that they are native to the region, but they are not found settled in large
numbers in Bangalore.[17] Speaking Kannada, they do not celebrate the Karaga
jatre (although they can be present as an audience), nor do they have any
temples within their control dedicated to Draupadi, although they represent themselves as a fire lineage. In terms of political organization, one of
the oldest associations of this community, the Agnikula Kshatriya Sangha,
was started around 1950 with the assistance of a leading member of the
community, an industrialist and agriculturist named Byaterangappa from
Nelamangala. Byaterangappa was an associate of Sir M. Visvesvaraya, the
diwan of Mysore, and dreamed of making his hometown of Nelamangala
near Bangalore an industrial center. He owned a sawmill and sugar factory
there.

According to a speech delivered by Byaterangappa to the Sangha in
1951, the Agnikula Kshatriyas were born of the lineage of the hero Agni
Banniraya. Although of royal descent, in time they lost their land and settled near various bodies of water, chiefly in Tumkur and Bangalore districts. Their people were divided into four separate jurisdictions with their

own headmen.[18] The first signs of political unity in the community came in 1924, when leaders of various villages and headmen came together in a common assembly. This became a full-fledged movement by 1948, when a campaign was begun to get women of their community to wear blouses to cover their breasts, a move that had the blessings of the religious head of a nearby monastery. The next step was the formation of the Sangha in 1950 to carry out welfare work in the community. Byaterangappa tried to get the community included in the legal list of Backward Tribes before his death in the late 1960s, but faced a great deal of opposition in the group. Other Agnikula Kshatriya organizations today include the Education Development Society for educational uplift, started about twenty-six years ago, and the Tigala Welfare Development Society, started about three years ago.[19] The community has a number of other institutions associated with it. These include a students' hostel, a girls' high school, a cooperative bank, a college, and a community hall (under construction in 1996) at Rajajinagar in Bangalore city on land that was donated by the erstwhile chief minister, Dev Raj Urs.[20] Byaterangappa's grandson, Narendra Babu, is an active member of the community today and is a City Corporation Council member from the Nagapura Ward. He claims that both the Vahnikulas and the Agnikulas originally belonged to Karnataka, whereas the Shambukulas came from the Tanjavur region of Tamil Nadu. The first two groups, he states, existed in Karnataka from the time of the Kadambas (fourth to sixth centuries) and Gangas (fourth to tenth centuries). Once a ruling class, they lost their land and were reduced to being horticulturists residing close to bodies of water.[21]

The Shambukula (or Jambukula) Kshatriyas, most of whom arrived in Bangalore at the turn of the twentieth century, appear to be the latest group. Some of them may have been in the employ of the British in various "native" regiments. It is certain that many of them came to work in the new textile factories set up by the British, such as the Binny Mills, but also in the locally managed Raja Mills and Minerva Mills. At that time, most of the workers who used to work nine- or ten-hour days would get a daily wage of about half a rupee. Many of them were employed in the weaving sections of the mills, where about 80 percent of the workers spoke either Tamil or Telugu. Speaking Tamil, the Shambukula Kshatriyas are today to be found concentrated in the areas of Binnypet, Cottonpet, Magadi Road, Kalasapalyam, Srirampuram (all in Bangalore), and Krishnarajapuram on the outskirts of the city (see Map 11). Many of their names reflect their older occupational base: "Naicker" (heads of small areas), "Gounder" (agriculturists), and "Padaiyichi" (foot soldiers).[22] They also celebrate a Draupadi festival, but their practices differ from those of the Karaga *jatre*. According to Ramaswamy Naicker, the president of the Mysore Shambukula Kshatriya Association: "We hold the recitation of the *Mahabharata,* perform plays and the fire-walk. None of these is done in the Tigalarapet Karaga."[23] They regard themselves as descendants of the sage Shambu, born in the lineage of Vira Vanniya, who rose from the sacrificial fire of the sage (see Figure 10). They are considered closely linked to the Vahnikula Kshatriyas, because Draupadi, the patron deity of the latter group, was also born from fire.

A pamphlet circulated by Ramaswamy Naicker (Kaliyaramurtti 1990)[24] traces the birth of the hero Vira Vanniya from fire for the purpose of destroying demons:

> When sage-kings were ruling, seated in state beneath white canopies, the royal lineages were known as "sages of the solar race." Unable to endure the oppressions of the demons in the world, the sages and the people petitioned Parvati and Shiva [the goddess and her consort]. As Lord Shiva had manifested Lord Murugan from the eye in his own forehead, now Parvati desired to manifest a son to destroy these demons. The man-child manifested in this manner should not be born either from woman's womb or from man's agency! The gods also petitioned that only one who appeared thus could destroy the demons. In this manner, Uma [Parvati], separating from the left side of Lord Shiva, manifested from her own power the fire called "Kamakshi." The whole world was full of light. Through the grace of the goddess who resided in this fire, by means of her own supreme power, a beautiful man-child appeared. It was he who would become the great king Vira Rudra [Supreme] Vanniya, who deigned to come and protect this world. Kamakshi gave him the name of Vira Vanniya and raised him, instructing him in the laws and settling his inquiries or questions as mother and teacher. Because of this, Kamakshi is truly the mother of fire. When her son had developed all his power, she directed Vira Vanniya to kill the demons. In that manner Vira Rudra Vanniya destroyed the demons and worked hard for the benefit of the land. He accepted leadership for the army of the land; this is the opinion of the *purana.*

According to the next passage in the writing, the career of Vira Vanniya overlaps that of the sage Shambu, also born from fire:

> The six-headed lord [Murugan] had a body bestowed by Shiva in order to destroy the demon called Surapadma. During the battle to destroy Surapadma, he [Surapadma] enclosed Murugan inside

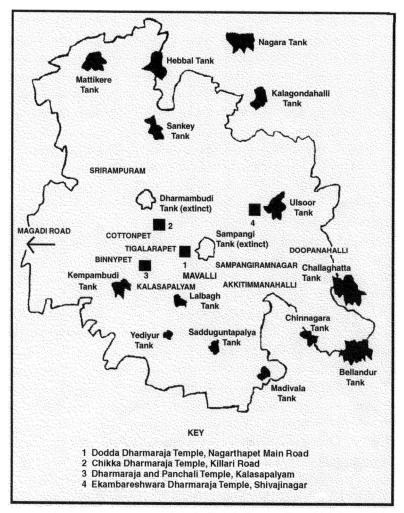

Map 11. The four Dharmaraja temples and central tanks in Bangalore in the 1990s.

a great boulder. When Murugan cried, "Amma [Mother]," Shiva opened the eye in his forehead. From the eye emerged frightful sparks of fire. From these sparks appeared the great sage, Sri Shambu. He helped Murugan to destroy Surapadma. Because the great sage, Sri Shambu, was born from the great fire from the great Lord's forehead eye, he received the title of "The One Born in Fire." Those who continue to follow in his path are called Vanniyakula Kshatriyas. This is the opinion of the *purana*.

தமிழக - கருநாடக - புதுவை மாநில
வன்னியகுல சூத்திரிய
சமூகப்புரட்சிமலர்

ஸ்ரீ சம்பு மாமுனிவர் யாகத்தில் முதலில் தோன்றிய ஸ்ரீ உருத்திர வன்னிய மாமன்னர்

மலர் வெளியீடு 2 - 10 - 90   மலர் விலை ரூ. 10

குடந்தை குறுவட்ட வன்னியகுல சூத்திரிய சங்கம்
5, கருணைகொல்லைத் தெரு கும்பகோணம் - 612001

Figure 10. The birth of the fire hero Vira Vanniya.

The efforts of the sage Shambu, on the insistence of the goddess, Kamakshi, the principal deity of the city of Kanchipuram or Kanchi, led to the birth of the hero Vira Vanniya, as the pamphlet continues to describe:

> After petitioning the holy one, the goddess met the great sage, Sri Shambu, in Tiruvanaikka near Tiruchi. In order to destroy giants and to support the holy, she ordered him to engender the sacrificial flame. The great sage, Sri Shambu, in that way engendered the sacrificial flame established out of a desire for a son. In the Uttara constellation of Panguni month, on the day of the full moon, on the auspicious day of the month called Somavatara, in the Simha [Lion] solar sign, the great king Vira Rudra Vanniya appeared out of the sacrificial flame with ornaments on his mountain-like shoulders, with a jeweled crown on his head resembling the effulgence of the sun, and wearing rings in his ears. He bore a spear in his holy hand and was mounted with his banners on a horse like fire. He destroyed the demons and the gods were overjoyed. The great king, Vira Rudra Vanniya, received the salutations of sages who praised his warlike skills. Then three [maidens]—Samudradevi, Indrani, and Kopaladevi—with joyous minds presented the hero his lion throne. They put [the god] Indra's mystical garland of holy prosperity on Rudra Vanniya, bestowed a crown, gave him a mystical sword, and petitioned that he conduct a benevolent reign.

The piece ends by suggesting that the word "Vanniya" is a northern term and that the community migrated from the northern plains of India, where they were members of the ruling class, to other parts of the country, including Kanchi, where the goddess Kamakshi has an important temple, and took other names:

> The community god of the Vanniyas would become Kanchi's Kamakshi. The Vanniya community's lineage would become the lineage of the great sage Shambu. In every land there are four castes. In that very way in the land of Magadha [in north India] there would be four castes called priests, rulers, merchants and cultivators. In this [classification], the Vanniyakula Kshatriyas would become members of the ruling community. One may read in many books and inscriptions matters concerning the Vanniyas. One may note that they take on many customs connected to the solar race and to the lunar race. [But] a king born in Shambu's community is called Shambuvarayan [a Shambu king]. The Vanniyas are called Shambukula Kshatriyas in Karnataka;

Agnikula Kshatriyas in Andhra Pradesh; Dipakula Kshatriyas in Gujarat; Indrakula Kshatriyas in Bihar; Vanniyakula Kshatriyas in Tamil Nadu; Suryakula Kshatriyas in Uttar Pradesh; and Suryakula Kshatriyas in Rajasthan.

The president of the Mysore Shambukula Kshatriya Association (established in 1946), Ramaswamy Naicker, came from Tamil Nadu about 1940, when he was about seventeen years old, to work in the Binny Mills. Members of the community had already formed small associations by that time that used to meet at the community temple in the mid-1930s, but these were not registered bodies. The association, with which Ramaswamy Naicker has been closely associated from its early years, currently runs a student hostel, extends scholarships and free tuition to poor students, and draws a major portion of its funds from a three-floor shopping complex and marriage hall where the association's offices are also located. It also acts as a marriage bureau for members of the community, and in some cases conducts free marriages. According to Ramaswamy Naicker's estimates, the number of persons in the Shambukula Kshatriya community is 200,000. Today the majority of them appear to be engaged in various petty trades, as factory workers, and as laborers. Some, like Ramaswamy Naicker, who runs a small-scale industry called Allied Machineries and General Supplies— as well as Mr. Muniram and Mr. Madhavan (engineers) and Mr. Perumal (an elected state representative)—were or are influential members of the community. In fact, it was in the residence of Mr. Muniram in Bangalore that the three groups—the Agnikula, the Shambukula, and the Vahnikula—first assembled in 1974 to form an alliance.[25] Asked about the implications of Tigala unity, some members of the association stated that it created a cultural and political alliance, because it brought together those groups that were fire-born and it allowed the giving and receiving of brides between the groups. In the early days, they affirmed, there was little communication among the three groups because of the differences in the patterns of migration and because some Tigalas had forgotten the cultic connection that has become more obvious today.[26]

The Cultic Terrain

The cultic imagination of these groups and their connection with others as Bangalore has changed socially and spatially is localized in the city in four temples dedicated to Draupadi (see Map 11). These temples are also sometimes called "Dharmaraja" or "Dharmaraya" temples after Dharmaraja or Yudhisthira, the eldest of the five Pandava brothers who are married to

Draupadi in the classical *Mahabharata*. The first temple lies in Tigalarapet in the City and is associated with the Vahnikula Kshatriyas and the Karaga *jatre*. It is called the Big Dharmaraja Temple *(Dodda Dharmaraja Devastana)*. The second, the Small Dharmaraja Temple *(Chikka Dharmaraja Devastana)*, is also in the City. This temple does not have a large festival associated with it, but its devotees revered the Karaga in a subdued fashion on the night of the full moon of the same lunar month, as do those of the Big Dharmaraja Temple. The temple belongs to the Gollas or Yadavas, legally considered a Backward Class, who were traditionally cowherds in this region. They regard themselves as descendants of the deity Krishna, but in reality form a heterogeneous social group. [27] The area around the temple has seen the migration out of many Golla families, and today, in the immediate neighborhood, there are only about eight or ten families left. The Karaga festival occurs with the help of contributions from various business communities that reside in the area. The chief deities in the temple are Krishna and Dharmaraja; Draupadi, whose image is found in the temple precincts, is worshiped chiefly as the "sister" of Krishna, the lineage deity.[28] The image of Potha Raja, "Draupadi's sister's son," is also found in the temple precincts. Unlike at the Big Dharmaraja Temple, where a goat sacrifice is made to Potha Raja, no animal sacrifice occurs at this temple, "because the Yadavas tend animals," according to the priest of the temple, Mr. Dhananjaya. Inside the temple area is a white image of the Sufi shrine of Tawakkul Mastan, although it does not seem to be especially revered. The main rituals here are dedicated to Krishna, and rituals offered to male deities appear to take precedence over rites dedicated to Draupadi.

The Shambukula Kshatriyas patronize the third temple, the Dharmaraja and Panchali Temple, which is found close to the walls of the old fort in Kalasapalyam. Besides the images of Draupadi, Krishna, and Dharmaraja, the temple complex also holds a separate shrine dedicated to the deity Rama, as well as the tomb of Muthayala Ravuthar, Potha Raja's "brother." Potha Raja is regarded here as the charioteer of Dharmaraja during the Kurukshetra War in the *Mahabharata*. Tamil soldiers in the employ of the British constructed the building as a "camp temple," and according to the priest it has been in existence for about 250 years. The Karaga *jatre* begins here with rituals dedicated to Annamma, a virgin goddess considered the "elder sister" of Draupadi. The most important feature of this temple's forty-eight-day festival is the culminating ceremony of the fire-walk, in which the ritual players and the populace walk across embers of coal in a pit about twenty-seven feet long.[29] Mr. Manickkam, the erstwhile priest of the temple (the temple now has a Brahmin priest) stated that this act is performed in imitation of Draupadi, who stayed with each of her husbands for one year. When she went from one to the other, she walked through fire to prove her chastity and purity.[30]

Ramaswamy Naicker, who is also associated with the temple trust, claimed instead that the fire-walk commemorates Draupadi and her brother, who were both born of fire. The festival as a whole takes place in consequence of a vow made by Draupadi after her disrobement in a public assembly when her husbands, the Pandavas, lost her in a game of dice to their cousins, the Kauravas. Ramaswamy Naicker said: "She swore that she would braid her hair and have a bath only after the blood of Duryodhana [one of the Kaurava brothers] was put in her hair. Earlier, a blood sacrifice used to be offered at the temple, but this does not happen any longer because the government has banned it."[31] The theme of the braiding of Draupadi's hair with blood is found in a number of local cults and in the Tamil *Mahabharata* of Villi.[32] It is dramatized the evening before the fire-walking ceremony in plays that are performed by troupes of workers who train for months before the festival for a small fee of 1,000 rupees. Narrators also recite the Tamil epic during the festival for about a month. Although the nine days before the festival are important and the priest bathes at nine different spots around the City Market area, the apex of the festival is the final procession and the fire-walk. Some of the heads of other religious institutions also attend this event, along with government officials and ministers. The Karaga, accompanied by Virakumaras from the community of Shambukula Kshatriyas, visits the tomb of Tawakkul Mastan and other sites in the K. R. Market area in a chariot procession.

The fourth temple, the Ekambareshwara Dharmaraja Temple, is in the Cantonment market and associated with Chettiars and Gounders, who are corn merchants, oil-millers, fruit-sellers, and other kinds of traders.[33] Until about two decades ago, this temple celebrated the Karaga *jatre*, known chiefly as the "Draupadiamma fire-walking festival" because of the giant fire-walk. Today, however, the "Drowpathy Amman Firewalking Devotees Association," members of which belong to various castes, conduct the festival at a goddess shrine on a parallel road.[34] At the end of the festivities, the association and its office-holders disperse, then reconvene the next year, their official existence dependent on the festival. The fire-walk arouses as much attention today as it did in the early years of the last century when it was reported by Aiyangar (1910–11) in the annals of the Mythic Society, the course of events almost unchanged although the organizational locus of the festival has altered. A newspaper report reads:

A young boy, all of eight years old, his face smeared with turmeric and a small pouch of lemons tied around his waist is about to go through his first trial by fire. He is just one of the 450 people who walked over red-hot coals in homage to Draupadi in RBANMS High School grounds on Sunday. A huge pit, 15 feet by 23 feet, six inches deep, was covered over by hot coals that heated the enclosure in which the walk would take place. The festival is held to commemorate Draupadi who was supposed to have walked through fire to prove her chastity in the Mahabharata. A member of the festival committee, Mr. Sriramulu says: "We have a month long celebration which began on May 9 and culminates with the fire-walk. The previous day to the fire-walk, we also hold a ceremony where a sword is made to stand atop a pot. We believe that when the fire-walk starts, the sword kept in the temple will fall." ("Test by Fire: Draupadi Devotees Celebrate," *Bangalore Age*, June 9, 1997, 10–11)

Devotees who want to walk register their names at the association and have to sleep over at the temple the previous day. They wear clothes soaked in turmeric, and some of the men dress as women in imitation of the goddess. The more fervent male devotees wear saris and flowers in their hair. The fire-walkers may also tie lemons, a "favorite fruit of the goddess," around their waists, and give offerings of fruit and milk to the goddess before the walk.

Although all of these groups have a connection to fire, fire-born ancestors, and fire lineages *(agnivamsha)*, the Vahnikula Kshatriyas, accepting that the Shambukula Kshatriyas and the Chettiars or Gounders are also worshipers of Draupadi, see the latter two groups as partly distinct from themselves. The Vahnikula Kshatriyas, they say, belong to the "lunar" lineage, dynasty, or race *(chandravamsha)*, whereas the others belong to the "solar" lineage *(suryavamsha)*. This assertion seems to be linked largely with the ritual calendars that are followed by the three groups. Among the solar lineages, the festival of Draupadi ends a month after the festivities of the lunar lineages and takes place during the daytime. The lunar lineages celebrate their festival after moonrise and before sunrise. This kind of categorization suggests that the idea of solar and lunar lineages can be used to express differences among groups in the city that are otherwise linked to a common cultic terrain.[35]

The elements of this cultic terrain, as we have seen, are complex. Some of the groups are related to each other because they have fire-born ancestors, a common language and migration history from Tamil Nadu, or the same occupation. The three groups are also linked to one another and other communities in the city through a complex of temples where fire-walks or Karaga festivals "based on the *Mahabharata*" are conducted. There is also a common repertoire of figures—Draupadi, Dharmaraja, Krishna, Potha Raja, and the Sufi Tawakkul Mastan—even though their relationship to each other varies from temple to temple and group to group. These criss-crossing ties have, in recent decades, provided a symbolic language for the creation of an alliance between the three groups—the Agnikula, Shambukula, and Vahnikula.

The Backward Classes Movement

In preindependence Karnataka, six different bureaucracies governed the state. These included the princely state of Mysore (which also had jurisdiction over Bangalore city), the Bombay Presidency, the Madras Presidency (which controlled the Cantonment in Bangalore), the bureaucracies of the Nizam of Hyderabad and the chief commissioner of Coorg (who was also the British resident at Bangalore), and the princely state of Sandur. The non-Brahmin movement, directed against the dominance of upper-caste Brahmins in public affairs, the government, and education, was largely localized in the princely state of Mysore.[36] The British had reinstated the Wodeyar kings of Mysore in 1881 after they had been deposed from power due to the peasant revolts of 1831. Many of the rulers' political efforts from 1881 to 1947 were aimed at creating a model state through the services of government officials, who tended to be drawn from urban educated classes and were chiefly Brahmins. Between 1881 and 1910, mainly Madras Brahmins and some others from the Madras Presidency were recruited to government posts: the British, in the period before 1881, had also tended to recruit persons from the same Presidency, as they were more qualified educationally.[37] This recruitment policy continued under the diwans, who were special administrators of the state under the kings.[38] Also, although the higher posts in the administration were filled with Madras Brahmins, half those in the Police Department and many of those with posts in the palace were Brahmins from Mysore, creating a struggle in the state between the two groups. This controversy between Madras and Mysore was partially resolved when M. Visvesvaraya, a Brahmin from Mysore, was diwan from 1912 to 1918.[39]

After 1910, the form of non-Brahmin agitation changed. For some time, attention had been directed toward the rivalry between Madras and Mysore Brahmins; a new cleavage now came to the fore due to the lack of representation of non-Brahmin communities in extralocal, nonvillage politics. It has been argued that the rulers governed through bureaucracies in which Lingayats and Vokkaligas, who were dominant, landed communities at the village level, had little representation. A gap existed, therefore, between the local and the extralocal levels.[40] In the early years of that century, large numbers of Vokkaligas and Lingayats who had gained a modern education and an awareness of urban, regional, and national events aspired for representation in supralocal politics and the economy. This desire also took the form of resentment of castes and groups that were dominant in the bureaucracy and the urban sectors, especially Brahmins.

One of the contexts for this non-Brahmin agitation, however, was the creation of a base for popular participation in politics and society. For instance, in 1881 the Representative Assembly had been created, and in 1907 a Legislative Assembly had been established; in addition, a number of schools and community associations were also created.[41] In 1917, some 100,000 rupees of the state budget were set aside for scholarships for students declared "backward," a term that did not refer to a legal category as much as to economically and socially depressed castes.[42] The legal connotations of the term emerged more forcefully after 1918. The year 1917 saw the formation of the Praja Mitra Mandali, an association of non-Brahmin communities, for the purpose of securing quotas and reserved seats for their communities and special recruitment in administration, and the Mandali sent a deputation to the king a year later agitating for these demands. The Mandali was probably inspired by the formation of the South Indian People's Association (later the Justice Party) in Madras, an organization of non-Brahmins.[43]

All these efforts bore fruit in 1918, when the Miller Committee was appointed to look into these issues. According to the committee's definition, all castes except for Brahmins were classified as "backward." The committee used three criteria for this definition—educational backwardness, literacy in English, and employment in government service—using the 1911 Census data as a base. Some castes clearly could not be considered backward according to these criteria, but the committee included them in this category nevertheless. These castes included relatively affluent trading castes such as Mudaliars and Pillais, and Indian Christians, who tended to have better educational qualifications than those in many other groups. Based on the findings of the Miller Committee that only one-third to one-fourth of government posts were filled by non-Brahmins, the government of Mysore passed an order in 1921 mandating reservations in the administration and schools, establishing scholarships for students, and abolishing competitive examinations. The objective was to increase the number of qualified non-Brahmins in state services to 50 percent in seven years. The government order clearly had an impact, although the Lingayat and Vokka-liga castes gained more than other communities and castes, because there were no special provisions for really depressed groups.[44] The non-Brahmin movement, therefore, was fractured along various caste lines.

Non-Brahmins had also been agitating for the appointment of a non-Brahmin diwan in the state, and this finally led to the appointment of Kan-tharaj Urs as the diwan after Visvesvaraya in 1918. Albion Bannerjee, who belonged to a Hindu reformist association (the Brahmo Samaj), and Mirza Ismail (a Bangalore Muslim) succeeded him. In the decade or so that fol-lowed, the non-Brahmins advocating "Home Rule" for India worked with the Congress Party in the state, also dominated in early years by Brahmins. As time went by, this movement was gradually taken over by the Lingayats and Vokkaligas, many of whom were lawyers, but for a while the Congress Party and the independence movement in India largely coopted the non-Brahmin agitation. After 1947, independent India also institutionalized "reservations," quotas reserved for designated castes and tribes (Sched-uled Castes and Tribes) whose members were socially, politically, and eco-nomically disadvantaged, in education, government, and so on. This meant that in various states the non-Brahmin movement had to contend with new caste and tribe groups and legal categories that were constitutionally upheld by the courts. Therefore, in addition to various Backward Classes and degrees and categories of "backwardness" (More Backward, Backward Tribe, Backward Caste, and so on), each state discussed what the total per-centage of reserved quotas should be.

By 1947 the Vokkaligas had gained control of the Congress in Mysore. Between 1947 and 1956, every chief minister of the state (except one) was a Vokkaliga. Between 1956 (when the territories of "Karnataka" were unified) and 1972, every chief minister was a Lingayat, for in the enlarged state Lin-gayats outnumbered Vokkaligas.[45] It can be argued that it was really after 1956 that the non-Brahmin movement became transformed into a strong Backward Classes movement in Karnataka.[46] Throughout the period of Congress rule in the state—up until 1983, when it lost the elections for the first time to the Janata Party—certain concessions were made to more dis-advantaged groups among the non-Brahmins, and various Backward Classes commissions were created. Before 1956, the scope of the term "Backward Class" and the commissions' recommendations about reservations and ap-pointments were more or less the same as those of the Miller Committee. But after the reorganization of the state boundaries in 1956, each area had its own list of Backward Classes. The Nagana Gowda Committee was ap-pointed to examine these issues in 1960.[47] It argued that 57 percent of the population of the state (other than those classified as Scheduled Castes/ Tribes) were backward and that this category included Muslims and Christians. The committee recommended 68 percent reservation in the state (including Scheduled Castes/Tribes). Based on its report, the government passed an order in 1962, but this and subsequent orders were challenged by the courts, and it became increasingly obvious that another commission and different criteria for defining backwardness were necessary.

Some of these concessions and efforts were mere tokens, and others, such as the land reforms of 1961 and 1974, had a greater impact, although the effect of the reforms was unevenly distributed throughout the state because of different landholding patterns in various regions.[48] The 1974 land reform was an important element of an entire series of initiatives of the Congress chief minister, Dev Raj Urs, between 1972 and 1980, to help non-Brahmin groups. This included welfare schemes as well as appointments of large numbers of persons to posts in the government and the administrative apparatus. An important impetus in this move was the recognition, which became increasingly apparent to later chief ministers as well, that the support of other castes was necessary for rule. After all, the Lingayats and Vokkaligas together constituted only about one-third of the population of the state.[49]

In 1972, the Havanur Backward Classes Commission was appointed, and for the first time the commission had no Lingayat, Vokkaliga, or Brahmin members.[50] Several caste organizations sent their representatives to the commission, which presented its report in 1975. According to its report, 44.52 percent of the population of the state was to be treated as "Other Backward Classes" besides the 14 percent who formed Scheduled Castes and Tribes.[51] For the first time, this commission classifed Lingayats (excluding a few subcastes among them) and four other castes besides Brahmins as "forward" castes and stated that caste-related backwardness applied only to Hindus. The centerpiece of the Dev Raj Urs program was the proposal to act on the recommendations of the Havanur Commission report that a major share of positions in schools and government services (32 percent) should be reserved for members of Backward Classes. At this time, Dev Raj Urs was creating a powerful coalition of Backward Classes in Karnataka against the Lingayats.[52] He was also trying to establish a power base for himself in the Congress Party after its split in the state in 1969. Therefore, although he accepted the recommendations of the Havanur Commission (the First Backward Classes Commission), he also modified it by adding seven more castes to the list of Backward Classes, including his own, and Muslims.[53] Further, he actively encouraged the establishment and revival of a number of caste associations, especially among numerically weak, disadvantaged, or scattered groups. To a lesser or greater degree, this attention to Backward Classes has been continued by subsequent chief ministers and political parties in the state.

Some of the recommendations of the Havanur Commission were subsequently questioned in the Supreme and High Courts, and as a result the Venkataswamy Second Backward Classes Commission was appointed in 1983. At this point in time, the Janata Party headed by Ramakrishna Hegde was in power in the state. The two dominant castes, the Lingayats and the Vokkaligas, supported him although he was a Brahmin. This acceptance of Brahmin leadership represents a shift in the Backward Classes movement. To balance the various groups in the state, the Venkataswamy Commission was entirely composed of nondominant backward groups.[54] It excluded thirteen castes, including the Lingayats, from its recommendations. The commission's report raised a furor in the state, and because of pressure from the two dominant castes, the government rejected the report. It passed an interim order on reservation that brought practically all castes, including the Lingayats and Vokkaligas, back within the purview of reservation. This order was subsequently extended under the Congress Party's rule in the state.

The extension occurred even after the Chinnappa Reddy Third Backward Classes Commission had submitted its report in 1990 after its appointment the previous year.[55] It recommended 56 percent reservation in the state (including Scheduled Castes/Tribes). The report was placed on the floor of the legislature for public debate, and the previous interim order was extended three times. During this time while the report was under state government consideration, the Supreme Court of India gave a judgment in 1992 relating to reservations and the state government felt the need to modify its report, which it did in 1994. This was done by passing two orders, in April 1994 and in July 1994. The latter order divided "backward" groups into four main categories and raised the level of total reservation to 57 percent.[56] It also included the dominant castes, the Lingayats and Vokkaligas. Therefore, in effect the older reservation policy, which clearly granted unequal rights to many castes, continued, as the nondominant Backward Classes in Karnataka were too divided and concerned with sectional interests to force the government to act on their demands.

Three more forces in the state have emerged in the last two decades that keep the Backward Classes movement from achieving substantial gains: first, the farmer's movement, which has basically been spearheaded by the Lingayats and Vokkaligas in opposition to the various measures undertaken by Dev Raj Urs, especially land reforms; second, the increased importance of the communal issue, which has, following the destruction of the Babri mosque in Ayodhya and other events, led to the Muslims' perceiving themselves as a distinct minority in the state rather than as part of the Backward Classes movement; and third, the migration of Backward Classes from the neighboring states of Andhra Pradesh and Tamil Nadu into Karnataka, which has changed the balance of power locally.[57]

Within the legal framework of the state, the Vahnikula Kshatriyas were recognized as a Backward Class even in 1960, although part of a larger "Tigala" group. The estimates of the Tigala population in the state have varied in the various Backward Classes committees and commissions. All of them have classified the Tigalas (including the Shambukula, Agnikula, and Vahnikula Kshatriyas) as "backward," but they have given different percentages for them as part of the total population of the state. In 1960 the Nagana Gowda Committee gave an estimate of 152,700 persons, 0.72 percent of the total population of the state; in 1972 the Havanur Commission estimated 223,279 persons, 0.74 percent of the total population of the state; in 1984 the Venkataswamy Commission estimated 217,107 persons, 0.60 percent of the total population of the state; and in 1988 the Chinnappa Reddy Commission gave an estimate of 240,118 persons, 0.5446 percent of the total population of the state.

The variety of names associated with the Tigala category emerges in the Karnataka State Government Order, dated April 20, 1994, which modified the recommendations made by the Third Backward Classes Commission headed by Justice Chinnappa Reddy, which had submitted its report in 1990. According to this order, a variety of groups, "Tigala, Agnivamsha Kshatriya, Agnivanni, Agnikula Kshatriya, Dharmaraja Kapu, Palli, Shambukula Kshatriya, Thigala, Vanniar, Vannikula Kshatriya, Tigler and Kuravan," are listed in Category II (More Backward) among the Backward Classes.[58] These groups were reclassified as Category IIa (Relatively More Backward) according to a new government order dated July 25, 1994.[59]

As can be seen, the estimates show a declining percentage of these population groups, however defined, through the years. This fact, the need to counter the force of other landed communities in the state (particularly the Lingayats and Vokkaligas), and their displacement in the city have probably been key mobilizing factors toward the creation of a Tigala alliance. Unlike their caste brethren in Tamil Nadu, the Vahnikula Kshatriyas have been relatively late players in the Backward Classes movement in south India. Their somewhat more strenuous efforts in this regard have been made through an alliance formed between three groups in Bangalore in the 1970s, which is largely geared toward accruing benefits from the government. All the groups are conscious of the fact that the earlier, preindependence, social system in which headmen administered local jurisdictions, even in urban areas, prevented a political alliance. The only links between different groups at various sites were those forged by ritual and kinship. Today, however, the alliance has been made possible by opportunities that have opened up outside the local patron-client economy through education, improved means of communication, and the Backward Classes movement. Thus, paradoxically, the transformation of the cityscape from a world of gardens and water into an urban armature and the disappearance of their control over the material basis of the city have led to the emergence of a more inclusive urban association for the Vahnikula Kshatriyas as "Tigalas." At one level, this alliance is due to the Backward Classes commissions and the creation of a legal category by the state. At another level, the alliance is embedded in different institutions and associations in Bangalore, ranging from the City Corporation to ritual bodies.

The Gardener as an Urbanist

Between 1949 and 1995, there were ten elected councils of the Bangalore City Corporation (BCC). Until 1961, the representation of the Tigalas in the BCC was poor, but it increased dramatically after the creation of the Havanur Commission and the period of Dev Raj Urs. In 1949 and 1954, there was only one representative from the Vahnikula Kshatriya community in each council; in 1961, there was one councilor each from the Vahnikula and the Shambukula Kshatriya communities; and in 1965, the Vahnikula Kshatriya community had two representatives, whereas the Shambukula Kshatriyas had one.

After the 1971 council, the number of Tigalas on the BCC Council—including the Vahnikula, Agnikula, and Shambukula Kshatriyas—rose sharply, although most of the councilors were from the two major parties in the state, the Congress and the Janata Parties (see Table 4).[60] The Congress Party dominated state politics until 1983, when they lost the elections for the first time to the Janata Party. In the BCC Council as well, this trend is apparent: from the statistics available it can be seen that there were no Janata Party representatives in the BCC Council election before 1983. However, there were other parties, such as the Dravida Munnetra Kazhagam Party, that were represented in 1971. Although this party, along with the All India Anna Dravida Munnetra Kazhagam (AIADMK), is influential among the Backward Classes in Tamil Nadu, no Tigala candidate has ever belonged

Table 4

Tigala participation in Bangalore City Corporation Council

Party	Election years			
	1971	1983	1990	1995
Congress I	29 (1V)	11 (1S)	34 (1V, 1S)	19 (1V)
Janata	0	56 (1A, 2V,1S)	18	39 (4V)
Muslim League	5	2	0	0
Bharatiya Janata Party	3	4	8	26
AIA Dravida Munnetra Kazhagam	0	7	3	0
Dravida Munnetra Kazhagam	8	2	3	1
Independents	4	4	18 (1A, 1V)	11 (1V, 1S)
Kannada Chaluvali	5	0	0	0
Samsta Congress	2 (1A)	1	0	0
Powra Samiti	7	0	0	0
Nava Nirmana Vedike	0	0	0	3 (1A)
Karnataka Congress	0	0	0	1
Communist Party of India-Marxist	0	0	1	0
Samyukta Samajwadi Party	0	0	3	0
Total number of Councilors by party	63	87	100	100

Note: V = Vahnikula; S = Shambukula; A = Agnikula Kshatriya. The numbers in parentheses represent the numbers from these three groups who served as councilors as opposed to the total number from their party.
Source: Bangalore City Corporation records.

to these parties. The Tigalas seem to have identified themselves firmly with the vicissitudes of Karnataka state politics in spite of their mythic and historical connections with Tamil Nadu. Another feature of the composition of the City Corporation after 1971 is the increase in the number of independent candidates as well candidates from the Bharatiya Janata Party (BJP), particularly in the 1995 BCC.

Tigala candidates since 1990 have included independents, showing that the domination of the Congress and Janata Parties has been broken among them, at least in the BCC. Even before the 1995 elections, a number of Tigala leaders were wooed by the BJP, and the State Legislative Assembly member from the Chamrajpet constituency (under which Tigalarapet falls),

Premilla Nesargi, belongs to the BJP. From interviews with some Tigala leaders between 1995 and 1996, there appeared to be indications that the relationship between the BJP and the Tigalas could become closer given the right response to their specific interests in the city. The Tigalas as a whole captured about 8 percent of the total seats on the BCC Council in 1995, an impressive win given the small population of the community. As the breakdown in Table 4 demonstrates, among the Tigalas, the Vahnikula Kshatriyas have had the greatest representation on the BCC Council; their presence was recognized especially in the 1995 election, when they won six out of eight seats won by Tigalas. The 1995 elections were also significant in that for the first time female candidates were elected to the Corporation Council (three, all from the Vahnikula Kshatriya community and all Janata Party nominees). One of the major reasons for the continuous visibility of the Vahnikula Kshatriyas on the BCC Council is the importance of the Karaga *jatre* itself in the central business district of Bangalore.

A key figure among the Vahnikula Kshatriyas in the period after the formation of the BCC was S. M. Munivenkatappa (1913–93) who won the single Tigala councilor's seat even in 1949. In the early years, he was an associate of many well-known Congress Party politicians in the city. He was also responsible for many initiatives with respect to the Karaga *jatre*, because he was a member of the temple committee. These included circulating invitations to the performance, enlarging the temple area, and writing a number of books on the Karaga *jatre* and on the role of the gardeners in the state. He also responded to the Havanur Commission by providing information on the community. The interpenetration of his political role with themes of the Karaga *jatre* and gardening telescope the forces that are at work in the larger alliance as well.

In 1944, S. M. Munivenkatappa wrote a prizewinning essay entitled "Grow More Vegetables" for an essay competition organized by the National War Front Organization at the state level. The essay, which was reprinted in the book *Vegetable Produce* (published in English in 1945 and in Kannada in 1949), began: "The war started in Europe. From that time, the price of food products rose. The cost of vegetables and fruits increased with the summer and heat. . . . To begin with, Indians do not have a diet that is healthy. Those who use vegetables are in an aggravated situation. For many living in towns, growing more vegetables has become a key purpose. There is not enough produce for those defending the nation. We should grow more vegetables and also become self-reliant" (my translation, Munivenkatappa 1950, 64).

The book as a whole is an eccentric mixture of styles and issues. It speaks about the need for self-reliance in horticulture to fulfill the needs of citizens in villages and cities, the aesthetic delights of gardening, its physical benefits as an exercise, and the role of gardeners. It pays serious attention to the minute details of growing various vegetables in summer and winter.[61] In separate articles in Bangalore newspapers, Munivenkatappa spoke passionately about fruits grown in the region, such as apples and grapes.[62] The prizewinning essay, which meanders through the correct soil and weather conditions for vegetables and the contribution to nation-building that gardening could make, ends with the rallying cry: "For the play of children, for the food of adults, for the pleasure of city-dwellers, for the income of villagers, grow more vegetables! For the soldiers who protect the nation, for the health of citizens, grow more vegetables!" (my translation, Munivenkatappa 1950, 74).

This curious book and essay contained many of the elements of Munivenkatappa's urbanism. It was his second publication after he graduated with a master's degree in economics from the Maharaja's College in Mysore, the first graduate from the Vahnikula Kshatriya community.[63] The ability to make connections between the horticultural enterprise of the community, the Karaga *jatre*, and civic needs remained a stable element of his political thinking and career until the end. The two main phases of his career were the periods 1945–75 and 1975–93.

In the first period, the public role of Munivenkattappa seems to have been firmly embedded within the politics of Bangalore and the niche that the Vahnikula Kshatriyas/Tigalas (he used these terms interchangeably) as gardeners occupied within it. In the latter period, as political events in the state created a greater basis for the mobilization of Backward Classes, his efforts were directed toward the creation of an alliance of the Vahnikula Kshatriyas/Tigalas with organizations and leaders of other communities. By the end of his career, other individuals had assumed leadership of the movement, and their political thought was no longer linked purely to the role of Vahnikula Kshatriyas/Tigalas as gardeners. Mediating both phases of his career, and of the alliance as whole, was the Karaga *jatre*.

Although Munivenkatappa had been appointed to the Representative Assembly of Mysore state between 1945 and 1949 and had been a member of the Senate of Mysore University earlier, his influence was largely on Bangalore's politics. He was elected unopposed to the City Municipal Council (later the Bangalore City Corporation Council) in 1948 and became its vice president. When the first City Corporation was founded a year later, he became the leader of the Congress Party in the council. At this time, he was engaged in writing many of his books on gardening, and by the time the second edition of *Vegetable Produce* was published in 1950, it included a new preface that was basically an appeal to the government. He was increasingly concerned about the dispossession of land owned by the Vahnikula Kshatriyas/Tigalas in the city and about the lack of voice of the gardeners in public spheres:

> In the Mysore region, growing vegetables, flowers, and fruits is the community occupation of the Tigalas (Vahnikula Kshatriyas). This labor is of national importance. Rulers and the common populace desire vegetables and fruits that Tigalas produce. From their efforts, waste is turned into nutritious foods for citizens. Yet gardeners have not been given sufficient encouragement. In the past 30–40 years, the government and the Municipality have annexed many of the gardens attached to Bangalore. It can be estimated that this annexation covers about 800 acres of land. This has occurred in the name of the growth and beautification of the city. In spite of repeated appeals, the government has not given gardeners even a small bit of land. . . . The Congress government must provide succor to the Tigalas of Bangalore. I appeal that the land on the banks of the Koramangala Tank be provided to them. (My translation, Munivenkatappa 1950, ii)

At the time that the Second Five Year Plan was on the anvil in the country, Munivenkatappa issued another pamphlet, *Help Tigala Class*, which was more explicitly a manifesto than had been earlier pieces:

> For the past three to four centuries, a class of people whose full-time occupation is gardening has been residing in Mysore [as Karnataka state was earlier known]. These professional gardeners are known as "Tigalaru," otherwise known as "Vahnikula Kshatriyas," whose population is said to be about 50 lakhs [5 million] in the Madras State. As per the 1941 census, the Tigala population in Mysore was 101,706. On the basis of natural increase and migration from the neighboring Madras State, our population can now be estimated to be about 125,000 in Mysore . . . It is unfortunate that mainly because Tigalas remain a minority and backward community they have not so far been able to receive timely attention and encouragement. (Munivenkatappa 1957, 1–2)

Munivenkatappa went on to argue, as he had earlier, that 800 acres of land in the city that could have been cultivated by the Vahnikula Kshatriyas/Tigalas of Bangalore for its growing population had been acquired for planning extensions and the beautification of the city. At the time that the Koramangala Tank land was acquired, he stated, the government paid half the cost of the land. He suggested that this land, which measured about 150 acres and was being used for growing grass, be leased or sold to the Vahnikula Kshatriyas/Tigalas, who could then use it to grow vegetables to counter food shortages in the city. He also put forth a series of demands to the state and central governments as well as the Planning Commission in the pamphlet: a horticultural survey on a scientific basis should be organized in the state; in places other than Bangalore, landless Vahnikula Kshatriyas/Tigalas should be provided with suitable garden land, either free or at minimal cost; monetary assistance should be granted by way of long-term and seasonal interest-free loans for gardening; and marketing conditions should be improved in cities and towns to fetch a fair price for gardening produce.

These demands did not have a great impact. In 1962, Munivenkatappa became the founding president of the Vegetable and Fruit Merchants Association at the City Market in Bangalore and renewed his efforts through means other than the City Corporation. One of the first acts of the association, accomplished by means of a statewide agitation, was to demand removal of a tax on fruits that had been in effect in the city since 1957. It appears that by this time Munivenkatappa was becoming conscious of the need to create various associations for the amelioration of the conditions of the Vahnikula Kshatriyas/Tigalas in the city. Therefore, from the late 1950s onward, he participated in a number of initiatives such as the Gardeners' Cooperative Association, the Nurserymen's Cooperative Society, and the Youth Association, in addition to efforts at raising money for a student hostel.

By this time, Munivenkatappa had been appointed convener of the Dharmaraja Temple committee that organized the annual Karaga celebrations. He held that post for fourteen years, from 1948 to 1962. He took an active interest during this time in the cultural world of his community, applying to it the same combination of realism and mythic vision that he had applied to gardening in the city. In that connection, he published a number of pamphlets on prominent members of the Vahnikula Kshatriyas such as the wrestler Annaiappa.[64] In *Karaga Mahotsava* (The Great Karaga Festival), a slim but popular volume, he spoke about the origins of the Vahnikula Kshatriya community from the sacrificial fires of the sage Shambu. He attributed the four important ancient and medieval kingdoms of south India to this same lineage. The book details the roles of various participants in the festival and locates the festival's rationale in the *Mahabharata*. The festival, according to him, had a symbolic role, depicting the birth of the Primal Goddess and the creation of cosmic and social order.

The book is of less interest than the various initiatives Munivenkat-appa launched during his tenure as a temple committee member. The architectonic representation of this vision can best be seen in the changes he effected in the temple. Until his tenure as a committee member, the Dharmaraja Temple was a small structure separated from other temples near it: for instance, a Muthyallamma Temple stood outside it on the boundary of the neighborhood. He created a boundary wall that bound the two temples to each other and also got a Ganesha Temple built on the periphery of the compound as a site complementing the Muthyallamma Temple. Within the Dharmaraja Temple, a Krishna shrine was also built, "for Krishna and Draupadi were brother and sister." The chariot of the temple that used to be assembled every year was now made into a permanent structure, and a shed was built outside the compound wall of the temple for housing it. He also built shops nearby for the purpose of generating temple revenue. For the first time in the history of the Karaga *jatre*, there was a systematization of the rites on different days. A calendar of events was drawn up (and is still followed today), and it was circulated in a pamphlet to all households in the area, fixing the roles of the various players and committees. Even the choice of the Karaga priest was standardized: Munivenkatappa believed that the priest should be chosen on the basis of election rather than hereditary status, and that someone whose height and weight were best suited to the purpose should be selected.[65]

A rationalism was visible in Munivenkatappa's efforts that prompts comparisons of him with another great leader of depressed castes in Maharashtra who also belonged to the gardener caste, Jyotirao Phule (1827–90). Phule's efforts as a reformer stressed the importance of education and campaigns against the caste system; equally, he recognized the importance of cultural practices that created a certain communitas and camaraderie among these castes, practices that did not stem from the worldview of higher castes. Therefore, he actively promoted festivals such as those dedicated to Bali Raja, whom he idealized as a lower-caste, peasant hero subjugated by higher castes. Like Phule, whose family was associated with the palace as gardeners, Munivenkatappa married into a family that supplied fruits and vegetables to the palace. Munivenkatappa also appears to have realized the importance of the Karaga *jatre* to a number of groups besides the Vahnikula Kshatriyas of the city. He drew attention to this fact by inviting government officials to the festival, thus extending its base of political legitimacy. Perhaps there is no greater evidence of this than his effort to make the Corporation Day holiday (Kempe Gowda Day) coincide with the day of the Karaga procession! Up until this moment, the significance of the Vahnikula Kshatriyas in the state and the city had been centered in three of their roles: as gardeners, as wrestlers (many of them well known throughout Mysore state), and as ritual players in the Karaga *jatre*. Although the Wodeyar kings had occasionally patronized the *jatre*, Munivenkatappa seemed conscious of the need to carve out a larger political and cultural base for the community through the regular intervention of the state.

The Creation of Tigala Unity

Although various associations among the three "Tigala" groups existed in the 1940s, either as community welfare institutions or as temple trusts, and there were Dharmaraja and Draupadi temples associated with them as well as other groups, it is not clear that they had self-consciously articulated a frame of unity, mythic or political, among themselves until the 1970s. The creation of a political alliance among the three groups—the Vahnikula, Shambukula, and Agnikula—coincides with the latter period of Munivenkatappa's career—that is, the period after 1975. In Munivenkatappa's writing, the term "Tigala" had most commonly been used to mean the group that celebrated the Karaga festival and those who were traditionally gardeners.[66] In May 1975, the "Karnataka Tigalara Vokkuta Samsthe" (Karnataka Tigalas' Unity Organization) was registered in Bangalore under the Karnataka Societies Registration Act (1960), and the term "Tigala" came to stand for all three "sects"—the Vahnikula, the Shambukula, and the Agnikula. In the years before this time, Munivenkatappa seems to have been actively involved in dialogues with the leaders of other groups in the city and the state for the creation of an alliance. These efforts crystallized in his report and those of other leaders to the Havanur Commission, in which the term "Tigala" came to largely define three groups instead of having the loose and somewhat shifting meanings adopted earlier.[67] After 1975, Munivenkatappa more or less retired from political life, but continued to play an advisory role in the public affairs of the community.

Other groups and leaders emerged within the Tigala community, now defined as an amalgamation of three groups. A few leaders of all three groups were driving forces and went on to hold offices within the new organization.[68] According to the memorandum of the Vokkuta Samsthe, one of the main objectives of this alliance is to bring together members of the three sects of the Tigala Kshatriya community within the jurisdiction of Karnataka state.[69] The emblem of the organization clearly represents this alliance and its mythic basis (see Figure 11). The pot containing fire is an al-

Figure 11. The emblem of Tigala unity.

lusion to the Karaga icon and the origin of the three sects from fire—either from Draupadi, who was born of fire (the Vahnikula Kshatriyas), from the sacrificial fire of the sage Shambu (the Shambukula Kshatriyas), or from the fire hero Agni Banniraya (the Agnikula Kshatriyas). The two flags represent the sun and the moon, because the three groups see themselves as belonging to the "lineages" of the sun and the moon, with somewhat separate ritual calendars. The sides of the triangle containing the pot and the flags stand for the three groups and their unity. The triangle and the pot are set within three circles, emblematic of time (the twenty-four-hour day), the sky, and the universe.

Quite often, members of any one group will separately identify themselves as a "caste." It is clear, however, that many of the features of their community have evolved not with reference to some pan-Indian or even south Indian caste scheme, but according to the history of their settlement in the city. In this history, corporate group characteristics coagulated around the veneration of the goddess, certain martial cults, and shrines that often connected them to other shrines because of a shared repertoire of figures and stories. Intersecting this complex is language (Kannada or Tamil) and, for some, the community's relationship to landownership in the city (the Shambukula Kshatriyas did not hold land). The alliance may be best described as a "paracommunity," a voluntary association that is not based merely on ascriptive status and enables members of a community to pursue political power, economic opportunities, and social mobility.[70] The most important basis for the Tigala paracommunity is a cultic terrain that has mobilized separate groups into a political alliance.

Between 1976 and 1996, four committees of office bearers of the Vokkuta Samsthe were elected; the total number within each committee was nineteen. The membership of the organization is open to all Tigalas over age eighteen for a small fee, and a number of meetings are held annually at various temples, school buildings, and houses of members. The president of each committee is chosen by rotation among the three "sects." Therefore, the first president belonged to the Shambukula community, the second to the Agnikula, the third to the Shambukula again, and the fourth to the Vahnikula. The general secretary, however, has been drawn mainly from the Vahnikula Kshatriyas, as is the treasurer, and it appears that the Vahnikula Kshatriyas are the driving force behind the organization (see Table 5). The Central Committee today consists of 3,000 to 5,000 members besides some life members and donor members. There are female members as well, numbering some hundreds, but the Vokkuta Samsthe is clearly male dominated, as are the Karaga *jatre* and the Tigalas' representation on the City Corporation Council.

The career of S. Srinivas, the treasurer of the Vokkuta Samsthe from 1985 to 1996, is fairly typical of many others in the organization. He was born in 1946, and his family were long-time residents of Tigalarapet. After studying in the Mission School, he acquired a degree in commerce from a Bangalore college in 1972, candidly admitting that he had neither the grades nor the linguistic capabilities to earn another degree. In the late 1970s, the only child of his dead father, he spent a number of years while working as a supervisor in an electronics workshop petitioning to keep family land. This amounted to fifteen to twenty acres spread out in different areas that had come under the purview of the Urban Land Ceiling Act and the Slum Clearance Board. Through his efforts, a few acres were retained as garden land, and in addition he now has his own private business for metallurgical work. Even as a young man, he was active in helping senior members of the community found the Vokkuta Samsthe. The basis for this political work lay in his involvement with older organizations in the community, such as the Youth Association (a cultural body that helped students with their studies), and also in putting on plays and taking part in wrestling competitions. As a youth, Srinivas used to accompany the Karaga priest when the latter used to train in the gymnasium; he himself was a wrestler, participating in state-

Table 5.

Main office holders of the Karnataka Thigalara Vokkuta Samsthe

	Terms of office	
Offices	1976–80	1980–82
President	M. Muniram (S)	T. V. Thimmegowda (A)
Vice president	T. V. Thimmegowda (A)	M. Venkataswamygowda (V)
Vice president	M. Parthasarathy (S)	V. Ramaswamy (S)
Vice president	M. Muniswamappa (V)	T. V. Thimmaiah (A)
General secretary	E. Krishna Narayana (V)	M. Ramaiah (V)
Treasurer	L. Lakshminarayan (V)	P. Chikka Krishna (V)
Associate	H. D. Venkataswamy (S)	C. G. Marigowda (A)
secretary	T. V. Thimmaiah (A)	R. Muniswamy (S)
	1982–85	**1985–96**
President	V. Ramaswamy (S)	C. Krishnappa (V)
Vice president	E. Krishna Naryana (V)	Betappa (A)
Vice president	H. D. Venkataswamy (S)	M. Ramaiah (V)
Vice president	R. Muniswamy (S)	R. Muniswamy (S)
General secretary	P. Chikka Krishna (V)	M. Mutappa (V)
Treasurer	M. Ramaiah (V)	S. Srinivas (V)
Associate	S. Srinivas (V)	C. G. Marigowda (A)
secretary	P. Raman (S)	P. Raman (S)

Source: Minutes of General Body meeting, December 15, 1996; and interview with K. Lakshmana, September 30, 1999.

Note: V = Vahnikula, A = Agnikula, and S = Shambukula.

level wrestling events. Eventually, he joined the Vokkuta Samsthe as a member and rose to hold various positions in it as well as in other bodies such as the Mysore Horticultural Society. He suggested, however, that there is still some division within the Vahnikula Kshatriyas between college graduates and educated persons on the one hand and, on the other hand, those who cling more steadfastly to older political ties under local headmen. Some of those associated with the temple and the Karaga *jatre* maintain a certain distance from the Samsthe, because they are suspicious of ties to other groups.[71]

Between 1975 and 1979, the Vokkuta Samsthe held forty-two executive meetings. This period was clearly the most successful phase in its history according to many leaders of the Samsthe:[72]

We conducted this phase like an agitation and struggled to bring awakening among the community of the Tigalas. We held numerous meetings where we would invite ministers like [Dev Raj] Urs and others as well so that the Tigalas and the ministers felt pride in the community. In one meeting at Neelasandra, we invited four important ministers—Mallikarjun Karge, Veerappa Moily, Dharam Singh, and Kagodu Thimmappa. At this time, in 1974–75, Kemp Raj Urs, who was the brother of Dev Raj Urs, was the president of the Karnataka Backward People's Association, where I was also an office holder. (Interview with E. Krishna Narayana, December 30, 1996)

This was a "zoom period," as one person characterized it; through political patronage and the community's networks within government bureaucracy, a number of Tigalas began to acquire social and occupational mobility. In December 1975, Vokkuta Samsthe members attended the Southern Vahnikula Kshatriya Conference in Madras, which brought together "caste" brethren from all over south India. This was an important factor in their consciousness of the links of the fire-born communities with other such groups in Tamil Nadu and Andhra Pradesh, although this has not grown into a broad political base yet.[73] Most of their efforts during this period, however, were directed toward the protection of horticultural land in the city:

In the 1970s, as a result of the Land Reforms Act of Dev Raj Urs, which made tenants the tillers, a number of Tigalas stood to gain, since in many areas they did not directly own land. The Samsthe provided information about the Urban Land Ceiling Act, the Karnataka Land Reforms Act, the Urban Land Tax Act, and the Karnataka Slum Clearance Act, and at some sites, such as Tumkur and Kolar, it is estimated that Tigalas became owners of hundreds of acres of garden land. One of the main triumphs of the Samsthe in this period was the denotification of sixty-one villages in the 1970s which were being acquired by various municipal and city authorities for development purposes. The organization actively campaigned among its community members against this acquisition. Through its efforts, it prevailed upon the chief minister, Dev Raj Urs, to issue an order in 1976 directing the Bangalore Development Authority, the municipalities of various towns, the Bangalore City Corporation, and the Housing and Urban Development Department not to acquire lands being cultivated by the Tigalas. (Interview with E. Krishna Narayana, December 30, 1996)

Dev Raj Urs seems to have played a significant role in the eyes of the same member from the Vokkuta Samsthe. It was under his rule as chief minister that the Tigalas were given the status "More Backward" within the Backward Classes:

> Dev Raj Urs recognized the Tigala community more than any other chief minister. He made an order that the land of the Tigalas should not be acquired, since it was needed for their traditional occupation, gardening. It was also during Dev Raj Urs' period that the Tigalas were made part of the "More Backward" category of the Backward Classes. Now we want Backward Tribe or Scheduled Tribe status, and we have approached Deve Gowda [previously chief minister of the state] about it, but he has now become prime minister. However, we are trying to approach [him] through other Backward Classes ministers such as Jalappa, Scindia, Siddaramaiah, and Jayakumar. All these are in the Janata Dal, but when we conducted our conference [in 1996] we invited all parties because the conference was conducted on community, and not on political, lines. Using the previous order issued during Dev Raj Urs' time, we are trying to stop land acquisition in Anekal, Tumkur, Kanakpura, and other suburban areas. (Interview with E. Krishna Narayana, December 30, 1996)

The Mythic and Political Universe of the Alliance

From 1978 onward, the Vokkuta Samsthe held seven state-level meetings at different towns in the southern parts of the state besides numerous other smaller meetings organized on social occasions. Many of the groups associated with the Vokkuta Samsthe, which regards itself as an umbrella organization of about 150 bodies, include Vahnikula Kshatriya organizations associated with the Karaga *jatre*. The first state-level meeting was held in Korategere, Tumkur district, in 1978. This initial meeting was addressed by then-Chief Minister Dev Raj Urs, and it appears that about 100,000 people gathered there.

At the second conference, held at Malur in Kolar district in 1987, the minister for home affairs, R. L. Jalappa, was invited as one of the chief guests. In a petition to him and the other members of legislature who were invited, the three groups of the Tigala community defined themselves as the lineages of fire and children of Draupadi and Dharmaraja, their patron deities. The petition stated that the Pallavas, the ancient rulers of Kanchipuram in Tamil Nadu, belonged to the same lineage. As warriors in various regional armies and as small migrating groups, Tigalas had spread to different parts of south India, becoming gardeners as they settled near various bodies of water. This was the reason for differences in their language, although their basic customs remained the same. Today, the petition said, they are 1 million in number and are economically and educationally extremely backward. On the occasion of the Malur meeting, the Vokkuta Samsthe made four main demands. First, they stated that the government should compensate the Tigalas for the land they had lost through the growth of Bangalore by means of allocating to them lots of land elsewhere. Second, they wished to be classified as a Backward Tribe and not as a Backward Caste, because in the Backward Caste category in which they had been placed by the Havanur Commission there were 119 other castes and hundreds of subcastes, some of them economically and socially very powerful. Third, the Vokkuta Samsthe sought special measures to increase the literacy rates in the community (which stood at 0.3 percent) through scholarships and reservations. And last, it sought adequate representation for the community in the state legislature.

The Samsthe held other meetings; it conducted a mass marriage ceremony at Malur, Kolar district, in 1988, another mass marriage ceremony at Kolar in 1989, and a meeting at Bangalore city in 1990. All the demands made at Malur in 1987 were made again, in an only slightly modified form, in other state-level meetings and to other government ministers and party representatives. The Malur petition itself was largely based on the petition submitted earlier by Munivenkatappa to the prime minister, Indira Gandhi, at the Lalbagh conference of Backward Classes, Scheduled Castes, and Tribes in 1973. The main difference between the two was the proposal in the Malur petition that their status be changed to Backward Tribe.

This demand was raised more forcefully in the two public meetings held after the Chinnappa Reddy Commission report had been discussed in the legislature and the government had passed two orders modifying it by including new groups. The Chinnappa Reddy Commission report's classification of the Tigalas and their "synonym groups" in Category II of the Backward Classes along with 102 other groups denied the Tigalas any appreciable benefits. The Samsthe held two rallies to indicate its opposition to the report. The first (on August 7, 1994) was held near the Dharmaraja Temple in the City and included many members of the community as public speakers, some of them Bangalore City Corporation councilors and others belonging to various government departments, such as the police and the education department. This meeting also included a procession. The second rally (on September 25, 1994) was held in a large plot of open land at Tumkur town, Tumkur district, and the chief minister, Veerappa Moily, was invited to inaugurate it.[74] The Memorandum to the Chief Minister presented on that occasion reiterated the same demands made at the Malur meeting, but added that the number of Tigalas in the state was 2 million. The Samsthe argued that in neighboring states some castes had changed their categories under the reservation policy to procure greater benefits.[75] It demanded that the Tigalas be reclassified as a Backward Tribe, Scheduled Caste, or Scheduled Tribe.

The demand made at Tumkur was changed back to a plea for Backward Tribe or Scheduled Tribe status at the next meeting, perhaps due to opposition by members of the community to Scheduled Caste status, which was considered especially low. On August 11, 1996, a rally of various Tigala organizations called the "Karnataka Tigala People's Great Conference" took place near Town Hall in Bangalore.[76] Another group, the "Awakening Association," joined with the Vokkuta Samsthe to organize this meeting.[77] This group, founded in 1993 with K. Lakshmana as the secretary, was trying to work with Vahnikula Kshatriyas outside of Bangalore toward an awareness of their rights and unity with other groups. Lakshmana, who holds a law degree and craftsman certificate, described the history of Vahnikula Kshatriyas in Bangalore city as a continuous migration out of the city to its peripheries as the gardeners followed the distribution of bodies of water, striving to cultivate their gardens as their lands within the city were acquired. Somewhat poetically, he said: "We followed in the trail of water. First we cultivated land at Siddigatta Tank near the City Market. We lost our land there. Then we settled near Lalbagh garden, only to once more lose our land, and were pushed towards Koramangala and Doopanahalli. After that land was acquired, we moved to Varthur. Now with the Singapore Technology Park being planned there, we have been pushed out towards Malur town" (interview with K. Lakshmana, August 11, 1996). E. Krishna Narayana, one of the leaders of the Samsthe, stated more emphatically: "By birth we are tribals. We move from place to place in search of water for gardening. The government should give us this tribe status."[78]

Leaders and community members from various districts attended the August 1996 meeting, coming by truckloads to the Town Hall. Since the hall itself could not house all the people—estimates were that there were about 25,000 persons, chiefly from Tumkur, Kolar, and Bangalore city—tents were put up outside, and people sitting there watched the proceedings by means of closed-circuit television. The Vahnikula Kshatriya association of the Dharmaraja Temple boycotted the meeting, as members claimed that they had not been consulted about planning the meeting. Leaders of the community as well as prominent state ministers addressed the rally.[79] Although the chief minister had been invited to attend, he did not do so, and this led to a protest by youth from the community, who blocked the main road in the area for about an hour, leading to a huge traffic jam.

The demands made at this public meeting are instructive. Although ministers addressing the gathering urged the Tigalas to consider all Backward Classes as their "caste," the Tigalas themselves demanded, first, that the government compensate them for the loss of their land with 1,000 acres of other land. Lakshmana claimed, in an interview that day, that 80 percent of the land acquired by the government in the city had belonged to the Tigala community. Although the Vokkaligas had managed to retain their lands by a variety of means, the Tigalas had not because they were educationally and economically less powerful. Second, the leaders stated that the Tigalas' inclusion within Category II of the Backward Classes was meaningless, because in the very same category there were 102 other groups. This classification denied the Tigalas adequate economic benefits and representation. The leaders demanded that the Tigalas be included in the category of Scheduled Tribe or Backward Tribe. While the speeches were going on, many of the young men of the community danced and sang outside the hall to the accompaniment of drums and other musical instruments. There was also an exhibition of fruits and vegetables grown by the Tigalas.

One of the demands that has been raised by the movement in recent years is that the Tigalas be allowed to select a candidate for the Legislative Council of Karnataka (the upper house in the state legislature) from the Tigala community. Although this demand was made at the 1987 meeting in a muted form, it rose again with particular force in 1994. Memorandums were circulated among the various Tigala organizations asking support for the candidacy of E. Krishna Narayana as a member of the Legislative Council. Krishna Narayana had previously held the post of director of Printing, Stationery, and Publications at the Government Press in Bangalore. He held a master's degree in physics besides various diplomas in printing from London and had been the member of various sports groups in the state, such as the Cyclists Association and the Football Association. He had long been politically active in the community, having been one of the founder members of the Vokkuta Samsthe and held office in it in positions such as general secretary. His candidacy received wide support from various organizations, including the Karnataka Vahnikula Kshatriya Tigala Youth Association (established in 1936), the Mysore Shambukula Kshatriya Association (established in 1946), and the Akhila Karnataka Vahnikula Kshatriya Tigala Jagruti Sangha (established in 1994).

The scale and momentum of the movement increased after 1987, with greater income and expenditures than in previous years (see Table 6).

Table 6

Income and expenditure of the Karnataka Thigalara Vokkuta Samsthe, 1980–95, for the calendar year January 1 to December 31, in Indian rupees

Year	Income	Expenses	Balance	Comments
1980	6778.65	1107.50	5671.15	Most of the expenditure went toward printing (760.00), whereas donations by members (1544.00) to conduct meetings provided the main income.
1981	5084.00	6083.27	999.27	Scholarships (3104.00) were the main expense, whereas income came from a lottery (3879.00).
1982	1830.18	3007.64	1177.46	General Body meetings were the main expense (1690.00), whereas members' contributions (780.00) were the main income.
1983	1883.05	5272.83	3389.78	Meetings were the main expense (3016.55), and income was mainly derived from donations (1350.00).
1984	1004.60	980.00	24.60	The main expenses were for coaching classes for the Karnataka Public Service Commission exam (880.00), and the income derived from it was 980.00.
1985	1707.90	3841.40	2133.50	The main expense was for conducting marriages (1000.00) whereas the main income was from members' contributions (1395.00).
1986	1281.00	1498.50	217.50	All were petty income and expenses.
1987	15000.10	10306.04	4694.06	The main income came from donations of members (12342.00), while expenses went chiefly toward scholarships (2300.00).

Table 6 (continued)

Year	Income	Expenses	Balance	Comments
1988	8425.35	11655.15	3229.80	The main expense was toward conducting a mass marriage (7629.00), and the main income was donations for this purpose (7500.00).
1989	18006.25	13733.30	4272.95	The main income came from donations for mass marriages (15015.00), and the expenditure went toward printing (5477.00) and scholarships (2900.00).
1990	20234.75	20294.50	59.75	Donations for (19602.00) and expenses (12095.00) toward the state-level conference were the main income and expenses, respectively.
1991	158.20	410.90	252.70	No significant activity.
1992	2779.75	2715.67	64.08	No significant activity.
1993	877.50	1424.60	547.10	No significant activity.
1994	6677.50	7807.40	1129.90	The main income came from members' donations (5500.00), and the main expenditure was for printing and stationery (3850.00).
1995	45366.73	5615.70	39751.03	The main income came from a bank deposit of the Samsthe (39,499.00), and the main expense was toward the printing of bylaws copies (4000.00), presumably regarding the proposal of a candidate to serve as a member of the Legislative Council.

Source: Proceedings of the General Body meetings and balance sheet accounts, 1980–95.

Until 1987, the income of the Samsthe was largely derived from donations of members for General Body meetings, the first of which was held in November 1979. Hardly any income was collected from membership fees, a pattern that continues today. In 1987, the income collected in the form of donations from ordinary members, which had been less than 1,500 rupees per year, increased to 12,342 rupees, rising to an all-time high in 1990, with about 19,602 rupees collected thus. A large portion went toward conducting mass marriages in the community and holding public meetings. Although there were lean years between 1991 and 1993, the scale of activity and public mobilization has remained high since 1987.

The outflow of political energy and the manner of organization of the state-level meetings of the Vokkuta Samsthe mimic the cycle of Karaga performances in the City and in surrounding towns. This is one of the modalities in which the cultic terrain interacts with the reservations made available by the state and the Backward Classes movement. The meetings of the Vokkuta Samsthe have been held in the three main districts in which the Karaga *jatre* is held—Tumkur, Kolar, and Bangalore—and almost always with the support of the organizations at the local level that hold the performance itself. The center of activity and inspiration, however, seems to be Bangalore.

The setbacks that this movement has received in recent years, especially in terms of the lack of protection of the horticultural land of the Vahnikula Kshatriyas, will probably focus attention more than ever on the cultic terrain. For instance, interviews with various leaders of the Vahnikula Kshatriya community, clearly the driving force in the alliance, demonstrate their awareness of the need to broaden the base of the paracommunity. Their efforts include a recasting of their history and the political community: many claim more vociferously than ever that the founder of Bangalore was a Tigala. Lakshmana, a prominent leader, argues that there are other groups in the state who have a putative descent from heroes and figures of the *Mahabharata*, although they are not conscious of their unity with the other Tigalas.[80] For all the three groups in the alliance, he argues, Vyasa, the author of the *Mahabharata*, and the grandfather of the Pandava heroes in it, is the origin; Kunti herself, the mother of the Pandavas, came from Karnataka, whereas the other wife of their father (Pandu), called Madri, came from Madras. The only difference is that the Tigalas have migrated from different regions: the Agnikulas are old residents of Karnataka; the Vahnikulas migrated from the middle parts of Tamil Nadu; the Shambukulas came from the southern part of Tamil Nadu.[81] The language distribution shows this connection: the Agnikulas speak Kannada, the Vahnikulas

Tamil and Kannada, and the Shambukulas Tamil. All three languages are derived from a protolanguage called "Aravu," which combines the two languages of Kannada and Tamil as well as Telugu and Sanskrit, Lakshmana claimed.[82] Lakshmana's mythic universe can obviously be extended to accommodate other groups. For instance, in the same interview he stated that the relationship between the Vahnikula Kshatriyas and the community of the Small Dharmaraja Temple, who claim Krishna as their patron deity, was like the relationship of the Pandavas to their cousin, Krishna.

As represented in Munivenkatappa's philosophy and life, Vahnikula Kshatriya–Tigala political action is essentially based on local experience within the city and not on a regional vision of the masses. It works through political and social institutions and public spaces within the city: the City Corporation, alliances with other urban groups, demonstrations at the Town Hall, and the Karaga festival. The largest presence of the Vahnikula Kshatriyas-Tigalas, after all, is in Bangalore. Occasionally, as in the representation made to Prime Minister Indira Gandhi at the South Zone Conference of Backward Classes, Scheduled Tribes, and Scheduled Castes at Lalbagh in 1973, the Vahnikula Kshatriyas–Tigalas have categorized themselves as a "rural" class. This representation seems a matter political expedience on that occasion, for the Vahnikula Kshatriya–Tigala households in Karnataka are largely town or city dwellers. Where they are not, the "villages" they live in are on the periphery of urban agglomerations and cannot really be described as rural. In concrete terms, most of their efforts seem to be directed toward securing gains within the city. Therefore, in 1979 the chief minister was invited to inaugurate a Vahnikula Kshatriya student hostel and marriage hall in Bangalore. One of the appeals to the chief minister on that occasion was that the day after the Karaga *jatre* should be declared a local holiday because it is a night-long festival and the thousands of persons who participate in it in the city lose sleep that night! Larger legal or constitutional changes are sought only when they are required for these advances. It is only in very recent times that the movement's vision has broadened to include efforts to acquire civic representation on not just the BCC Council, but also on the State Legislative Council. This reflects, in part, the enlarged mythic-political universe of the alliance that is spilling over the boundaries of the city, but it is still too early to reflect on what form this alliance will take.

5

The Primal Goddess, the Polyandrous Spouse, and Celibate Warriors

The Creation of a Landscape of Memory

The cultic terrain of the Karaga *jatre,* together with other legal and institutional interventions, opens up a realm of political action for Vahnikula Kshatriyas in Bangalore, and facilitates the construction of a wider alliance with other Backward Classes in the city. These mobilization efforts encode some elements of the terrain—fire-born ancestors, fire sacrifice, fiery lineages, and their location in the narratives and practices of key shrines in Bangalore. Specifically, the Karaga *jatre* is embedded in topological and institutional coordinates drawn from the many urban models of Bangalore and the flows between the various axes of the performative complex that center on goddess temples, the figures of warrior deities, and Sufis. These coordinates and axes create an arena of operation for the Karaga *jatre* that also embodies them through ritual, oral, and kinetic practices. This chapter focuses on the kinetic practices that compose the *jatre* and the ideas of the body that underlie them. The next chapter focuses on another compositional device, the oral epic. The descriptions of the ritual process and preparations for it, which are drawn from observations made across three years— 1995, 1996, and 1997—give us the moments, movements, vistas, babble, and colors of the Karaga *jatre.* This chapter, however, does not focus intensively on rituals, icons, implements, meanings, or ritual officiants related to these except where they provide a basis for analyzing the time-space units that emerge from the kinetic practices of the *jatre* every year.

There are four aspects to these time-space units, each unit of which I call a "kinetograph": a representation of spatial movement in time that emerges from the ritual process. First, the kinetograph, suggesting a type of dance notation, includes direction and orientation and refers to temporal flows and spatial boundaries. For instance, the procession that occurs on the last night of the Karaga *jatre* charts a route through the City that, when represented by its chief nodes, stops, and directions, reveals how the *jatre* is located within other discursive and historical processes. Highlighted at different phases of the *jatre*, the kinetograph "fills in" or "lays out" public spaces in the metropolis and gives us a framework to grasp how meanings are created within the *jatre*. Above all, these meanings are related to an understanding of the spatial character of and temporal flows within the metropolis and its social history, architecture, and changing economic and cultural bases.

Second, each kinetograph creates a particular representation of locality and temporality so that, taken as a "set" together with the oral epic, they allow for an understanding of how the performance acts as a mnemonic. It is this matrix that makes possible the landscapes of urban memory, being, as it were, tools for their creation. These themes are taken up again in the conclusion. Suffice it to say here that although kinetographs are abstract and formal categories, they involve material sites in the city. They gather up or "re-collect" spaces such as temples, markets, streets, bodies of water, gardens, factories, stadiums, gymnasiums, and certain locations within the performative complex and urban models into particular sections of time. For instance, the Sufi shrine in the City is connected to the Anjaneya temples as well as other sites in one of the last phases of the *jatre*.

Third, although each kinetograph creates a "map" of the city, these maps must not be understood merely as cognitive categories. As I pointed out in chapter 1, urban social memory is transmitted and transformed through the performance and through practices of the body linked to it. The ritual players move through the metropolis, walking, praying, or creating altars in different parts of the city during the days of the *jatre*. It is crucial, therefore, to understand the social nature of these practices and the cultural ideals embodied in them. The Karaga *jatre* involves a yearlong preparation by the Vahnikula Kshatriyas. This includes training in gymnasiums on the part of Virakumaras and the Karaga priest as well as making other arrangements as the time of the festival draws closer. This chapter describes these preparations and the ideas about the body that underlie them, such as ideas about the circulation of blood, its transformation into semen, and the connection between sexual energy, celibacy, and strength. The *jatre*, as well as its phases and cosmology, is also related to conceptions of the "heating" and "cooling" of the Primal Goddess, as Draupadi is portrayed in the performance. Further, there are parallels between the ritual and civic body, such as the conservation and channeling of bodily fluids and the flows between bodies of water and gardens in Bangalore.

Fourth, the kinetographs in the City's Karaga *jatre* parallel those that appear in Draupadi performances in other towns surrounding the metropolis and Bangalore's new suburbs, to which they have spread in the last fifty years or so. What we have here is not a "regal cult" with its structure of performances, such as the Ramlila in Banaras,[1] nor a model of "galactic polity" embodied in ritual, as in the cult of Pattini.[2] Instead, theoretically, theatrically, and practically, it is a model that can be extended to cover new segments that are linked to previous ones through modes of alliance and correspondence, a "theater of the civic." Therefore, as Bangalore grows and incorporates new suburbs and towns in the larger metropolitan region, so has the Karaga *jatre* come to be performed in new areas.

The Gymnasium

The central role in the Karaga *jatre* is held by the Karaga priest, who comes into contact with the power of the goddess as the bearer of the Karaga. For the past five decades, the role of the Karaga priest has rotated between three families.[3] The man who is a Karaga priest must be married; he leaves his house on the night that the flag of the festival is hoisted and comes to stay in the temple. His wife removes all insignia of marriage and is considered to be in a state akin to widowhood for the period of the festival, and she is prohibited from seeing her husband's face. All these prohibitions are lifted when he returns home after the festival and the two are once again "married." The priest's marital state is explicitly related to the process of coming into contact with *shakti*. He approaches this power in part through training and in part through the establishment of correct sexual relations with his wife, who embodies this power. Asceticism and sexuality are terms of a unified field of discussion about the body and its transformation in the Karaga *jatre* rather than being opposed. Therefore, through the observance of certain taboos and the establishment of ritual distance from his wife during the festival period, the priest achieves power and, in effect, becomes a sort of substitute for her. This is common to priests in many goddess shrines as well as other bearers of the goddess's power in other parts of India.[4]

The Karaga is said to weigh about fifteen to twenty kilos. So training is required on the part of the priest to be able to bear its weight on his head for nearly ten hours and move all over the city on the final day of the performance. In Malur town close to Bangalore, the Karaga priest often begins his training about three months in advance; among other things, this involves his running every morning with a sandbag weighing about twenty-five kilos on his head and practicing special dances in the courtyard of the temple. On the day of the *jatre*, the Karaga in Malur is said to contain pots inside of which are placed the image of Draupadi, jaggery, a couple of kilos of rice, and a few other articles, such as bangles and turmeric. The weight of the jasmine garlands decorating the Karaga alone is about ten kilos.[5] There are special families of florists who supply the jasmine for the Karaga in Bangalore, and fifteen to twenty persons are specially appointed to make garlands inside the temple for this purpose. There are norms about how the Karaga should be structured, although these are not divulged, being considered a secret. After it is covered with jasmine, representations of the insignia of the goddess—the conch, the discus, the trident, the mace, and the drum—are stuck on the flowers.[6] Once the Karaga is mounted on his head, the priest may not touch it; in his right hand he carries a dagger, in his left a magical stick.[7] On the day of the Karaga procession, he is dressed in a turmeric-colored sari and blouse. On his hands are black bangles, and around his neck are strands of pearls, rubies, and diamonds. He also wears a gold waistband and, thus adorned, is considered to have been transformed into a fit support for the goddess.

The "hero-sons," Virakumaras, who accompany the priest, are distinctively attired in white pants, white turbans with gold work on their fringes, and red- and white-checked scarves. Nearly all members of the Vahnikula Kshatriya community send at least one male member to the *jatre* as a Virakumara. These males take a vow either at the beginning of the festival period or, more commonly, on the day of the Karaga's first emergence, to perform the service of guarding the deity. During this period, they must remain celibate, separated from their womenfolk (especially their wives), and must eat only one meal a day, usually uncooked food or that cooked in a special pot; they do not eat meat or drink alcohol during this period. They also do not visit a house where a marriage or a death has occurred or where there is a menstruating woman. The symbols of their allegiance are a wristband and a sword (see Figure 12). The sword is in possession of every family that supplies a Virakumara and has been exempt, according to folklore, from the Arms Act from the time of Mark Cubbon over a hundred years ago. Brahmin priests tie the wristband, since this is regarded as a sort of sacred thread of celibacy. It binds the hero-son to the goddess and represents the strict demands made on his character and his sexuality during the Karaga *jatre*.

Along with the Karaga priest, the Virakumaras also train regularly in a gymnasium *(garadi mane)*. Indian-style wrestling *(mallayuddha* or *kusti)*

Figure 12. The Virakumaras perform blade service.

is a form that dates back at least to the period of the *Mahabharata* (probably about the beginning of the first millennium BCE). There are many scenes in the Sanskrit epic and in south Indian versions that speak about the martial talents utilized by various characters in the narrative as well as instruments such as the mace. Certainly martial heroes were venerated, as is evidenced by the number of hero-stones commemorating their deeds that are found all over south India dating from the early periods of the last millennium. Kings were also celebrated for their prowess: the Pallava ruler Narasimhavarman I (630–668 CE) had the title of "Mahamalla" or "The Great Wrestler." There are descriptions of wrestling at the court of the Vijayanagar emperor, Krishnadevaraya, who ruled over much of south India in the sixteenth century. One historian remarks that duels and contests were very common in the court of the emperor and lands were granted tax-free for running gymnasiums.[8] As Zarrilli (1994) notes, there are variations among local martial traditions. Some like "Varma Ati," found in the southern part of Tamil Nadu and the Kanyakumari region, do not employ weapons, whereas these are emphasized in "Kalarippayattu," a martial discipline practiced in Kerala since at least the twelfth century that has elements both from Tamil Sangam culture (fourth century BCE to 600 CE) and the *Dhanur Veda* ("Bow Knowledge") tradition. The *Veda* encompasses a number of traditional fighting arts and is claimed by both the *Mahabharata* and the *Ramayana* as a means of education in warfare. Kalarippayattu was linked closely to forms of worship such as Teyyam in North Malabar, and religious ideologies and a complex set of interactions between the human microcosm and the macrocosm shaped the martial skills of the practitioners.[9]

In north India, wrestling may have absorbed some elements from the Mughal form of wrestling brought to the subcontinent by Persian armies; there might even be some features of it that are owed to the Greek classical wrestling style introduced by the armies of Alexander. Technically, both northern and southern types resemble Western free-style wrestling although the theories of the body in the two systems differ. As Alter (1992 and 1995) shows, central to Indian wrestling is the belief that sexual energy and celibacy are linked and that strength is a function of structuring sexual energy: the variety of exercises that are part of the wrestlers' daily regimen include jackknifes and knee bends, which are linked to the production and control of semen; the possession and storage of semen is important for strength, although it has to be kept in balance and should not be in excess. In many medical traditions, such as Ayurveda and Siddha, which are popular in south India, semen is regarded as a transmutation of blood and it is thought that processes that increase the digestion of food and the circulation of blood also lead to the production of semen. For a wrestler these processes include maintaining the correct diet (vegetables are important here, especially leafy ones, as well as milk and clarified butter); breathing during exercise; engaging in vigorous workouts, including duels and weightlifting; and receiving oil massages. Breathing practice and assuming physical forms, inherited from yogic paradigms, that are meant to increase and manifest power are also deployed. Alter (1995) suggests that the effulgence and heat of the body produced by exercise should be likened to ejaculation. The wrestler becomes virile by channeling his sexuality, and is strong because of his self-control.

The main deity in Vahnikula Kshatriya gymnasiums is Anjaneya or Hanuman, a son of the god of wind. The wrestlers revere Anjaneya because he was a great devotee of the deity Rama and was unmarried, celibate, and therefore able to contain all his "strength." Yet this control is always tenuous. As one wrestler told me, once, while Anjaneya was flying over the ocean, a drop of his sweat [semen?] fell into the water and was swallowed by a fish; from that "union" was born his son, Anjan. Anjaneya has many resonances with Bhima, one of the five Pandava brothers, who was, like Anjaneya, the son of the god of wind (Vayu) and was admired by many for his strength as a wrestler and fighter. Besides the Karaga *jatre*, the other important festival celebrated around August by the Vahnikula Kshatriya community is "Bhimana Amavasya."[10] The main worshipers at this festival,

Figure 13. The chariot carrying an image of Bhima goes through the streets of the City.

unlike at the Karaga *jatre,* are women of the Vahnikula Kshatriya commu-nity. A chariot carrying the idol of Bhima (see Figure 13) goes around the neighborhood where they live, stopping at various houses where rituals are performed. Bhima is especially revered for his undoubted valor and his devotion to Draupadi, the wife he shared with his other brothers. As Abhi-manyu, the Karaga priest in 1996 and 1997, narrated:

> During the period of exile in the forest, the Pandavas and Kunti, their mother, were staying in the house of a Brahmin. Nearby lived a ferocious demon that had been daily eating one male member of each family in the settlement by turn. Kunti awoke to hear the family of the Brahmin wailing one night; when she asked, the whole matter was revealed to her. It was the turn of the Brahmin family to send their son to the demon, their only son. Kunti decided that since she had five, one son could be sacrificed for this purpose. So Bhima was sent. He fought with the demon and killed him. It is to commemorate this victory that Bhimana Amavasya is celebrated. It is also the day that Bhima was born. (Interview with M. Abhimanyu, August 3, 1996)[11]

Bhima is also considered the only one of the five brothers who was able to satisfy each desire of Draupadi. Therefore, during Bhimana Amavasya women perform rituals for their husbands, and unmarried girls, who tie yellow wristbands on their wrists, pray for a husband like Bhima, whom the Vahnikula Kshatriya men are directed to emulate.

The gymnasium is an important focus for the community's men, even for those who are not serious wrestlers, and for the boys and girls who train there during childhood. After a girl child menstruates, or even a few years before that, she is withdrawn from the gymnasium, although I was given the impression that it has become increasingly uncommon for females to attend it at all. For some years, however, girls may also train in a variety of gymnastics and perform during the Karaga *jatre* as part of a public display. Adult women are strictly prohibited from entering the gymnasium premises. For men and boys, however, the gymnasium continues to be a meeting place, a site for an everyday regimen of the body and preparation for the performance. It is also associated with their roles as militia in the armies to which they were historically attached.

The gymnasium is usually a large room with traditional instruments (sticks, maces, stone weights, and clubs). The floor is covered with red earth, and a mirror is leaning against one wall. Invariably a picture of Anjaneya is found gracing another wall. The area is protected from the elements, and there the wrestlers carry out daily exercise or engage with others in practice wrestling. There are three gymnasiums belonging to the Vahnikula Kshatriya community in the City, each of which is visited during the Karaga *jatre* by the priest and his troupe and is named after a famous wrestler or teacher.[12] During the Karaga *jatre*, a ritual is performed at each wrestling house; the instruments are decorated and worshiped, and a conical image is made out of the red soil on which the wrestlers exercise (see Figure 14). This is decorated with jasmine and vermilion and surrounded by fruits; this image closely resembles the Karaga itself. The soft red soil, which is meant to balance "heat" within the body of the wrestlers, is brought from distant villages. This earth covers the wrestler's body and maintains a critical level of heat within it after exercise.

These are not the only gymnasiums in the city, for many communities in Bangalore, Hindu and Muslim, have their own gymnasiums, some with old historical associations, where men and boys train daily. It is claimed, for instance, that Haider Ali attended the Cottonpet gymnasium in the City during his youth. Many are named after their teachers, who are household names, and there is a main street in the City named after a famous wrestler from the community of gardeners. Competitions are still held within and between various gymnasiums in open spaces, and these are attended by large crowds and local politicians.[13] When the king of Mysore still ruled, grand contests patronized by him would be held in the expansive grounds

Figure 14. A conical image made of red soil from the gymnasium.

near his palace. Even in the period after his patronage, figures such as Phelwan Jayaram of the gardeners participated in the 1968 Indian National Games.[14]

The *Karnataka State Bangalore District Gazetteer* (1990, 200–201) mentions ten important gymnasiums in which wrestling and competitions are held today in the City, the Cantonment, and new extensions, and names a number of different wrestlers from various Hindu and Muslim communities in Bangalore. Titles such as "Mr. Olympic," "Mr. Karnataka," and "Yuvakarnataka" ("Young Karnataka") are conferred on men winning these competitions. These gymnasiums are generally equipped with rings, dumbbells, parallel bars, stall bars, iron shoes, and medicine balls. In the early decades of the 1900s, pupils were also coached in textbooks on gymnastics in Kannada, *Vyayama Deepika* being one of them, and the gymnastics included wrestling, boxing, and so on. In some of the newer gymnasiums in Bangalore, such as "Steve's Gym" in the Cantonment area, "gymnastics" refers mainly to bodybuilding, weightlifting, and floor exercises, and this type of bodywork is of a different form from that of the older places, reflecting influences from modern American or European gyms.

The Karaga priest trains regularly in the gymnasium, for the physical strength built up there allows him to perform many of the strenuous activities in which he must engage during the performance period. The hero-sons also train. For those accompanying the priest, the training is as demanding as that of the priest, for all the main rituals during the *jatre* are performed after moonrise and before dawn with subsidiary rites occurring during the day. During the performance, the priest and most of the hero-sons go without much sleep for almost nine days in a row. Strength and celibacy are interconnected during the performance and in everyday life. It must be emphasized that "training" is not a sporadic activity, but a life-long investment. Apart from making visits to the gymnasium, little boys will go with their fathers and other men who are Virakumaras to accompany the Karaga troupe all over the city. By the time initiation as a Virakumara occurs for these boys and men, roles have already been ingrained through years of experience, practice, and observation. Their transformation may be more or less complete. Especially for those players such as the Karaga priest and the Virakumaras, the time span of the performance and the observances involved—the control of diet, the restrictions on sexuality, and the strenuous physical regimen—alter the sense of the body. The body is molded to such an extent that even when Virakumaras do "blade service" *(alagu seve)* for Draupadi, where they repeatedly strike their chests with their swords, no pain is purported to register in the body and no blood is shed.

The Goddess Shrine and the Seven-Circled Fort

The gymnasiums cluster around the Dharmaraja Temple, the main locus of the Karaga *jatre*. The temple itself (see Map 12) is situated on Nagarthapet

Road (now named after the temple) and is surrounded by other neighborhoods such as Nagarthapet, which is associated with jewelers, Kumbharpet, associated with potters, and Ganigarpet, associated with oil-pressers. Across the main road from the temple on its north side is the main police station of the area, the Halsur Gate Police Station. This police station is so called because one of the gates of the old settlement, the Halsur Gate, is said to have stood in this area. Across from the police station and the Nagarthapet Road on the east side are the Corporation Offices of Bangalore. The crossroads is one of the busiest in Bangalore, crowded with pedestrian and vehicular traffic. Nagarthapet Road is lined with dozens of shops and forms the east-west artery of the City and its markets. At festival time, the market area remains functional through almost the entire night, as city dwellers are to be found out on the streets, either making the rounds of the temples in the area (practically every street has a small shrine), listening to scriptural recitations, or transacting business. In previous years, movie theaters even ran an extra late-night show for viewers.

The spire of the Dharmaraja Temple, surrounded by a tall wall and heavy gates, can be seen from the road. The temple owns a few square feet of open land in front of it; on this is a large tree, under which the snakestones stand. The temple itself stands surrounded by about five feet of circumambulatory space outside the main building. The main building has a sanctum (shown in Map 12 as the innermost rectangle) that houses five images (A to E in Map 12), an upper level where devotees stand to get a glimpse of the images from railings that cordon it off, and a lower level that, on any given day, people can be seen using as a public space for meetings and conversations. Most of the visitors to the temple are members of the Vahnikula Kshatriya community, although many people from the neighborhoods surrounding the temple area, such as members of the potter community or the community of weavers, also visit. The spire as well as certain parts of the temple, such as the decorations within, are brightly painted; the oldest part is built in the Dravidian style of architecture, perhaps dating from about 1800, as some officiants claim.[15] The festival flag of the temple is yellow. It is mounted on a long bamboo pole with 101 rings (sometimes, it is said, 56) and brought from the Jaraganahalli forest on the south side of the city by twenty-five Vahnikula Kshatriya families before the festival begins.

The temple was refurbished at different times. At the entrance are two temples, one an old shrine engulfed by the Dharmaraja Temple and the other a more recently built structure. The former (shown as I in Map 12) is the temple of Muthyallamma, a boundary and pox goddess, which

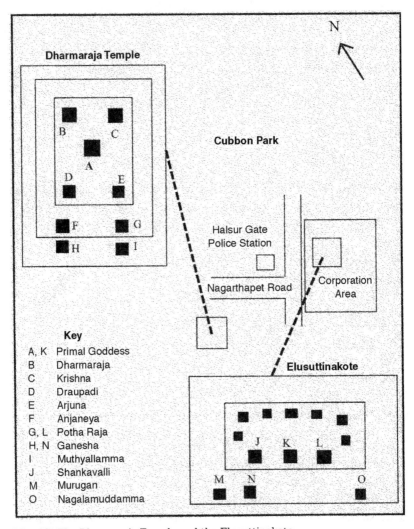

Map 12. The Dharmaraja Temple and the Elusuttinakote.

marks the Halsur Gate of the settlement. The latter (shown as H in Map 12) is a temple for Ganesha, the elephant-headed deity, built about the 1930s. Each of these has its own priest, although all the priests are members of the Vahnikula Kshatriya community. Daily rituals and special weekly ones— for instance, during the full moon every month—are conducted at the shrines. On entering the wall that encloses the temple, there are two guardians to be found: figures of Anjaneya and Potha Raja (F and G, respectively, in Map 12). The significance of Anjaneya has been already mentioned; about the latter, I have something to say later.

The sanctum of the Dharmaraja Temple (see Figure 15) houses the central image of the Primal Goddess *(adi shakti),* the principle of female divinity. Behind this are two images, of Dharmaraja and Krishna; to the right of the goddess (as one faces her) is Arjuna, and to her left is Draupadi. The iconography here is also reflected in the cry that accompanies the end of every ritual at the temple and elsewhere during the Karaga *jatre:*[16]

> At the feet of Krishna, Govinda [Krishna]!
> At the feet of Dharmaraja, Govinda!
> At the feet of the five Pandavas, Govinda!
> At the feet of the Primal Goddess, Govinda!
> At the feet of Panchali [Draupadi], Govinda!

Surrounding the image of the Primal Goddess are the processional icons of the Pandava brothers and Potha Raja. The iconography thus resonates with two aspects of Draupadi in the festival, the first that of "Panchali," the one from the region of Panchala who married the five Pandava brothers, the second, that of the Primal Goddess herself, as depicted in various scriptures. This dual nature also emerges from three oral accounts told to me during the *jatre* in 1996.[17] The first is that of Ramdas, a ritual player in the performance who died late that year:

> There was a demon called Timmarasu. He was hiding behind a
> rock in the forest when Draupadi was passing by alone. He called
> out to her and made advances. The blood of the demon was such
> that if a drop fell on the ground a thousand prototypes were born
> from it. Draupadi, angered, shook the portion of her sari covering
> her breasts. From that sprang the Durga Pujari, the Gante Pujari,
> and the Ganachari [all three are ritual players in the Karaga].
> When she shook it again, out sprang the Virakumaras. They
> fought the battle against the demon, but each drop that fell gave
> birth to a hundred thousand more. Finally the goddess felled him
> with one stroke, and before the demon's blood could reach the
> ground, she licked up the blood and also swallowed him whole.

An officiant at the temple narrated the second account during the festival:

> In the *Swargarohana Parva* [the last section of the *Mahabharata*
> epic], it is told how Draupadi and Dharmaraja were sitting on the
> balcony of their palace. The Kurukshetra War was over, and

Figure 15. The sanctum of the Dharmaraja Temple.

Dharmaraja and Draupadi had been crowned as rulers of the kingdom. Looking out, they saw a man walking down the road carrying the slippers of his wife on his head; the young woman was riding a horse, and the man's old mother was hobbling along on the road in the hot sun. Dharmaraja realized from these signs that the Kali Age [the last in the cycle of four ages, each of them literally thousands of years] was dawning. Meanwhile, news arrived that Krishna had passed away, and with him the Dwapara Age, and the Yadavas [the community he ruled] had decimated themselves. The Pandavas realized that it was time for them to ascend to heaven. On the way, Kali Purusha [the personification of the Kali Age] accosted Draupadi in the form of a demon. The brothers were so weakened by the passing of Krishna that they could not help her. So she decided to take matters into her own hands, and the deities Parvati and Shiva, whom she prayed to, also gave her their own powers. She was instructed to make a pot, and Parvati's and Shiva's power was installed in it. Then were born the Ganachari, the Gante Pujari, and the Virakumaras. The last were born for her protection. After some time Draupadi passed away, but left her *shakti* behind to be born again and again. The Vahnikula Kshatriyas were thus born with the dawn of the Kali Age for the protection of her *shakti*.

The third account, by an old widow who cleaned the temple daily, ran as follows:

On the route to heaven, all the brothers fall away by the roadside, one by one. The first to fall, however, is Draupadi. After some time, she "awakens," having been merely unconscious, and finds herself left alone by the wayside and confronted with the demon. Both Shiva and Parvati appear in answer to her prayers and give her their *shakti* in the form of a Karaga pot made from the flowers of the forest, chiefly jasmine, to defeat the demon.

There are obviously many variations on the theme of Draupadi and the Primal Goddess that are seen in these oral accounts. The powers of Draupadi, sometimes her own and sometimes powers given to her by the gods, allow her to swallow the demon and his blood and also to produce the Virakumaras nongenitally. In all these tales, Draupadi appears in her one "birth" as the Primal Goddess herself, whereas in another she is Panchali, the spouse.

Across from the Dharmaraja Temple is the Elusuttinakote, which occupies a tract of land within the grounds of the Corporation Offices of Bangalore. This is a circular temple with its main entrance facing away from the road. Surrounding it are large government buildings with their constant traffic of officials, petitioners, and workers. Some trees frame the temple, but its blue dome can be seen rising above a metal cage that forms its body. The temple is quite overshadowed by the other structures, roads, and parking lots of the Corporation Offices. Only very regular visitors to the area may notice this site, which has come to be totally enclosed by bureaucratic offices of the city, forming an enclave from an earlier time period in their midst. The name of this temple literally means "Seven-Circled Fort," and it houses the other figures central to the Karaga *jatre*.[18] It is not a large structure, having been refurbished in recent years; all the images within the temple were furnished in the 1960s by an association of the Virakumaras.[19] From oral accounts it appears that a cruder and somewhat nondescript structure existed before the temple was fashioned in this form. Most Vahnikula Kshatriyas claim that the land nearby belonged to the temple and was appropriated for the purposes of constructing the Corporation Offices. Occasional visitors to the temple worship the images, whereas regular rituals are performed morning and evening. As is common to many goddess temples, on certain days of the week and month—for instance, the nights of the full moon and the new moon—special rites are carried out and the frequency of visitors, most of them from the neighborhood, increases. The priests at this shrine are Vahnikula Kshatriyas, members of a family who recite the oral epic during the *jatre* and are called the "Gante Pujari."

The images inside the Elusuttinakote include stone plaques of the "Seven Mothers" that were established in 1988 (see Map 12).[20] The representations of these aspects of the Primal Goddess, usually seen as her forms, ring three other images, one of which (depicted as K in the map) is the form of the Primal Goddess herself. The mustached figure of Potha Raja kneels on one bent knee, a sword in his right hand and a goat in his left.[21] He and his wife, Shankavalli, are found on either side of the Primal Goddess (represented as L and J, respectively). Outside are fairly recently built shrines dedicated to Murugan and Ganesha (M and N in the map), sons of Shiva and Parvati. Icons of the nine planets were established in the summer of 1996 and occupy a corner of the fence that circles the shrine itself (not shown in the map). Also outside the shrine is the image of Potha Raja's sister, Nagalamuddamma (O in the map). The role of the figure of Potha Raja and the connection of the husband-wife and brother-sister pairs to the figures of the Pandavas and Draupadi was narrated to me in 1996 by a temple officiant:

When the Pandavas escaped from the wax palace, they moved southwards to the kingdom of Potha Raja and the city of Elaipur, also known as Shivananda Pattana or Kalyanapuri. At this time they were in disguise and went around begging for food. At the end of the day, they would divide it between themselves: half the portion used to be given to Bhima, and the rest apportioned among the other brothers and Draupadi. Bhima, with his legendary appetite, complained that he was not getting enough to eat and was becoming weak. He decided to become a woodcutter and sell his logs for food. One day, after cutting down a huge tree, he came to the city of Elaipur and set his tree against an old fort to rest from his labors. The tree was so huge and the fort so old that it fell down. This angered the king, Potha Raja, who had him thrown into prison. The king, a lustful and fierce Shiva devotee, had decided that he would sacrifice 101 persons to Shiva and garner the lord's favors. Bhima would be the 101st sacrifice. Meanwhile, nightfall had come and Bhima had not returned. Krishna with his powers of vision saw the entire situation; he and Arjuna, in disguise as a beautiful nomad woman, arrived at the city-fort of Elaipur or Elusuttinakote. They stayed in the house of a nomad.

The king heard about the beauty of Arjuna and came to visit the house. He was enamored. He wished to marry her. Krishna said that he would allow the marriage on two conditions: first, the king must free all the prisoners; second, he must eat raw flesh. The besotted ruler agreed to both ruses: thus Bhima was freed and the king's penance was defiled, because as a Shiva worshiper he was not to touch raw meat. Krishna also revealed to the king Arjuna's true identity. It now remained for Krishna to fulfill his end of the bargain. From his conch emerged the figure of Shankavalli, the daughter of Pandu and Madri, sister of the Pandavas, who was then married to Potha Raja. To cement the relationship further, Dharmaraja was married to Potha Raja's infant sister, Nagalamuddamma. Potha Raja then became the leader of the army of the Pandavas at Kurukshetra, and continued to hold the fort for the Pandavas when they departed for heaven. Potha Raja was a protector of the goddess in the Dwapara Age just as the Virakumaras are in the Kali Age.

The correspondences that emerge from this account are many. Elusuttinakote forms the counterpoint to the Dharmaraja Temple within the context of these relations and the structure of the Karaga *jatre* at three levels: first, by linking Draupadi and the Pandavas to a local version of the *Mahabharata*, as suggested by the preceding account; second, by pointing to a city (Elaipur, Kalyanapuri, Shivananda Pattana, Elusuttinakote) that is believed to have existed, sometimes literally, sometimes metaphorically, in Bangalore's current location (Potha Raja at Elaipur is the archetype of the Virakumaras-to-be in the current city of Bangalore); and third, by signaling the emergence of Draupadi in her second birth as the Primal Goddess in the Kali Age along with the Vahnikula Kshatriya community itself.

Draupadi's Body

Cultural ideas about the body embed and connect these three arenas— the Dharmaraja Temple, the Elusuttinakote, and the gymnasiums—with the ritual processes of the Karaga *jatre* and the preparations preceding it. The control of male and female bodies in the festival and in everyday life is linked to the power that is felt to inhere in heat, blood, semen, and sexuality. The maintenance of celibacy by men during the performance is fragile and dependent on women's acquiescence, and in a way draws from their self-control. Although women are circumscribed by this ideology, during the performance Draupadi's role, which is the central focus of the performance, is not amenable to a similar construction and she has to go through several stages before she can be contained within it.

Goddesses who appear alone or without consorts are seen as possessing dangerous powers: most village or boundary goddesses are of this nature in south India.[22] As Kondos (1986, 180) points out, such goddesses should be read not as malevolent beings, but as formidable protagonists because they possess destructive powers. Or, as Tapper (1979, 18–19) states, the word "Mother" *(Amma)* used to designate her is less a description of her attributes of motherhood than an "euphemistic disguise" for her un-controlled powers. When the goddess's heat is extreme, pox or disease (with which she is identified) results. At this time, in many temples dedi-cated to the goddess, "cool" substances such as yogurt as well as blood sacrifices are offered. It is her heat that counteracts the heat of the fire-walking pit that a devotee enters in her name after taking a vow during many festivals. There is also a story (though not voiced often) that Drau-padi is married to each of the Pandava brothers for a certain number of months. The first lunar month, in which the Karaga *jatre* occurs, marks the end of her union with Bhima and the beginning of her marriage to Arjuna, one among the five brothers who won her in a competition for her hand. But in the period from the beginning of the Karaga *jatre* to the last day, she stands alone in her unmarried and singular state, being joined to Arjuna only on the final day. She is represented as bloodthirsty, martial, and angry. The crowning symbols of her power are the jasmine flowers that during the *jatre* decorate the Karaga as well as the hair of the priest. Jasmine, which is white, is considered "hot like fire." Only the "marriage" on the last day of the festivities returns Draupadi to a state in which the heat can be con-trolled, although, paradoxically, this heat is channeled through the body of a man who has become the medium of the goddess.

A theory about the body and its interaction with the macrocosm un-derlies these practices, as well as the training in the gymnasium. White (1996) states that common to various traditions such as yoga, Ayurveda, Siddha, and cults around the goddess are concepts in which a threefold structure of fluid-fire-wind *(rasa-agni-vayu)* interacts with ideas of the hu-man, the divine, and sacrifice.[23] The polarity between the human and the divine, or the microcosm and the macrocosm, is mediated by the act of sacrifice, which allows a transfer from one domain and substance to the other. According to different domains of usage, this triad has taken the form of moon-sun-wind, semen-blood-breath, and mercury-sulfur-air. In other words, fluid, moon, semen, and mercury and fire, sun, blood, and sulfur are mediated by the active element of wind, breath, and air in the sacrificial structure.[24]

In the healing tradition of Ayurveda, the relation between the three substances is worked out in terms of the body, disease, and the environ-ment and has parallels in the models developed by yoga. As White states, the cycle of seasons and life and death are reduced to the dynamic interaction between the sun and the moon, in which the maintenance of moisture and vital fluids is the goal. The year is divided into two semesters: the fiery (when the sun rises higher in the sky and drains the moisture from living beings) and the lunar (when the moon is relatively higher than the sun in the sky and rains moisture on the world). The first semester corresponds to the period between the winter and summer solstices, the second to the period between the summer and winter solstices. The turning points between them fall approximately on January 14 and July 14. The connection between the rejuvenation of the moon and that of human bodies is an explicit one. Food in the body can be "cooked," and the end product of digestion is, in males, semen, which is lunar. The waxing and waning of the moon during the year and the lunar month subjects semen to the same dangers as the moon experiences in relation to the sun. The lunar month is the time it takes for the food that males ingest to become semen and for females to produce ova.[25] As White says: "These perceived dangers to the very survival of the male sexual fluid are compounded by an Ayurvedic identification of the female uterine blood with the fiery (agneya) sun that drains the ecocosm of all its vitalizing moisture in the first semester of the year: the 'lunar' semen a male is capable of producing is but a drop in the fiery maelstrom of his partner's sexual fluid" (White 1996, 26).

In traditions of yoga, the lower abdomen is associated with the female sun; the head is the locus of the cooling moon, whose fluid is semen, carried upward by yogic practices and transformed into nectar, the drink of immortal life. These traditions and seasonal festivals emphasize customary practices for channeling and balancing this polarity.[26] The idea that the polarity between the sun and the moon, heat and cold, needs to be balanced is also at play in the Karaga *jatre*. Practices for channeling heat include control of the breath, exercises performed in the gymnasium, and blood sacrifice or the offering of other substances. There is also a difference in the substances offered by men and women to the Karaga *shakti:* jaggery, a "cool" substance, is offered by women to the idol at the temple, whereas men offer lemon juice and "cool" fruits and also receive them as offerings. During the "hot" months of March and April when the Karaga *jatre* takes place, men and women both offer cool substances to the Primal Goddess, but the dominant imagery is one of heat that has to be kept constantly in check by counterofferings of "cool" substances. This need to maintain a tenuous balance is spatially perceivable in the separation of male and female members of the community during the festival: women remain almost totally apart from ritual sites during the festival and have few roles as ritual players. Men's heat, too, especially of those who are the hero-sons, is in constant danger of overflowing and must be contained through a variety of practices.

However, it is the heating of the goddess and her embodiment in the priest that reveal most fully the ambiguities and ambivalences involved in the construction of the body in the performance.[27] As, on the one hand, the heating of the Primal Goddess gradually escalates during the performance, on the other hand, it is a man who comes to embody her hot power, and the sign of this heat is the headdress of jasmine that the Karaga priest wears. Carried by the force of the Karaga, the priest begins a special dance that is regarded as a sign of the goddess's presence. Until this moment, the priest has been called by a variety of terms, usually "master" or "the Karaga priest"; now he is referred to as "the Karaga" and is neuter in gender. People say, "It came by," "It danced," or "The hero-sons made it play." It is the heating of the goddess that leads to the manifestation of the Karaga. In fact, the "hot" dominates the "cool" until the night of the procession that marks the end of the nine-day festivities. On the night that the Karaga is manifested as a gleaming, bejeweled, red-colored cone decorated with jasmine flowers, the priest carries it on his waist; during the procession, the Karaga rests on his head. Members of the community associate this positioning with the power and heat of the Primal Goddess and see the power as having traveled from the priest's waist up the length of his full form, producing a state of tremendous energy and bliss. The two positions are also reflected in the dress of the priest. On the night of the Karaga's emergence, the priest is bare chested, wearing only a turmeric-colored waistcloth reaching from his waist to his feet *(dhoti)*, which is associated with men's wear, but during the procession he wears a turmeric-colored sari and blouse covering his full form. This transformation of the body also achieves form in the three stages of the performance:

1. From the period of the hoisting of the flag at the temple to the seventh day of the festivities (the "Hasi Karaga" day), we witness the gradual emergence of the Primal Goddess in the form of the Karaga icon. Here Draupadi is regarded as the Primal Goddess. We can term this the stage of "incarnation."

2. Two days later, the "Pete Karaga" (on the night of the full moon) and the "marriage" of Arjuna and Draupadi occur, Draupadi's "hot" form now contained. We can term this

process the stage of "personification," and it includes the Karaga's procession through the City and the arrival of processional chariots from other temples in Bangalore at the City Market.

3. On the day after the Pete Karaga, the chariot of Arjuna and Draupadi, now duly married, is brought to the grounds of the Elusuttinakote, led by the figure of Potha Raja. There, along with the Karaga priest, who is still dressed in a yellow sari but without a headdress, surrounded by an audience drawn from the neighborhood, a ritual player narrates the story of Potha Raja and his connection to Draupadi. This we can term the stage of "localization."

Therefore, the three stages of the performance—incarnation, personification, and localization—are the processual parallels of the juxtapositioning of Elusuttinakote, the Dharmaraja Temple, the gymnasium, the images at the three sites, and the themes and motifs emphasized in the oral narratives. The relationship between myths, *sacra*, rituals, and the body is, however, not one of closure, because although there are coordinates between one plane and another, it also produces symbolic structures that are mobile and produce different effects at different sites within the city. This is dramatically evident in the spectacle seen in the city as the Karaga troupe hurtles down the street visiting various temples, houses, gardens, and tanks: the Karaga priest, his head covered with a scarf, carries a dagger in his right hand and a sacred staff in his left. A flag accompanies him, with five colors embodying the five brothers. One person carries a trident as a symbol of the Primal Goddess and leads the way. An umbrella accompanies the priest. Pounding down the road is the Gante Pujari, who carries various *sacra* in a bundle. Among these are a whip that is used to initiate the Virakumaras, a container of turmeric powder, four silver anklets that belong to Draupadi, bells, a drum, and a silver container that has representations of the brothers etched on it.[28] These *sacra* are set down at various sites during the nine days and worshiped, and each becomes a miniature stage during the period of the Karaga *jatre*.

The Phases of the Performance

Every year, the Karaga *jatre* begins with the raising of the flag at the Dharmaraja Temple in the City on the seventh day of the luni-solar month of "Chaitra."[29] This corresponds to the beginning of the Tamil New Year, which the Vahnikula Kshatriyas tend to follow for the most part. Festivities go on for eleven nights, including the first and the last day, when the flag of the temple is raised and lowered.[30] The events are fairly standardized, and the sequence of rituals held does not alter from year to year.[31] The only difference is a variation in dates, because the Karaga *jatre* follows a luni-solar calendar. The "Vahnikula Kshatriya Sangha," formed in 1965, is an organization whose primary function is to organize daily rituals at the temple and the Karaga festival. Prior to the formation of the association, a somewhat ad hoc group used to come together to perform these duties. In addition to the association, temple trustees appointed by the government and elders of the community have a role to play in arrangements for the *jatre.* Although the temple does not have a Brahmin priest, according to many of the ritual players there has been evidence of a certain systematization in the order and timing of temple rituals and the addition of what are considered "standard" temple rites.

The creation of a permanent association for organization of the festival has parallels with other processes of temple reform from about that period. For instance, in the mid-1950s a boundary wall was added to the temple, and later a row of shops was added near the wall for the purposes of producing temple income. The chariot of the temple that used to be assembled every year with wood from the forest was instead replaced by a permanent structure. In 1974, for the first time, a Karaga bearer (Shiv Shankar) was chosen by a process of selection rather than hereditary family position, an event that continues to attract a great deal of discussion, and sometimes censure, in the community. In the 1980s, the icon of the boundary goddess Muthyallamma was replaced by another idol because the older one needed animal sacrifice. Many of these processes of reform date from the final period in the career of Munivenkatappa and coincide with efforts to build Tigala unity and the Vokkuta Samsthe (see chapter 4). The standardization of ritual processes and the creation of a permanent infrastructure appear to be complementary to the attempts to widen the cultic terrain and bases of political unity.

The calendar of events for 1996, as published in a pamphlet that is widely circulated prior to the Karaga *jatre,* is given below. The festival covers a period of eleven days (nine if we exclude the flag hoisting and lowering, which tend to be rather small events), and the following are the most important phases of the ritual process with the dates on which they occurred in 1996. Nearly all of the significant events occur after sunset and before sunrise:

March 26	On the seventh day *(saptami)* of the month of Chaitra, the festival begins at 10 P.M.; at 3 A.M. is the flag hoisting at the Dharmaraja Temple.
March 27–30	Various rituals in the Dharmaraja Temple and around it from 7.30 P.M. onwards.
March 31	On the twelfth day *(dvadashi)* of the month, lamps are brought to the Dharmaraja Temple by the women of Vahnikula Kshatriya families from all over Bangalore from 3 A.M. onwards.
April 1	On the thirteenth day *(triyodashi)*, Hasi Karaga occurs at Sampangi Tank from 3 A.M. onward and concludes at the Dharmaraja Temple.
April 2	On the fourteenth day *(chaturdashi)*, sweet-rice is brought by women of the community to the Dharmaraja Temple and distributed as a sacred offering.
April 3	The full moon (fifteenth day, *purnima*) is the occasion of the Pete Karaga from 10 P.M. onward, which begins at the Dharmaraja Temple. (In 1996, the festivities concluded before 2 A.M. because of a lunar eclipse.)
April 4	On the day after the full moon *(padyami)*, the oral epic is recited at the Elusuttinakote from 2 A.M. onward. At 4 A.M., a black goat is sacrificed to Potha Raja in the Dharmaraja Temple.
April 5	On the seventeenth day of the month *(bidige)*, spring festivities occur from 4 P.M. onward at the Dharmaraja Temple, when men of the community play games with turmeric-colored water brought by women of the community to mark the end of the festival. The flag of the festival is lowered after midnight (April 6).

Before the events begin, the temple and households are scenes of increased activity. Music from movies, usually devotional tunes, is broadcast through loudspeakers in the temple. This music can be heard all around the neighborhood as houses are cleaned and painted and relatives arrive from other towns. The temple is decorated with lights, the images are polished, and invitations are sent out to government departments such as the Karnataka Electricity Board, the Public Works Department, police officials, the Home Ministry, and the Prisons Department (in case some of the prisoners want to attend). On the Kannada New Year's Day, the first day of Chaitra, a week before the actual festivities begin, the headman of the community sends an invitation to the Vahnikula Kshatriyas in Jaraganahalli village (now part of the metropolitan area of Bangalore). This invitation asks them to make arrangements to provide the bamboo pole for the flag-hoisting ceremony. This bamboo pole is selected about six months before the festival, and special rituals related to it are performed from that time. This pole is brought to the temple in the early hours of the morning of the first day of the festival on the shoulders of Vahnikula Kshatriya men from the forest area near the village.

At the temple, devotional songs have been playing since the evening before, and a special troupe belonging to the barber caste that plays all the music at the festival has also gathered at the temple. The headman and other elders go to the house of the Karaga priest and bring him to the temple, followed by other players. The man who plays the role of Potha Raja carries the temple flag, and this is tied to the bamboo pole after Brahmin priests perform suitable purification rites. The Karaga priest, carrying a silver staff and a dagger and wearing a red-colored shoulder cloth, performs rituals to the chariot containing the images of Arjuna and Draupadi. The chariot then goes around the streets of Tigalarapet along with community elders, musicians, and others led by the image of Potha Raja, the trident, and the five-colored flag. On the way, women present offerings to the chariot and the priest. On their return, the flag of the temple is hoisted; it is almost dawn by this time. A Brahmin priest also ties wristbands on the wrists of the officiants of the Karaga performance and a few select elders.[32] Many informants say that the whole festival mimics the celebration of marriages in the community: the flag hoisting is like the betrothal ceremony; nine days after the betrothal, the marriage of Arjuna and Draupadi occurs; the headdress of flowers worn by the Karaga priest is similar to those worn by brides at their weddings; and the procession of the chariot through the city is like a marriage procession. Yet underneath this simple explanation, not only is the identity of Draupadi in the *jatre* ambivalent, but the valorized celibacy and warriorhood of the hero-sons are posited against ideas of the body that are located in the uncertainties related to the control of heat.

Daily during the *jatre*, rituals are performed at the Muthyallamma and the Ganesha temples on either side of the Dharmaraja Temple. Small groups of people gather for these rituals every evening. In addition, the Karaga priest bathes at nine points in different parts of Bangalore, accompanied by his troupe of Virakumaras and other ritual players. These events are not widely attended by persons from outside the community, although a large number of Virakumaras may sometimes be present. The three most significant days of the performance, in terms of public attendance, are the "Arati Dipa," which occurs on the twelfth night of the month, the Hasi Karaga, which occurs on the thirteenth day of the month, and the Pete Karaga, which occurs on the night of the full moon. There are slight differences between these three events: Arati Dipa is a part of the festival where, for the first time since the festival has begun, women have a public role to play. The Hasi Karaga and the Pete Karaga involve the male members of the Vahnikula Kshatriya community in an active role; women are absent here as performers, although they are present within the temple and its environs as spectators.

During Arati Dipa, four bands of persons depart from the temple in the evening, each band including a man carrying a bell, a bearer of the trident, and musicians. All of these bands go in separate directions to localities in Bangalore where Vahnikula Kshatriya households are present in large numbers in order to invite the women to participate in the Arati Dipa and also to shield and cleanse the neighborhood. The persons going in the southern direction carry the image of Potha Raja.[33] At the threshold of each house stand women carrying a plate with two oil lamps and an offering. They wash the feet of the trident bearer, who represents the goddess, and pray to the trident. During the Arati Dipa, women start arriving at the temple about 2 A.M. Large lamps with sacred pots inside are carried aloft, usually, but not necessarily, by women from households that supply Virakumaras (see Figure 16). Each lamp is made of pounded rice and jaggery syrup and decorated with jasmine flowers. The lamp can be extremely elaborate, standing sometimes three to six feet tall and costing anywhere between 500 and 1,000 rupees. All the women arrive at the temple by about 3 A.M. and after performing individual rituals congregate outside the temple in rows, carrying their lamps aloft. Outside the temple, firecrackers, lanterns, and torches are lit and acrobatic feats and swordplay are performed by children of the community who are training in the gymnasium (see Figure 17); this is the only time that the children have a public role to play in the ritual.

The women carrying lamps follow the Karaga troupe, minus the Karaga priest, around the localities surrounding the temple. The route forms the normal boundary of public space for women in their everyday lives in the area. All along the route, people can be seen perched on their balconies or standing by the roadside to watch the procession, the torches of fire, and the acrobatics. The purpose of the festival of lamps is to invite the Primal Goddess to visit individual households so the residents can fulfill vows or

Figure 16. The festival of lamps.

pray to procure strong husbands like Bhima. But there is another set of meanings that becomes visible in the ritual. Jaggery, a "cool" substance, is offered by women to the *shakti* at the temple, whereas men, and especially the priest, undergo increasing heat, which has to be kept in check by various substances.[34]

Figure 17. A young girl performs gymnastics during the festival.

On the day before the Hasi Karaga, when the heat of the goddess and the Virakumaras becomes most evident, the ceremony for initiation *(diksha)* of new Virakumaras is performed. This is generally considered a secret rite and is hard to witness because of the cordon of Virakumaras and men present around the sanctum, where it is performed. According to accounts of those present, it appears that a new initiate must sit down in front of the sanctum. He is usually wearing a bare minimum of clothing and a garland of jasmine. Turmeric paste, a "cool" substance, is rubbed on his chest, back, stomach, and tongue. Gathered are the senior members of the community, the headman (the Gowda), and the spiritual instructor of the priest (the Ganachari). The Gante Pujari, a ritual officiant who sings songs that invoke Draupadi, begins to chant a hymn, wraps his whip around the wrists of the Virakumara-to-be, and swings it back and forth gently. Then the initiate, the Gante Pujari, and one elder huddle beneath a white cloth for a few seconds and then reemerge with the Gante Pujari announcing to those present the sacred society to which the initiate belongs. The Virakumara is believed to give his "affiliation" to the Gante Pujari in a trance. The latter also asks that the initiate vow to maintain the strictures of purity befitting the status of a Virakumara. The new initiate then performs blade service for the first time in front of the sanctum, cheered on and aroused by the chants of "Alla Lalla Lalla Di" (a magical formula that the Virakumaras chant when they perform blade service) from those gathered. During the initiation ceremony in 1997, the Karaga priest-designate for 1999 and his wife were also initiated in a special ritual.[35]

Hasi Karaga is so called because the Karaga is said to be prepared every year from unbaked clay by a potter. It is untreated, or "raw" *(hasi)*, as it were. This is brought to the area of the Sampangi Tank by a small group of Virakumaras, the Karaga priest, the Gante Pujari, and the Ganachari, about fifteen persons in all. At about 11:30 P.M., the Karaga priest, the Gante Pujaris, the Ganachari, and a few others go to the Upnirinakunte, a small pond in Cubbon Park, now virtually dried up, in a ritual procession. The road to the site cuts through Cubbon Park in front of the State Central Library, which, apart from a few streetlights, is all dark. There are hardly any passersby at this time of the night. In the darkness, the small group conducts secret rites that no one, not even other members of the community, may witness. The Virakumaras with their swords are entitled to ensure the exclusion of nonmembers of this select group.

Gathered in the bed of the former Sampangi Tank are other Virakumaras and the general public. The level of excitement is high in the triangular area that has been left over from the construction of the Kanteerava Stadium, which looms behind what remains of the once large body of water (see chapter 2, Map 7). The roads are devoid of vehicles, but all around the area devotees are awake and waiting for the appearance of the Karaga *shakti.* Only the Vahnikula Kshatriya women are absent from the scene, customarily excluded from witnessing the feat of the birth of the goddess. The compound is bustling with activity as flower sellers sell handfuls of jasmine buds that are thrown on the priest as he passes by with the Karaga, as well as peanuts and other refreshments. A pillared hall stands at the edge of the tank bed. This is completely dark, but one can make out the outline of a white tent inside, large enough for five or six men to sit inside. At about 2 A.M., one hears drums and other instruments begin to play again. Accompanied by this drumming and the wailing of horns (called *banka*, resembling hunting horns), Virakumaras rush in from the entrance to the tank bed accompanying the Karaga priest, who is shielded from the public gaze by a moving curtain made of scarves. They disappear into the tent in the hall amidst cheers from the crowds.

For the next hour or so, on the grounds of the tank, groups of Virakumaras are getting wristbands tied by Brahmin priests. Their swords are lined up in a formation the shape of a crescent moon. Suddenly, lights are turned on in the hall and the musicians begin to play. Drums echo the shouts of "Govinda" by the Virakumaras and the public. The tent has begun to tremble and shake. In a few moments, the swaying of the tent is over and it is thrown off to reveal in its midst a Karaga covered with a ruby-red cloth, decorated with jasmine, and with a diamond-studded chain around its neck (see Figure 18). The Karaga *shakti* has manifested itself.

All the rituals of the past few days have been geared toward inviting the Primal Goddess to incarnate herself. There is a virtual stampede around the hall as Virakumaras push forward to throw jasmine on the Karaga as it sits shining in the spotlight. For the next hour, the crowd does not slacken. Meanwhile, the priest, who has also emerged from the tent, goes toward the area where the swords are kept. He bathes and is dressed in a turmeric-colored waistcloth that reaches to his ankles, jewelry, and an elaborate headdress made of jasmine that reaches to his feet. The Virakumaras have smeared their chests with turmeric paste, and they wear jasmine garlands. At this point, like the *shakti* whose children they are, they are in a "hot" state. After a rite is performed near the swords, the priest returns to the hall accompanied by the Virakumaras, who have picked up their swords. Again, a chant goes up among the crowds: "Govinda, Govinda!" The priest stands in the hall for a few moments, and in a flash the Karaga "sits" on his waist, his left hand curved around it. The Karaga is said to leap onto his waist of its own power. A curved dagger is held in his right hand. The frenzy of the crowd is great. At this moment, the priest becomes a support of the Karaga *shakti* as its bearer (see Figure 19). He begins to sway and dance, stepping in a pattern that is carried out only by him; the community does not have any special dances in the repertoire of the *jatre*. He goes around the hall a few times, carried by the force of the Karaga *shakti*. His face is grave. After a few circles, he goes down the steps of the hall and begins to

Figure 18. The Karaga manifests itself.

regally move clockwise around the grounds. The members of the public gathered have lit camphor all over the field to welcome the appearance of the Karaga *shakti,* and the priest and his troupe step on these flames as they move across the ground. The Karaga is supposed to be "dancing" with beatitude.

Figure 19. The priest carries the Karaga on Hasi Karaga night.

By carrying the sacred pot, the Karaga priest himself is transformed. The power of the Karaga appears to take over his body, causing him to begin his special dance. Henceforth he is referred to as "the Karaga." The Karaga itself is beyond gender, although Draupadi and the Primal Goddess are referred to in the feminine. The state of the priest is less akin to possession by a sacred being, although at times it has a family resemblance to it, and is more a state of transformation through previous bodily preparations and present contact with the Karaga. To receive the touch of the priest while he is carrying the Karaga, or a lemon (considered to have curing properties), is to be especially blessed.

After a few circles around the area, the number of which is always a matter for discussion (Will the Karaga dance three times or more this year?), the Karaga, accompanied by the Virakumaras carrying their swords, moves to the Elusuttinakote to ritually circle the images there, and then the procession enters the Dharmaraja Temple. Inside the temple precincts, as outside, the audience is thick, and there is scarcely room to enter. The spectators include those from other communities as well as Vahnikula Kshatriya men and women. The Karaga dances around the sanctum (nine times in 1996 and twenty-seven or more times in 1997), and all along the way camphor is lit and jasmine buds are thrown at the Karaga. Afterward, the Karaga disappears into the sanctum and the viewers disperse. It is usually around sunrise by this time.

The Karaga, as a sacred icon, is related to the popular story of Draupadi's "second birth," which I cited earlier and which is suggested in the oral epic recited after the procession on the night of the full moon. There is also a subtext to the story, told to me by a temple officiant in April 1996, that explains the community's affiliation with the monastic seat *(peetha)* of Dattatreya:

> Swayambhuva Manu and Satpura, born from the right and left
> portions of Brahma [the Creator], together gave birth to Devahuti,
> who was married to Prajapati. The latter couple gave birth to nine
> virgins, of whom the second one was Anasuya, whom the sage
> Atri married. One day at their hermitage, Brahma, Vishnu, and
> Shiva appeared to test the chastity of Anasuya. They asked to be
> served food, but before Anasuya could do so, they demanded that
> she serve them in her naked form. Anasuya realized by her vision
> that these were the gods themselves. To fulfill their request and to
> preserve her chastity, she sprinkled some water over them,
> whence they were turned into infants and she suckled them. The
> gods offered the couple a boon, and they requested that the three

gods be born to them as their children. The gods then manifested themselves in a son, Dattatreya, who contained the forms of the three gods. Likewise, the Karaga that Draupadi made to vanquish the demon Timirasura contained the powers of the three.

During the Hasi Karaga, Draupadi appears as the Primal Goddess, possessing the powers of the three gods or sometimes the powers of Shiva and Parvati. This aspect is not stressed on the Pete Karaga day, when the Primal Goddess returns to her guise as Draupadi and, further, as the wife of Arjuna. This transition is mediated by an event called "the offering of sweet rice" *(pongal seve)*, in which the main theme is that of Draupadi's various disguises.

This ritual is performed on the night before the Pete Karaga. The Gante Pujari and his troupe gather near the sanctum of the temple at about 2 A.M. Around this time, women of the community have also started drifting in: theirs is not a very large number, about twenty-five in all. They carry with them kerosene stoves, rice, milk, and sugar to make the sweet-rice preparation inside the temple compound. The Gante Pujari's troupe, accompanied by anklets and drums as musical accompaniments, begins to recite stories in Tamil about the period of Draupadi's exile in the forest, when she wandered around as a gypsy.[36] One member performs this recitation, and then a chorus joins him from time to time. The cycle of stories is never completed; indeed, it would take days to do so, and a fragment is recited until the sweet-rice preparation has been made and the Karaga priest performs the dawn rituals. There are not many people present to hear it, either, about six to ten persons in all. (In 1996, these stories were not recited at all, and in 1997 a fragment was recited for about two hours or so.) The whole frame of the "gypsy cycle," as it is known, encapsulated for me by Krishnappa, a Gante Pujari, during a break in the ritual in 1997, runs thus:

> Years of exile have passed. The Pandavas and Draupadi are leaving the tenth forest and passing to the eleventh one for their next period of exile. Draupadi wants to visit Hastinapura city and see her relatives there. She goes disguised as a gypsy and has the youngest Pandava twin [Sahadeva] strapped to her back. Gandhari [the mother of the hundred Kaurava cousins of the Pandavas] is present, and Draupadi becomes her attendant. She is involved in a fortune-telling episode that arouses the suspicions of Duryodhana [the eldest of the hundred brothers] about her true identity. He wants to imprison Draupadi, but meanwhile Arjuna arrives there, also disguised as a gypsy, and begins to threaten his cousin.

Duryodhana is persuaded to let the gypsies go free for a "fee" of sweet-rice. He gives Draupadi boiled grains, however, which will not sprout, and she cannot make sweet-rice from it. But she sows them anyway, and as they escape from the city, whole stalks of rice come up behind them, having grown to their full length in a day. On this day, therefore, women make sweet-rice in memory of that event. This is consecrated and then offered as sacrificial rice and placed in nine directions to satisfy the nine planets.

The event, though not attended by the large crowds that mark the others, is as central to the Karaga *jatre* as the other rituals. It offers a moment, as does the recitation of the oral epic a few days later, of framing the performance through an important narrative. The oral epic connects the classical epic and its sites with local heroes and the present city. The gypsy story connects the two forms of Draupadi, the Primal Goddess and the wife of the five brothers, through a narrative privileging disguise and duplicity and mediates between the forest and the city through the image of a sown area. The connection between the forest and the city is again suggested at the end of the festival in the oral epic, just as at the beginning of the festivities the bamboo pole brought to the temple for the flag-hoisting ceremony linked the forest to the city.

This ritual also mediates the transition between the Hasi Karaga and the Pete Karaga. At noon of the Pete Karaga day, the priest bathes again at Upnirinakunte. The Virakumaras who return from this site carry branches of a special tree.[37] This is used to decorate the site within the temple where a fire sacrifice will be offered that afternoon. After returning to the temple, the Karaga priest places the sanctified rice preparation made by the women of the community around the temple to mark it as a ritual space and also to ward off evil forces. In the afternoon, the Karaga priest is adorned in the temple with black bangles by a local bangle seller. Both men and women from the community come to watch this event. A fire sacrifice performed by Brahmin priests is then offered with the Karaga priest seated at the fire. From the temple, a procession of ritual players move toward the house of the priest, carrying with them a sari, a blouse, and other items necessary for the "wedding" of Draupadi: puffed rice, dried coconut, and a basket with nine varieties of saplings that have been kept growing from the day of the flag hoisting.[38] The priest takes leave of his family and goes to the "groom's house"—that is, the temple. In the late evening, he leaves for Upnirinakunte to bathe again, carrying his dagger and staff. Afterward, proceeding under a veil of scarves, he goes to the pillared hall in the Sampangi Tank area to be dressed in a yellow-colored sari, a long-sleeved yellow blouse, and a headdress of jasmine. Once he returns to the temple, he quickly enters the sanctum. Inside, the marriage of Draupadi to Arjuna is performed. This rite takes place in secrecy, and there is no public event until the emergence of the Karaga from the temple after 10 P.M.

Outside the temple, elaborate precautions and arrangements have been made by the police, because the crowds that come to witness the Karaga's emergence from the temple and procession are gigantic. The chief guest in 1996 was the chief minister of Karnataka, H. D. Deve Gowda, who later went on to become the prime minister of India. The other invitees included the minister of revenue, the minister of home affairs, the leader of the opposition parties in the legislature, and various other members of the state legislature. Outside the compound of the temple stands the chariot that will carry the images of Draupadi and Arjuna; it has been standing outside the temple since the third day of the festival. The images of these two are brought out, along with the processional image of Muthyallamma, which is seated in a separate chariot. The chariots of both of these will go down the main temple road and return to the temple after the Karaga procession leaves.

A little before the Karaga priest emerges from the sanctum, the Virakumaras present an elaborate display that mainly involves their swords' touching their bodies; they never draw blood unless the Virakumara has been "impure." This swordplay *(alagu seve)* literally means "service with the blade"; little boys as well as older men beat their chests with the swords to the chant of "Dik-Dhi, Dik-Dhi" or "Govinda, Govinda," the former a magical formula and the latter a name for Krishna. The courtyard inside the temple and the open space outside it, where spectators are seated, is thick with these cries. The cries and blade service themselves are intended to excite the goddess so that she will appear again. After a few hours, the Karaga emerges from the temple. The priest is on his knees with a huge headdress of jasmine (this time, the Karaga is within it). Gunshots are fired outside the temple and shouts of "Govinda, Govinda" fill the air. The devotees gathered inside throw jasmine buds on the Karaga, and sometimes people, mainly women, go into a trance. The Karaga "dances" around the courtyard of the temple, stepping on the flames of camphor that has been lit by devotees, before going onto the road outside the temple walls. It moves back and forth a few times on the main temple road, and then suddenly, accompanied by shouting Virakumaras, it leaves as part of a procession for a tour across the City (see Figure 20).

Once the Karaga procession has left the Dharmaraja Temple, all the chariots from various shrines gathered outside the temple slowly make their

Figure 20. The Karaga moves through the streets on Pete Karaga night.

way to the City Market. Different temples in the city patronized by several caste and community groups bring these chariots. The Karaga *jatre,* like many other goddess festivals, is held in the hot months of March, April, and May due to the luni-solar calendar that is followed in this region. A number of goddess temples that are otherwise unconnected to the *jatre* complete their festivals around this time. The chariots from these temples congregate near the Dharmaraja Temple a little while before the Karaga priest emerges from the temple precincts on the night of the festival with a full moon. All along the City's roads, processional idols can be seen in their tractor-driven chariots, decorated grandly with lights and a variety of flowers. After the Karaga procession has begun from the temple, these make their way to the City Market area, where they will stand all night for citizens to pay their respects to the audience of deities. In this company of gods and goddesses, a number of new chariots can also be witnessed as recently established temples, saints, and cults are drawn into the Karaga cycle. The reverse is also true: a new goddess temple may also have its own Karaga *jatre*, although this may actually be confined to the few streets that surround the temple or to its immediate neighborhood.

All along the route of the Karaga procession, city dwellers stand with jasmine buds to throw on the Karaga or to offer prayers. The city appears a vast pilgrimage site or a fairground, with houses, streets, stores, and temples lit with lights and thousands of people milling about. The procession makes a number of stops at different shrines where prayers are offered. (In 1996, the Karaga procession returned to the temple a little after midnight in order to avoid the lunar eclipse, which was considered inauspicious.) Most years (as in 1997), the procession does not return to the temple until sunrise. By now it is the sixteenth day of the month.

After a few hours, the priest emerges from the sanctum. He is still dressed in a yellow sari and carrying the staff and the dagger, but the Karaga itself has been placed inside the sanctum on a platform, and the priest's head is covered with a yellow scarf instead of the floral headdress he wore earlier. He sits in an armchair inside the temple while people come to him to make offerings of money and receive his blessings. These offerings, apparently, form the only monetary compensation that the priest receives from the Karaga festivities as a whole. The priest is in a liminal stage at this point: since entering the temple on the flag-hoisting day (where he has stayed along with other members of his troupe), all rituals have been geared toward the appearance of the Primal Goddess and his support of her form. On this day, he is once again separated from her form, but still bears some sacrality connected with his previous contact and continues to stay within the temple.

After midnight, a small chariot carrying the images of Arjuna and Draupadi and the Karaga priest, led by the image of Potha Raja, arrive at the Elusuttinakote, trundling down the street that separates the two sacred sites. Here the Gante Pujari narrates the oral epic that deals with the history of Potha Raja, the origin of the Vahnikula Kshatriya lineage, and the sacrifice of the goat to Potha Raja in fulfillment of a promise made by Krishna and the Pandavas to the local hero. Potha Raja is a ritual figure found in some parts of south India who is usually a servant or a guardian of the local goddess; his role in her cult seems to be associated with a blood sacrifice. In the Karaga *jatre*, his role is to become part of the Pandavas' alliance through marriage to their sister after he has been tricked and defeated by them. Among the audience at Elusuttinakote, which includes a small number of Virakumaras and temple officiants as well as some people from other neighborhoods in the City, is the Karaga priest, still dressed in a sari, his hair covered with a scarf. After the epic is narrated, prayers are offered to the chariot's idols and to the idol of Potha Raja.

The troupe then moves to the Dharmaraja Temple, where a goat is sacrificed to two men (belonging to the same family) who embody Potha Raja. They rush outside their house carrying whips and proceed to the temple screaming. They are in a frenzied state, and it is believed that they are possessed. They roar at the group, their bodies smeared with white powder or ash and their heads covered with headdresses of jasmine like the priest's on the Hasi Karaga day. Sometimes they strike themselves with a whip, which increases their possession and the crowd's excitement. At the temple, an offering of rice cooked by the women of their family has been placed next to the sanctum. A live black goat is brought to the temple. The two possessed men circle around it screaming. It is held still with a whip or struck with it, and the Gante Pujari bends over to ask it a question while it is covered with a white cloth. The goat is supposed to give some acknowledgment of its sacrificial identity or magically identify Potha Raja (I received both explanations). Then the two men identified with Potha Raja leap on it and bite its neck and suck its blood. If the goat was not dead by this time, it certainly is by the time that this process is over. Blood runs from corners of the men's mouths. The heat of their possession is "lowered" by stuffing their mouths with huge balls of curd-rice, a "cooling" substance; these, with traces of blood on them, are regarded as containing some powers and are given to children to make them "fearless." The dead goat is gifted to the family of Potha Raja. The two men then sit on the steps outside the temple sanctum, in a bit of a daze still, while people prostrate themselves before them.[39]

The next day (the seventeenth day of Chaitra), preparations are made for the spring festival *(vasantotsava)*. Games are played with turmeric-colored water that is also used to douse grooms and brides after weddings. A square wooden frame is set up, on which hangs a thick rope. The headman holds one end of the rope. On the other end hangs a gunnysack with coconuts inside, which men of the community have to pound to pieces with the poles used to pound rice. Some men stand near drums filled with turmeric water and throw it on the others holding the poles, making the task of the latter difficult; in turn, the headman pulls the rope to make it swing violently. As men slip and fall in their attempts, the crowd, which now includes women, is filled with laughter, the seriousness and the period of penance of the festival having come to an end. That night, meat is consumed in most houses, because the period of restrictions is over. The seventeenth day marks a further point of transition in the performance sequence. Just as the separation between men and women comes to an end, so also does the Karaga priest become accessible to women of the community. At midnight, the flag of the festival is lowered, and the Karaga priest returns home to his wife. The two are once again "married" at his house, the period of separation between them having ended. The last event that occurs after the festivities are over is the immersion of the Karaga. Just as the Gante Pujari and other officiants are responsible during Hasi Karaga for the manifestation and birth of the *shakti* in the form of the Karaga, they are also responsible for its dissolution. They are reputed to immerse the icon in the waters of the Kaveri River near Srirangapattanam town, the Karaga returning to the element of water, from which it had earlier emerged.[40]

The Suburbanization of the Performance

Following the Karaga *jatre* in the City, two cycles of other performances emerge in suburbs of Bangalore and in certain towns in Bangalore, Kolar, and Tumkur districts. Although each of these is regarded as a Karaga *jatre*, the motifs and sequences of events are not identical to those just described. This is evident even in the pamphlets of invitation, which are circulated prior to the *jatre* at different sites.[41] Yet there are topological coordinates as well as certain events that form parallel structures among these sites. This can be demonstrated by making comparisons between the City *jatre* and performances in Doopanahalli and Hoskote town in the vicinity of Bangalore on the Old Madras Road. Many of these *jatre* are described as "Flower Karaga" *(Huvina Karaga)*.

As discussed in chapter 2, Doopanahalli is a locality of Bangalore that, up until the 1970s, was an outlying village close to the large Damlur Tank. The gardens in the area have since been swallowed up by the growing metropolis and incorporated into new residential localities. The larger area around it today is a middle- and upper-middle-class neighborhood.

The gardeners here are remembered for the large potatoes that they culti-vated and sold as far as the City Market. In Doopanahalli, which hosts a Karaga *jatre* about three days after the one in the City, the number of Vah-nikula Kshatriya households is about one hundred. During the Karaga fes-tival in 1996, about sixty households sent Virakumaras to the festival in their neighborhood. Like the City, this area also has a gymnasium where the Virakumaras train, and the temple flag is hoisted on a bamboo pole brought from a nearby forest by the men. The temple associated with the Karaga *jatre* is dedicated to Muthyallamma.[42]

The calendar of events for the 1996 festival at Doopanahalli is given below.

March 31	Flag hoisting.
April 1	Ritual bathing of the priest; vermilion decoration of the image.
April 2	Ritual bathing; decoration of image with mint leaves.
April 3	Ritual bathing; decoration of image as the goddess Parvati.
April 4	Ritual bathing; decoration of image as the goddess Bhudevi.
April 5	Ritual bathing; festival of lamps.
April 6	Ritual bathing; Hasi Karaga.
April 7	Ritual bathing and the offering of sweet-rice.
April 8	Ritual bathing, Flower Karaga, and festival of processional chariots.

The routines of the Doopanahalli *jatre* are similar, in essence, to those of the City celebration. The Karaga priest trains in preparation for the festival; a body of water (in this case, a well) is the site of the Karaga's emergence; and there are officiants called the Gante Pujari, the Ganachari, the Gowda, and others here, although they are more tattily dressed than the City's participants. Changes in the topography of the area have created shifts in the way the performance occurs. The laying out of roads on a grid pattern, the disappearance or lack of access to many wells because of mid-dle-class residential construction, and the sale of garden land have moved many sites of the Karaga priest's visits to the interiors of temples. Often there have been violent consequences: in 1984, it is said that one of the Vi-rakumaras doing his blade service got his sword stuck in an electricity wire and was electrocuted. There are some stark differences as well: unlike the City *jatre*, this one is more isolated while being festive; the rest of the mid-dle- and upper-class neighborhood of the area is asleep. Only a few pockets within it are awake and decorated with lights. One finds here the appearance of tiger-dancers—usually some persons, Hindu and Muslim, who dress as tigers *(huli vesha)*—who have disappeared from the City *jatre.* However, the market in the erstwhile village is busy, and many storeowners selling grains, vegetables, clothing, and household implements or running restaurants do a lively business.

Hoskote lies about thirty-five kilometers from the heart of Bangalore en route to Madras. The route is heavily industrialized and includes the Indian Telephone Industries and various chemical factories. According to informants, Hoskote has about 400 Vahnikula Kshatriya households. Most of the Vahnikula Kshatriya households are engaged in rose and grape cultivation. In 1996, about 160 households supplied Virakumaras to the Karaga performance in Hoskote, but at least a hundred large and small villages on the periphery of Hoskote contributed monetarily toward the performance. The temple that hosts the Karaga *jatre* houses an image of Draupadi in the main shrine.[43]

In 1996 the calendar of events at Hoskote was as follows.

April 25	Flag hoisting.
May 1	Rituals to the nine planets, and a fire sacrifice; Hasi Karaga after midnight.
May 2	The festival of lamps.
May 3	Flower Karaga.
May 4	The spring festival, the goat sacrifice, and recitation of the *Mahabharata.*

The Karaga *jatre* at Hoskote is presented on the night of the full moon of the second luni-solar month, "Vaishakha." The rituals form a compressed series. One of the reasons for this is that most of the Vahnikula Kshatriyas are involved in work in their gardens; nonagricultural occupations among them are rarer than at the other two sites of the *jatre.* Therefore, the Virakumaras tie wristbands only on the day of the Hasi Karaga, and it is not necessary that the wife of the Karaga priest be secluded; she must only not see the Karaga itself. In 1996, the Hoskote festival was commonly held to involve some degree of "risk": The Karaga priest and various members of his family had been sharing the responsibility of carrying the Karaga for about twenty years. The priest's younger brother died about the time the festival began, and, given that he had certain duties during the funeral ceremony, the Karaga priest was able to observe only some of the required restrictions on the day before the Hasi Karaga, when he moved into the temple.

At all three sites—the City, a suburb, and a satellite town—certain common features emerge even though the sequence of events is relatively mobile. In the case of the City Karaga *jatre*, the events always begin on the seventh day of Chaitra, also the Tamil New Year's Day. The events on the days from the seventh day to the full moon are fixed in the City. In other areas, not all the rituals performed in the City are necessarily found, nor are they in the same order. However, there appears to be a core structure that is found at all sites: the flag raising and lowering, the festival of lamps, the Hasi Karaga, and the chariot procession. The fire-walking ceremony, the sacrifice of the goat to Potha Raja, and the recitation of the epic appear to be optional. For instance, the fire-walk is present in Hoskote, but not at the other two sites. The sacrifice of the goat and the recitation of the epic are present in the City and in Hoskote, but not in Doopanahalli. The *shakti's* incarnation, personification, and localization is the dominant ritual structure for all the performances, but the goddess is not a fixed icon: in the case of the City, the Primal Goddess/Draupadi shares her charisma with the Seven Mothers in Elusuttinakote, as well as boundary goddesses such as Muthyallamma. In the other settlements, where the Flower Karaga takes place, the goddess does not have a unitary identity, but shares her power with her "siblings." In the case of Doopanahalli, the central shrine holds the twin images of Muthyallamma and Sathyamma, who are considered to be sisters, along with five other goddesses.[44] They are regarded as siblings of Draupadi, and Potha Raja is regarded as their "brother." In Hoskote, where Draupadi is the main icon in the temple, the Karaga shares its sacral field with the goddess Gangamma, whose temple near the tank where the Karaga is born is patronized by fishermen; Gangamma is regarded as the second wife of Shiva. One local narrative states that Gangamma decided to leave the tank one year (that is, overflow its banks), and the person who normally handled the sluices of the tank pleaded: "Wait here till I tell the village elders of your decision!" Gangamma promised to do so, but when the gatekeeper went to the headman, his head was cut off, and Gangamma, arrested by her promise, continued to inhabit the tank.

This centrifugality is balanced by the fact that each Karaga *jatre* acts as a centripetal force in the area for other temples, influential families, and business interests. Various temples (regardless of denomination) send their chariots and palanquins to the final day of the festival. Gods, goddesses, and saints in their chariots and even wandering mendicants carrying photos of their deities assemble on the final day of the festival in a central street or market area. People from the region come to pay their respects to the gathering of gods and goddesses as well as to admire the artistic flower decoration of the chariots. Each chariot from a temple is patronized by the temple trust itself or by some influential devotee. This patronage supports a priest, a decorator, an assistant to the priest, a couple of men who operate the chariot—which today is not hand drawn, but usually a Massey-Ferguson tractor—and a band of musicians.

For temples in the suburbs or satellite towns this procession is a kind of performance-directed urbanism. Temples and their patrons on the periphery of the city acquire an urban veneer, because they have an opportunity to display their influence. In turn, many landlords who have moved to Bangalore revisit their villages during the Karaga *jatre,* because these villages normally also have the festivals of their temples during this period. The contributions of different villages and suburbs to a Karaga *jatre* in the region create a field of financial offerings where status, political power, and upward mobility can be exhibited. Business interests are closely tied with the Karaga performances at all sites. The market area and shops are kept open throughout the nights of the festival, and consumers from various areas pour in. The scale of business activity is greater than usual; hotel owners and shopkeepers also make financial contributions to the Karaga. The Karaga *jatre* has gained the level of symbolic acceptance that it has in all these areas because the performance allows the play of not only different sectarian interests, but also economic activity. The ritual consumption of the *jatre* is intimately linked to the productive activity of the area.

All sites display of the template of market-settlement, fort, and tank that informs the Karaga *jatre* in the City. In Hoskote, there are the remains of an old fort that was constructed by a Palegara of the area. There is also a "Seven-Circled Fort," a small shrine with seven platforms called the Elusuttinakote (see Figure 3, chapter 1). The Hasi Karaga rituals are performed close to a tank called the Chickkere, and the Karaga emerges from a well in the bed of the tank. Every Friday, a market is held in the main street of Hoskote that almost invariably coincides with the final day of the Karaga *jatre* there. The periodic market attracts villagers from the surrounding regions to buy and sell all kinds of products, from cattle to fruits.

The Hoskote event is as old as the City Karaga *jatre,* according to informants. The *Mysore Gazetteer* shows that this Karaga *jatre* was performed in Hoskote about 1930 and drew about 8,000 persons; at that time, the same performance in Bangalore led to an assembly of about 20,000.[45] The Doopanahalli *jatre,* however, has been developed more recently, dating back about thirty years or so. The members of the troupe there were "trained" by the ritual players and elders of the City *jatre,* and the performance is, in many senses, affiliated with the City. The fort closest to

Doopanahalli is near the City, and there is no separate temple there called the Elusuttinakote. Although there have been no large tanks in the vicinity of Doopanahalli since the Damlur Tank vanished, the Karaga emerges from a well near the temple. The area of the settlement around the Muthyal-lamma Temple is also the area of its market. Therefore, the combination of a body of water, a fort, and a market-settlement seems to be integral and formulaic to the urban performance of the Karaga.

Kinetographs in the Karaga *Jatre*

This template of the fort, settlement-market, and body of water is present in kinetographs of the Karaga *jatre*. The kinetographs appear as representations of temporality and place within Bangalore and are constructed through ritual movements that are made during the *jatre*. These space-time units constrain and inform meanings of the *jatre* as a whole, and they also function as a mnemonic. It is as if each kinetograph creates a cross-sectional perspective of the metropolis's history viewed through the social experience and realms of life of the Vahnikula Kshatriya community. Each is a mode in which material objects, places, events, relationships with other groups, shrines, streets, and other public arenas are gathered up and organized into a map. A kinetograph suggests directionality in the metropolis, a way of orienting the audience and the participants in time and history in relation to public space. Four kinetographs can be identified within the performative process: alternation, circumambulation, procession, and the suburban cycle. Each of these suggests a specific axis within the *jatre*, and, taken as a set along with the oral epic, they create landscapes of urban memory.

Alternation

Each day, there is an alternation of rituals between the two sites of the Dharmaraja Temple in the City and "the Seven-Circled Fort," Elusuttinakote (indicated as A and B in Map 13 and connected by a dotted line). Although rites are performed at both these temples on a regular basis throughout the year, they have a special character during the festival period. The Karaga troupe visits both these sites during the *jatre*, and every afternoon and evening rituals are performed at the two locations. Women can be present at these ceremonies. What is significant about this alternation is that with the decline of the fort's importance in Bangalore after the establishment of the British Cantonment, the Elusuttinakote appeared as a ritual counterpoint to the Dharmaraja Temple in the City, a transfer from the political

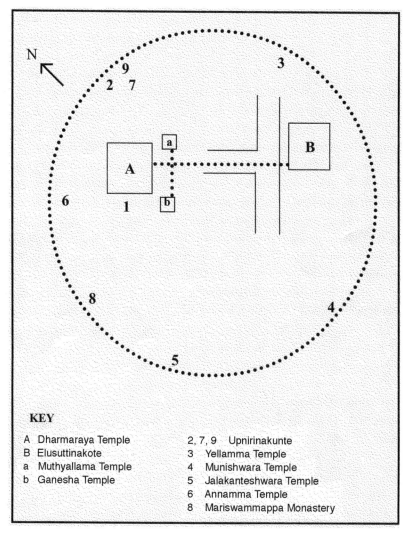

Map 13. Alternation and circumambulation in the Karaga *jatre*.

KEY

A	Dharmaraya Temple	2, 7, 9	Upnirinakunte
B	Elusuttinakote	3	Yellamma Temple
a	Muthyallama Temple	4	Munishwara Temple
b	Ganesha Temple	5	Jalakanteshwara Temple
		6	Annamma Temple
		8	Mariswammappa Monastery

realm to the symbolic. This recombined fort and City forms the first axis of the *jatre* and is spoken about in the language of kinship and domesticity among the Vahnikula Kshatriyas. The Vahnikula Kshatriyas describe the Dharmaraja Temple as "the in-law's house" because this is where Draupadi lives after her marriage to the Pandavas, and the Elusuttinakote as "the mother's house" because this is the location of the Primal Goddess. Viewed from the perspective of the goddess inside the sanctum of the

Dharmaraja Temple, the two shrines form the northwest-southeast spatial axis of the performance.

In addition to the alternation between the Elusuttinakote and the Dharmaraja Temple, rituals are performed at the Muthyallamma Temple and the Ganesha Temple, both situated outside the walls of the Dharmaraja Temple (indicated as a and b in Map 13 and linked by a dotted line). Every evening, a variety of decorations and oblations are carried out by different families of the Vahnikula Kshatriya community at the temples for a fee ranging from 1 rupee for entrance to the ritual to 100–501 rupees for honors at the rite. In contrast, therefore, to the other axis of the performance, this is linked to the neighborhoods where the community resides. These two temples are situated close together and form the northeast-southwest spatial axis of the festival when viewed from the perspective of the pilgrim facing the temple. The decorations of the deities at the two temples in 1996 and 1997 (the list is more or less standardized) are given below. These decorations are mainly products of gardens that are items of household consumption. In the rituals, they are displaced from their locations in the house, the field, and the garden, and sacralized by use in the temples.

Decorations at the Ganesha Temple

March 27, 1996	Turmeric
March 28, 1996	Vermilion
March 29, 1996	Flowers
March 30, 1996	Pulses
March 31, 1996	Peas
April 1, 1996	Jasmine
April 2, 1996	Pulses
April 3, 1996	Lunar eclipse; no decoration
April 15, 1997	Turmeric
April 16, 1997	Vermilion
April 17, 1997	Flowers
April 18, 1997	Pulses
April 19, 1997	Jasmine
April 20, 1997	Butter
April 21, 1997	Peas
April 22, 1997	Butter

Decorations at the Muthyallamma Temple

March 27, 1996	Turmeric
March 28, 1996	Vermilion
March 29, 1996	Peas

March 30, 1996	Wheat flour
March 31, 1996	Pulses
April 1, 1996	Flowers
April 2, 1996	Rice
April 3, 1996	No decoration
April 15, 1997	Turmeric
April 16, 1997	Vermilion
April 17, 1997	Peas
April 18, 1997	Wheat flour
April 19, 1997	Flowers
April 20, 1997	Betel-nut leaf
April 21, 1997	Rice
April 22, 1997	Butter

Circumambulation

On nine days of the *jatre*, excluding the days of flag hoisting and lowering and ending with the procession across different parts of the city, the Karaga troupe travels to nine ritually marked points where the priest bathes and changes his clothes. The Gante Pujari unpacks the *sacra* at various locations, and the Karaga priest performs rituals to them. The flag staff of the Karaga priest and his dagger are also placed along with these *sacra,* and surrounding them are a variety of fruits and flowers, bananas, watermelons, lemons, grapes, and jasmine (see Figure 21). If the location is a garden, the altar is a tree. If it is a temple, most of the ritual is performed in its vicinity, although not always inside its precincts. Each day, the bathing occurs at midday at one of the following sites.

Day 1   The Dharmaraja Temple itself.
Day 2   Upnirinakunte (the pond at Cubbon Park).
Day 3   The Yellamma Temple, now in Sampangiramnagar (in the Sampangi Tank area).
Day 4   The Munishwara Temple near Lalbagh.
Day 5   The Jalakanteshwara Temple (in the Kempambudi Tank area).
Day 6   The Annamma Temple (in the Dharmambudi Tank area).
Day 7   Upnirinakunte.
Day 8   Mariswammappa Monastery.
Day 9   Upnirinakunte.

If we refer to the space of the City itself, beginning from the temple (marked 1 on Map 13), the troupe moves around the City in a circumambulation of the temple (indicated by a dotted circle marked 2–9 for different

Figure 21. The altar at Upnirinakunte.

bathing sites covered on different days, as shown on the map). This forms a clockwise spatial axis for the performance, with nodes formed by three types of bodies of water—a pond, tanks, and wells. On the second, seventh, and ninth days, the troupe returns to the Upnirinakunte, a saltwater pond that does not exist today except as a small sealed well in Cubbon

Figure 22. The priest and the troupe at Upnirinakunte.

Park (see Figure 22). On three other days (days 3, 5, and 6), it covers sites in the vicinities of three tanks, the Sampangi, Kempambudi, and Dharmambudi Tanks. All these tanks have been taken over in a variety of ways by the city: the Sampangi Tank holds the Kanteerava Stadium and sports complex; the Kempambudi Tank receives sewage from the city and contains some housing colonies that have eaten into the tank bed; and Dharmam-budi Tank holds the bus terminal of Bangalore. On two days (days 4 and 8), the troupe visits sites that were earlier near two large wells. These do not exist today, so the troupe stops instead at temples in the wells' vicinity.

Informants state that up until the 1950s, the priest as well as other members of the troupe would bathe at the bodies of water.[46] In fact, the bathing originally occurred at the gardens belonging to the community that were near these bodies of water. The gardens were cultivated using wells and canals leading to the tanks that carried organic waste for manure purposes. These activities do not occur any longer, either because the tanks and wells themselves have disappeared or because the sewage canals contain industrial and chemical waste. Four drainage systems existed in the city, according to one informant. These fed the horticultural cycle until the early 1960s. Each of these formed an interlocking system with tanks and other bodies of water, large and small, and some of these appear within the Karaga *jatre*.[47]

Although one may read any number of meanings into the gardener-wrestlers' performance, there is a relationship between earth and potency and the ambivalent identities of the Primal Goddess and the priest that becomes visible through the kinetograph of circumambulation. The valorized celibacy and martial representations of the hero-sons and the increased heating of the Goddess are today posited against a context in which the gardeners are faced with increasing impotence as they lose their land in the city and the waters that feed these gardens become extinct. This gives the images of virility and controls over heating and cooling another level of meaning: not only is there an orderly regimen of the body in wrestling and during the *jatre*, but this is related to the vicissitudes of the body politic. As tanks and gardens gave way to concrete after the 1950s, the occupations of members of the community changed from being gardeners to being part of an urban working class and petty bourgeoisie. As members of urban classes, fewer men attend the wrestling-house than even fifty years ago, and hardly any own land in the city. Thus the fluids of the city, waste and water, have dried up, and no circulation occurs; the priest metaphorically recreates the flow to cool the "hot" bodies of the hero-sons and himself. Potency through self-containment, although a dominant trope in the performance and in the ethics of the gardener-wrestlers who struggle to keep heat from spilling over, is a deeply fragile construct in this context.

The nine-point city circumambulation by the Karaga troupe has changed over time to incorporate new sites into its structure, usually temples in place of bodies of water and gardens. Of the list given earlier, the only two temples that seem to have been part of the cycle before the twentieth century are the Annamma and the Yellamma Temples. The former is a significant site, as mentioned earlier (see chapter 3): the Annamma Temple is part of the old quadrilateral goddess structure of Bangalore, and the temple also marks one of the gates of the City. The temples of these boundary goddesses have been in the control of various communities who live in the City area: therefore, the community of oil-pressers controls the Annamma Temple. The Yellamma Temple, controlled by the Vahnikula Kshatriyas, is another significant shrine, because the Vahnikula Kshatriyas consider themselves related to the lineage of the sage Jamadagni and Yellamma, as narrated to me in this account by the Yellamma Temple priest in April 1996:

> The king, Renukaraja, had twenty-one wives, of which the main one was Bhogavati. He, however, was childless, and after a long penance to Shiva and Parvati, had a daughter, Renuka Paramjyoti or Yellamma, born to him from the sacrificial fire. The other wives were jealous of this child and tried to kill the baby by putting a cobra in the cradle, but Yellamma killed it. When Yellamma grew up, she was not only beautiful, but also virtuous. Sage Jamadagni arrived at the court of the king. He saw Yellamma and was desirous of marrying her. The king granted his wish rather than anger the sage, who was known for his terrible temper. At the hermitage in the forest, it was Yellamma's duty to bring a pot of water made from her own hands out of sand. The pot would rest on her head on a coiled cobra.
>
> One day, as she walked back from her labors carrying the pot, she saw a king and a queen lovingly tending their child together. Wistfully, she thought how wonderful it would be to have a child born to her. At this point, the pot developed holes and the water flowed away. This incurred the wrath of Jamadagni, who cursed her, and her beauty was marred by pox. In time, Yellamma had three sons born to her. The sage asked them to behead Yellamma; the elder two sons refused, but the youngest, Parasurama, agreed and chopped off the head of his mother. The head splintered into 108 pieces. The sage was pleased with the obedience of his son and granted him two boons. The first one that Parasurama asked for was that his father should give up his anger. The second was that his mother's life should be restored. The latter event occurred, however, through a process of regeneration: each of the 108 pieces of Yellamma became an aspect of the Primal Goddess.

The goddess Yellamma resembles Draupadi because, like the latter, she was born from a fire sacrifice. She is also regarded as a boundary goddess associated with pox and is petitioned for healing a variety of afflictions because she too received a curse of the pox. Her decapitation is of great significance for the Karaga *jatre*. Each of the pieces of her decapitated head regenerated into wholeness, and in narratives about the Karaga *jatre* at several sites outside of the City, the goddesses of these shrines are conceived of as splinters of her head. Therefore, Yellamma's head serves as a paradigm for the links between the City and the suburbs just as her presence in the City serves to mark its boundaries.

Among the nine points at which the priest bathes, those not associated with the Vahnikula Kshatriyas show the links of trade and commerce that exist in the City where the Vahnikula Kshatriyas reside or work. For instance, the monastery visited on the eighth day is associated with the Lingayat community; today Bangalore has sixty-three such centers.[48] In Bangalore, the Lingayat community controls a number of financial activities in the City—for instance, moneylending and the operation of provision stores and other shops. The Vahnikula Kshatriyas, like many others in the area, rely on them for these services. Again, the temple visited on the fifth day is associated with cloth merchants, traditionally weavers of silk and fine embroidered cloth, called the Pattegaras. Two groups besides the Vahnikula Kshatriyas draw the chariot carrying Draupadi and Arjuna on the final day of the Karaga: oil-pressers (Ganigas); and weavers of cotton (Devangas). Both these groups live in neighborhoods bordering Tigalarapet, and weavers, in fact, have looms in houses of Vahnikula Kshatriyas landlords.

Apart from the nine points at which the priest performs his ritual bath, the troupe daily visits a number of temples, houses, and wrestling sites that the Karaga priest has been invited to grace (see Table 7). These have also changed over time: it appears that earlier, most of the houses visited belonged to Vahnikula Kshatriyas, and in addition, the temples were usually those of deities associated with non-Brahmin communities. Today, the list also includes a temple manned by a Brahmin priest as well as a garment factory run by a Vahnikula Kshatriya.

Procession

On the night of the full moon, the Karaga, accompanied by hundreds of Virakumaras, moves in a procession through the City. The Karaga troupe has a designated route that it traverses through the night, up until the early hours of the morning. The route itself is a kinetograph, with the starts and stops of the procession serving to mark out sites on the way. Beginning

Table 7.

Sites visited by the Karaga troupe during the nine-day performance

Festival day	Sites visited
Day 1	Flag hoisting at the Dharmaraja Temple.
Day 2	Commencement from the temple—*Upnirinakunte*—Elusuttinakote—Dharmaraja Temple.
Day 3	Dharmaraja Temple—Hasi Karaga site in the Sampangi Tank bed—Ganesha Temple opposite the Kanteerava Stadium—*Yellamma Temple* at Sampangiramnagar—headman's house in Sampangiramnagar—Annaiappa gymnasium—Dharmaraja Temple.
Day 4	Dharmaraja Temple—*Munishwara Temple* near Lalbagh—garment factory near the City Corporation premises—Dharmaraja Temple.
Day 5	Dharmaraja Temple—*Jalakanteshwara Temple* near Kempambudi Tank—Ganesha Temple near the K. R. Market—Venkatadasappa gymnasium—Dharmaraja devotional center—Dharmaraja Temple.
Day 6	Dharmaraja Temple—*Annamma Temple* near Kempe Gowda Road, City Market area—Sitaram devotional center in the Nagarthapet area—Dharmaraja Temple.
Day 7	Dharmaraja Temple—*Upnirinakunte*—Hasi Karaga site—rituals at the house of Mr. Jayaram, the person in charge of the Kunjanna gymnasium—Kunjanna gymnasium—Dharmaraja Temple.
Day 8	Dharmaraja Temple—*Mariswamappa Monastery* at Kalasapalyam—Dharmaraja Temple.
Day 9	Dharmaraja Temple—*Upnirinakunte*—Dharmaraja Temple.

Note: Dashes indicate direction; italics indicate places at which bathing usually occurs; unless otherwise mentioned, all sites are in the Tigalarapet area. The troupe also visits the Elusuttinakote daily, though it is not mentioned here, once while leaving the Dharmaraja Temple and once while returning to it.

from the Dharmaraja Temple, the procession passes by a number of smaller shrines, houses, and stores. Special prayers, however, are said at four other sites that form edges extending from an uneven parallelogram, another axis of the performance. The Karaga enters these sacred arenas, and the ritual officiants greet the troupe and the Karaga by offering prayers to it or extending a blessing. The crowds at these points are enormous, many people conscious that these are vantage points from which to view the Karaga or to receive its beneficence. These people are usually members of other communities who live in the various neighborhoods in which the shrines are located. The shrines themselves are specially decorated with lights, the images within them ornamented with flowers, and the priests and ritual officiants within them waiting eagerly for the stop of the procession. The night of the Karaga procession is one on which many of these sites receive the largest number of visitors, who continue to offer prayers and money before and after the stop of the Karaga troupe.[49]

The route is depicted in Map 14. The shrines are indicated by the numbers 1–5 and are marked as squares on the diagram. The letters A–F mark the route that the procession takes. Therefore, setting out from the Dharmaraja Temple (1), the procession moves along Nagarthapet Road (A) in an east-west direction. It then turns southwest on Avenue Road (B) toward the Kote Anjaneya Temple (2). Returning by the same route until it joins Chickpet Road (C), the procession turns in a westerly direction and then southward on Old Taluk Cutchery (OTC) Road (D) until it reaches the Hazrat Tawakkul Mastan Shrine (3). After prayers at this shrine, the procession moves northwest on Subedar Chatram Road (E) to visit the Annamma Temple (4). Then it turns east on Killari Road (F) to proceed to the Yelahanka Gate Anjaneya Temple (5). It returns via Avenue Road (B) and Nagarthapet Road (A) to the Dharmaraja Temple.

Of these, the Chickpet Road and the Avenue Road are the busiest areas of the City. They are the sites of frenetic markets for goods ranging from vegetables to gold. Both of them—and, by extension, Nagarthapet Road—form the two main axes of the City. Killari Road forms the northern boundary of the City. Although this is not always clearly visible because of the traffic on the road and buildings in the area, Killari Road lies north of the extensive low-lying area that forms the City. Subedar Chatram Road extends out of the old boundaries of the City toward another market area called the Kempe Gowda Market. The five shrines at which the procession stops mark boundaries of the City in one way or the other, lying on its extremities although they are today integral parts of the metropolis.

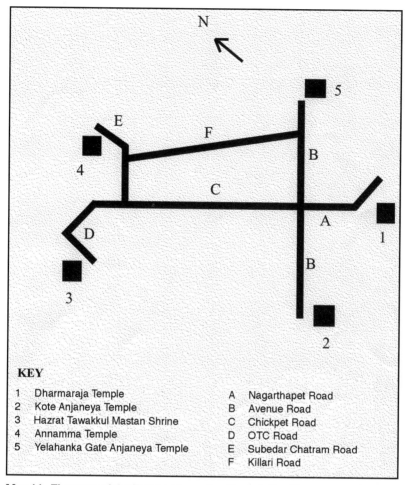

Map 14. The route of the Karaga procession through the City.

KEY

1	Dharmaraja Temple	A	Nagarthapet Road
2	Kote Anjaneya Temple	B	Avenue Road
3	Hazrat Tawakkul Mastan Shrine	C	Chickpet Road
4	Annamma Temple	D	OTC Road
5	Yelahanka Gate Anjaneya Temple	E	Subedar Chatram Road
		F	Killari Road

It is as if slices of specific historical periods of the City's development and current existence are represented in this kinetograph. Above all, the representation refers to the fort-City just as the earlier kinetograph referred to bodies of water of the precolonial urban model. It also signals the axes of the urban performative complex. Therefore, the Annamma Temple is a node within the quadrilateral goddess complex along with the celibate warrior Anjaneya, who guards the "gates" of the fort on the north and south. The Hazrat Tawakkul Mastan Shrine is a reminder of the period of the construction of Tippu Sultan and Haider Ali's fort, the settlement of a large number of Muslims in the City during that period, and the connection that developed between the goddess and the Sufi. The Dharmaraja Temple is the locus of the central civic ritual of the City and part of the axis of goddess worship of the performative complex. As can be seen from the map, there is a certain complementarity between the City and the fort that is signaled by the Karaga procession's stops. There is also a certain symmetry in the sexual identities of the sacred beings at these sites: the Annamma Temple houses a goddess who is considered a virgin goddess, whereas the Dharmaraja Temple houses Draupadi in her twin aspects of the Primal Goddess and the wife of the five brothers. Anjaneya is a celibate warrior, and the Sufi is "married" to God. These aspects of complementarity and symmetry, as well as the movements east and west, north and south, toward the center and toward the boundaries, inform axes of this kinetograph.

The Suburban Cycle

The last kinetograph represents the integration of a number of suburbs and towns in the Bangalore metropolitan region into the cycle of the performance after the Pete Karaga is over. Map 15 shows the main towns in the three districts and the suburbs of Bangalore that form part of this cycle (compare Map 15 with Map 2, chapter 1). It is significant that many of these Karaga performances are recently established ones. In 1930, only two Karaga *jatre* were mentioned for the Mysore region, out of a total of 159 festivals: one in Bangalore City and another in Hoskote town (both in present-day Bangalore district), the former drawing 20,000 persons and the latter 8,000.[50] The spread of the Karaga *jatre* seems, from all accounts, to have occurred largely after 1950. As mentioned in the previous chapter, the Vahnikula Kshatriyas are settled mainly in Bangalore, Tumkur, and Kolar districts. The largest number are to be found in the City, but in Bangalore itself they inhabit a number of suburbs that were earlier villages connected to the City primarily through the marketing of vegetables. Today, these areas are either industrial or residential tracts of the city. In these suburbs, as well as in towns close to Bangalore, performances take place in two cycles after the completion of the Karaga *jatre* in the City. The suburbanization of the Karaga, therefore, has a certain form that is referred to regularly by members of the community themselves:

1. The first cycle occurs in the ten-day period following the night of the full moon of the first luni-solar month, Chaitra. This cycle is indicated by a thick line in Map 15. Karaga *jatre* takes place at Vijipura, Chikballapur, Anekal, and

Mayasandra on the same day as the Bangalore Karaga *jatre*. Vijipura and Mayasandra are small suburbs of Bangalore and are not shown in Map 15. Anekal is a town in Bangalore district, whereas Chikballapur town is in Kolar district. Both are a few hours away by road from the metropolis. In 1996, the Kengeri *jatre* occurred three days after the Pete Karaga. Kengeri is an important satellite town of Bangalore; it is on the road to Mysore, barely forty-five minutes away from the center of the City. In 1996, four days after the Pete Karaga there were smaller performances at Malur, a town in Kolar district, and this was followed by the *jatre* at Doopanahalli, described earlier. These performances are presented more or less on the same schedule every year.

2. The second cycle occurs during the ten-day period following the full moon night of the second luni-solar month, Vaisakha. This cycle is indicated by a double line in Map 15. The *jatre* at Yelahanka, a suburb of Bangalore, takes place a day prior or a day after the full moon. Karaga *jatre* then occur at Hoskote, Malur, Devanahalli, Chikballa-pur, and Dodballapur. Of these towns, Hoskote, Devana-halli, and Dodballapur are in Bangalore district. Malur and Chikballapur towns are in Kolar district.

Karaga performances take place at Tumkur and Kolar towns in Tumkur and Kolar districts, but these seem to be somewhat more distant events for the Vahnikula Kshatriya community in Bangalore. Although some attend the Karaga *jatre* at the towns and suburbs just mentioned, most do not seem to attend the ones at Tumkur and Kolar; these form almost the outer limits of the ritual cycle. The densest cluster of towns and suburbs is in Bangalore district itself, as Map 15 shows, forming interweaving twin axes of performances that essentially seem to be presented within a fifty-kilometer radius.

The performances in many of the towns and suburbs are simpler than the one in the City. At each of these sites, the same structure of bathing at nine points, visiting a variety of temples, and the fort-City dyad (which is generally present in the large towns such as Hoskote and Malur) is repli-cated. At nearly all of these sites, a Sufi shrine is part of the ritual process. Sometimes other communities celebrate the Karaga *jatre*. For example, in Dodballapur members of the weaver community (Devangas) also have a

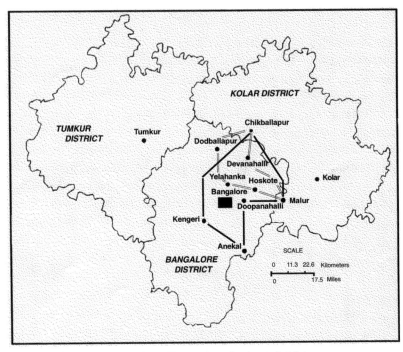

Map 15. Suburban cycles of the Karaga *jatre* in three districts.

role to play. At each of these sites, the Karaga *jatre* may or may not be dedicated to Draupadi. The connections between these sites and the City Karaga are chiefly achieved through the image of the death and rebirth of Draupadi, on the one hand, and the dismemberment of Yellamma, on the other hand. One method of rationalizing the performances related to goddesses elsewhere, as mentioned, is to regard all these goddesses as portions of the decapitated Yellamma.[51] Therefore, the goddess Draupadi's power, intimately linked to territory and its inhabitants, is circumscribed by the power of other goddesses in neighboring localities, and she has to enter into relations with the others.

The kinetograph suggests another kind of historical boundary for the Karaga *jatre:* a ring of fort-settlements around Bangalore, the establishment of many of them coinciding with or occurring prior to the development of Bangalore by the Palegara Kempe Gowda. These settlements were usually controlled by local chieftains and commanded a view of the areas within the jurisdictions of the chiefs, besides being key settlements for inland trade. Francis Buchanan's journey through these areas from Madras around 1800 presented a view of the settlements that formed part of the precolonial geography of these areas. In his account he spoke of the rich trade of Bangalore—especially in betel nuts, textiles, black pepper, and sandalwood—with other centers such as Calicut and Mangalore on the west coast, Hyderabad, the Arcot districts, the range of communities involved in their manufacture, and other residents of the cosmopolitan urban site.[52] He pointed to the division of lands in this region into watered lands and drylands, the former comprised of gardens called *tota*, whether utilized for palm plantations, betel-nut and fruit gardens, or kitchen gardens growing vegetables. These were watered partly by tanks, he observed, by channels from rivers, or by machines drawing water.[53]

What is significant about Buchanan's narrative is that it linked the ring of forts (called *kote* or *durga*) to gardens cultivated by gardeners that he called "Palliwanlu." He stated that all the gardens in this area were east of Sira and Srirangapattanam and the fortified strongholds that ran north from Capaladurga (see Map 16, adapted from the map of Buchanan's route). These included the forts Melkote, Huliurudurga, Hulianadurga, Savanadurga, Bhairavanadurga, Shivaganga, Niddigal, Devarayanadurga, Koratagiri, Chinrayandurga, Madhugiri, and Chandragiri. Turning east, these included the forts of Mahakalidurga, Nandidurga, and Ambajidurga. The ranges of hills to the east of Bangalore were a major watershed for several rivers and fortified settlements, and there do not appear to have been any major forts that ran northeast to southwest. The forts seem to have formed a ring north, west, and south of Bangalore, with the mountains on the east forming another kind of fortification. Buchanan also emphasized in his account the sites that today perform the Karaga *jatre* in the two suburban cycles described: Kolar, Chikballapur, Dodballapur, Tumkur, Devanahalli, Hoskote, Malur, and Anekal. As can be seen from Maps 15 and 16, the sites of the Karaga *jatre* today are all within the ring of forts or in close proximity to them. Buchanan's account in 1800 and the present suburban cycles of the *jatre* suggest that these forts form the boundaries of gardeners, gardens, and a horticultural universe in the Bangalore region.

These boundaries are also significant in terms of the ways in which various publics and sites can enter the events of the Karaga *jatre*—the "regime of participation," as it were. The regime is mediated by kinetographs in the same way that the significatory practices of the performance as a whole achieve location through them. Topological, institutional, and historical inputs create a specific aesthetics for the performance, and there are civic modes of participation that are nonindividualized modalities; instead they are social practices that follow certain cultural pathways and memories of place. According to Bakhtin (1990), if no social practice or

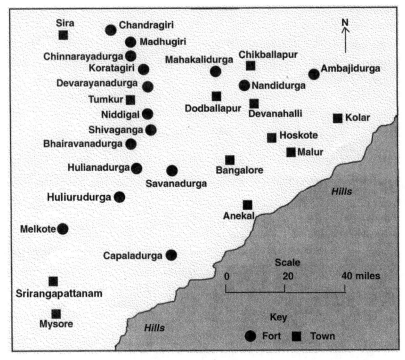

Map 16. The ring of forts and boundaries of garden lands in the Bangalore region. Source: Adapted from Buchanan 1870.

history is perceived to exist beyond the individual participant, delimiting and situating him or her from outside, such a consciousness cannot be "aestheticized." Communion is possible, but not an aesthetic event. Further, what this implies is that the theatrical public is not constituted through a unified, monadic relation to the external world. Rather, this constitution occurs through the operation of dense, multiple, and overlapping networks of discourses, cultural practices, and institutional structures.[54] In the case of the Karaga *jatre*, ways of participating in the performance are channeled primarily through spatial and temporal coordinates that also inform the kinetographs. People gather at various shrines along the route of the procession at which the Karaga troupe stops. Again, the modes by which new shrines, audiences, and publics within the metropolis can enter the frame of the performance is by becoming part of the circumambulatory space or by creating chariots that join the procession. New towns and suburbs similarly must fall into the two suburban cycles described. Nearly all the new sites of the *jatre* are also part of the jurisdiction of the metropolitan region of Bangalore of the 1990s (see Map 2, chapter 1). Therefore, aesthetics and participation are structured through kinetographs where historical, institutional, and discursive practices intersect. It must be emphasized, therefore, that the extension of the Karaga *jatre* to new publics and sites, as has been occurring in the past fifty years, will probably be done through frames and practices suggested by these kinetographs.

6

Cities and Forests

The Recitative Topos

The oral epic about the origins of the Vahnikula Kshatriya community, the *Karaga Purana* or the *Vahni Purana,* is recited outside the Elusuttinakote on the night after the full moon and the Karaga procession through the City. The recitation usually begins after midnight (in 1996, for instance, the recitation began at about 2 A.M.) and goes on for two or three hours. The recitation is done by a ritual officiant known as the "Gante Pujari" (literally, "The Bell-Priest"; see Figure 23), and there can be more than one. The Gante Pujari's family are priests of the Elusuttinakote. The person who had been reciting the epic for at least two decades was Venkataswamappa. He passed away some months after the Karaga *jatre* in 1996, and no one from his family was found to replace him effectively in 1997, as a result of which the narration was not presented that year. In 1998 and 1999, his brother, Krishnappa, recited the *Purana.* In 1996, I recorded Venkataswamappa's recitation outside the Elusuttinakote as he presented it, and it was later translated and transcribed from Telugu and Tamil, the two languages of the oral epic.

The recitation creates a shift from the previous nine days of the performance by introducing a new narrative within the structure of events (see Figure 24). A number of story lines about Draupadi have emerged on different days of the *jatre* and run their course as the phases of the performance are completed. These are the stories of Draupadi's birth as the Primal Goddess (on the seventh day of the festival), of Draupadi as gypsy (on the eighth day in connection with the making of the sweet-rice), of Draupadi and other gods and goddesses (introduced through the sites linked with the priest's bathing), and of Draupadi's marriage to Arjuna (emphasized on the ninth day of the festival), which all stress different aspects of

Figure 23. The Gante Pujari sings at the Dharmaraja Temple.

Draupadi's nature. On the night of the *Karaga Purana* (on the tenth day of the festival) the dominant narrative is that of Draupadi in the forest, followed by that of the alliance of Draupadi and the Pandavas with a local ruler, Potha Raja.

This new story line allows a "recitative topos" to emerge alongside kinetographs that have given contours to the metropolis through the ritual

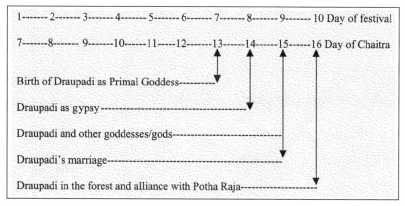

Figure 24. Story lines about Draupadi in the Karaga *jatre.*

processes of the previous few days. If the kinetograph is a representation of place and time through movement, the social, temporal, and mnemonic locus evoked through the act of recounting the oral epic may be termed a recitative topos.[1] It is the narrative stage, as it were—forest, fort, sea, underworld, or hut—on which events are played out. There may be more than one locus in the recitation, and locales may follow each other sequentially or be presented in particular combinations. They necessarily imply the passage of time and the memory of things past. In this sense of being space-time units, they inform and constrain meaning-making possibilities.

The recitative topos of the *Karaga Purana* refers to the period of exile of the Pandavas, and especially Draupadi, in the forest. It invokes the forest in a way that the *jatre* itself has so far only suggested. The Karaga *jatre,* for instance, begins with the act of preparing a bamboo pole to hold the flag of the temple. Members of the gardener community bring the wood from the Jaraganahalli Forest to the temple in the early hours of the morning of the first day of the festival.[2] The theme of the forest is also echoed, time and again, in narratives about goddess shrines in Bangalore that form part of the urban performative complex. A constant theme in these accounts is how settlement is predated by the occupation of the goddess in the forest, which, with the passage of years, gives way to human habitation. When forest turns into settlement, the forest and the goddess come to form an "internal" symbolic boundary of the city. The destinies of the settler-goddess and the newcomers, the forest and the city, are entwined, and rather than forming separate domains, interpenetrate each other through various events and practices. Again, this interpenetration is explicitly conjured up during the gypsy cycle of stories recited during the ritual of "the offering of sweet-rice" in the *jatre:* moving from the tenth forest to the eleventh one in the period of exile, Draupadi, in disguise as a gypsy, visits the capital city of Hastinapura from the forest. Therefore, although the forest forms an indispensable backdrop to the festivities in the city, the *jatre* is presented almost entirely within the city. On the day after the Karaga procession through the city, in the early hours of the morning, the events of the *jatre* turn once again to the memory of the forest.

As the oral epic unfolds and we hear stories being told and songs being sung in a chorus, the recitative topos of the forest appears to be extremely nuanced. The oral epic begins with an invocation of the lineage of the Lunar Dynasty and that of Potha Raja. The events, then, turn immediately to the occasion of the Pandavas' losing their kingdom in a game of dice to their cousins, the Kauravas. The Pandavas leave the city of Hastinapura and wander through the forest among its denizens. For the audience as well as the participants listening to the epic, memories of the city are led into the space of the forest because the central reference of the *Karaga Purana* is to the exile of the heroes and Draupadi. However, there are transitions in the narration from the city to the forest and back again, along with transactions between the city and the forest, which, like other oral accounts about goddess temples, reflect a landscape in which the city and the forest are boundaries of each other. In the interaction between city and forest, therefore, a number of subsites and details appear. The claims made in the *Karaga Purana* are not just about origins; there are also topographic claims relating to urban history, social space, and spatial geography; we shall return to this theme in the last section of the chapter.

Multivalence in the Karaga Purana

Although self-consciously presented as a classical text by the Gante Pujari, the *Karaga Purana* does not belong to the Sanskrit *purana* scheme. The *purana* are defined by Indologists as a class of Sanskrit literature that is divided into two categories: first, the *mahapurana,* which are eighteen in number and deal with creation, recreation, genealogies, cycles of time, and the histories of dynasties more or less summarily; and second, the *upapurana,* which are written in much the same style, but deal more extensively with local cults and sects. The *Karaga Purana,* however, shares the character of other texts that have been written, chiefly between the twelfth and the seventeenth centuries, which claim to be *purana,* but do not deal with the themes just given and largely discuss the origins of particular castes or places.[3]

In the Tamil literary tradition, the composition of *purana* is said to date back to the earliest period of literary activity. Several Sanskrit *purana* existed by the end of the fifth century, copies of which were made in Tamil in the medieval period. It is likely that the idea of composing on Sanskrit models existed at the same time that other literary forms were borrowed. We also know of the existence of Jain *purana*, belonging to the tenth century, and other Tamil *purana* of the twelfth century from inscriptional evidence. The distinctive character of Tamil *purana*, as Shulman (1980) points out, is the localization of mythic action through two spatial forms: first, the shrine is seen as the center of the universe and of the myth; second, an ideal landscape connects different worlds. These forms distinguish the Tamil *purana* from the Vedic sacrificial system, which is inherently mobile. In the Tamil case, the deity emerges, radiates, or is revealed at a specific site, and efforts to move it prove futile: the only way in which it can be moved is through a chariot procession along a circumscribed route.[4] In the *Karaga purana*, the forest is presented as an ideal landscape, and the central events of the epic are localized at the Elusuttinakote, the abode of the Primal Goddess.

The *Karaga Purana* is also similar to many Telugu *purana* in which goddesses are a central focus: Narayana Rao (1986 and 1989) states that most discussions of south Indian goddesses locate them among "right-handed" agriculturists and landowning castes. Although he refers to the Telugu country, his observations can probably also be extended to other parts of south India. In the epics of these groups, men aspire to heroic warrior status and keep women under strict control. Yet there are also other social groups, "left-handed" trading and artisan castes, in whose epics the female warriors heroically defend the integrity of the group against hostile powers. Although the Vahnikula Kshatriyas nowhere describe themselves either as left-handed or right-handed, their *purana* has the characteristic of left-handed castes in that a female warrior goddess is the apex of the narration; it also shares the character of epics of right-handed castes in that the men claim warrior status and origin in it.

The *Karaga Purana* is based on characters and themes that are "from the *Mahabharata*," according to the Gante Pujari. Many themes and motifs, however, are from sources independent of the classical Sanskrit *Mahabharata* attributed to the sage Vyasa, as is true of many other *Mahabharata*-based performances in south India.[5] I will not explore here how the *Karaga Purana* is related to other myths, folktales, epics, or drama or how the classical epics were themselves influenced by folk themes, except to agree with Hiltebeitel (1991a, 413–16) that many of the south Indian versions of the *Mahabharata* and folk epics linked to them—the Tamil *Elder Brothers Story*, the Telugu *Epic of Palnadu*, and the mythology of the Draupadi cult in Tamil Nadu—have a family resemblance in certain ways. They celebrate Kshatriya values and are linked to castes connected with land (although I would add that they may not always be dominant in the region); and apart from certain recurring themes from the *Mahabharata*—dice matches, disguises, alliances—they have certain "minimal features" that link them to each other. First, they deal with a heroine who represents a goddess (quite often a virgin, or at least in a single state). Second, the heroine has low-status companions or guardians. Third, each of the heroines is linked or identified with Draupadi. In folk versions, notably the *Epic of Palnadu* and the Draupadi cult mythology, the figure of Potha Raja is an important one, just as he is in the *Karaga Purana*. The accounts of Draupadi as a gypsy and the Potha Raja cycle can be described as the "surplus" of the Sanskrit *Mahabharata*.[6]

Many commentators agree that the earliest southern *Mahabharata* was that of Perundevanar (in Tamil) and that Pampa's *Mahabharata* (in Kannada) and Villiputtur Alvar's (in Tamil) tend to follow Perundevanar's in significant ways.[7] In the extant versions of Perundevanar (ninth century) and Pampa (tenth century), the *Mahabharata* concludes after the Pandavas' victory over their cousins, the Kauravas, in the Kurukshetra battle.[8] The emphases of the two are, however, different: in Pampa's, the *Adi Parvan* (the first book of the classical Sanskrit epic that describes the genealogy of the Lunar Dynasty to which the Pandavas belong) occupies an important place, whereas in the existing Perundevanar version it is the *Udyog Parvan* (the fifth book in the classical Sanskrit epic, which tells of the preparations for the Kurukshetra battle). The emphasis on characters also shifts in the two texts: for Pampa, it is Arjuna who is the hero.[9] For Perundevanar, it was Krishna who was the focus.[10] In the *Karaga Purana*, the main character is not Krishna (for Shiva also appears to be a significant figure) or Arjuna, but Draupadi in her various guises and thus refers to the *Aranyaka Parvan* (the third book in the classical Sanskrit epic that deals with the period of exile of the Pandavas for twelve years). One such guise of Draupadi is her incarnation as the Primal Goddess.

Perhaps one of the central references of the *Karaga Purana* is to the *Devi Mahatmya*. This is one of the most famous of all texts devoted to goddess worship, probably written about the fifth or sixth century around the Narmada Valley, and comprises fewer than six hundred verses.[11] In the

Devi Mahatmya, the ultimate reality in the universe is understood to be feminine. Devi's complex relationship to various deities reveals aspects of her nature, but she is never merely a consort. The outline of the text is as follows (Coburn 1996, 32–33): there is a frame story and three myths in the *Devi Mahatmya.* The first half of the frame story tells how a king and a merchant seek refuge from various adversities in a forest. They meet a sage who tells them that their problems are due to *mahamaya* ("she who possesses great deceptiveness" or "she who is the great deception"). He then recounts three myths about Devi, each more extensive than the next. The first outlines her cosmic status. The second involves her origins on earth and her martial activities and ends in her conquest of the buffalo-demon Mahisa. The third celebrates her various forms and their role in the victory over the minions of the two demons, Sumbha and Nisumbha. The residual half of the frame story ends up with the king and merchant worshiping Devi, who appears to them and answers their prayers.

It is perhaps the second and third episodes that have the greatest resonance with the *Karaga Purana.* In the second episode, Devi, with the combined splendor of Brahma, Vishnu, Shiva, and other gods, defeats the buffalo-demon who is threatening the gods. There has already been a suggestion in the oral accounts in the previous chapter that the Karaga combines the forces of these three deities. In the *Karaga Purana,* Draupadi as the Primal Goddess also defeats a demon identified with a buffalo. In the third episode of the *Devi Mahatmya,* Devi multiplies her forces, and from her emerge the Seven Mothers. The Seven Mothers are present iconographically in Elusuttinakote and also appear, somewhat obliquely, in the recitation by the Gante Pujari. It is beyond my competence to show how widely prevalent the *Devi Mahatmya* is in Karnataka (or, more generally, in south India), although manuscripts, performances, and art influenced by the *Devi Mahatmya* or forms of the Devi have been identified in Mysore and on the western coast of Karnataka.[12] However, I will reiterate the importance in neighboring Mysore of the Dassera festival dedicated to the Chamundeshwari (Devi) who defeats the demon Mahisasura; a popular temple of the former and a statue of the latter are found on the hill near the city.

Both Telugu and Tamil are present in the *Karaga Purana* recitation. Tamil is used for the poems that are sung to musical accompaniments, chiefly bells and a drum, and Telugu is used for the prose. This interspersing of prose and poetry is common to old Tamil as well as old Kannada.[13] The Tamil and Telugu of the *Karaga Purana* are not classical; its languages are closer to the spoken word, especially the speech of such spaces as the market, the street, and other public sites. Some of the Telugu prose, in fact, shows an admixture of Kannada as well. There is a constant presence of more than one voice in the recitation, because the narrator and the audience are not clearly separated from the dramatis personae of the narration itself. Potha Raja, Draupadi, and Arjuna are present as processional images to hear the epic, and the audience members speak among themselves and to the Karaga troupe during breaks. This effect of multivocality is also achieved by the switching between a first-person and third-person voice and between nonprose and prose sections of the recitation.

As traders and gardeners in the city, not only do the Vahnikula Kshatriyas have an enviable mobility between and interaction with different groups and milieus, but their *purana* also achieves the effects of cultural mediation through intertextual surfaces. By "intertextual surface," I mean motifs and themes that emerge from, parallel, are opposed to, interrogate, or converge with other cultural texts, traditions, and narratives.[14] Themes from various classical texts that are bracketed off from each other historically or socially because of their literary history, period, language, or social spread are incorporated in the recitation and thereby dialogized. This incorporation is by no means discordant or chaotic, but deliberate in its efforts to achieve multivalence. Therefore, while listening to the epic, one cannot simply refer to Tamil *purana* or Kannada or Telugu epics; instead, one draws from a fund of motifs and images from various traditions and languages. This multivalence is specifically related to the urban nature of the performance. In the context of the city and given the diverse constituency of the audience, different themes of the recitation obviously appeal to the cultural memory of various listeners. Some are struck with the echoes of Villi's *Mahabharata* or that of Pampa. For others, Draupadi appears to be like the fierce goddess of the *Devi Mahatmya*. Throughout the recitation, the songs in Tamil salute the deity Rama, although it is to another avatar of Vishnu, Krishna, rather than Rama that the Pandavas are related. In the same way that it creates links to the larger world of Vaishnavism in its nonprose, Tamil sections, in the prose, Telugu sections the epic refers repeatedly to the figures of Shiva and Parvati. Draupadi as goddess is linked to these figures in several crucial ways, as I shall show later. It needs to be mentioned here, however, that the epic's ability to mediate several of the religious universes in south India parallels the way in which the text mediates other textual traditions. The Vahnikula Kshatriyas, in fact, see themselves as nonsectarian in contrast to many other communities in south India who are sometimes strongly Shaiva or Vaishnava.

Dramatis Personae

The recitation of the *Karaga Purana* cannot begin until the arrival of a chariot carrying the images of Arjuna and Draupadi (now duly married), the Karaga priest, other members of the troupe, and the drummers and horn players. A place is also made for the processional image of Potha Raja. The crowds who have slowly gathered over nine days for the procession have dispersed, and there are only a few people, besides the ritual players themselves, who hear the recitation of the *Karaga Purana*. To this audience, kings and divine beings mingling with commoners, the epic is recited with the accompaniment of a few simple musical instruments. The area surrounding the temple is quite silent; the hectic activities of the past few days are over. It bears all the debris of the events of the past few nights, including bananas thrown at the chariot by the crowds for luck and the fulfillment of wishes, jasmine buds, and food. Sleeping groups and workers from distant parts of the metropolis lie around. Gathered at the Elusuttinakote are forty to fifty persons, many of them from other communities, and in fact, most members of the Vahnikula Kshatriya community do not attend, worn out by the strenuous activities of the past nine days.

There are two groups of ritual players within the Karaga *jatre*, all of them members of the Vahnikula Kshatriya community, and both groups are present at the Elusuttinakote. The first group comprises the following: the goddess Draupadi and her bearer, the Karaga priest, the Gante Pujari, the Ganachari, the Virakumaras, and Potha Raja, a group that has mythic origins. Persons in the second group derive their roles as members of the Vahnikula Kshatriya community and have parts to play in other ritual and secular realms. This group includes the Gowda, the Kula Purohit, the Bankadasi, and the Kolkara.[15]

I have already dealt with the Virakumaras and the Karaga priest in previous chapters. Except for the role of Virakumara, which any adult male of the community may adopt, and that of Karaga priest, which belongs to certain families, the enactment of the roles of each of these players is the preserve of a few families belonging to households that have a common genealogical origin, usually from a male ancestor. There is one family designated as the Ganachari's family; one Gante Pujari family; two families each of Potha Raja, the Kolkaras and Bankadasis; and five Gowda families.[16]

The Ganachari is considered the "chieftain" of the lineage of Vahnikula Kshatriyas. He was the first to be born from Draupadi, and just as the deity Ganesha is propitiated before any other rituals are undertaken, the Ganachari is given first honors. He is the one who takes care of the religious matters of the community, and during the Karaga *jatre*, he accompanies the Karaga priest constantly, overseeing, as it were, all rites and rituals. On the Hasi Karaga day, he sits inside the tent in the pillared hall conducting rituals before the emergence of the Karaga. On the night of the procession, he is the only one allowed inside the sanctum along with one other player, and both together position the Karaga on the head of the priest.

The Gante Pujaris are those who emerged from the Primal Goddess ringing bells. There are usually three or four main persons who are Gante Pujaris. During the Karaga, they instruct the Karaga priest in various ritual observances, set up the altar on different days of the performance, sing an invocation to the goddess at the temple and at different sites, and, along with their bells, make the priest "dance" when he carries the icon. It is through their invocation and prayers that the goddess makes an appearance. The chief among them is known as the Durga Pujari (a reference to the *Devi Mahatmya* perhaps, and the worship of goddess Durga), and he is sometimes the one among the Gante Pujari family who recites the *Karaga Purana* on the day after the Karaga procession. The Durga Pujari is also the one who gives the Karaga priest the mystical formula, the "seed-word" *(bijakshara)*, as a preparatory aid so that he can come into contact with the Karaga.

Potha Raja's role is to see that all family and community rituals are carried out without impediment.[17] He is present in two primary modes during the Karaga *jatre:* as an image and in the role of a man or men who represent him. His image is taken out first during the Karaga procession, leading all the other idols, and must be generally present when other idols are. Throughout the festival, the man who represents Potha Raja is also constantly present at all the main rituals. During the sacrifice of the goat, "Potha Raja" (who is sometimes in reality two persons, but is referred to in the singular) is dressed up with an elaborate headdress of jasmine and sways and screams inside the temple. This state is usually described by the phrase, "The god has come," a phrase that suggests possession. There, a black goat is given to him, and blood is sucked from its neck. This act imitates the gift of a goat to Potha Raja, an event that is narrated in the *Karaga Purana.*

In addition to these persons, there is the Gowda, who is the headman of the Vahnikula Kshatriyas in the Tigalarapet area. He oversees, along with the temple trustees, all the arrangements for the Karaga *jatre.* The Bankadasi are three or four in number and play wind instruments somewhat like hunting horns meant to invoke the spirits. The Kolkar is a bearer of news about ritual events in the community. The Kula Purohit is a Brahmin who is present at the initiation of the Virakumaras, performs the fire sacrifice that is a preparation for the "marriage" of Draupadi and Arjuna on the last day of the performance, and purifies the flagpole before the flag is raised at the beginning of the festival. He is also the chief officiant at wedding ceremonies of Vahnikula Kshatriyas.

At the Elusuttinakote, having placed the Karaga in the temple the night before, the Karaga priest returns in fairly simple dress. He is still wearing the sari of the previous night, but the headdress has been removed, and he covers his head with a yellow scarf instead. He performs a rite to the small chariot containing the images of Arjuna and Draupadi, which has also arrived at the Elusuttinakote (see Figure 25), and to the image of Potha Raja, which is placed in front of the chariot. He sits down by the side of the chariot. Often during the recitation he can be noticed dozing, quite exhausted after the strenuous procession the previous night. After a salutation to the gods, the recitation at Elusuttinakote begins, bilingually, with the songs in Tamil and the prose in Telugu.[18]

The Recitation

A song:

I am a living being,
Have compassion on me, O Kind-Hearted One,
Please protect us, who are your children,
Give me the words to praise you,
I pray to you wholeheartedly,
Ganesha, who fulfills wishes, auspicious Ganesha, salutations to
     you,
The All-Pervasive One, salutations to you,
Rama Raghurama Jagatswami [The Master of the World].[19]

The prose:

Eminent people, relatives, and parents: I request you to forgive me even if there are some mistakes in my recitation and to bless me. This day I will narrate the story of Potha Raja. I will trace the beginnings of the Vahni Dynasty, narrate how it began and how it became eligible to serve the Mother. It is for this reason that we are reciting the epic today.

Gurulinga Raju was the son of Aralinga Raju. Shivalinga Raju was the son of Gurulinga Raju. Shivalinga Raju's son was Potha Raja. This is the dynasty of Utdanda Potha Raja.[20]

Now we come to the dynasty of Yayati. The father of Pandu, Chitrasena, and Vichitrasena was Santanu. Their father was of the family of

Figure 25. The Karaga priest arrives with the images of Arjuna and Draupadi to hear the oral epic.

Yayati. This was the son of Gangeya. Chandrasena also belonged to this dynasty. The Pandavas belonged to the Lunar Dynasty.

A song:
Our Rama, we who have unnecessarily played dice,
Our Rama, we have lost all our property and kingdom,
We take refuge in you, Rama Raghurama.

The prose:
The Pandavas of the Yayati Dynasty and Dharmananda [Dharmaraja] ruled the kingdom of Hastinapura that is our present Old Delhi and New Delhi. Duryodhana [the eldest of the one hundred Kaurava brothers] wanted to acquire half of this kingdom at any price. With this in mind, Duryodhana invited the Pandavas for a feast on a festival day. At this meal, they were served a sweet dish mixed with poison. Bhima, being a voracious eater, ate a lot of the sweet and fell unconscious. At this moment, his enemies threw him into a river. Krishna [who was a cousin of the Pandavas] and Vidura [the uncle of the Pandavas] saw this. They saved Bhima and blessed him with prosperity in the future.

The Pandavas had played dice and lost all of their kingdom and property and were sent into exile. When they completed their tenth year and entered their eleventh year of exile, the gods, the sun, the moon, and others sang in praise:

A song:
Our Rama, the dweller of Dwaraka [the capital city of Krishna],
Our Rama, the Blue-Skinned One,
Rama Raghurama Jagatswami.

The prose:
All the gods came to Dharmananda and Draupadi in the forest and pleaded that they be saved from the two demons, Ambasura and Timirasura. These demons were drinking and making merry. Whenever Ambasura would get angry, he would go and fight with the gods, rob their treasures and bring it back with him. Timirasura was the elder of the two demons and spent his time with women and wine. So one day, the gods came to the Pandavas and pleaded that Bhima and Draupadi should do something about Timirasura. Timirasura had a boon from a god that he could not be killed by anyone other than the Mother, the Supreme Strength and Light. He got this

boon through penance. When the gods complained, Dharmananda called out to Krishna:

A song:
Our Rama, the dweller of Dwaraka,
Our Rama, the Blue-Skinned One,
Our Rama, with Garuda [his eagle mount] as his vehicle,
Our Rama, who stood by us,
Our savior, Rama, we take refuge in you,
The gods, and eight guardians of directions, praise you thus.
Rama Raghurama, our hands pray to Krishna,
Rama, through whom we can attain salvation,
Rama, through whom we can increase our vigor,
Rama, through whom we can increase our wealth,
Raghurama, we take refuge in you.

The prose:
Lord Krishna said: "This Timirasura cannot be killed by anyone except a woman." So Lord Krishna directed Draupadi to kill the demon. He blessed her and sent her to kill Timirasura.

There are two mountains, Endagiri and Suvarnagiri. This is where Parvati and Shiva live. In a cave below this mountain the demon Ambasura had made his dwelling. He had collected all the wild animals that he had killed and stored them in his cave. When Shiva used to come down the mountain to bless people, Ambasura, triumphantly twirling his mustache, ate their animals. Parvati smelled this meat and said to Shiva: "We have Shaivas [devotees of Shiva] living here, and this demon is eating nonvegetarian food. Is there no solution to this problem?"

Then Shiva said to Parvati: "Oh Parvati! A woman's mind is narrow and moves like a fish in water." He told her that she was always creating some problem or the other. He then brought a huge boulder and blocked the cave after pushing the demon inside it. The demon was imprisoned inside the cave for three days. He was not able to push the boulder aside. He kept peeping through a small hole to see if some passersby could save him.

Draupadi was passing through this way on her path to kill Timirasura. There was a footpath next to the mountain that Draupadi took. She heard someone calling out to her but could not see anyone when she looked around her. Then Ambasura told the Mother that he was behind the rock. Ambasura said: "Oh Mother, Oh Mother! I am behind this boulder. Shiva has pushed me inside. I have been here for three full days. Please help me move this boulder!" Draupadi tried but was not able to move the huge rock. She then prayed to Lord Krishna:

A song:
Our Rama, the dweller of Dwaraka,
Our Rama, the Blue-Skinned One,
Our Rama, who has Garuda as his vehicle,
I meditate on you, Rama Raghurama Jagatswami.

The prose:
Then Draupadi kicked the boulder away with the tip of her toe. Ambasura said: "Oh Shiva! You have locked me in for three days in the cave without food or water. Therefore, I take a vow that I will cause obstacles in your penances. Otherwise, I am not fit to call myself 'Ambasura'!"

When Draupadi was proceeding to fight Timirasura, Ambasura said: "Mother, you have saved me from three days of starvation. So I will follow you wherever you go." Draupadi told him that she was going to battle and asked if he would follow her. Ambasura agreed. This Ambasura or Potha Raja trailed behind Draupadi. They found Timirasura surrounded by women, drinking wine, and making merry. Draupadi wondered how this intoxicated fellow would be able to fight her. She called out to him three times: "Hey, demon! Hey demon! Hey demon!" There was no response from Timirasura. Then Draupadi shot an arrow at him. The problem was that Draupadi did not follow the rule that she should prostrate herself and pray before shooting the arrow, the correct method. Timirasura saw the arrow fall in front of him. He thought: "What? Has a woman come to fight me?" And he asked her to turn back. Then Draupadi got very angry. She was standing on a small mound. She shot a second arrow that pierced Timirasura's right shoulder. It started bleeding. Wherever a drop of blood fell, an army of men sprang up. Then Draupadi realized that Timirasura was no ordinary man; he was a demon whose every drop of blood gave rise to hundreds of men. She prayed to Krishna:

A song:
Our Rama, the dweller of Dwaraka,
Our Rama, the Blue-Skinned One,
Rama, to you I pray.

The prose:

She took another arrow and shot it at Timirasura's neck. The demon prayed, and this turned into a garland. Timirasura smiled and said that he was one who had the powers of illusion and other special powers and told Draupadi that she could not harm him. He then advanced on her. Draupadi, thinking about how a drop of the demon's blood gave rise to hundreds of soldiers and warriors, had to devise another plan.

She assumed her cosmic form. She lifted one lip toward the sky and another toward the underworld. She spread her tongue on the earth. All the warriors who emerged from the demon's blood came rushing toward her shouting. Draupadi gathered them onto her tongue along with Timirasura in the middle. She cut off the head of the demon and threw it across the seven seas. Then she swallowed all of them whole. Rama Raghurama Jagatswami!

During the battle, the portion of Draupadi's sari draped across the breasts fell and split into three pieces. When the first piece fell, the Ganachari was born. When the second piece fell, the Gante Pujaris were born and began to ring their bells and pray to the Mother. When the third piece fell, 101 Virakumaras were born. They shouted: "Alla Lalla Lalla Di" [a magical formula] and started fighting alongside the Mother. Even then nothing happened, which is why Mother spread her tongue on the earth and swallowed all the demons. She protects her children, and that is why we sing: "Mother, who emerged from the fire, Divine Mother, to you we do ritual oblations."

Everyone was afraid that Draupadi would enter the city in her cosmic form and destroy people there. So Brahma [the Creator] came and tried to entice and pacify the Mother to become her normal self. This did not work. Then Shiva [the Destroyer] came and asked her to put an end to her form, but that also did not work. Then Vishnu [the Preserver] came down and said: "Oh, Mother! Why are you so angry? Calm yourself down." With this, the Mother was pacified. The Ganachari, the Gante Pujaris, and the 101 Virakumaras also sang together in praise of the Mother:

A song (to Draupadi):

Our Mother, Saraswati [the goddess of learning and the wife of the
    Creator],
Mother, you are the only one to ward off obstacles,
Mother, you were born out of fire,
Mother, you are worthy of ritual oblations,
Mother, you are the wife of the five brothers,
Mother, we welcome you, Supreme Mother,

Mother, the wife of the Pandavas who went to the forest,
Mother, you are a source of support for our lineage,
Mother, we welcome you,
Mother, we will not forget your feet,
Mother, as followers, we will not forget your greatness.

The prose:

In this way, everyone meditated on the Mother. The 101 Virakumaras chanted: "Govinda, Govinda" and "Alla Lalla Lalla Di." This chant is so powerful that it can pacify the Goddess. The Mother gave up her cosmic form and returned to her earlier one. She looked around her and saw her sons. She made up her mind to bless them and guide them in the right path. She materialized figures of the five Pandavas and Draupadi; these images were given to the Virakumaras. She asked them to meditate on her and become gardeners. She pacified all of them and went back. Even the demon Ambasura went on his way.

One day, Parvati and Shiva were strolling in the forest, and Parvati asked Shiva: "Can I ask a question?" Shiva said: "A woman's mind, a small mind, the mind of a fish in the water, all these are one and the same! Ask me your question, and I shall try to reveal whatever I can." Parvati said: "Shiva, here in the forest where sages are doing penance, the animals are mating and are very happy; when I see all this, I also desire intercourse." Shiva said: "A woman's mind, a small mind, the mind of a fish in the water, all these are one and the same! For a woman, the sari itself is ornamentation. It is not proper that you should have intercourse whenever you feel like it." But Parvati insisted on this.

Then the two took the form of eagles, flew in the sky, and mated there. During this procedure, a drop of semen fell on the ground. Ambasura, the demon, was watching, took the form of a three-month-old baby, swallowed the semen and started crying. When Parvati and Shiva came down, they saw this baby and Shiva said: "I told you that a demon could be watching us and that unforeseen things could happen, but you did not listen!" Parvati, however, was attracted to the baby and put him on her lap. The baby played there. Then Parvati and Shiva took the baby and placed it in front of their house so that they would not get a bad name. Since the demon had the powers of illusion and was a receiver of boons, he grew in one day how much he should have grown in many years.

During the churning of the ocean of milk [at the beginning of creation], the snake that was used as a rope spat out poison. In order to save the world from becoming poisonous, Lord Shiva drank up the poison and

Parvati stopped the poison in his neck with her hand. The neck became blue, and thus Shiva came to be known as "Nilakantha" [the Blue-Throated One]. Lord Krishna took the form of the damsel Mohini and distributed the nectar, playfully avoiding giving the nectar to the demons and only giving it to the gods. At this moment, a demon joined the gods by the process of illusion and drank up some of the nectar. Vishnu in the form of Mohini, realizing what had happened, sent his discus to kill the demons. The demons ran hither and thither. The discus returned to Vishnu; he aimed it again at the demon who had joined the gods, and it cut his body in two—the head and the rest. From this were born Rahu and Ketu.

Ambasura, who was a child now, was always outside the house. He was always in search of food. The gods who came to visit Shiva came riding on some animal or the other. When they were inside with him, the baby devoured the animals. Devendra came on his horse, and the baby devoured it. Yama came on a buffalo, and that too was eaten. After two days of this, Yama decided to keep watch and see who was killing all the animals. Looking through a small hole in the door, he saw that the baby had transformed itself into a demon and was swallowing the buffalo whole. So he caught hold of the animal's legs and called out to Shiva. Shiva came out and saw that the demon had devoured most of the buffalo, and only the tail and the hind legs were left. Shiva then said to Yama: "Leave him alone or he will devour you too! He is a demon, and his only aim was to spoil my penance. We cannot keep him here anymore. When Devendra left his horse here, he ate it up; he ate up your buffalo as well." Shiva decided that the baby would have to be sent away.

At this juncture, Aralinga Raju's son Gurulinga Raju, Gurulinga Raju's son Shivalinga Raju, lived in the city of Kalyanapuri or Shivananda Pattana. The whole city was built within a fortress. Shivalinga Raju and Kalyani Devi were ruling the kingdom. Around this fortress, Parvati had drawn a decorative pattern made from rice flour.[21] The couple did not have children and were engaged in penance for a child. Shiva went to them and handed over the three-month-old child and asked them to take care of it. At the same time, Parvati gave a ripe mango to Kalyani Devi and asked her to eat it after prayers, and from this was born a daughter.[22] Shivalinga Raju and Kalyani were proud of their son and praised the Lord:

A song:
Our Rama, dweller of Dwaraka,
Rama, they strung out pearls,
Rama, they tied festoons,

Rama, they heaped up pearls,
Rama, they drew decorative patterns,
Rama, the city was the abode of happiness,
Rama, all the people of the city blessed the child,
Rama Raghurama Jagatswami.

The prose:

All the people celebrated the birth of a son to Shivalinga Raju and Kalyani. They sang lullabies and praised the child. The sages, however, said that this child was a demon and asked what harm it could do in the future.

The baby, Potha Raja, grew up, and at the age of twelve, in the prime of his youth, began to rule the kingdom. The Pandavas were in their tenth year of exile. Bhima was a voracious eater and was used to princely fare. In the forest, he would divide the food into half for the five others and keep the other half for himself. One day he got an urge to eat rich food and told his brother this; his brother said that this was not possible, as they had lost their kingdom and property. Bhima then replied that he would go in search of food.

In the forest, Bhima saw a person with legs like coconut trees, hands like banana trees, and a head the size of a mountain standing in the midst of trees which were either dried up or burnt. Bhima bent and collected the dried wood and tied it into a bundle sixty measures in width and ninety-six measures long. But he was not able to lift the bundle. He looked around him to see if anyone was there to help. Lord Krishna decided to teach him a lesson and came in the guise of an old man. Bhima shouted out to him for help to lift the bundle. The old man said that this was not possible and asked: "Who is your father who created such a bundle?" Bhima then remembered his father [Vayu, the wind god], and Krishna disappeared. When he contemplated his father, a whirlwind appeared and lifted the whole bundle into the sky, and Bhima put it on his head. He walked toward Shivananda Pattana. Cowherds in the hills who saw him got fearful and ran into the city shouting that this was a demon with a devilish bundle. Bhima went to the fortress and put down his wood against the walls.

The fortress around which Parvati had drawn a pattern crumbled. Potha Raja came out angrily and asked: "Who is this who has destroyed my fortress?" He saw Bhima, beat him, and put him into prison for three days without food and water. Bhima meditated while imprisoned: three drops of honey fell down from the sky, he licked that, his hunger was satisfied, and he went to sleep. Dharmaraja, Arjuna, Nakula, Sahadeva [the other Pandava brothers], and Draupadi were all concerned about Bhima. They all meditated on Lord Krishna:

A song:
Our Rama, the dweller of Dwaraka,
Rama, the Blue-Skinned One,
Rama, on whom we meditate,
Rama, our savior who gives us salvation,
Rama, who increases our valor,
Rama Raghurama Jagatswami.

The prose:
Then Krishna arrived on his vehicle, Garuda. The brothers collected jasmine and different varieties of flowers and showered it on his feet and prostrated themselves before him. Krishna told them that Bhima was safe and was in the fort of Shivananda Pattana. He said that Potha Raja was a strong, clever king and one who had received many boons. Therefore, they had to think of a plan to get Bhima out by cheating Potha Raja. Then Krishna and Arjuna bathed in the Kalyani River, sprinkled water on themselves, and turned into women—Krishna into an old lady and Arjuna into a twelve-year-old girl. They went around the city shouting: "Combs for sale!"

Potha Raja was twelve years old, in his prime, full of passion, his eyes red. He was sitting on the wall of his fort. The two nomad women were going around, and Potha Raja ordered two peons to bring them to him.[23] The women went to him and told him that the husband of the younger woman had been missing for three days and they were searching for him. The king was enamored of the girl and asked: "Is your husband so handsome that you are going in search of him?" The young girl replied: "Yes. He has legs like the coconut tree, hands like the banana tree, and his head is as big as a mountain." Then the king told her that there was a man in his jail who resembled the description that she had given him. The king asked a peon to accompany the women and show them the man in prison. The young girl admitted that the person was her husband. Then Potha Raja said: "You are so beautiful and petite and this man is so huge like a demon. How is this?" For when Arjuna donned a woman's guise, he became brighter than the sun and the moon. Potha Raja said: "I will release your husband if you fulfill my desire." The young girl agreed and asked the king to come to the second hut where she was staying, which was among six other huts, and shout: "Billa bai paducha" [reference unclear, although this was described as a magical verse]. The king released the husband, and the girl and the old lady took Bhima away. Bhima realized the true identity of the women and was overjoyed that his brothers had come to save him.

Krishna knew that Potha Raja had in his possession two Shiva *linga* [phalluses, each a representation of Shiva], a trident, a drum, and five sacred images in his prayer room and that he performed rituals to them every morning before sitting on the fort.[24] Bhima and Arjuna expressed their desire to see the prayer room, and once inside they carried away these articles. Potha Raja told them that he would definitely come in the night to their hut and the young girl must satisfy his desire. Everyone left the palace. Dharmananda was very pleased at the safe return of his brothers. He reminded them that they were in exile and that they must not be recognized by anyone.

Potha Raja went in the middle of the night to the second hut and called out: "Billa bai paducha!" Bhima was sleeping in the second hut; he came out and carried Potha Raja without any effort to the platform of the peepal [the sacred fig tree]. He beat him, but Potha Raja did not retaliate; he was a tiger behaving like a cat. Sitting on the wall of his fortress later, he met the women again, who asked him why he had not come to their hut. Why had he gone to the second hut when they had asked him to come to the third hut? They invited him to come to the third hut that night. This set of events occurred the next night as well. The third night, the women told Potha Raja that they would definitely fulfill his desire that night and that he should come to their hut again.

Potha Raja had a sister, Nagalamuddamma, who emerged from the mango fruit given to Kalyani by Parvati. This baby used to cry throughout the night and did not allow anyone to sleep. Potha Raja waited till his parents fell asleep, took an ax, and cut their throats. Then he took the baby on his shoulder and went to the hut. There he gave a leaf from which milk trickled to the baby to suckle so that she would not cry.[25] He then went to the fourth hut. Arjuna and Bhima decided that this was a good time to attack Potha Raja again; they carried him to the peepal tree and beat him with tamarind tree twigs. Potha Raja was hurt badly and in great pain. He then resorted to his cosmic form. Bhima caught hold of one of the plaits of the hair of this form and twisted him around as if he were a toy. This fight continued till each of the three plaits was severed and returned to the three gods: one plait to Shiva, one to Vishnu, and one to Brahma. The gods complained that their disciples were fighting among themselves and someone should put an end to this battle.

Parvati then claimed Potha Raja as her son and gave him refuge. The entire area became covered with a forest of leaves, and its cover protected Potha Raja. This forest, except for Bhima and Potha Raja, who came outside it, covered everyone. The huts, Dharmananda, everything was covered by leaves. Then Krishna thought it over and said to Dharmananda that Potha Raja was the type of person who had decapitated his own parents. Unless he was married he would continue to trouble all the brothers in the future. Dharmananda said he would agree to whatever plan Krishna suggested. Then Krishna brought forth Shankavalli [the sister of the Pandavas] from his conch.

When King Pandu died, the water on his chest was collected and poured into a conch and given to Ganga, the river. Nobody even realized that the Pandavas had a sister. Krishna transformed her into a goat and let her graze on the leaves. Wherever the goat defecated after grazing, a Shiva *linga* emerged. The demon wondered how it was that this forest and mountain of leaves was reduced to nothing. He wanted to catch the goat. Dharmananda and others watched this. Another goat was materialized, and Shankavalli was replaced by it. The story of the event being narrated today—the sacrifice of the goat—is the event that will occur after the recitation is over.

Dharmananda and Krishna, after discussions with all the gods, performed the marriage of Potha Raja with Shankavalli saying that the time was auspicious. Nagalamuddamma had been left at the side of the Ashwatha [peepal] tree when Potha Raja began his fight with Bhima. The gods decided that Nagalamuddamma should marry Dharmananda, since he would not have a marriage in the future [reference unclear]. He tied the marriage necklace around Nagalamuddamma. Rama Raghurama Jagatswami! The time was good, and the stars were auspicious, and the marriages of Dharmananda and Potha Raja were performed. All the gods blessed the two couples.

A song:

Rama, the one who strung the pearls,
Rama, the one who tied the festoons,
Rama, the one who heaped the pearls,
Rama, the one who drew the decorative pattern,
Rama, the one who performed the weddings of Dharmananda and
    Potha Raja.

A song:

Our Mother, Saraswati,
Mother, you are the only one to ward off obstacles,

Mother, you were born out of fire,
Mother, you are worthy of ritual oblations,
Mother, you are the wife of the five brothers,
Mother, we welcome you, Supreme Mother,
Mother, the wife of the Pandavas who went to the forest,
Mother, you are a source of support for our lineage,
Mother, we welcome you,
Mother, we will not forget your feet,
Mother, as followers, we will not forget your greatness.

The recitation by the Gante Pujari ended thus, with the Gante Pujari's sons and nephews singing a hymn in praise of Draupadi. Everyone shouted: "Govinda, Govinda!" The Gante Pujari then said: "We have tried to explain to the best of our knowledge the greatness of Draupadi and why this ritual is performed. We hope that everyone will benefit from it. We surrender to Krishna!" The Karaga priest broke a coconut in front of the idols and performed a rite. By now it was dawn, and the audience made their way back home or to the temple. They were preceded by the image of Potha Raja, who was carried aloft by one of the men, the chariot (the Karaga priest sat perched on the chariot with the images of Draupadi and Arjuna), and the musicians.

Intertextual Surfaces

The beginning of the recitation frames the *Karaga Purana* within two narratives: the story of Potha Raja, and the origin of the Vahnikula lineage and their relationship to the Mother, Draupadi, as Primal Goddess. There is a bifurcation in the recitation between the forest and the fort-city of Shivananda Pattana as the sites of the two narratives. The origin of the Vahnikulas from Draupadi as Primal Goddess in the forest leads into the fort-city of Potha Raja, where the Pandavas encounter, dupe, battle, and then strike an alliance with Potha Raja. Draupadi and the Vahnikula Kshatriyas disappear from the stage of the fort-city, whereas the Pandavas, who are only nominally present in the forest, appear more strongly in Shivananda Pattana. The connection between the two appears to be the demon Ambasura who, having accompanied Draupadi in her battle against Timirasura in the forest, reappears as the son of Shivalinga Raju, now renamed Potha Raja, in the fort-city. Draupadi, who transforms herself into her cosmic form and then back again, is absent from Shivananda Pattana, but in her place is Arjuna dressed in woman's guise as a nomad, recalling the story of

Draupadi the gypsy. This doubleness of the demon and the doubleness of Draupadi's identity (and others' identities) are themes of central importance in the recitation, as is the duality of the topos.

The recitation initially locates the Pandavas in the kingdom and the city of Hastinapura. There, the brothers lose their kingdom ignominiously to their cousins, the Kauravas. This act immediately shifts the scene of the recitation from the city to the forest, where the Pandavas must spend several years in exile. In the topos of the forest, the central character is Draupadi. She appears in the epic in various bodies, chiefly that of the Primal Goddess, whose main role is to vanquish demons. Rao (1978, 12–17), for instance, states that the origins of the Karaga performance as a whole and its various players can be traced to two episodes of the *Mahabharata:* one that is found in the *Adi Parvan* in the southern rescension and another that is not found in the classical version. The first is the event of Draupadi's marriage and her union with the five Pandava brothers. Here Rao introduces a story of how Draupadi was the daughter of a sage in her previous birth. She prayed that she might find a husband who was the repository of all virtues. Shiva, responding to her prayers, said that not one, but only five husbands would be able to fulfill this requirement. In her next birth, she was born out of the sacrificial fire of her royal father and came to marry the five brothers.[26] The Karaga performance, he claims, speaks of the marriage of Draupadi. The second episode occurs when the Pandavas are on their way to heaven. Draupadi is the first to fall on the journey; the brothers leave her behind, thinking that she is dead, and move on. However, she is only unconscious, and when she comes to, she is faced with Timirasura, a demon who covets her and wishes to carry her away. She then assumes the form of the Primal Goddess and kills him. The Virakumaras are present with her at this battle. Rao points out that, etymologically, the demon's name suggests "darkness," and therefore the Karaga procession, which begins at night and returns to the temple at dawn after a tour of the city, is representative of the victory of light (and the Primal Goddess) over darkness.

Yet within the *Karaga Purana* itself, no mention is made of the incident of journeying to heaven or of the marriage of Draupadi that Rao cites. Instead, as Hiltebeitel (1988a, 8) points out, the forest Draupadi is one who goes beyond her role as portrayed in the classical *Mahabharata* and instead is a heroic, fierce form. The effort of the oral epic seems to be to use and transform motifs from other classical traditions. In the *Devi Mahatmya*, for example, Devi is said to underlie or pervade the cosmos, and she assumes different forms to maintain the cosmic balance that is threatened by enemies. In different episodes of the text, different battles are featured, but the third episode is one in which the goddess Kali appears as an ema-nation of Devi in her battle against the demons Canda and Munda. During the battle, a group of seven goddesses known as Mothers also appear cre-ated from certain male gods.[27] The key episode in the *Karaga Purana* that speaks of the origins of the Vahnikula Kshatriyas is the one in which Drau-padi, in her cosmic form as the Primal Goddess, fights and vanquishes Timirasura. The demons Ambasura and Timirasura resemble the demons Canda and Munda, whom Kali defeats in battle. The term *kali* etymologi-cally means "the dark or blue-black one"; to the extent that it is related to the masculine noun *kala*, it shares the meaning of "time" or "the fullness of time," and, by implication, time that "brings all things to an end, the de-stroyer."[28] Draupadi, sometimes known as "Krishnaa" in south India, is also the dark one, and in the role as the vanquisher of Timirasura she is akin to Kali. In the *Devi Mahatmya*, Kali defeats the two demons Canda and Munda, and because of this deed, Kali is known as Chamunda. Another demon in the *Devi Mahatmya*, Raktabija, who has been difficult to defeat because each drop of his blood gives rise to others like him, is also killed, because Kali drinks up his blood and his offspring.[29] In the *Karaga Purana*, Drau-padi slays a similar type of demon that seems to inhabit a region near the mountains on which Shiva and Parvati reside.[30] Draupadi, in her cosmic form, is linked to the goddess Kali by two other features. Kali is represented with unbound hair and a lolling tongue, which characterize her nontradi-tional and liminal character.[31] Although in the *Karaga Purana* there are no indications of the first, the Karaga priest's hair is supposed to be unbound, and in fact, his headdress of jasmine, which reaches down to his feet on Hasi Karaga day, is said to represent the unbound hair of the goddess Draupadi.[32] Although the unbound hair may allude to a social distinction—for instance, married women do not keep their hair unbraided—it also suggests a cosmic dimension. Kinsley (1997, 84) states: "Considering Kali's identification with the cremation ground and death, her loose hair may suggest the end of the world." Hiltebeitel (1981, 186–87) also points out that this unbound hair is related to Draupadi's appearance in the assembly hall after her husband wagers and loses her in a game of dice; she is made to undress, and her unbound hair suggests that she is menstruating. Many Vahnikula Kshatriya informants relate the unbound hair to a vow that Draupadi makes that she will bind up her hair only with the blood of the Kaurava responsible for her humiliation, a theme that is present in the *Ma-habharata* of Villiputtur Alvar. The image of the lolling tongue appears in the *Karaga Purana* when, in her cosmic form, the Primal Goddess spreads her tongue on the ground and swallows up the demon. The tongue can also signify tasting the forbidden and the polluted as well as a desire for sexual gratification.[33]

The spilling of the demon's blood reinforces the connectivity of blood and other substances, such as food and semen, that has appeared in a different manner in the Karaga *jatre* so far—for instance, through the Virakumaras' training in the gymnasium and the priest's transformation through contact with the Karaga. As Shulman points out (1980, 90–97; 103–8; 131–34), in the Shaiva *purana* tradition, sacrifice is needed for the creation of new life. The symbol of the new life produced from the sacrifice is the fiery seed equated to the remainder of the sacrifice after all oblations have been made. This sacrifice is needed for the foundation of a shrine and also for the origin of a dynasty, and Tamil folk traditions also offer numerous examples of the idea that blood sacrifice is needed for the construction of a sacred edifice. Two traditions are thus combined here: Vedic sacrificial concepts are joined with ancient Tamil ones in which blood is regarded as the source of life. For instance, the shedding of blood in war is equated to the harvest of grain or the production of food from the soil. Blood sacrifices are also offered to memorial stones erected in honor of dead heroes. Creation by blood is seen as an alternative to sexual procreation. The blood of a sacrificial victim (a goat or a buffalo) is often drunk by one or more participants in rituals or poured into the mouth of the image of the goddess so that the power and life force of the victim may be transferred to the goddess or the participants.

The sacrificial victim who is also the seed of new life in the *Karaga Purana* is the demon Timirasura, who is a "Raktabija" (literally, blood-seed) whose every drop of blood produces more prototypes like him. This sacrifice leads to procreation, and in the *Karaga Purana* the moment of sacrifice of the demon is also one in which the goddess's sari, draped across her breasts, splits into three pieces.[34] This tripartite separation strikes a parallel with other Tamil narratives. In the moment of the sacrifice, women can lose a breast, as in the myth cited by Shulman (1980) about the goddess Minakshi, who loses one of three breasts and is transformed from being an embodiment of abnormal womanhood into another state. The reverse is also possible. In the third-century Tamil epic *Silappadikaram*, the heroine Kannaki tears off her left breast after a miscarriage of justice and hurls it at the city of Madurai, whence it burns in a fire.

Just as in the Dharmaraja Temple sanctum Draupadi is depicted as both the spouse of the Pandavas and the Primal Goddess, at the moment of sacrifice of the demon in the *Karaga Purana*, Draupadi reveals herself in her cosmic form. The moment of revelation is also the moment of origin of the Virakumaras and the other ritual players of the *jatre*. The thirst of the Primal Goddess for blood is ultimately pacified by the presence of her children, who sing her praise, and she gives up her cosmic form and is transformed back into Draupadi. She grants them ritual figures of the five Pandavas and Draupadi and urges them to become gardeners. The ritual objects will reappear in Potha Raja's possession in the second part of the recitation.

This doubling of Draupadi, as spouse and Primal Goddess, is embedded in bodily disguise: the terrible goddess in her cosmic form returns to her guise as Draupadi after giving birth nongenitally and from her breasts to the hero-sons and the other ritual players in the Karaga performance.[35] Meanwhile, the procession the night prior to the narration has ended with the wedding of the goddess and the transformation of the priest into a woman as her power moves through his form while he bears the icon.[36] The doubling of demons in the *Karaga Purana* parallels this disguise. Tamil myths, according to Shulman (1980), reveal an attempt to remove a male deity from the arena of sacrifice, which is considered partly polluting because of the sacrificial act. This removal occurs through a surrogate, who might be a bull, a devotee, a human, or a demonic enemy. Lurking beneath the surface is always the identity between the surrogate and the deity. In the case of the *Karaga Purana*, it appears that the sacrificial surrogate is at least double, if not multiple. There is one demon, Ambasura, who is the enemy of Shiva because Shiva has imprisoned him in a cave, but becomes an attendant of the Primal Goddess; there is another demon, Timirasura, who is the enemy of the goddess and whom she slays; and there is the mysterious demonlike Potha Raja.

The slaying of the demon by a goddess is embodied, above all, in the myth of Chamundeshwari and Mahisasura, where the buffalo-demon, Mahisasura, is a potential suitor. He is challenged to a contest and dies at the hands of the goddess. At the moment of death, it is revealed that he bears or wears a sign of identification with Shiva, whose devotee he is. Therefore, his death is tantamount to the murder of Shiva, whom the goddess seeks as a mate.[37] In the *Karaga Purana*, the linkage of the buffalo-demon with Ambasura and Potha Raja is made in several sections of the tale, although initially Timirasura is identified as the main demon killed by the goddess. On Timirasura's death, the narration moves to the story of Ambasura and Potha Raja (see Figure 26). Ambasura swallows a drop of Shiva's semen during the intercourse of Shiva and Parvati, a tale that is similar to the popular tale of the birth of Shiva and Parvati's son, Skanda, due to an interruption of their lovemaking. Ambasura thus reveals that he is iden-

Figure 26. The image of Potha Raja.

tified with Shiva, having swallowed a drop of Shiva's semen. The demon is called Ambasura while he is in the forest. When he takes his place in Shivananda Pattana with foster parents, he is called Potha Raja. The disguise of the goddess is matched by the duplicity of the demon. The identification of Ambasura/Potha Raja with the buffalo—he almost eats it whole—and the connection to the buffalo-demon is therefore made quite eloquently.

The recitation thus seems to split the epic into two parts: the first, where the central parallels are the *Devi Mahatmya* and Tamil *purana;* and the second, which resembles certain street dramas from the Draupadi cult in Tamil Nadu in which Potha Raja is a central figure. However, the period of wandering and disguise that is the main motif of the *Karaga Purana* allows the entire story to be constructed in terms of episodes in which the characters who appear in one are paired with characters in the other, as is the case with the pair Ambasura and Potha Raja. Again, the Primal Goddess and Draupadi, as well as Shiva and Krishna, appear as pairs. There is also an internal pairing that takes place in each episode: Ambasura and Timirasura, Krishna and Arjuna, Potha Raja and Dharmaraja, and Draupadi and Ambasura. This kind of pairing has the effect of urging the audience to make narrative connections with other episodes and myths as well as endowing each event with irony through various strategies. If A of one episode is also B of another, this double-voicedness brings in a certain narrative ambiguity and open-endedness. There is another type of pairing that is referred to by members of the Vahnikula Kshatriya community: Potha Raja is supposed to have become the commander-in-chief of the Pandava army after the marriage alliance with the Pandavas' sister. This is reminiscent of Draupadi's brother Dhrishtadyumna, also born of fire, who, in the Sanskrit version of the *Mahabharata,* is the chief of the army. A further type of pairing is that of sex reversal, which can suggest an internal pairing within the body; for instance, Vishnu gives rise to the form of Mohini or the disguise of Arjuna as a woman.[38]

The "civilizing" of Potha Raja (through battle and, finally, through a marriage alliance with the Pandavas) within the frame of the *Karaga Purana* is the central element of the latter portion of the epic. The conquest of the demon-king by the goddess is a motif that is more common to a settled population than to pastoral groups.[39] The Vahnikula Kshatriyas are explicitly such a population, as is their audience, and it is particularly appropriate that the story should end with the incorporation of Potha Raja by Draupadi's spouses. The domestication of Potha Raja, believed to be a local ruler of the area that is now Bangalore, by the heroes of the *Mahabharata* parallels the localization of the epic story by the *Karaga Purana.* There is another aspect of this localization. The incorporation of Potha Raja through marriage at the end of the tale moves the *Karaga Purana* back from the forest to the city, just as the city had been replaced by the forest at the beginning of the narrative.

Bhima mediates the movement from forest to city. Bhima, the son of the god of wind, is, like wind and air, an active ingredient in the epic. He gathers wood in the forest and, with the assistance of his father in the form of a whirlwind, he carries the wood to the city. He sets it up against the walls of the fort, an action that mimics the carrying of the bamboo from the forest to the temple at the beginning of the *jatre*. Potha Raja imprisons him because his actions lead to the fall of the fort walls. Bhima also resembles Potha Raja/Ambasura in that he is a voracious eater. In the recitation that follows these events, two marriages occur in a classical south Indian pattern of sister exchange: Potha Raja's sister marries Dharmaraja, and Dharmaraja's sister marries Potha Raja.[40] This is similar to the patterns of marriage in the Vahnikula Kshatriya community. [41] In a general sense, one marriage necessarily leads to other alliances given the system of preferential mating in this part of south India.[42] These lead to a system where two people may be related in more ways than one.

Potha Raja's marriage is a substitute for Potha Raja's desire for Arjuna in the guise of a nomad woman whose combs are marks of fortune-telling abilities.[43] The guise of a nomad woman that Arjuna adopts when he moves from the forest to the city is similar to the disguise of Draupadi as gypsy in the "gypsy cycle" recited in the Karaga *jatre*, when she travels from her exile in the forest to the city of Hastinapura. If the disguise of Arjuna and Krishna evoke the disguise of Draupadi as gypsy, they also allude to a vow that Draupadi has made to dress her unbound hair with the blood of the Kaurava brother responsible for her humiliation using a comb made from his ribs. Hiltebeitel (1991a, 404–5) states that in a chapbook drama called *Turopatai Kuravanci* Draupadi, disguised as a gypsy fortune-teller, tells Duryodhana's wife and mother of his fate: she will tie up her hair after the battle is over on the battlefield, taking up a handful of his blood and separating his ribs for a comb. Hiltebeitel points out that it is usually Krishna who ties her hair up with red or orange flowers. The phrase "combs for sale" thus is a sinister and bloody allusion to Draupadi even though she is absent from the events in this part of the narration.[44]

Potha Raja's sources of strength are objects that resemble the *sacra* carried by the Karaga troupe during the *jatre*, including a trident, a drum, and five images, part of the mobile altar carried by the Gante Pujari. The idols in Potha Raja's prayer room are also reminiscent of the images given by Draupadi to the gardeners in the epic, although in the story here, the Pandavas steal these *sacra* from Potha Raja. The action in the forest by Draupadi is paralleled by the Pandavas in the city. The theft of the *sacra* weakens Potha Raja so that his adversaries can humiliate him.

Potha Raja beheads his foster parents, an act that is a prelude to the revelation of his true form. The manifestation of his cosmic form is similar to that of Draupadi as the Primal Goddess except that in the city Potha Raja holds center stage. The reference to the plaits of Potha Raja suggests not only hairiness, which in many local cults is associated with demonic and bestial qualities, but also a connection with three gods and perhaps the signs of special powers from them that returned after the plaits were severed.[45] The theme of hair continues, obliquely, in the next prose section. Parvati, coming to Potha Raja's rescue, covers the entire area with a forest of leaves. As Olivelle (1998, 29–30) suggests, hair is frequently associated with grass and plants in myths and rituals: there is the association in the *Rig Veda* (8.91.5–6) between hair on the head and in the pubic region and grass in fields. Other texts link the hair of the creator to vegetation and fertility. The cover of vegetation that Parvati offers Potha Raja when she claims him "as her son" implies fertility and hair; earlier, as Ambasura, he has "played in her lap."

Potha Raja, in the heat of passion, kills his parents. This shedding of blood has to be pacified, converted, and transformed by the act of marriage, a domestication that is similar to the marriage of Draupadi at the end of the *jatre*. Potha Raja's mate is Shankavalli, who is formed from the interaction of the "waters" of King Pandu with the female river, Ganga. The marriage is likened to a sacrifice; Shankavalli is replaced in the epic by a goat that Potha Raja seeks to devour. In the early hours of the morning after the epic has been recited, the blood of a real goat is ingested by a person called Potha Raja at the temple. The cycle of transformation between blood, sexual union, and food is completed when the infant sister of Potha Raja is married to Dharmaraja. This final event directly connects Potha Raja with Draupadi through a system of parallel exchanges.

The Social Space of the Epic

The epic relates other temporalities to the space of the city, including mythic times such as the exile of the Pandavas in the forest and the origins of the Vahnikula Kshatriyas. The presence of Draupadi and Arjuna in the chariot along with Potha Raja and other ritual players at the recitation also brings previous histories into the present. This annihilation of temporal barriers between periods is a central aspect of the epic, because it is "living memory." The epic, when recounted, also evokes a recitative topos that is composed of four interlocking levels. At the level of relations within the *Karaga Purana*, a social space is created in which persons are tied to others in more than one way: Draupadi is married to all the brothers, but primarily to Arjuna; she is linked to Krishna, as she is also dark like him and is called "Krishnaa"; the two sometimes have a relationship of implied siblingship; again, Krishna's sister is married to Arjuna, and in fact produces the heir to the Pandavas.[46] Arjuna, in disguise as a young maiden, is desired by Potha Raja, who instead marries his sister Shankavalli. Potha Raja's sister is Dharma-raja's wife. Potha Raja himself replaces Draupadi's brother (Dhrishtadyum-na) as the leader of the Pandava legion. The relationship between Draupadi and Potha Raja here is one of nonprocreative symmetry and implied sib-lingship. What is central is the horizontal nature of relations between the main characters. This is represented in Figure 27. Every character is linked in more than one way to another, producing, on the one hand, a tight set of overlapping relations, and, on the other hand, a fundamental ambiguity in spite of the tightness of structure. This makes the epic inherently "double-voiced"—that is, it "serves two speakers at the same time and expresses si-multaneously two different intentions" (Bakhtin 1981, 324).

The second level of the recitative topos's social space is created through the numerous languages of the epic. A language is not only strati-fied according to dialects and formal linguistic markers, but is stratified as well "into languages that are socio-ideological: languages of social groups, 'professional' and 'generic' languages, languages of generations and so forth" (Bakhtin 1981, 272). The numerous plots and subplots of the narra-tion, the various intertextual surfaces within it—the *Devi Mahatmya,* the Tamil *purana,* the *Mahabharata,* the Potha Raja story—and the several re-ligious traditions that the oral epic refers to, assume a "heteroglot" world, one in which many languages, groups, and voices interpenetrate one an-other. At a site where cultural consensus is established, only a single narra-tive pathway is needed for the audience to pick up cues. But if the context is a multicultural city with various social groups present, multiple points of entry must be provided into the body of signs. By providing a range of lan-guages and symbolic pathways, the epic works against categories giving expression to forces of social and cultural centralization.

At a third level, the recitation of the *Karaga Purana* suggests a different model of social organization where political authority does not flow from a single hierarchy. Just as the kinship system within the epic and among the Vahnikula Kshatriyas is one in which self-perpetuating exchanges are pos-sible between (minimally) two horizontally linked groups through sister exchange, the model of the political system is one in which groups, the Pandavas and the lineage of Potha Raja, are connected through various re-lationships of reciprocity. In the previous chapter, I suggested that the Karaga *jatre* could be replicated theatrically and practically in any number of new

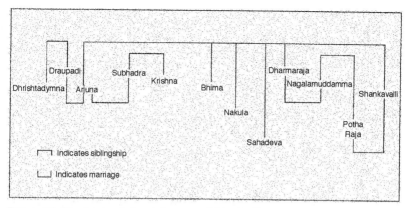

Figure 27. The horizontal social space within the Karaga epic.

suburbs of the metropolis through various kinetographs. In the same manner, the model of the political system that emerges through the *Karaga Purana* is one in which relationships between social groups can be established through exchange and equivalence. This exchange forms the mythic complement of the Tigala alliance that is being forged today by the Vahnikula Kshatriyas in the metropolis of Bangalore with other Backward Classes. It suggests that for Backward Classes in the urban context, political networks are often couched in the language of kinship and that goddesses and mythic heroes, whether those of lineages or of corporate groups, occupy a pivotal role in creating this reciprocity.

At a fourth level, the social space invoked by the epic suggests flows between the city and the forest that offer a memory of an urban landscape in this part of south India that we should reconstruct briefly.[47] This is a landscape that is not brought into existence by the state or a regional polity, but precedes and is outside them. Kempe Gowda is credited with the founding of Bangalore in the mid-sixteenth century; he constructed a fort near or around the settlement with gates, and also built two intersecting roads in it. Certain artificially constructed bodies of water were also created in and around the fortification. This implied that he had control over resources, both personnel and material. However, even before the fortification was built, settlements inhabited by a number of occupational groups—from shepherds to ritual officiants engaged in relations of trade and other types of exchange with each other—existed in the area, which was covered by a fairly dense forest.[48] The oral accounts of many goddess temples and deities of blood and power in Bangalore also testify to this historical scenario. The creation of a fortified city by Kempe Gowda was therefore a departure from an earlier urban model. In this earlier model, the settlements were not just isolated "villages" in the midst of the forest, but were part of a disaggregated landscape in which nodal settlements were related to each other through ritual, commercial, or kinship systems. It is clear from inscriptions that by the ninth and tenth centuries, if not earlier, religious institutions in south India such as temples stood at the core of expanding spatial, political, agricultural, and commercial networks and that urban sites began to develop around ritual centers.[49] The condition for this transformation was a locus of cultivators, traders, and ritual specialists who were situated around a ritual site. Later on, many such settlements became part of more extensive linkages, complex polities, and the transactional networks of more central urban sites, including forts and bodies of water such as tanks.

It seems clear from the topos of the *Karaga Purana* that we are provided with a memory of this development from forest and its settlements to the city-fort and also of the continuing transactions between the forest and the city. Although the *Karaga Purana* mentions Hastinapura and the Pandavas in north India, this is a reference to a period of urbanization in north India that began far earlier in the first millenium BCE and was localized along the Ganga River, further northwest, and also in central India. The *Karaga Purana* itself quickly moves to a forest and fort-city network that is south Indian in its scope and localization. The forest topos described is variegated in its inhabitants and settlements. There are, of course, deities such as Shiva and Parvati living on the mountains, but also cave dwellers ("demons") and sages. There are also forest gardeners, it is clear, from the Vahnikula Kshatriyas origin; some occupations connected with wood, as Bhima's efforts attest; and cowherds on the hills who see the wood-carrier coming to the fort city. Nomads who come to the fort-city of Potha Raja to sell their wares arrive at a site that seems to be quite complex. There is a settlement and a fortification comprised of a wall, a prison, and a palace, a stratified society that consists of a ruler, his peons, and the huts of other occupational groups. There is a suggestion that either within or outside the fort, where these huts are located, there are many kinds of trees and even perhaps a grove with tamarind, peepal, and other trees.

Although this could very well describe the Bangalore of Kempe Gowda's time or other such sites in the sixteenth century, I would like to suggest that two subtle absences in the epic refer to an urban landscape that predates the fort-City-tank model of which the Dharmaraja Temple later became a part. There is no mention of gardeners within the fort-settlement, unless the trees are some kind of oblique reference to them, which is significant considering that the *Karaga Purana* purports to tell the story of their origin. And, more centrally, there is not a single mention of a tank. The memory thus presented through the *Karaga Purana* is a frontier world in which the forest-people, of which the gardeners were a part, are encountering the walls of a fort-city before they become absorbed within it—for instance, through recruitment into armies. Historically, this would be a period that extended from the ninth or tenth century to the sixteenth century. This is also a period of the fort-city before extensive water systems such as tanks were constructed or became central to the urban site. It is interesting, therefore, that although tanks and other bodies of water are part of the kinetic aspects of the Karaga *jatre,* they are not part of the oral aspects, as evidenced in the *Karaga Purana.* This memory of the forest and the city and their mutual relations therefore provides another model in addition to the ones that came into existence in Bangalore after the sixteenth century, and it is a reminder of an earlier history of urbanism in south India.

Conclusion

The Circus Comes to the City

From the time of Bangalore's founding in the sixteenth century until 1800, the model of the city was composed of three elements: the fort, the tank, and the settlement-market. Interlaced with these were forests, horticultural gardens, and other green spaces emerging from an older history of urbanism in south India. After the last Anglo-Mysore battle in 1799, a "park and garden" model that depended on the physical and social separation of the City and the Cantonment through Cubbon Park overlay this model; the Cantonment was also dotted with smaller parks, boulevards, and parade grounds. In 1949, when the Cantonment and the City were combined into a single political and civic unit, a new model premised on a grid plan and a system of radial roads became dominant. Within this model, the most important feature was the disappearance of bodies of water and gardens and their replacement by new landmarks and nodes such as stadiums, bus terminals, housing colonies, bureaucratic offices, and industrial estates. By the 1990s, Bangalore had emerged as a center for high-technology research and software production. Monitoring these developments in the second half of the twentieth century were the Comprehensive Development Plans for the city whereby a monolithic vision came to govern "city planning," itself a new linguistic and discursive field in the management of Bangalore.

The transformations of the city's built environment over the centuries have been linked to various performances and spectacles.[1] For instance, in November 1996, more than six months after the annual Karaga *jatre*, a procession began from the City Railway Station near the erstwhile Dharmambudi Tank. The procession was moving toward the Windsor Manor Hotel, which housed many of the invitees and contestants for the Miss World beauty pageant in Bangalore when about six hundred protestors, led by the Communist Party of India (Marxist), were rounded up by the police. This event was one moment in a series of controversies that dogged the contest after the decision was made by the Amitabh Bacchan Corporation, Ltd. (ABCL) to hold the pageant in Bangalore.[2] The corporate sponsors for the contest included national companies and multinational ones such as Citibank, Motorola, Siemens, and the Welcome group of hotels. Some of the disputes that were a run-up to the contest included stays by the High Court on the serving of alcohol during the contest and protests by the right-wing Bharatiya Janata Party and some women's organizations in the city against "the demeaning public display of a woman's body." There were also charges that the state's chief minister, J. H. Patel, was a stooge of the ABCL; he vigorously supported the contest, claiming that it would bring in revenue from tourism for the state. Corporate executives from the information technology industry threatened a strike. They were trying to draw attention to the terrible conditions of the Hosur Road linking Bangalore to the "Electronic City" on the outskirts even while the chief minister was launching expensive plans for the beautification of the city on the eve of the pageant. The last time that such efforts had been made in the city had been when the South Asian Association for Regional Cooperation (SAARC) summit of South Asian world leaders was held in the city in 1986. The comparison was not far off the mark if one considers issues other than merely "beautification" plans. Due to the protests against the pageant from various quarters and threats by a "suicide squad," it was estimated that 12,500 policemen had been deputed to oversee security (this figure excluded paramilitary forces that were on hand and a bomb squad that had been called in). The contingents of the police force exceeded the arrangements made for the SAARC summit held exactly the same month a decade earlier.

The pageant was one of the most important spectacles in the city that year. In fact, several newspaper articles claimed that henceforth, for tax purposes, beauty contests should be included within the category of "entertainment" along with sports and films to bring greater tax revenue to the state. Beneath the hysteria and the many conflicts and ironies of this pageant, and in the interstices between the forces that linked this science city of India with global processes of consumption, other local issues became visible. The beautification plan for the city was the other face of a not-so-aesthetic process of takeover of space in the city that had progressed almost unchecked since the 1950s. In this process, garden land, open areas, and tanks in the city had increasingly given way to stadiums, golf courses, and other landmarks such as the city's central bus terminal. The most recent moment in this history of internal environmental colonization was the occasion of the Indian National Games, held in the summer of 1997, when another tank was converted into a huge housing project for participating athletes despite protests from a range of civic groups.

Three agencies have had key roles to play in these processes of city development. The Karnataka Urban Infrastructure Development and Finance Corporation (KUIDFC) was a nodal agency, with a board of governors, including the chief minister of Karnataka as chairman, coordinating the disbursement of funds for the improvement of urban infrastructure under the rubric of the Mega City Project. The schemes proposed within the project fell into five categories: traffic-related works (plans for overpasses, road widening, pedestrian subways, ring roads, and new bus terminals); decongestion of the city (proposals to shift markets and develop truck terminals on the outskirts of the city); water supply schemes; city beautification plans; and commercial projects (including the development of new markets). In 1998, ten projects estimated at over 2 billion rupees had either been sanctioned or were in progress.[3] The various projects included plans for land acquisition in the city, including defense land or land from the Department of Forests, inviting tenders and studies from the private sector and funding from banks such as the Asian Development Bank, which assists the KUIDFC.

The second agency was the Bangalore Development Authority, which, along with the Bangalore City Corporation, was trying to deal with the traffic congestion in Bangalore. Addressing a vehicular population that grew nearly 700 percent between 1977 and 1994 involved two giant initiatives. One scheme was the Elevated Light Rail Transit System, conceptualized as a public-private joint venture meant to cover a ninety-six-kilometer route and a network of six main routes. Proposals had been invited from various private institutions such as United Breweries. Although the complete system was to be fully operational by 2008, the scheme had not begun to be implemented by the end of 1999. The second scheme was the development of the "Outer Ring Road," the alignment of which was finalized in 1991–92 with a route to cover 62.09 kilometers.[4]

The third and most important agency was the Bangalore Metropolitan Region Development Authority (BMRDA), which was entrusted with the role of preparing a structure plan for the Bangalore metropolitan region as a whole. Its goal was "to change the landscape of investment opportunities of Southern Karnataka, so that development is appropriately managed in the BMR [Bangalore Metropolitan Region] and successfully promoted in the surrounding SKR [South Karnataka Region]."[5] BMRDA's draft structure plan attempted to induce population growth and generate employment generation in satellite towns, growth centers, and nodes on the periphery of the metropolitan region, effectively doubling their populations, and aimed at containing population within the Bangalore Metropolitan Area at around 7.60 million by the year 2011. Towns in the eastern and western segments of the metropolitan region, such as Anekal, Hoskote, Devanahalli, Dodballapur, Nelamangala, Magadi, Ramnagaram, Channapatna, and Kanakpura—many of which were towns where the Karaga *jatre* was performed (see Map 15)—were target sites for dispersed development. Along with a number of other projects, such as the development of Devanahalli International Airport, an expressway to neighboring Mysore, and industrial estates, the draft structure plan set the stage for a large-scale transformation of Bangalore and the denudation of the green belt. Although it recommended participation from various local bodies, the plan itself was prepared largely in the absence of public discussion.

The full effect of the schemes of all these agencies would radically alter the topography within Bangalore, the nature of various public spaces in the city, and the rights to these spaces of different communities and institutions. The projects were debated among groups in the city insofar as scanty information about them was made available or the potential effects on the city became visible. Certain Vahnikula Kshatriya leaders, such as K. Lakshmana, expressed concern over the proposed international airport at Devanahalli town on the outskirts of the city, where Vahnikula Kshatriyas owned garden land. Another scheme approved by the Mega City Project sanctioning committee included a project involving the Kempambudi Tank, the only surviving tank of the three that were crucial to the Karaga *jatre*. In 1996, the debate was begun as to whether the tank should be restored or converted into a park. Other projects included plans for traffic circles in the vicinity of the Elusuttinakote in conjunction with plans for the Elevated Light Rail Transit System. None of the Vahnikula Kshatriyas—nor, indeed, most civic organizations—was consulted regarding any plans for their neighborhoods or their understandings of the city.

Publics, Power, and Civic Performance

How can we understand the articulations between these processes of planning and production and performances within the city, including the Miss World beauty pageant and the Karaga *jatre*? One reading of history is that performances such as the Karaga *jatre* have mutated gradually because of colonial penetration and the developmental state. Therefore, the political emasculation of the Mysore state by the British paralleled the extension of patronage by the princely rulers to royal and martial performances. Nineteenth-century Bangalore witnessed the slow growth in and popularity of the Karaga *jatre* in the City, hitherto a performance organized by a relatively small population of Tamil speakers that was rivaled only by the celebrations at St. Mary's Church in the Cantonment. Under the developmental state, local performances can be seen as mutating further to participate in or be represented within the theme park of nationalism or regionalism. The annual Dassera procession at Mysore, for instance, today presided over by ministers of the state, is a portrayal of various "folk" traditions in Karnataka through dancers, musicians, floats, costumed men and women, and animals alongside marching schoolchildren, the National Cadet Corps, or the mounted police.

This transformation of local performances into "little traditions" accompanies planning models in the city that have tended to emphasize large-scale construction projects, grid patterns for the use of urban space, radial road systems, public-sector industries, and centralized and opaque civic authorities. From the 1950s to the 1980s, this seems to have been the predictable civic landscape of most Indian cities. Rituals of sport in the city have matched such displays of the prowess of the state apparatus. The sites of sport such as cricket are marked clearly in space, usually by gigantic buildings that are visible vertically for miles off and inside which spectators have their vision directed in sloping lines toward a central arena. The enormous Kanteerava sports complex that looms in a rather sinister fashion behind the Karaga hall in Bangalore is an example. Contrast this with the sites of the Karaga *jatre*, where the entire city is the stage of the spectacle and the priest moves through city streets in a horizontal relationship to standing, praying, and walking spectators. In contrast to public or civic space that is dispersed in many sites—temples dedicated to various deities, crossroads, and markets—the stadium is a forum in which civic space is no longer multicentered. The creation of an urban armature by the developmental state has led to the focusing of public activity in certain central areas of the city.

The redirection of routes in the city around central landmarks is not merely a state-sponsored project, however. With the liberalization of the Indian economy from the 1980s onward, the appropriation of civic space for new theatrical displays has been increasingly undertaken by a number of commercial interests, including local ones. Therefore, on the Airport Road leading into the business area of Bangalore stands "Kemp Fort" (an abbreviation, it has been suggested, for "Kempe Gowda Fort"), a multistoried shopping complex described as the "ultimate shopping fantasy," which was constructed to resemble a medieval European castle with a moat (see Figure 28). The owners opened their first outlet about two decades ago in the City area and another one in the fashionable business district of Mahatma Gandhi Road before Kemp Fort was constructed. In front of all three centers, trying to lure local tourists and busy citizens, are Disney-type animals and men in knightly armor dancing to Hindi film or pop music. The displacement of the "fort" from the City could not have been more complete and fantastic.

In the 1990s Bangalore was being marketed as an icon of a world city, both through the production of software and through the consumption of mega-spectacles, more than in the previous decade. The Miss World pageant and the National Games, although they added another layer to the various spectacles witnessed in Bangalore, stood at the intersection of national and international capital and urban planning interests in Bangalore rather than emerging as performances linked to communities in the city. Capital and planning were converting the city into a theatrical space, but without acknowledging older axes of the city, recovering its fragments, or bringing neighborhoods into the process of planning and acquisition of power.

This exclusion may be exacerbated given the political scenario in the state. On the eve of the midterm elections in India in August 1999, an alliance was struck between regional and national parties in the state of Karnataka. The Bharatiya Janata Party, historically a right-wing party, attempted to broaden the base of its operations in the wake of its fall as the national ruling party after about two years in power. It created electoral adjustments with a motley bunch of parties espousing various local, communal, and liberal causes, and stressed the place of Backward Classes in this equation. In Bangalore the question was, Which party would the Backward Classes vote for? If the Bharatiya Janata Party and their "National Democratic Alliance" came to power in the state, how would the performance of the Karaga *jatre* and the Vahnikula Kshatriyas be influenced by this development?[6] Performances and festivals such as the Karaga *jatre*, as well as institutions within which they are embedded, such as gymnasiums, youth associations, or neighborhood groups, have been penetrated in many Indian cities by right-wing organizations. Having become occasions for violence in many cases, they have been accompanied by increasing state surveillance. The link between performances and terror in late-twentieth-century cities is borne out by examples across the world, from the Brooklyn Carnival in New York to the Ganesh processions in Bombay.

Transformations of the ecological landscape of Bangalore accompanied changes in the deployment of symbolic regimes and the construction

Figure 28. Kemp Fort.

of civic space. Urban environmental movements have emerged, seeking to save spaces such as forests, tanks, parks, nurseries, or grazing lands that previously wove together the urban fabric. A powerful argument for the civic role of performances such as the Karaga *jatre* and the classes associated with them is their potential as allies for those engaging in ecological struggles. How does one place this somewhat millenarian possibility within the context of globalization and late-twentieth-century capitalism?

Manuel Castells argues that the rise of the network society based on the disjunction between the local and the global calls into question the construction of identity for most groups. Except for the elite inhabiting the timeless space of flows of global networks and their nodes, "there is no longer continuity between the logic of power-making in the global network and the logic of association and representation in specific societies and cultures" (Castells 1997, 11). Therefore, the creation of identities for a great number of groups takes the form of the construction of "defensive identities" that are based on communal principles. What are the implications of this argument for cities? Looking at a range of movements from religious fundamentalist organizations to the Greens and the feminists in different areas of the world, he points out that in the 1980s and 1990s territorially based identities took four main routes. First, local governments absorbed urban movements and actors directly or indirectly through systems of citizen participation, and this created the possibility of a reconstitution of political control. Second, local communities sustained an influential grassroots environmental movement, particularly in middle-class suburbs, exurbia, or an urbanized countryside. Third, a vast number of poor communities survived through the development of communal organizations aimed at the means of their survival. Fourth, particularly in segregated urban areas, movements took the form of violent attacks against the "walls" of the city. In all these cases, the struggles focused on three realms of the network society: time, space, and technology.

In contrast, Jane Jacobs states in her study of aboriginal claims to space in Perth that these struggles produced meanings that officials, courts, and other powers were not able to read. They "reactivated a (pre-) modern knowing of space within the specific conditions of modernity" (Jacobs 1996, 127). The contests she describes were over an area near the Swan River that had been used by the colonial government to establish a depot in 1833 as part of measures to contain and exclude the Aborigines. In the 1980s, this area, for some time the location of a brewery, became a site for development by corporate interests into a brewery and hotel chain with theaters, office spaces, and a theme park. Laws about aboriginal land had tended to place claims to sacred territory far away from urban centers. In this case, aboriginal claims located the spiritual firmly, and inconveniently, within the area of the Swan Brewery. Aborigines occupied the area for a while in 1989, and this occupation and controversy between "beer, work, tourism and sport" and "urban dreamings," as Jacobs categorizes the two sides, put into sharp relief a number of issues. First, sacredness was unpredictable, and the separation between the sacred and the secular was part of the imaginings of the nation-state. Second, the view of a Public Nature put forth by the Aborigines was against both private and government interests, which could accommodate less problematic formulations of the aboriginal worldview only as long as they could commodify it. Third, Jacobs demonstrates that these struggles over space are structurally linked to other contests in cities such as London. Although the Aborigines' struggles failed and the area was given over to development, Jacobs argues that the aboriginal occupation not only brought the sacred back into the city, but set off an "anxious" politics of occupation by the government and developers.

Although both Castells and Jacobs present influential arguments, the Vahnikula Kshatriyas performing the Karaga *jatre* do not really fit these profiles, and it is important to outline why this is so. Although they have been represented in local government bodies such as the BCC Council, they have not been absorbed by them, but instead have largely functioned through community-level associations. They are by no means completely disempowered, and their political mobilization efforts are geared toward reclaiming their means of production and the construction of alliances with different groups in which symbolic capital is a crucial component. They are not middle-class suburbanites or those who belong to an urbanized countryside at the forefront of an "environmental" movement, but comprise the city's working class and petty bourgeoisie. The sacred is the center of their claims to the city, but their understanding of the sacred is deeply tied to the definition of the urban realm itself rather than to "public nature," as represented in the aboriginal view that was less rooted in the urban.

Toward a Model of the Civic

In the period before the establishment of the Cantonment, the Vahnikula Kshatriyas played several roles in the ritual, political, and economic structure of Bangalore. They were recognized for their contribution to the Karaga *jatre* and the armies of various Nayakas and Palegaras, as well as their horticultural efforts. Some of these functions continued when the Cantonment was established, especially with the growth of demand for vegetable and fruit produce as the population swelled. Again, as wrestlers, many men of the community received encouragement for their sport in competitions organized locally in Bangalore and in events patronized by the Wodeyar kings. After 1949, the lands of the gardeners slowly disappeared under concrete, and the occupations of many members of the community came to be tied to the informal sector of the economy, where they worked as sellers of vegetables, fruits, and flowers or in petty self-employment. Given their educational and financial constraints, only a few achieved positions within the formal economy, whether in the public or private sector or in the bureaucracy. All this occurred cheek by jowl with the growing numbers attending the Karaga *jatre* and with its spread to new suburbs and towns in the metropolitan area. Although this can be read as part of a history of displacement, disenfranchisement, and marginalization in spite of dramaturgical visibility, we can also understand the Karaga *jatre* of the Vahnikula Kshatriyas as producing a model of the civic in Bangalore that is kinetic, oral, mnemonic, spatial, and ultimately political. Further, this is a model of actions and transformations that provides us with a method of also understanding the logic of urban plans and metropolitan development.

"Regimes of the body"—constructs about the body and sacred mediation, as well as practices tied to them—are a means of ingress into this model. The Karaga *jatre* involves the preparations of the Vahnikula Kshatriya males in gymnasiums. Both the Virakumaras and the Karaga priest undertake to direct their strength and sexual energy in order to come into contact with the *shakti* of Draupadi. The control of male and female bodies of players and the flows between food, blood, and semen are expressed through a language in which the categories of heating, cooling, and transmutation are central. The transformation of Draupadi through the phases of incarnation, personification, and localization occurs through the channeling of her heat. The stage of incarnation is one in which the condition of heat (brought on by the practices of the priest, Virakumaras, and citizens) becomes so excessive that the Primal Goddess emerges as the Karaga. The heat travels up the body of the Karaga priest from waist to head, a moment of tremendous excitement for those gathered. Set upon the head of the priest, who is controlled by its presence, the Karaga directs a path through the city in which time and space are reconfigured. The hot form of the Primal Goddess is then contained through the marriage of Draupadi and Arjuna. On the night when the *Karaga Purana* is recited and a blood sacrifice to Potha Raja is carried out, the epic, the goddess, and the community are localized within the Elusuttinakote. Beyond these events, the Karaga *jatre* spills out into numerous suburbs and towns of the metropolis.

Following this process through, we can see the *jatre* producing a model of the civic with four levels (see Figure 29). Each of the levels is mediated through successive transformations of the body, memory, and the city in a dynamic chain. If regimes of the body constitute the first level, the somatic transformations produced feed into the second level, which is the *jatre* as a whole. The *jatre* has two compositional devices, kinetic and oral. The rituals carried out by the priest and his troupe, the procession routes that are taken, and the sites at which *sacra* are set down create kinetographs through motion. The narration of the *Karaga Purana* situates the mythical origins of the community as a fire lineage and its history of settlement within the topos of the forest and transactions between forest and city. It is through these kinetic and oral practices that urban memory is altered. This occurs through several processes:

1. Orienting cultural materials in a different spatial and temporal direction, which may take the form of reversal.
2. Creating clusters that form a significatory overload in the configuration of social meaning or concentration.
3. Replacing one object with another in the same position.
4. Replacing one object with another in a chain of meaning.
5. Dispersing meanings and events across various sites.
6. Creating new patterns of meaning through parallelisms and complementarities between sites and objects.

Volosinov ([1927] 1987) suggests a similar logic for the manner in which the "social unconscious" operates. He sees four processes (dispersal is not one of them, nor is the positing of parallels or complementarities)— which he terms "inversion," "condensation," "substitution," and "displacement"—at work in the unconscious and language. He claims that the unconscious is a social product and is not different ontologically from the conscious. The conscious is merely the "official conscious" that expresses the ideology and practices of hegemonic groups, whereas the "unofficial conscious" reflects all those forces that are centrifugal to the system and interrogate it. Therefore, certain linguistic forms and verbal utterances, which are his main concern, reflect the oblique strategies used by groups to express the censoring or control of expressions, moralities, and worldviews. Again, Halbwachs (1992) argues that the laws governing the memory of groups include changing the traditions of older groups by rewriting their positions in time and space; renewing them through unexpected parallels, oppositions, and combinations; concentrating meaning and events; and the duality of sites.

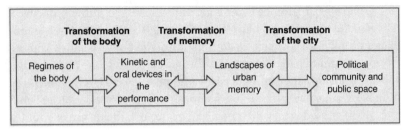

Figure 29. A model of the civic.

Within the Karaga *jatre*, too, bodies of water and shrines are re-collected from their everyday spatial location into a clockwise "victory over direction" *(digvijaya)* around the Dharmaraja Temple. The procession route through the City aligning goddess shrines, warrior-gods, and Sufi saints along with other sites creates a dense pattern of meaning. One object is also replaced and substituted by another. The Seven-Circled Fort, the Elusut-tinakote, emerged after the old fort had been largely destroyed and the boundaries of the City had opened out toward the military garrison in the Cantonment. Seen in the context of Bangalore's history, the *jatre* inverts the relationship between political and symbolic power. Meaning is also dispersed: goddess shrines, warrior-gods, and saints form part of the code-pendent narrative of the Karaga *jatre*. The oral epic also takes up the tradi-tions of older groups and texts, but reworks them within the context of the *jatre*. It prioritizes the period of exile in the forest and transforms Draupadi into a *Devi Mahatmya* type of goddess. Like the goddess who undergoes several transformations, the audience must traverse the forest, along with many characters in the epic who are disguised allusions to figures from other narratives, to arrive at the figure of Potha Raja in the city.

The reconfiguration of memory, time, and space generated by kine-tographs and the recitative topos links the second level in this model with the third, which are the landscapes of urban memory. These recollections are spatially marked readings of the city that posit a variety of relationships between cultural materials drawn from different historical periods and time frames. One kind of landscape is the interaction between the city and the forest, with the forest people depicted as encountering and interacting with the walls of a fort-city. Historically, this was a period in the growth of urban settlement in south India extending from the ninth or tenth century up to about the sixteenth century. Although the forest is depicted as inhab-ited by a number of different personages and spaces, the fort-city is por-trayed as one without extensive water systems such as tanks. The memory of the forest and the city and the interaction between their groups—kings, sages, demons, herders, nomads, wood sellers, and goddesses—is inserted into the experience of contemporary Bangalore.

Another landscape is the ring of forts, bodies of water large and small, and transactions with the settlement-market. Although in a generalized sense such a topos was prevalent in many other cities of south India from about the sixteenth century onward, the landscape of memory that emerges here is less abstract and more specific. The circle of forts of which Bangalore is part is simultaneously the boundary of a horticultural universe. Bodies of water appear as a set of three types—tank, pond, and well—linked to each other in a structure of flows. These are associated with ritual centers patronized by different communities within the settlement-market, such as oil-pressers, moneylenders, and weavers. The boundaries of the fort and the settlement-market are structured in terms of sites associated with goddesses, celibate warriors, and Sufi saints. There is also a landscape of memory involving a range of green spaces that emerges from the *jatre*. The offerings of flowers, pulses, vegetables, and other products on various altars connected with the festivities suggest horticultural gardens and agricultural fields, whereas the narrative of Draupadi as gypsy suggests the sowing of rice in these fields. The *Karaga Purana* and the other ritual events create a dense panorama of forests, grazing lands, agricultural fields, tree groves, and horticultural gardens devoted to flowers, fruits, and vegetables.

The transformation of the city, spatially and temporally, through these landscapes of urban memory is the link between the third and the fourth levels of the model, the creation of a political community and the claims to public space in the city. Although these follow from the *jatre*, they also feed into it, and the model of the civic should be read as an analytical construct of interlocking levels rather than as a unidirectional hierarchy of cultural and historical flows. Therefore, although in this book the creation of Tigala unity and the cultic terrain has been analyzed before the *jatre*, political mobilization and community formation are both required for the performance of the *jatre* and flow from it. The construction of a political community by the Vahnikula Kshatriyas has intersected with new developments in the state and in the city. The three groups of Tigalas, the Vahnikula Kshatriyas, the Agnikula Kshatriyas, and the Shambukula Kshatriyas, as they define themselves today, have diverse origins, occupations, and histories of settlement in Bangalore. It is claimed that the Agnikula Kshatriyas were aboriginal horticulturists in this region, although today few of them are engaged in horticulture. There is some evidence that the Vahnikula Kshatriyas probably migrated to Bangalore in several waves after the tenth century. The Shambukula Kshatriyas were the last arrivals; some of them were in the employ of the British army, but most became factory laborers. The occupations of all these groups have since diversified, while at the same time a corporate identity based on their origin as a fire lineage has been sustained. It is primarily through the legal structures that the various Backward Classes commissions have created and through the language and practices of the cultic terrain that a "Tigala" alliance between the three groups has been constructed.

However, this kind of corporate group is not enough. More than any other figure, S. M. Munivenkatappa represents the features of this new political community. As he recognized in a self-conscious manner, this community includes five elements: a performance such as the Karaga *jatre*, economic associations in the city such as horticultural cooperatives, sites such as gymnasiums, civic bodies such as the Bangalore City Corporation, and the creation of an alliance among fire-born groups. The flows of political energy for the Vahnikula Kshatriyas, clearly the most active members of the alliance, are closely tied with those of the associations that organize the Karaga *jatre* and the mobilization that is necessary for it, whether in the City or in the suburbs. Therefore, most of the members of the Tigala alliance from this community are also members of the various youth associations that hold the Karaga *jatre* in their areas. This community is completely urban, and Bangalore is the hub of the political efforts. The political community being suggested here is one that includes a range of associations for "bodywork" and economic and ritual production apart from those that provide local political representation. These often overlap with each other so that a largely horizontal network of associations emerges within the space of the city.

Among the demands that the Vahnikula Kshatriyas have been making for the last twenty-five years, the one they have made the most vociferously is that the government compensate them for the loss of their garden lands in the metropolis. This claim must be placed within the context that the rights to the city articulated by the Vahnikula Kshatriyas stem from an experience of gardens and bodies of water as part of the urban landscape. This experience contrasts with development plans for Bangalore that have increasingly sought to exteriorize these spaces by putting them in the category of the "green belt" or to reduce them to a single-use construct of "recreation areas" or "lung spaces." However, within the Karaga *jatre* sacrality is regularly spatialized and space sacralized, lending a different ontological status and meaning to the Vahnikula Kshatriyas' claims to the city's space.

In the model of the civic presented here, we also have an explanation for the creation of public spaces in the metropolis in the form of stadiums, theme parks, software cities, or scientific projects through the matrix of development plans and capital investment that threaten garden lands or bodies of water. Shifts in the definition and control of public space and the nature of the city's political community through planning and capital are effected in the same chain of transformations and levels that are depicted in Figure 29. The creation of new kinds of spaces and publics is brought about through reconfiguring the body, memory, and space and time in the city. Alongside the infrastructure of new regimes envisaged for the civic body—ring roads, elevated light rail systems, overpasses, expressways, development corridors, and satellite towns—are regimes of transformation of the citizens' bodies. The urban armature being created not only alters the sense of the body in the urban, but also expresses it through events such as the Indian National Games and the Miss World beauty pageant. Stadiums replace tanks, circular routes around the city bypass older flows, and meanings are dispersed in new sites and concentrated in new clusters. These stand as signposts marking the changing contours of civic memory.

The significance of the model of the civic discussed in this book lies in two spheres: first, in the understanding that it provides of processes of city planning, whether in Bangalore or in Manhattan or Atlanta; and second, in the recognition of the fact that, although they are a minority in terms of the population of metropolitan Bangalore, the Vahnikula Kshatriyas, along with other groups in the Tigala alliance, represent the characteristics of a vast number of urban communities. It would not be an exaggeration to state that groups such as the Tigalas comprise the largest percentage of the urban populations of most cities. These are urban strata that occupy certain niches in the city, including sectors of the informal economy, petty trade, and some sites of the formal sector of the economy, groups that resist definition as purely migrating peasants or factory workers, traditionally the classes that have interested labor historians. Rather than representing them as a parallel reality of the contemporary city, we have to move past the flicker of images projected by high technology and its spectacles to recognize that these strata of society in fact produce the city in real terms. The recognition that constructs of place of these communities, relegated to civic amnesia or embedded within a grid plan, return regularly to civic consciousness is a deeply political act. It draws attention to groups who regard themselves as legitimate subjects of urban history, who actualize definitions of the metropolis through spatial and ritual practices, and who are involved in the act of renewing the meaning of the city.

Their political mobilization and rights to the city depend on these actions and complex positionings and draw on elements of theatrical, ritual, spatial, and somatic production. The intersection between the study of performance, topography, ritual processes, and political formation may therefore be the domain in which lies a deeper understanding of the civic in the contemporary city.

Survey of Vahnikula Kshatriya Households in Bangalore

A survey was conducted between March and August 1997 to document the changes that had occurred in Vahnikula Kshatriya households in the decades between the 1950s and the 1990s, during which the city underwent its most dramatic changes. The main shifts in the household economy were the loss of plots of garden land and occupational diversification.

The total population of Vahnikula Kshatriyas in Bangalore district, according to oral estimates, was about 250,000 at the time of the survey. The population surveyed in this study was 534 persons belonging to one hundred households—about 0.2 percent of the total Vahnikula Kshatriya population of the district. Three areas of residential concentration were chosen for this study. These areas were Tigalarapet, the area of the City where the maximum number of Vahnikula Kshatriyas reside; Sampangi-ramnagar, near the site where Karaga is "born" every year; and Doopana-halli, near Damlur Tank, in the Cantonment area. A sample from each study area was selected: sixty-two households with 328 persons totally from Tigalarapet; twenty-three households with 136 persons totally from Sampangiramangar; and fifteen households with 70 persons totally from Doopanahalli. Unfortunately, there are no official estimates of the total number of Vahnikula Kshatriya households in these or other areas.

The following tables based on this survey are shown for these three areas. Table A1 shows the acreage of land held by various Vahnikula Ksha-triya households in the three study areas in 1950 and 1997. Table A2 shows the locations of Vahnikula Kshatriya land ownership in 1950 (in the neigh-borhood under consideration, as well as other areas of Bangalore or out-side the city). Table A3 shows the main marketing patterns of the house-holds in 1950 for their products: the main markets (K. R. Market in the City,

Table A1.
Land ownership by Vahnikula Kshatriyas in three study areas, 1950 and 1997

	Number of households holding land of various acreages							
	0 acres		>0 to <1 acres		1 to <2 acres		2 to <3 acres	
Area	1950	1997	1950	1997	1950	1997	1950	1997
Doopanahalli	3	15	3	0	5	0	4	0
Sampangiramnagar	5	18	1	1	6	0	3	0
Tigalarapet	20	60	11	0	12	2	9	0
Total	28	93	15	1	23	2	16	0

	3 to <5 acres		5 to <10 acres		>10 acres	
Area	1950	1997	1950	1997	1950	1997
Doopanahalli	0	0	0	0	0	0
Sampangiramnagar	2	3	3	1	3	0
Tigalarapet	6	0	2	0	2	0
Total	8	3	5	1	5	0

Russell Market in the Cantonment, or both) and the main mode of marketing products (wholesale, individually owned shops, or sales on the street). Table A4 depicts the reasons for the loss of land by the Vahnikula Kshatriya households in the three study areas between 1950 and 1997, including land acquisition by the Bangalore Development Authority or other government institutions, sale or purchase of land, or both.

As Tables A1–A4 reveal, in 1950 Doopanahalli had three households that were landless (this mainly meant that some sale of land had already occurred by 1950 or that some households worked on land held by others). Three households held less than one acre of land, five held between one and two acres, and four held between two and three acres. The total number of households surveyed was fifteen. Of those that owned one of the larger plots in the village (between two and three acres), one belonged to the "Gowda" family, who are the headmen of the Vahnikula Kshatriyas in the village area. All households that cultivated land used wells as their main mode of irrigation. Most of these wells, as seen from the maps from

Table A2.

Locations of Vahnikula Kshatriya household landownership, 1950

Area of household residence	In the neighbor-hood	In Bangalore	Outside Bangalore	Not applicable	Total
	Number of households holding land				
Doopanahalli	7	4	1	3	15
Sampangiramnagar	9	7	2	5	23
Tigalarapet	0	40	2	20	62
Total	16	51	5	28	100

Note: Not applicable = landless households.

Table A3.

Marketing patterns of Vahnikula Kshatriya households, 1950

Area of household residence	K. R. Market only	Russell Market only	Both	Other
	Place of marketing			
Doopanahalli	5	0	6	1
Sampangiramnagar	17	0	0	1
Tigalarapet	38	0	2	2
Total	60	0	8	4

Area of household residence	Wholesale	Pavement shops	Both	Not applicable
	Mode of marketing			
Doopanahalli	8	3	1	3
Sampangiramnagar	14	4	0	5
Tigalarapet	23	17	2	20
Total	45	24	3	28

Note: Other = markets outside the city; not applicable = landless households.

Table A4.
Reasons for land loss by Vahnikula Kshatriyas in three study areas, 1950–97

| Area of household residence | Number of households losing land by 1997 | | | |
	Acquired by BDA and government	Sale	Both	Not applicable
Doopanahalli	8	3	1	3
Sampangiramnagar	6	9	0	8
Tigalarapet	13	22	5	22
Total	27	34	6	33

Note: Not applicable = landless in 1950 or holding land in 1997.

before 1950 shown in chapter 2, lay on the southern edge of the village on the fringes of the Damlur Tank. Seven households held land in the Doopana-halli area, four in other areas of Bangalore (usually neighboring villages that were then considered outside the city limits), and one held land out-side the city (in this case, in Devanahalli town on the outskirts of Banga-lore). The two main wholesale markets in the city are K. R. Market (in the area north of the fort) and Russell Market in the Cantonment area. Five households in Doopanahalli marketed the products they sold in K. R. Mar-ket, and six marketed products in both markets; one household marketed the products in Devanahalli itself, where it held land. Usually it was only the households with larger pieces of land that sold products in the city's K. R. Market, because that market lay at some distance from the village. Nearly all households grew vegetables, whereas one grew a combination of fruits, flowers, and vegetables. Most of the households (eight) did not own their own shops, but marketed their products wholesale; three had their own shops or sold vegetables and fruits on pavements in the market area, and one household used both modes.

Between 1950 and 1997, a number of changes occurred in the vil-lage. The chief transformation was that the area in and around Doopana-halli became an upper- and middle-class neighborhood, with gardens con-verted into housing sites, roads, and certain public and semipublic areas such as churches, temples, schools, and small parks. The driving forces be-hind this change were the Bangalore Development Authority (BDA), espe-cially in the period after the 1970s, and private developers in the decade of the 1990s. As Table A1 shows, not a single household in Doopanahalli held land in 1997. A majority of households (eight) lost their land when it came to be acquired by the BDA, the City Improvement Trust Board, or other institutions of the city (see Table A4). In many cases, the households received compensation for the land, although most households claim that this monetary amount was far less than the market value of the land at that time; in some cases, a tiny housing plot was received in exchange. Three households gave up their land when they sold it to private parties, and one lost land due to a combination of the two factors. The village area in 1997, as the maps in chapter 2 reveal, bore no resemblance to the area before 1950, having become a residential neighborhood. The garden lands were converted into large housing plots for middle- and upper-middle-class families, whereas the area in Doopanahalli was composed of numerous tiny households owned by both Vahnikula Kshatriyas and other communities, most of them low-income households. Many of these provided services to the higher-income groups as servants, shopkeepers, autorickshaw drivers, and members of other service groups.

In Sampangiramnagar (see Table A1), out of a total of twenty-three households surveyed, five were landless in 1950 (the members of one household said that the land had been sold before 1950, and those of another said they worked for others). The largest number of households (six) held garden land of between one and two acres; in Doopanahalli, too, this was the main pattern. Of these households, one belonged to the Gowda family of Sampangiramnagar. Another Gowda household held between two and three acres. In Sampangiramnagar, however, there were on the average three households each in other categories, and some also owned very large pieces of land—between three to five acres, five to ten acres, or more than ten acres. Among those households that held between five and ten acres, one belonged to the "Gante Pujari" family, which provided some of the ritual players in the Karaga *jatre*. Another family that held more than ten acres provided the priests of the Yellamma Temple in Sampangiramnagar to the village goddess whose shrine appears within the performance cycle of the *jatre*. In this area, too, most of the households (sixteen) cultivated their land through well irrigation, and a couple through a combination of wells and sewage canals that also provided organic manure. A majority (twelve households) grew vegetables, whereas one household each grew flowers or a staple exclusively, and four grew a combination of fruits, flowers, and vegetables. Most (nine) of the households with land held land in Sampangiramnagar; seven held land in other parts of Bangalore (see Table A2). Since this village lay close to the City, all except one household (seventeen) marketed their products in the K. R. Market, and fourteen of them marketed products through wholesale merchants (see Table A3). Sampangiramnagar had a number of households that had larger pieces of land compared to Doopanahalli, and this accounts for the wholesale mode of marketing.

In 1997, Sampangiramnagar had become one of the central neighborhoods of the city, close to the intersection of several main thoroughfares of Bangalore. It lay close to the market area, but also close to the administrative offices of the government, the Kanteerava Stadium, Cubbon Park, and many well-known schools and colleges in the city. The number of households in the neighborhood that possessed no land in 1997 was eighteen, more than three times the number in 1950 (see Table A1). Only those with three to five acres or five to ten acres had managed to retain their land. In the first case, there were two new households that gained land by 1997 and one that gave up its land in this area, increasing the number of households in this category from two to three. One of the new households had leased land around 1950 and regained this land by 1997 without any subdivision; this land lay at Hoskote town, east of Bangalore. Another household bought land in the city; this family had not owned any gardens in 1950, but the fortunes of the household had registered an upswing in the interim: two brothers in the household had received professional training, one as a doctor and the other as an engineer. The household had therefore purchased land of about four and a half acres on which it grew coconuts and flowers for wholesale trade. Regarding the older household, although it retained its total acreage of land, the gardens it owned were shifted from Lalbagh Road near Sampangiramnagar to Hoskote town outside of the city. In the category of five to ten acres, none of the original households held land in 1997; the household that did own land was a new one, and the land they bought was situated not in Bangalore city, but in Kolar town, a district on the east side of Bangalore district. Nine households had sold their land to private parties or developers in the interim, whereas six had had their land acquired by the BDA and other state institutions (see Table A4). In some cases, said informants, the land was acquired in the form of "layout charges" for the construction of roads and other public amenities, and no compensation was received.

Out of the sixty-two households surveyed in Tigalarapet, twenty were landless in 1950 (see Table A1). Of these, three had sold land before 1950, and the members of three others worked as gardeners elsewhere—for instance, in Lalbagh. Of the landless, over half (eleven households) had members who were ritual players in the Karaga *jatre*. Four households belonged to the family of the Karaga priest. Two households each belonged to the

"Ganachari" and "Gante Pujari" families; one each belonged to the "Banka Pujari," the "Kolkara," and the "Potha Raja" families. This factor presents us with an interesting feature of the Karaga *jatre*. The main ritual players seem to be those without land, whereas the Gowdas, who are the headmen of the Vahnikula Kshatriyas in different areas, belong to the middle range of garden landowners, creating a class difference within the community that is offset by ritual importance.

As in the other areas, most of those households in Tigalarapet that owned land in 1950 had less than three acres, the largest number (twelve households) holding between one and two acres, and a significant number (eleven households) holding less than one acre of land. In contrast to the other areas, however, in Tigalarapet all those households cultivating gardens held land outside the neighborhood, most of them (forty households) in other areas of Bangalore (see Table A2). This was because even a century before 1950, Tigalarapet was a completely built-up environment, because it was located in the City, as the map of that period in chapter 2 shows. The land of most of the households (thirty-four) was irrigated through wells, and the land of the others (eight households) was irrigated through a combination of wells and sewage canals. Of the two households that held land outside the city, one held between two and three acres in Hoskote town, and another held between three and five acres in Devanahalli town, both on the outskirts of Bangalore. Almost all those who held land in Bangalore (thirty-eight households) marketed their produce (chiefly vegetables) in K. R. Market, which was proximate to their residential plots, whereas two marketed their produce in the two markets of the city and two in other towns (see Table A3). More garden owners from Tigalarapet appeared to have shops or to be pavement sellers than in other areas (seventeen households), nearly half the total number of gardeners. A majority (twenty-three households) used wholesalers as did those in other areas.

By 1997, the same developments overtook these gardeners as those in Sampangiramnagar, because the areas in which they held their land were prime business and residential zones of the city (see Table A1). Sixty households were landless by 1997. As in Sampangiramnagar, the majority of the households in Tigalarapet (twenty-two) sold their land to private persons or developers, some (thirteen households) had their land acquired by city authorities, and others (five households) lost their land through a combination of these forces (see Table A4).

Predictably, these changes had far-reaching consequences for the occupational structure of Vahnikula Kshatriya households in Bangalore. Tables A5, A6, and A7 show the Vahnikula Kshatriya landholding patterns for all three study areas: the present sizes of households (in 1997) are shown against each stratum of land ownership as it was in 1950 for the three study areas. In Doopanahalli, the majority of households (five) across all strata of had either four or five members (see Table A5). In Tigalarapet and Sampangiramnagar, as well, more households fell into these categories than any other (see Tables A6 and A7). Between four and five members per household was the norm in 1997 in all three areas among the households surveyed.

The landholding pattern in 1950 is correlated to the changes in occupational structure after that period. As I stated earlier, all households claimed that gardening was their occupation in 1950, even when they did not own their own plots of land. In 1997, out of the one hundred households surveyed, only seven had some land, increasing the number of landless households from twenty-eight to ninety-three.

Tables A8, A9, and A10 depict occupational patterns of Vahnikula Kshatriyas in all three study areas, the number of males and females in each landholding stratum in 1950, and the occupations of various members of the households in 1997. The occupations themselves are not differentiated according to gender because, in all the households surveyed, only two women, one in Sampangiramnagar and another in Tigalarapet, worked in any occupation other than housework; both these women did some tailoring work within their homes. The category "housework" shown in Tables A8–A10 refers to women only. Gender difference with respect to occupation is thus very marked in the community. Nearly all the women work at home, and even those with some educational qualifications do so either in their natal or affinal families. This gender bias can also be related to the Karaga performance. Men chiefly perform the Karaga *jatre;* women have

Table A5.
Landholding and family size of Vahnikula Kshatriyas in Doopanahalli

Amount of land of each household, in acres, 1950	Number of family members in each household, 1997						
	2	3	4	5	6	7	Total
0	0	0	0	2	0	1	3
> 0 to < 1	0	0	1	1	1	0	3
1 to < 2	1	1	3	0	0	0	5
2 to < 3	1	0	1	2	0	0	4
Total	2	1	5	5	1	1	15

Table A6.

Landholding and family size of Vahnikula Kshatriyas in Sampangiramnagar

Amount of land of each household, in acres, 1950	Number of family members in each household, 1997								
	3	4	5	6	8	9	10	16	Total
0	0	1	1	1	0	1	1	0	5
> 0 to < 1	0	0	0	0	0	0	0	1	1
1 to < 2	0	1	4	1	0	0	0	0	6
2 to < 3	0	2	1	0	0	0	0	0	3
3 to < 5	0	0	0	2	0	0	0	0	2
5 to < 10	1	1	0	0	1	0	0	0	3
> 10	0	2	0	0	1	0	0	0	3
Total	1	7	6	4	2	1	1	1	23

Table A7.

Landholding and family size of Vahnikula Kshatriyas in Tigalarapet

Amount of land of each household, in acres, 1950	2	3	4	5	6	7	8	9	11	12	Total
0	1	0	5	4	7	2	0	1	0	0	20
> 0 to < 1	0	1	3	3	2	0	0	1	0	1	11
1 to < 2	1	1	4	5	0	1	0	0	0	0	12
2 to < 3	0	2	2	2	2	0	0	1	0	0	9
3 to < 5	0	1	0	1	2	0	0	1	1	0	6
5 to < 10	0	0	1	1	0	0	0	0	0	0	2
> 10	0	1	0	0	0	0	1	0	0	0	2
Total	2	6	15	16	13	3	1	4	1	1	62

Table A8.
Vahnikula Kshatriya occupations in Doopanahalli, 1997

Household landholding, in acres, 1950	Occupations of family members				
	Males	Females	NA	S	H
0	12	5	1	5	5
> 0 to < 1	10	5	0	2	5
1 to < 2	14	8	1	9	5
2 to < 3	9	7	1	6	4
Total	45	25	3	22	19

Household landholding, in acres, 1950	Occupations of family members				
	G	P	F	PS	PL	U
0	0	0	2	0	4	0
> 0 to < 1	0	0	0	0	8	0
1 to < 2	0	0	0	4	3	0
2 to < 3	0	0	0	5	0	0
Total	0	0	2	9	15	0

Note: NA = not applicable (old or very young); S = student; H = housework;
G = government employment; P = professional work; F = factory work;
PS = petty self-employment; PL = petty labor; U = unemployed.

few and extremely circumscribed roles during the festival. Most women are present at the temple on some occasions, but they may not be present at the site where the Karaga is born, nor may they take any main ritual roles in the performance except in assisting their husbands, brothers, or fathers to do so. Tables A8–A10 also show those unemployed (again, all males) and those who do not work (old or retired men and small children). Students include both boys and girls, although the data revealed that most girls did not study beyond high school. Most of the older generation had no educational qualifications at all (these statistics are not shown in the table), as literacy in this community is a fairly recent phenomenon, essentially dating from the 1960s.

The occupational groups shown in Tables A8–A10 require some explanation. "Government employment" refers to work for various departments in the city's bureaucracy—for instance, work in the Government Press, as accounts officers, and so on. All those who were surveyed in all

Table A9.
Vahnikula Kshatriya occupations in Sampangiramnagar, 1997

Household landholding, in acres, 1950	Occupations of family members				
	Males	Females	NA	S	H
0	16	18	2	11	9
> 0 to < 1	7	9	0	4	6
1 to < 2	19	11	5	5	7
2 to < 3	6	7	2	2	5
3 to < 5	7	5	2	3	3
5 to < 10	8	7	2	4	4
> 10	7	9	0	6	6
Total	70	66	13	35	40

Household landholding, in acres, 1950	Occupations of family members				
	G	P	F	PS	PL	U
0	3	3	1	4	0	1
> 0 to < 1	3	0	0	0	0	3
1 to < 2	1	0	0	4	4	4
2 to < 3	0	0	0	2	1	1
3 to < 5	1	0	0	2	0	1
5 to < 10	0	0	1	3	0	1
> 10	0	0	0	4	0	0
Total	8	3	2	19	5	11

Note: NA = not applicable (old or very young); S = student; H = housework; G = government employment; P = professional work; F = factory work; PS = petty self-employment; PL = petty labor; U = unemployed.

three of the study areas (thirteen persons) fell in low-income categories rather than those with high positions in the administration. "Professional work" includes work as doctors, engineers, lawyers, and insurance agents, and there were only four persons in this category in all three areas. The "factory work" category includes twelve persons who worked for public-sector factories such as Hindustan Aeronautics, Ltd., or Bharat Electronics or in the private sector factories. The majority of men (eighty-two) worked

Table A10.

Vahnikula Kshatriya occupations in Tigalarapet, 1997

Household landholding, in acres, 1950	Occupations of family members				
	Males	Females	NA	S	H
0	53	54	22	16	34
> 0 to < 1	32	31	9	14	19
1 to < 2	31	22	12	6	17
2 to < 3	25	20	6	10	14
3 to < 5	20	20	6	13	12
5 to < 10	6	3	0	5	2
> 10	5	6	1	2	3
Total	172	156	56	66	101

Household landholding, in acres, 1950	Occupations of family members					
	G	P	F	PS	PL	U
0	3	0	1	18	10	3
> 0 to < 1	1	1	1	8	7	3
1 to < 2	0	0	3	9	6	0
2 to < 3	0	0	0	8	5	2
3 to < 5	0	0	3	6	0	0
5 to < 10	0	0	0	2	0	0
> 10	1	0	0	3	0	1
Total	5	1	8	54	28	9

Note: NA = not applicable (old or very young); S = student; H = housework;
G = government employment; P = professional work; F = factory work;
PS = petty self-employment; PL = petty labor; U = unemployed.

in "petty self-employment," which included small operations that they ran and owned as limestone merchants, vegetable or other vendors, printers or binders, electricians, carpenters, operators of small engineering works, mechanics with garages, and so on. Those in "petty labor" (forty-eight persons) worked chiefly in the informal sector, with no businesses of their own or without ownership of their means of production; these included gardeners for houses or companies, drivers, screen printers, or those who worked for others in various petty businesses. Twenty men were unemployed, most of them younger men who had just finished their studies.

As Tables A8–A10 reveal for each landholding stratum, primarily those households with less than three acres of land in 1950, nearly all of which had lost these plots by 1997, had family members who worked as petty laborers. Again, it was mainly these groups who worked for the government as low-level employees or as factory workers or showed unemployment among their members. Nearly all households across all strata had men employed in some petty business or trade. Only Doopanahalli and Sampangiramnagar had households without such occupations in the stratum of landless or less than one acre, and only Doopanahalli had no persons who were government employees or professionals.

Notes

Introduction

1. The temple is also known as the Dharmaraya Temple.

2. Jois 1988; S. M. Munivenkatappa, no date, 13.

3. The word *jatre* is related to the Sanskrit word *yatra*, meaning "pilgrimage."

4. The Vahnikula Kshatriya community may also refer to him as "master" *(swami)*.

5. Therefore, as far as south India is concerned, Rowe 1973 supports Pocock's 1960 perspective in his analysis of Bangalore and Madras. Singer 1972, in his early study, also of Madras, similarly deterritorializes the category of the urban by emphasizing overarching civilizational continuities in India so that the fields of local and nonlocal forces are sometimes difficult to separate.

6. A representative but not exhaustive list of works on these themes includes Bapat 1981; Buch 1987; Dahiwale 1988; De Souza 1978; D'Souza 1968; Dobbin 1972; Fox 1969; Fox (ed.) 1970; Harris 1978; Joshi and Joshi 1976; Kosambi 1986; Lewandowski 1980; Lynch 1969; Mahadev 1975; Majumdar [1960] 1975; Majumdar and Majumdar 1978; Oldenburg 1976; Pantham 1976; Pethe 1964; Ramu 1988; Ray 1979; Rosenthal (ed.) 1976; Samaj 1958; Vidyarthi 1969.

7. For instance, Allchin 1995; Banga (ed.) 1991; Bayly [1983] 1988; Chakrabarti 1995; Cohen 1998; Dickey 1993; Hancock 1999; Haynes 1991; Llewellyn-Jones 1985; Luhrmann 1996; Manor 1993; Mines 1994; Misra 1998; Singer 1991; Tillotson (ed.) 1998; Yang 1999.

8. See Bakker 1986; Bhatnagar 1996; Blake 1991; Chaudhuri (ed.) 1990; Gollings 1991; Kalia 1987 and 1994; Luther 1995; Michell and Eaton 1992; Patel and Thorner (eds.) 1995a and 1995b.

9. See, for instance, Eck 1982; Smith and Reynolds (eds.) 1987.

10. See David 1997; Ghosh 1995; Nilekani 1998; Selvadurai 1998.

11. Shafi 1996, 20–21.

12. Srinivas 1995.

13. Srinivas 1998.

14. Srinivas 1997.

15. The use of the term "landscape" here is a direct allusion to the *akam* genre of classical Tamil poetry, in which five landscapes—the mountains, forest, lowland, seashore, and desert—are described (see Ludden 1985; Pillay 1975, 160–88; Ramanujan 1975). Differences in topography and water supply underlay the regions detailed in this early poetry. In this book, the landscape discussed is an urban one. Outside India, Schama's study of landscape and memory in the European tradition is a magisterial work (Schama 1995).

16. An exploration of similar themes occurs in Bodnar 1992; Favro 1996; Glassberg 1990; Jacobs 1996; Kammen 1991; Kasson 1978; Muir 1981; and Ryan 1997.

17. This is somewhat similar to the contrast between what Pierre Nora calls "environments of memory" and "places of memory." He sees the latter as artificial sites that have replaced the true and living memory of peoples, a characteristic of modernity (Nora 1989). Again, the distinction between "figured" and "disfigured" cities evokes a similar contrast (see Boyer 1995). See also Hannigan 1998, Sorokin 1992, and Wallace 1996 on the creation of theme parks, museums, and historical memory in the American city.

18. See, for example, Boyer 1996; Lefebvre 1991; Yaeger 1996.

19. Important works by scholars exploring these transnational circuits and port cities, Indian Ocean centers, and inland urban sites include Abu-Lughod 1989, Broeze (ed.) 1989 and 1997, and Chaudhuri 1990.

20. See, for instance, Amstrong and McGee 1985; Castells (ed.) 1985; Castells 1989; Sassen 2000.

21. This is largely true, for instance, of Harvey 1985.

22. This is, of course, a generalization, but see Jacobs (1996, 13–37) for a review of some of the trends within postmodern and postcolonial theories with respect to the city with which I generally agree.

23. See, for example, Ghannam 1998; Gregory 1998; Heitzman 1999b; Holston (ed.) 1999; Joseph 1999; Nzegwu 1996; Perera 1996; Taylor and Jamieson 1997; Watts 1996.

24. See, for instance, Arendt 1958.

25. For an elaboration of these definitions, see Seidman 1989; Sennet 1974.

26. Habermas 1991.

27. There is, of course, a wide range of scholarship on the public sphere. See especially Calhoun's discussion of the nature of the public sphere and civil society in China with respect to the 1989 students' movement (Calhoun 1994), as well as his earlier edited volume (Calhoun 1992), both of which examine, refine, and reformulate Habermas's idea of the public sphere.

28. On the suitability of practical discourse as a basis for discourse in the public sphere, see McCarthy 1992.

29. The literature on these themes is a growing, gargantuan body. My personal favorites are Uberoi 1978 and Visvanathan 1997.

1. Civic Rituals in the New "Silicon Valley"

1. Some believe that the new town was named by Kempe Gowda after a small hamlet near Hebbal Lake from which his mother, wife, and daughter-in-law hailed (Sundara Rao 1985, 4). It has also been suggested that the town's name derives from "Vengaluru," the town dedicated by the founder to the deity Lord Venkata of Tirupati

Hill, although the temple of Venkateshwara inside the fort was probably built much later, between 1687 and 1704 (see Hayavadana Rao 1924).

2. Many of the shrines built by Kempe Gowda were Shaiva, such as the cave temple of Gavi Gangadhareswara and the Basava Temple on the outskirts of the fort settlement. In later years, Kempe Gowda II built the Someshwara Temple in Halsur village on the east side of the fort, as well as the Ranganatha Temple in the fort area. Kempe Gowda II is also credited with constructing four towers on the outskirts of the settlement marking its boundaries.

3. See Rao, Shulman, and Subrahmanyam (1992, 82–92) for a description of similar towns in Tamil Nadu under the Nayakas.

4. I am aware that the nature and extent of Vijayanagar's authority and administrative apparatus and its relationship to the Nayakas is a subject of debate, with different interpretations followed by such authors as Karashima 1992 and Rao, Shulman, and Subrahmanyam 1992. It seems as if the descriptions of Kempe Gowda in popular accounts invoke at least some of the language and qualities described by Rao and others (55–56) with respect to the Nayakas in Tamil Nadu.

5. The Vijayanagar king, Achyutaraya, bestowed on Kempe Gowda ten villages: Halsuru, Varturu, Beguru, Jigane, Talaghattapura, Kengeri, Kimbalagodu, Hesaraghatta, Kannalli, and Chikkabanavara. These villages are part of Bangalore today (Sundara Rao 1985, 21).

6. Sundara Rao 1985, 121–24.

7. After 1881, they were called the Bangalore City Municipality and the Bangalore Civil and Military Station Municipality.

8. Hasan 1970, 180.

9. Bangalore Development Authority 1995, 1.

10. Ibid., 1.

11. This figure is given by the *Bangalore Metropolitan Region (BMR) Draft Structure Plan* (1998, 22).

12. Ibid. The concept of the "urban agglomeration" was introduced for census purposes in 1971 and represents the continuous urban spread of a town and its adjoining urban outgrowths or two or more physically contiguous towns, together with the contiguous and well-recognized urban outgrowths. According to the 1991 Census, there were twenty-two urban agglomerations in Karnataka, of which Bangalore was the largest (*Karnataka State Gazetteer Decennial Supplement* 1994, 84).

13. This is based on the *Comprehensive Development Plan (Revised)* of 1995 (Bangalore Development Authority 1995). See also *Bangalore Metropolitan Region (BMR) Draft Structure Plan* 1998, 22.

14. This figure is from the *Bangalore Metropolitan Region (BMR) Draft Structure Plan* (1998, 23). Bangalore district as a whole, covering an area of 8,005 square kilometers, is divided into Bangalore Urban and Rural Districts. Bangalore Urban District is now divided into the three subdistricts *(taluks)* of Anekal, Bangalore North, and Bangalore South. The subdistricts of the district itself, created in 1863, have varied in their boundaries from decade to decade.

15. *Bangalore Metropolitan Region (BMR) Draft Structure Plan* 1998, 24. This includes Bangalore Urban and Rural Districts and the Malur subdivision of the adjoining Kolar district.

16. Bangalore Development Authority 1995, 16.

17. *Karnataka State Gazetteer Bangalore District* 1990, 140–41. To my knowledge, there are no recent census figures on language distribution in the district.

18. Ibid. To my knowledge, there are no recent census figures on religious affiliation in the district.

19. He describes this mode as comprising technical relationships of production between labor and matter such that "knowledge intervenes upon knowledge itself in order to generate higher productivity" (Castells 1989, 10).

20. However, Heitzman 1997b speculates that, given the rate of population growth in the city, it is unlikely that both will be able to generate additional employment to balance population increases. Therefore, it may be private-sector enterprises, especially microelectronics and software producers with foreign links, that will cause growth in employment.

21. See also Gist 1986; Heitzman 1992, 1997b, and 1999a; Holmstrom 1994; Prakasa Rao and Tewari 1986; Rame Gowda 1977; Rowe 1973; and Vyasulu and Reddy 1985.

22. Venkatarayappa 1957, 58–60.

23. Ibid., 57–58.

24. Ibid., 61.

25. There were also 489 primary schools, 79 middle schools, and 41 high schools in 1948 (ibid., 70–77).

26. *Karnataka State Gazetteer Decennial Supplement* 1994, 213–14.

27. Ibid., 190.

28. Ibid., 213–14.

29. This estimate is provided by Heitzman 1997b.

30. "Government Pulls Out All Stops for IT Corridor," *Times of India* (Bangalore), November 17, 1999.

31. See Heitzman 1999a.

32. "Government Pulls Out All Stops for IT Corridor."

33. *Karnataka State Gazetteer Decennial Supplement* 1994, 190.

34. Bangalore Development Authority 1995, 41. The workforce of the city is defined as those belonging to the category of "main workers"—that is, those who are engaged in economically productive activity for a period of 183 days or more during the year.

35. Of these groups, the Bangalore Development Authority estimates that there are 3,000 certified goldsmiths, 2,500 certified silversmiths, 1,000 diamond setters and jewelers, and 3,500 licensed jewelers. In the transport sector, autorickshaws are a crucial mode of travel, and there are about 30,000 drivers of these vehicles. The document also estimates that about 2,000 brokers operate in the informal sector (Bangalore Development Authority 1995, 36).

36. Thippaiah 1993, 93–130, 116–19, 255, 297–319.

37. Bangalore Development Authority 1995, 39.

38. Immanuel Wallerstein 1974 describes the origins of the world economy as emerging out of Europe in the sixteenth century. His emphasis is on a network controlled by Europe as a unifying factor for understanding the first world system. King 1990 provides a somewhat similar emphasis through his examination of European

colonialism and urbanism. Abu-Lughod 1989 and Chaudhuri 1990 have a different perspective: they focus on the Arab and Asian worlds to a great extent and study the period before European economic or political dominance.

39. See Heitzman 1997a, who describes temple-directed urbanism in medieval south India, where temples provided modes of agrarian expansion and networks of control in the hinterlands. See also Appadurai and Breckenridge 1976, who show that up until the colonial period, the deity and the temple stood at the apex of a redistributive process.

40. My approach to the spatial arenas of the city differs from those of earlier studies of the "social ecology" of Bangalore, which also classified the city into separate zones. Venkatarayappa 1957, whose study is possibly the first comprehensive sociological study of Bangalore, divides the city into seven zones primarily through the nature and type of activities carried out in them. "A zone conceived thus is a unit typifying a particular activity in preponderance, though its total distribution may be scattered," he wrote. (123). Thus he divides the city into the business zone, the factory zone, the agricultural zone, the culture zone, the middle-class residential zone, the retired peoples' residential zone, and the military zone. This study heavily reflects preoccupations that were common to American urban sociology of the same period. Gist 1986, however, points out that the city did not demonstrate the type of features typical of a European or American city for various reasons. One of them is that residential segregation did not fall into a core/periphery pattern as in the United States, but was variegated according to religious or caste concentrations—for example, Muslims versus Brahmins or literates versus members of depressed castes. My own understanding of the zones of concentration and suburbanization does not depend so much on the type of activities or religious and caste segregation, but rather on the articulation of civic-spatial arenas and cult centers.

41. See Srinivas 1995.

42. See Srinivas 1999b.

43. See Srinivas 1995.

44. *Karnataka State Gazetteer Decennial Supplement* 1994, 693–700.

45. Ibid. See also Ashton and Christie 1977 on Yakshagana in Karnataka.

46. The first Kannada "talkie" was screened in 1934, and between 1981 and 1992 as many as 790 Kannada films were produced. The number in previous decades was about 702 altogether. The astonishing growth in the 1980s and 1990s was due to the scheme of the Government of Karnataka of granting a 50 percent tax exemption for each film in Kannada (*Karnataka State Gazetteer Decennial Supplement* 1994, 700–702). These figures, of course, exclude films shown in other languages in Bangalore and other parts of the state.

47. *Karnataka State Gazetteer Decennial Supplement* 1994, 688–93.

48. Beals 1964.

49. Hanur, ed., 1991, 475–83.

50. Ibid.

51. *Karnataka State Gazetteer Bangalore District* 1990, 196–97.

52. *Mysore Gazetteer* 1930, vol. 5, 29–31.

53. See Filliozat 1991, 151–52; Mugali [1946] 1990, 70–71; and Sinopoli 1993, 627.

54. See Beck 1982; Blackburn et al. 1989; Bruin 1994; Hiltebeitel 1988a; Roghair 1982.

55. Important contributions have already been made regarding performances related to the cult of Draupadi and the *Mahabharata* in south India, chiefly in Tamil Nadu. Hiltebeitel's work (see 1988a and 1991a) resulted in an extensive two-volume study of the Draupadi cult. He concentrates on the mythological and ritual dimensions of the cult, with data largely drawn from the recitations of the *Mahabharata* and the Terukkuttu performances during the festival cycle. The most detailed and sustained reference to Bangalore in his work is in Hiltebeitel 1991a, 30–34, where he discusses ritual officiants in the Draupadi cult. Frasca 1984 and 1994 carried out early work on the ritual, social, and aesthetic significance of Terukkuttu that focuses on themes from the *Villiputtur Paratam,* regarded as the Tamil *Mahabharata.* Bruin 1994 studied Kattaikkuttu, a Tamil theater form that uses motifs and themes from the *Mahabharata.* Other studies focusing on Draupadi temples and their ritual aspects outside Tamil Nadu include Tanaka 1991 on a site in Sri Lanka and Babb 1974 in Singapore, but this is not an exhaustive list.

56. In this, it differs from Hiltebeitel's hypothesis regarding the Draupadi cult in Tamil Nadu, its association with Islam in its militant forms, and the representation of this event in the figure of one of Draupadi's two guardian devotees, Muttal Ravuttan (see especially Hiltebeitel 1988a, 17, 101–27). I will not speculate here whether the militant figure is substitutable by the Sufi saint except to say that the latter is central in Bangalore.

57. There is an enormous and growing literature in a number of fields on the relationship between the body, individual or social, and the body politic. In sociology, the influence of Marcel Mauss and Émile Durkheim, both individually and jointly, has been enduring. I have been deeply influenced by their work as well as by that of Max Gluckman, Victor Turner, J. P. S. Uberoi, and others who emerged from the Manchester school of social anthropology and emphasized the interpenetration of these various bodies and the forms of control, exchange, and transformation that are possible. M. M. Bakhtin's corpus of work on language, oral practices, and their relationship to the body and performance is another important influence. In this study, I refer mostly to those works that locate the body in its relationship to the city.

58. This is the interpretation followed, for instance, by Rao 1978.

59. Biardeau (1989a, 128–31) suggests that other goddesses also played this role.

60. See Amstrong and McGee 1985 for a similar argument about noncapitalist production systems. Also see Sen 1975 for a powerful analysis of the "unintended city" of the poor in Calcutta.

61. I am grateful to Narendra Pani for asking pointed questions about the occupation of the priest one day in Bangalore, which sparked my detailed reflection described in the paragraph.

62. Variety of speech and the presence of multilingualism in cultures have been practices familiar to students of linguistics since the mid-1950s, emanating from the studies of Charles Ferguson 1959, William Labov 1966, and others. However, it was after sociolinguistics came into its own with the work of Dell Hymes and John J. Gumperz (see Gumperz and Hymes [1972] 1986) that a focus on the "ethnog-

raphy of communication" began to permeate studies of performance. See, for instance, Bauman 1986.

63. See Fabian 1990, 3–20, for a review of the deployment of the term "performance" in anthropology. Studies of performance within a larger historical and social context are visible occasionally in *The Drama Review* (see, for instance, Frasca 1994, Harris 1994, Huangpu 1992, and Kitazawa 1992).

64. See Worthern's critique (1995) in *The Drama Review.* This essentialism parallels the treatment of performance by folkloristics. As Appadurai, Korom, and Mills (1994, 467–68) remark, "folklore" is a term that needs to be problematized not only because of its European conceptual basis, but also because of its romantic essentialism.

65. This seems to be the implication of Fabian's work (1990, 12). Fabian appears to prioritize time over space (even though he accepts that space is also a dimension of performance) in his study.

66. See Bhandare 1993 for a study of the epistemological status of *smriti.* She does not emphasize the separation between *smriti* and *smarana.*

67. Therefore, Kersenboom (1995, 19–20, 93–94) argues that the Sanskrit word *smara* and the Tamil word *marapu* combine the ideas of love, memory, tradition, and worship and that memory is sustained by living gurus who transmit the tradition.

68. As Connerton (1989, 21–36) points out in his lucid exposition, "habit-memory"—the ways in which we habitually reproduce certain performances—has not really been dealt with by social scientists. Part of the problem is the reliance on a theory of language that separates "rules" and "application" or cannot deal with accumulative practices in which the skills of habit reside.

69. Chaitanya and the early Gaudiya Goswamis did this for Vrindavan in north India as well. I am grateful to Fred Smith for this reminder.

70. I am grateful to Barbara Kirshenblatt-Gimblett (personal communication) for this formulation. This intentionality with reference to the present moves us beyond the rather formal and hierarchical classification of performance traditions in India followed by Richmond, Swann, and Zarrilli 1990.

71. Lakshmana 1999, 59; Munivenkatappa, no date, 24.

72. Similar arguments have been made for "hegemonic masculinity" that is reworked into a context of social and economic marginalization: see Taylor and Jamieson 1997 on Sheffield, the "city of steel." Speaking about Buffalo Bill's Wild West, which presented spectacles of armed and costumed Plains Indian warriors in 1880s New Orleans, Roach argues that this show dramatized the closure of the frontier and the disenfranchisement of the American Indians. Again, border skirmishes enacted by Mardi Gras Indian gangs in the city, their particularly masculine emphasis, their fraternal organization, and their patriarchal dedication to the Big Chief recall post–Civil War rhetoric about resurgent Black manhood and the bravery of Black regiments on behalf of the Union cause (Roach 1996, 202–6).

73. M. M. Bakhtin 1981 uses the term "heteroglossia" to reflect on the ceaseless battle in language, society, and the individual between centripetal and centrifugal forces. Etymologically, heteroglossia means the variety of "tongue" or "voice" (a "voice" being not so much an individual's utterance, but a worldview harnessed to a discourse, ideological motifs, and a practice). His theory of language, unlike that of

Saussure, Jakobson, Chomsky, or Barthes, is set against strict formalization and the notion of a "system." It stresses the fragility and the ineluctably historical nature of language and social forms. Society is represented as a contradictory, polysemic world with different tongues. In such a world, there is constant interaction between meanings: a word, a literary form, or a dramatic performance becomes dialogized because of competing definitions assigned to the same thing. As Bakhtin writes, "Dialogism is the characteristic epistemological mode of a world dominated by heteroglossia" (426). The postulation of certain unmediated categories (and a single, unitary language) actually gives expression to forces working toward sociopolitical and cultural centralization. It ignores the fact that a word, discourse, or language can be "double-voiced," that is, it is a form that serves "two speakers at the same time and expresses simultaneously two different intentions" (324).

2. Models of the Garden City

1. Lynch (1960, 46–48) identifies five elements that are significant in organizing the "image" of the city, including "paths," "edges," "districts," "nodes," and "landmarks." These refer to physical forms, but also provide a system of orientation for citizens. See also Favro 1996, who uses the five elements of urban design identified by Lynch to analyze how the orchestration of various components of urban architecture occurred to create an unified and enduring urban image of Augustan Rome. In recent years, the works of Lefebvre 1991, de Certeau 1984, and time-space geographers such as Thrift 1996 have also emphasized the role of spatial practices and the body in movement to arrive at an understanding of the city.

2. As Gupta 1991 shows, the twelve largest towns in south India in 1871 continued to be those that had been central places even in the previous century: five of them were pilgrimage centers, four were strategic sites, and three were ports. Gupta argues that it does not appear that the British created any new pattern of urbanism apart from setting up enclaves in Madras and Bangalore.

3. This, of course, has historical parallels elsewhere. In ancient Greece, such as in old Athens and even in cities in Asia Minor that were colonized by the Greeks, the idea of public space was dispersed in many sites. By the second century, forums were created, such as the *agora*, in which civic space came to occupy the center of the city and power became increasingly personalized and centralized (see Ratte 1998 and Sennet 1996, 31–67). In Rome, similarly, the creation of an urban armature followed in the years after the Roman Empire reached its apogee, especially after Julius Caesar's death in the first century BCE. Many of these changes have been attributed to Augustus Caesar, who redirected the paths, nodes, and landmarks of the city to create an urban image of Rome as the locus and "stage" of the empire (see Favro 1996).

4. Bangalore's pattern was also common to some cities in Karnataka's neighboring state of Maharashtra, such as Pune. A variant is also found in the work of Pieper 1980, who describes the spatial structure of Suchindram town, located close to the southernmost tip of the Indian peninsula, as composed of five elements. These include a temple, an east-west ceremonial path, a circular processional road, two inland roads, and aquatic structures around the square tank and the river. The pattern of organization of the modern town is attributed largely to the Nayakas of Madurai, who developed this pattern in the middle of the seventeenth century. See also Gupta

1991 for an analysis of patterns of urbanism in south India in the eighteenth and nineteenth centuries and a description of a number of other cities in the region.

5. Fritz, Michell, and Rao 1984; Sinopoli 1997; Stein 1989.

6. These forts were at Magadi, Devarayana Durga, Hoskote, and other sites. Gupta (1991, 128) cites Colin Mackenzie, who makes a distinction between places that had the suffix *kotta (kote)* and those called *durgam (durga)*, both names for fortifications. Mackenzie sees the former as an earlier formation designed to protect all the inhabitants, whereas the latter grew up in the last days of Vijayanagar and was meant to protect the viceroy's family and retainers.

7. Sundara Rao (1985, 19, 96) states that Kempe Gowda's fort had seven gates: Halsur, Sondekoppa, Kengeri, Yelahanka, Yeshwantpura, Anekal, and Kanakanahalli Gates; by the mid-1700s, the main gates were Halsur, Yelahanka, Yeshwantpura, Anekal, Sondekoppa, and Mysore Gates. See also Jayapal 1997 for a description of Kempe Gowda's Bangalore and that of Haider Ali and Tippu Sultan.

8. This was the area that came to be known as Khalasipalya or Kalasapalyam (Sundara Rao 1985, 183).

9. Ibid., 361–62.

10. Sundara Rao (1985, 21) mentions that the Vahnikula Kshatriyas lived in the area around Halsur Gate from the time of Kempe Gowda and seems to suggest that the Karaga *jatre* associated with the Dharmaraja Temple has continued from that time onward.

11. Ibid., 23–26.

12. Morrison 1993 also states that tanks were found in large numbers in the Vijayanagar capital. These were often part of interlinked systems, with multiple tanks related to each other so that the runoff from one led to another and the tanks were connected to wells.

13. Agarwal and Narain 1997, 204–5.

14. Sundara Rao 1985, 326.

15. Agarwal and Narain 1997, 204–5.

16. Rau (1968, 11) writes that until 1897 the supply of potable water for the northwestern part of the City came from the Dharmambudi Tank, and water was let out into basins constructed at convenient points on the streets.

17. Sundara Rao 1985, 21, 96.

18. Hasan 1970, 212.

19. *Karnataka State Gazetteer Bangalore District* 1990, 236.

20. Koch 1998.

21. Hasan 1970, 212–13; *Karnataka State Gazetteer Bangalore District* 1990, 236–37.

22. In 1990, the list of plants in the gardens covered 127 families, and the gardens themselves covered an area of ninety-seven hectares (*Karnataka State Gazetteer Bangalore District* 1990, 237–38).

23. An eleven-foot statue of Queen Victoria was later unveiled in 1906, apparently a replica of a similar statue in Worcester, England, created by Sir Thomas Brock (*Karnataka State Gazetteer Bangalore District* 1990, 239). See also Jayapal 1997 for a description of some of the major statues in Bangalore.

24. See Chandy 1983 and Jayapal 1997.

25. Venkatarayappa 1957, 15.

26. Hasan 1970, 128.

27. Gundappa 1968, 25. The Glass House bore a family resemblance to the Crystal Palace in Syndenham, England, when it moved there in 1854 after its completion as a world exhibition hall.

28. Sir L. B. Bowring, the British commissioner of Bangalore in the 1860s, built the Miller Tank to supply water to the Cantonment, because the water pumped from the existing Halsur, Shoolay, and Pudupacherry Tanks was insufficient. The "Great Famine" occurred in 1875–77, and in 1882 the chief engineer of the Madras Sappers and Miners, Lt. Col. R. H. Sankey, built the Sankey Tank in the northern part of present-day Bangalore to augment the drinking water of the Civil and Military Station. In 1892, Sir K. Seshadri Iyer, the diwan of Mysore state, constructed the Hessarghatta Tank to supply water to Bangalore besides making improvements in the existing tanks, such as the Yele Malappa Chetty, Kakol, and Byata Tanks. In 1930, considering the fast growth of the city, the Mysore government gave its approval to the construction of a reservoir at the Thippagondanahalli Tank (see Hasan 1970 and Narendra 1993).

29. At the national level, the reports of the Committee on Urban Land Policy (1965), the Task Force on Housing and Urban Development (1983), and the National Commission on Urbanization (1988) are important documents. The first serious effort at laying down an urban land policy was the Third Five-Year Plan, where the control of urban land values was recognized, but from the Fifth Five-Year Plan onward, clearer guidelines were laid down and plans were made with respect to urban land policy (see Ravindra 1996).

30. Although there are a number of laws governing land, the following laws enacted by the government of Karnataka are applicable to Bangalore city (Ravindra 1996, 35–39). The Karnataka Town and Country Planning Act, 1961; the Bangalore Development Authority Act, 1976; and the Bangalore Metropolitan Region Development Authority Act, 1985, all control the use of land with a view to regulate its planned growth and development. The Land Acquisition Act, 1894, and the Karnataka Industrial Areas Development Board Act, 1966 can both be used to acquire land for public purposes, including industrial development. The Karnataka Municipal Corporation Act, 1976, and Zoning Regulations and Building Bylaws are aimed at controlling building activity and land development. Other relevant laws are the Karnataka Slum Improvement and Clearance Act, 1973, the Urban Land Ceiling Act, 1976, the Karnataka Land Reforms Act, 1961, the Karnataka Land Revenue Act, 1964, and the Karnataka Urban Development Authorities Act, 1987.

31. Ravindra 1996, 105.

32. These recommendations were embodied in the "Report of the Expert Committee Constituted by the Government for Submitting Proposals for Preservation, Restoration or Otherwise of the Existing Tanks in the Bangalore Metropolitan Area."

33. "The Charm of Greens and Serenity," *The Indian Post* (Bombay), November 2, 1987; "Changing Face of the City," *The Hindu* (Madras), August 13, 1988; Arun Bhatia, "Bangalore's Tanks Go to Seed," *Deccan Herald* (Bangalore), March 19, 1989; "Policy Options to Save Bangalore," *Deccan Herald* (Bangalore), April 25, 1989; "Above Normal," *Sunday,* June 6, 1993; "The Heat Is On!" *Indian Express* (Bangalore),

March 19, 1994; "Is Paradise Lost?" *Indian Express* (Bangalore), October 15, 1994; "City Green Belt Area Reduced," *Deccan Herald* (Bangalore), March 18, 1995; "Plans to Beautify Bangalore Gather Dust," *The Hindu* (Madras), June 5, 1995; "Citizens Get Together in a Bid to Save the Yediyur Lake," *The Sunday Times of India* (Bangalore), September 19, 1999.

34. Narendra 1993, 13–23.

35. It is estimated that 30 percent of the water needs of Bangalore can be met through harnessing rainwater runoff ("Role of Cities for Management of Urban Environment: Bangalore—An Environment Profile," *The Economic Times* (Bangalore), August 26, 1993. See also Agarwal and Narain 1997.

36. This committee was called "The High Power Committee on the Beautification of Bangalore." Whereas this report covered more ground (parks and "lung spaces," visual pollution, the role of the BDA, and other issues), in terms of its approach to tank, and green spaces in Bangalore, there was a continuity with the Lakshman Rau Committee report.

37. See also "Lake Grab," *The Week*, September 19, 1993; "A Landmark That Was," *The Hindu* (Madras), March 21, 1994; "Think Tanks," *Deccan Herald* (Bangalore), October 21, 1995; "Vanishing Lakes, Who Is to Blame?" *The Hindu* (Madras), July 15, 1996.

38. Gowda 1998.

39. By the mid-1980s, according to one estimate, 20 percent of the unauthorized construction was within the City Corporation limits, 70 percent in the conurbation area, and 10 percent in the green belt area ("Where Is the Green Belt?" *The Hindu* (Bangalore), August 9, 1987).

40. Bangalore Development Authority 1995, 78.

41. Bangalore Development Authority 1984, 109.

42. Bangalore Development Authority 1995, 207.

43. "The Tragedy of Bellandur," *CEERA Newsletter* 2 (3), 6.

44. See Heitzman 1999b for a discussion of the Indian National Games and the channeling of resources within the city toward the development of sports infrastructure.

45. "The Proposed DLF Township at T. G. Halli: A Death Sentence to Bangaloreans?" *Swabhimana*, 4 (Jan.–May 1999), 3.

46. "Lack of Vegetation Poses a Threat to Birds," *The Hindu* (Bangalore), August 6, 1999.

47. The report remarked that the tank was ill kept, with sewage water flowing into it. Portions of it had been converted into a swimming pool and a park, and there were encroachments on one side. The committee recommended that the waterfront be developed through the agencies of the Forest and Tourism Department rather than converted into parks and open spaces.

48. "BDA's Housing Plans Spell Doom for Siddapura Nurseries," *The Sunday Times of India* (Bangalore), July 13, 1997; "GO Permitting Buildings on Nursery Land Stayed," *Deccan Herald* (Bangalore), February 3, 1998; "Builders Eye Siddapura Nursery," *The Indian Express* (Bangalore), July 13, 1997.

49. *Karnataka State Gazetteer Decennial Supplement* 1994, 152–58.

50. Venkatarayappa (1957, 23–24, 130–33) points out that people in Mavalli, Siddapura, Kankanapalya, Munireddypalya, Palace Guthalli, and Hebbal were mainly

gardeners, but gardens for vegetables and fruits were also found in the north, south, and western edges of the city.

51. Venkatarayappa 1957, 89.

52. These were the parcels accounted for in surveys 58, 79, and 99 in Neelasandra village.

53. Sampangiramnagar forms part of District 9, as defined by the BDA (Bangalore Development Authority 1995, 174–75). The district as a whole, covering 688.25 hectares, is primarily residential in character (29.69 percent), although the area used for transportation, including roads and two main bus junctions, covers a larger area (31.45 percent). Parks and open spaces cover only 10.76 percent; they are exceeded by industrial areas (12.87 percent), but only marginally exceed public and semipublic areas (7.96 percent) and commercial areas (7.27 percent).

54. Doopanahalli forms parts of District 8A (with a total area of 1,622.97 hectares) as defined by the BDA (Bangalore Development Authority 1995, 167–69) and is described as comprising well-developed residential extensions toward the western part of the district and agricultural lands toward the east; there are thirteen "rural pockets." The residential area was 27.68 percent of the total area; industrial, 23.92 percent; parks and open spaces, 19.97 percent; transportation, 17.64 percent; public and semipublic, 8.00 percent; and commercial, 3.09 percent.

55. Stallybrass and White 1996 also make the point that for liminal categories, center and periphery are related symbolically and politically.

3. The Urban Performative Complex

1. The *Mysore Gazetteer,* which covered the Bangalore region in 1930 (although the boundaries of the district were different from the ones that exist today), reveals that of the thirty-four *jatre* in the district of Bangalore, nine were dedicated to goddesses (1930, vol. 5, 29–31). In 1990, of twenty-eight major *jatre* in Bangalore district, eight were dedicated to goddesses (*Karnataka State Gazetteer Bangalore District* 1990, 194–95). The data reveal that nearly all of these are boundary goddesses.

2. The *Karnataka State Gazetteer Bangalore District* (1990, 41) points out that neolithic remains have been unearthed in Bangalore and that about 1000 BCE it was a megalithic center.

3. The earliest Chola record is that of Rajaraja I (985–1016) and was found in Kamasandra in Hoskote subdistrict. Parts of Bangalore district were under two Chola provinces *(mandalas)*—Mudigonda Cholamandala and Nigaril Cholamandala (ibid., 48–49).

4. Champakalakshmi 1996, 45–46.

5. The priests of the latter temple and the Gadagamma Temple are Vaishnava.

6. The image dominating the sanctum, however, is a relatively recent one of the goddess Mahalakshmi, and it is paired with two other forms, those of Gajalakshmi and Vaibhavamurti.

7. James Heitzman, personal communication.

8. Sinopoli (1993, 627) points out that a number of images of Hanuman have been found in the archaeological surveys carried out in the Vijayanagar capital and were associated with roads and gates.

9. After India won its independence from Britain in 1947, the king was replaced by a golden throne carrying the figure of the goddess Bhuvaneshwari accompanied by a huge procession of floats, dancers from different parts of the state, the Palace Guards, the National Cadet Corps, and schoolchildren. The Mysore Agricultural, Industrial, and Fine Arts Fair, begun in 1888, turned into an annual exhibition along with a state-level sports event.

10. There are descriptions of the Dassera at Hampi, the imperial capital, by Abdur Razaak, a Moorish traveler, dating from 1443, and by Domingo Paes, a Portuguese traveler, from a century later.

11. Sinopoli and Morrison 1995, 87.

12. *Dasara Cultural Festivities 1981 Souvenir* 1981, 3–7, 25–33, 61–65, 67–70; Deepak 1993; Kamath 1987.

13. After the last Anglo-Mysore war, the British troops pulled out of Srirangapattanam near Mysore and moved to Bangalore. From 1831 to 1861, the Mysore king paid a sum of 50,000 rupees annually to the Madras government for the return of Srirangapattanam to Mysore. Further, in 1831 the British divested the king, Krishnaraja Wodeyar III, of his authority over the state and instead established a British Commission to rule it until 1881, when the commission was to come to an end. The "instrument of transfer," however, allowed the Cantonment to continue as a separate area of jurisdiction within the king's territories, with a British resident entrusted with its administration.

14. In Bangalore, the creation of the Cantonment had links with housing reforms before 1914 in Britain, which were centered in industrial cities with notions of providing some civic elegance. These reforms were often based on the contrast between working-class areas and landscaped suburbs as well as the creation of a corporate civic life through the building of the town halls or law courts (see Tarn 1980).

15. In 1932, there were three religious congregations of men (the Jesuits, the Redemptionists, and the Brothers of Mount Poinsur) and seven congregations of women (of which the Good Shepherd Sisters were probably the oldest). In 1988, the numbers of male and female congregations had risen to thirty and eighty-three, respectively (Simo, no date).

16. *Karnataka State Gazetteer Bangalore District* 1990, 143. To my knowledge, there are no recent census figures.

17. *Souvenir St. Mary's Basilica* 1974, no page number.

18. The British officers in the Cantonment attended St. Patrick's Church, by contrast.

19. *Karnataka State Gazetteer Bangalore District* 1990, 143. To my knowledge, there are no recent census figures.

20. See also Bayly 1989 and Eaton 1978.

21. *Karnataka State Gazetteer Bangalore District* 1990, 194–95.

22. Assayag 1993, 139.

23. The *Karnataka State Gazetteer Bangalore District* (1990, 940–41) states that Bangalore has nearly four hundred mosques, the oldest ascribed to the Mughals and built in 1687 in the City area. A mosque built more recently near the K. R. Market in the City area—the Jamia Masjid—was founded in 1940, whereas the Jumma Masjid in the Cantonment was built in the early part of the nineteenth century. The *Gazeteer* does not give us the number of *dargahs* in Bangalore.

24. According to Nissar Ahmed, a devotee of the saint familiarly called "Bawaji," the early part of Bawaji's education was due to the efforts of a Kutchi Memon in Madras whom Bawaji visited as a boy. When he was older, the father of Moulana Abul Kalam Azad, one of the heroes of the Indian independence struggle and the erstwhile librarian of Baghdad University, was his teacher. Later, Bawaji became Azad's mentor. He had also spent some years at Baghdad, and he was instructed to go to Lebanon to meet Saiyid Abdullah Jibli. According to Nissar, Abdullah Jibli was a contemporary of the Prophet Mohammad, and it is believed that he will live until the day of judgment. Bawaji became a disciple of Abdullah Jibli and was instructed to wear a black robe. He had been away from home for nearly seven years when the Prophet instructed him to return and serve his mother. There his family, having given him up for dead, were getting ready to perform his death anniversary, when he arrived in Kutch (interviews with Nissar Ahmed, 1994–95).

25. Nissar Ahmed, a Kutchi Memon devotee of the saint, states that the saint was unusual in that he was not only a mystic, but also a theologian, and was well versed in the four schools of Islamic law. He could trace his ancestry from the Prophet on both his mother's and his father's side. His mother belonged to the family of Sufis of the Chishti order of Ajmer.

26. The shrine houses important relics that make it an attraction to many Muslims. These include a footprint of the Prophet Mohammad on a marble slab that on the day of the Friday congregation exudes moisture considered to have healing properties, as well as a hair of al-Azam Dastgir and one of the Prophet. The latter two relics are exhibited on the death anniversary of al-Azam Dastgir and the Prophet's birthday, respectively. The footprint is displayed every Friday, the day when the largest number of people visit the shrine.

27. Cutchi Memon Jamath 1991.

28. These informants requested that their names not be disclosed.

29. The lineage of the Haider Shah Jilani is associated with Kutch-Bhuj in Gujarat, where there are almost three hundred shrines of the family, all associated with this Sufi tradition. The lineage is closely linked with the Kutchi Memon community, in Kutch as well as in other cities where the Memon community has migrated. It is said that the Kutchi Memons were converted to Islam by the efforts of Saiyid Abdullah, one of the two brothers (the other was Ali) who came from Syria about six hundred years ago. Later on, the Memons were advised by the saints to spread throughout the country, a condition of their prosperity, and so they began to settle in different parts of India. The largest Memon communities, apart from those at Kutch, are to be found in the major metropolitan cities of India. The Sufi saints also spread out to guide and provide spiritual succor to the various Memon families in different areas (Dadani 1971).

30. Khuddus Sahib related these and other accounts to me on various occasions during my fieldwork year, 1994–95.

31. O.T.C. Road is the Old Taluk Kutchery Road, which contained the "kutchery," or offices of the *taluk* or subdistrict.

32. The *Karnataka State Gazetteer Bangalore District* (1990, 942) remarks that Tawakkul Mastan hailed from Arabia and worked as a mason to build the fort of Haider Ali.

33. Bayly 1989, 111.

34. The devotion is associated with a statue, which was brought from Spain to Bohemia by a Spanish princess in whose family the statue was a treasured heirloom. This image was presented by the lady to her daughter, Princess Polixena Lobkowitz, who entrusted it to the Carmelites of Prague after her husband's death in 1623, apparently with the prophetic words: "Honor and respect the Child Jesus and you shall never be in want." In 1630, the Novitiate of the Carmelites was removed to Munich during the Thirty-Years' War and returned to Prague after the enemy withdrew from the city. Fr. Cyrillus was sent to the city to restore the sacred statue to its original place of worship, but found the statue mutilated, its hands missing. When he knelt before it in prayer, he heard the words: "Have pity on me, and I will have pity on you. Give me my hands, and I will give you peace." By a generous donation, the fathers sought to replace the mutilated statue. But scarcely had it been installed when it was destroyed by a falling candlestick and the prior struck down by a dangerous illness. The succeeding prior then restored the hands to the original statue, and its pleasure manifested itself when the prior fell ill to a citywide pestilence, but was saved after he offered mass before the image for nine days (*Prayer Book of Infant Jesus* 1979).

35. *New Catholic Encyclopedia* 1967, 500–501.

36. The church itself is the center of the parish where the Mass is celebrated. On weekdays, two Masses are celebrated every morning in Tamil, and there is one in the evening in English. On Thursdays, designated as the day of the Infant Jesus, nine Masses are celebrated, two each in English and Tamil; one each in Kannada, Konkani, and Malayalam; and two that are concelebrations in several languages.

37. They depict the following scenes: the birth of Jesus, the worship of the Infant by the shepherds and kings, Jesus at Nazareth, Jesus in the temple, the veneration of the Infant Jesus statue by the kings and queens of Europe, the transfer of the statue from Princess Maria to her daughter Polixena at her wedding in Prague in the sixteenth century, the gift of the statue to the Carmelites, the curing of Father Prior by the miraculous Infant, and the "tent" church of Viveknagar.

38. The hourly novena (to be said at the same time every hour for nine consecutive hours of one day), from a pamphlet distributed by the church reads: "O Jesus, who said: 'Ask and you shall receive, seek and you shall find, knock and it shall be opened to you,' through the intercession of Mary, Your Holy Mother, I knock, I seek, I ask that my prayer be granted. (Mention your request.) O Jesus, who said: 'All that you ask of the father in My name, He will grant you,' through the intercession of Mary, Your Holy Mother, I humbly and urgently ask your father in your name that my prayer be granted. (Mention your request.) O Jesus who said, 'Heaven and Earth shall pass away, but my word shall not pass,' through the intercession of Mary, Your Holy Mother, I feel confident that my prayer will be granted."

39. Rao 1994, 3–10.

40. Although the family of the Swamigal were members of the Srivaishnava sect, it appears that there were many incidents in his own life that associated him with the deity Dattatreya, Subrahmanya, Muslim teachers, and the Nath tradition (see Rao 1994).

41. Rao 1994, 29–50.

42. Ibid., 53–75, 87–106, 109–13.

43. Ibid., 118, 145–46, 145–46, 152.

44. The Kailash Ashram follows the Advaita philosophy of Adi Shankaracharya,

according to the *Karnataka State Bangalore District Gazetteer* (1990, 150), although Rao 1994 emphasizes that the Swamigal is dedicated to Sri Vidya.

45. Rao 1994, 155.

4. The Children of Fire

1. *Karnataka State Gazetteer Bangalore District* 1990, 173.

2. Munivenkatappa 1957, 1–2. The *Mysore Gazetteer* (1930, vol. 5, 33, 258, 400) states that about 1930 there were 31,644 Tigalas in Bangalore district, 11,914 Tigalas in Kolar district, and 21,783 Tigalas in Tumkur district; the numbers of Tigalas in other districts of the Mysore state were less than 10,000. The total number of Tigalas in these three main districts was 65,341.

3. Thurston [1909] 1975, 29–32. Another source states that the two main endogamous groups among the Tigalas are the "ulli" and the "aravu" (Iyer 1988, 609–11).

4. In the context of Vanniyars in Tamil Nadu, Hiltebeitel (1988a, 35–39), states that they derive their caste name from the Sanskrit word *vahni*, "fire," which in Tamil is *vanni*. He points out that a number of late-nineteenth- and early-twentieth-century scholars record versions of a common tradition in which Vanniyars were born from a primal sage, Shambu/Campuva/Jambhava. This is a name that is associated with the Campuvarayan kings, probably Vanniyars, who ruled over the Gingee area (in present-day North Arcot district in Tamil Nadu) in the fourteenth century. He also cites two legends. One is that the Vanniyars were born to fight two demons, Vatapi and Entapi or Mahi, who had received the boon of invincibility against everything except fire. The first Vanniyar, called Vanni Raja, Banniraya, and other names, was born from the flames of the sacrificial fire to defeat these demons. He then sired five sons who became the ancestors of various caste subdivisions. Hiltebeitel points out that the demon Vatapi is a personification of the Chalukya kingdom's capital, Badami, and that these legends probably allude to the defeat of Badami by the Pallava ruler around 643. Hiltebeitel also narrates a second account told to him by the Vanniyar caste leader at the Kailas Ashram in Bangalore, cited in the previous chapter of this book, that the Vanniyars were born from the gatekeepers of the "vanni" tree in which the Pandavas hid their weapons. The gatekeepers and their descendants worshiped Draupadi and migrated to Kanchipuram, where they served as warriors in the Pallava army.

5. Interview with T. M. Manoharan, September 30, 1999.

6. Munivenkatappa, no date, 39–40; Venkataswaminayaka Varma 1919, 2–9.

7. Puttaiya 1923.

8. Hiltebeitel (1988a, 13–31) remarks that although it can be established that the Pallava period supplies a number of elements to be found today in the Draupadi cult, there is nothing that resembles a total structure in that period. For evidence of the cult, one has to look to the disruption of Chola rule and the eruption of militant Islam into the south Indian political and cultic terrain in the thirteenth and fourteenth centuries. He suggests that the cult of Draupadi was consolidated by the end of the fourteenth century and postulates a core-periphery theory for the spread of the cult. He states that the Ginjee area was the core area of the cult from which it moved to other areas by a process of diffusion. The fourteenth century (the end of Hoysala rule and the rise of Vijayanagar), the sixteenth century in the heyday of the

Nayaka rule, and the eighteenth century marked three clear moments of this diffu-sion. He also makes the argument that the latter two periods marked the dispersal of the cults to towns from village areas. Looking at the spread of the cult across the three states of Tamil Nadu, Karnataka, and Andhra Pradesh, he states that the core area appears to have been the Arcot districts, and the cult there was largely rural. In the second period, there was still rural dispersal, but the cult was also to be found in high-population areas such as Chittor, Puttur, and Salem. Finally, the cult was found connected with urban areas, larger towns and cities such as Dindigul, Madurai, Coimbatore, and Bangalore.

9. Champakalakshmi 1996, 45–46.

10. See Hiltebeitel (1988a, 65–76) for a discussion of Draupadi's role as the goddess of the northern boundary of Gingee, where the temple faces east as well. Beyond the temple, north of the fort, lay the forest.

11. This analysis largely follows Baker 1984.

12. Karashima 1992, 43–58.

13. See Baker 1984.

14. For example, Yellamma by the Kammas, Kanika Parameshwari by the Ko-matis, and Draupadi by the Pallis (see Baker 1984; Bayly 1989).

15. These areas were chiefly North Arcot, Salem, and Coimbatore in Tamil Nadu.

16. There is another group called the "Thigala Holeyas" that has been docu-mented for a village between Mysore and Bangalore. This group is classified as a Scheduled Caste, and members have chiefly agricultural occupations and do not show any trace of Tamil in their speech. They claim that they arrived in this area from Kanchipuram and worked for Vokkaliga landlords and also as bodyguards for the Mysore kings. They do not celebrate any festival dedicated to Draupadi, al-though they worship other village goddesses. G. K. Karanth (personal communica-tion) suggests that along with the migration of the main Tigala groups, it is possible that a number of satellite castes also arrived in this area.

17. They live chiefly in Tumkur district and a few other areas in and around Bangalore city, such as Yelahanka, Channapatna, Ramnagaram, Magadi, and Nela-mangala.

18. These were at Tumkur, Kunigal, Turuvekere, and Kadaba near Bangalore.

19. These were the "Vidya Abhivridhi Sangha" and the "Tigalara Kshema Ab-hivridhi Sangha," respectively.

20. Interview with L. Narendra Babu, December 17, 1996.

21. Ibid.

22. Interview with Ramaswamy Naicker, January 10, 1997.

23. Ibid.

24. Translated from Tamil by James Heitzman.

25. Interview with Ramaswamy Naicker and N. Mahalingam, December 6, 1996.

26. Interview with Ramaswamy Naicker and M. Natarajan, January 10, 1997.

27. Mr. Dhananjaya, whose family members have been priests of the temple for more than sixty years, said that the Yadavas belong to three categories: the Pujari Yadavas, associated with the temple; the Tamil Yadavas, who are milk deliverers; and Telugu cowherds.

28. See Hiltebeitel (1988a, 10, 184–90, 221) on the relationship between Draupadi and Krishna as siblings and the Vanniyars and Yadavas, who venerate them as their lineage deities.

29. On similar fire-walking rituals in Tamil Nadu associated with the Draupadi cult, see Hiltebeitel (1991a, chapter 14).

30. This kind of explanation occurs at other sites where the fire-walk is done—for instance, at the Vahnikula Kshatriya festival of Draupadi at Malur town some distance from Bangalore.

31. Interview, January 10, 1997.

32. As Hiltebeitel shows, the Draupadi cult builds on pan-Indian popular traditions of a menstruating Draupadi who vowed after she was abused at the dice match between the Pandavas and their cousins, the Kauravas, that she would keep her hair unbound until she could dress it with the blood of the Kaurava Duryodhana's thigh. Bound and braided hair is associated with married and auspicious women, and Draupadi's unbound hair and bloody demands instead have their counterparts in festivals dedicated to the fierce goddess Kali (see Hiltebeitel 1991b, 388, 436; Hiltebeitel 1981; Hiltebeitel 1988a, 436–48).

33. This temple stands near Ulsoor Tank, and the central image is that of the deity Shiva. Many of the peripheral shrines appear to have been added after 1973, dedicated to Durga, Ganesha, and so on. There is, however, a separate side enclosure for the images of Dharmaraja, Draupadi, and the other Pandavas.

34. A narrator from Kanchipuram usually recites the *Mahabharata*, and the festival goes on for nearly six weeks. A series of dramas and storytelling episodes occurs, somewhat similar to those in the Terukkuttu theater of Tamil Nadu. The main image of veneration during the Karaga festival is that of Draupadi, a parrot in her right hand kept at the right-hand side of the Ankala Parameshwari image during the festival. The Karaga, a structure three feet tall covered with jasmine flowers—made four times during the festival at a Murugan shrine near the tank of Ulsoor—is carried each time by a different bearer.

35. Hiltebeitel (1988a, 37–38) argues that the notion of a Kshatriya fire race (Agnikula) goes beyond the formal claim in the *purana* that there are only two Kshatriya royal lines, the solar and lunar. According to south Indian traditions, the three kingdoms of the classical Sangam age included lunar Pandyas, solar Cholas, and fiery Cheras. It is possible, he states, that a prototypical Agnikula myth was present in different parts of ancient India, for similar stories about origins are found among the Rajputs in north India (see also the discussion in Hiltebeitel 1999, chapter 13).

36. There were various reasons for this focus on Mysore. These included the fact that the Kannada-speaking groups in the Madras Presidency were a minority, the districts of coastal Karnataka did not have much in common with those in the Bombay Presidency, and under the Nizam's autocratic rule no popular movement developed in Hyderabad (see Manor 1989).

37. In 1880–81, there were only 132 students in the two colleges of Mysore state; this number rose to 438 in 1910–11.

38. For instance, under the diwans Rangacharlu (1881–83), Seshadri Iyer (1883–1900), and Madhava Rao (1906–1909).

39. Kuppuswamy 1978, 41–43.

40. See Manor 1977 and 1989.

41. In Bangalore, for instance, many Tamil, Kannada, and Telugu institutions were running by the 1890s: Venkappa's Telugu and Kannada school, the Arya Balika Patasala, the Rai Bahadur Arcot Narayanaswamy Mudaliar school, the Mohammedan Sait Hindustani school, and schools run by the Wesleyan Mission and the London Missionary Society. Three community associations were formed: the Vokkaliga Sangha (1906), the Lingayat Education Association (1905), and the Central Mohammedan Association (1909). In 1913, compulsory primary education became the norm in fifteen centers of the state, and in 1916 the government directed that 25 percent of the posts of revenue inspectors should be filled by qualified non-Brahmins (see also Thimmaiah 1993 and Kuppuswamy 1978).

42. The next year, the government issued a directive that no one should be excluded from schools or any public bodies running on government funds on the basis of caste.

43. C. R. Reddy (the first chief minister of the new Mysore state after 1947) was the inspector general of education in Mysore and played a significant role in creating this alliance.

44. Dushkin 1974; Kuppuswamy 1978; Naidu 1996; Thimmaiah 1993.

45. Before 1956, Vokkaligas constituted about 23 percent, Lingayats 13 percent, and Muslims about 5 percent of the population of Mysore state. After 1956, Lingayats constituted 16 percent, Vokkaligas about 13 percent, and Muslims about 10 percent in the new state (Manor 1977 and 1989; Thimmaiah 1993).

46. This and the next few paragraphs rely heavily on Kuppuswamy 1978 and Thimmaiah 1993, especially for the analyses of the Backward Classes commissions' reports.

47. It based its findings on three criteria of backwardness: caste or community status, literacy, and representation in government service. At the time of its report, the Lingayats constituted 15.57 percent of the population and the Vokkaligas 12.98 percent; although Scheduled Castes and Tribes taken together were about 14 percent of the population, they did not constitute a political threat to these two dominant castes.

48. Manor 1989; Pani 1983; Rajpurohit 1982.

49. Manor 1980 and 1989.

50. The commission used elaborate questionnaires and urban and rural surveys for its report. It looked at class and not just caste or religion in defining backwardness, as well as residential, economic, and occupational criteria. It also projected data from the 1911, 1931, and 1941 Censuses.

51. It recommended not more than 50 percent reservation in the state, including Scheduled Castes and Tribes.

52. Manor 1989; Thimmaiah 1993.

53. The Vokkaligas continued to be part of this category. The total reservation, including Scheduled Castes and Tribes, rose to 58 percent.

54. It undertook a census of all households in the state and submitted questionnaires to various caste and community organizations and to governmental departments. Although it seems to have underestimated 15 percent of the urban population and 7 percent of the rural, it recommended that 32.98 percent of the population be considered "backward" and that there be 27 percent reservation in the state.

55. In the Venkataswamy report, Lingayats constituted 16.92 percent of the population and Vokkaligas 11.68 percent. According to the Chinnappa Reddy report, these figures were 15.33 percent and 10.80 percent, respectively.

56. The latter order is known as Government Order (GO) No. SWD 150 BCA 94, Bangalore, dated July 25, 1994.

57. Thimmaiah 1993.

58. GO No. SWD 75 BCA 92, dated April 20, 1994.

59. GO No. SWD 150 BCA 94.

60. The records of the six assemblies convened between 1949 and 1965 do not show the party-based division of candidates that became available at the City Corporation offices only from 1971 onward.

61. According to Munivenkatappa 1950, the summer ones included greens, eggplants, ladies' fingers, cucumbers, pumpkins, radishes, onions, garlic, corn, sweet potatoes, and gourds; the winter ones were potatoes, peas, tomatoes, kidney beans, cabbage, broccoli, brussels sprouts, cauliflower, carrots, beets, turnips, capsicum, leeks, parsnips, asparagus, celery, lettuce, spinach, and parsley.

62. He served as the subeditor of the Kannada paper, *Samyukta Karnataka*, and was a freelance journalist for others.

63. In 1941, he had published a collection of short stories called *Kumkuma*, the first of a series of fictional pieces in Kannada.

64. Annaiappa was the teacher at a well-known wrestling house in Tigalara-pet as well as a devoted participant in the Karaga festival, where he led his students during the acrobatics performance. Annaiappa apparently also performed the roles of Bhima and Arjuna during the *Mahabharata* plays held at the Draupadi Temple patronized by the Shambukula Kshatriyas in Kalasapalyam during their festival.

65. Interview with S. M. Raghu and S. M. Mohan (sons of Munivenkatappa) and K. Lakshmana, December 22, 1996.

66. For instance, about 1966 the Tigala Association was formed, but included only the Vahnikula Kshatriya group.

67. In the *Karnataka Backward Classes Commission Report* (1975, vol. 2, part 2, 46), the presidents of the Agnivamsha Kshatriya Vidyabhuvrudhi Sangha, the Mysore Shambukula Kshatriya Sangha, and the Vahnikula Kshatriya Sangha from Bangalore are shown as respondents to various questionnaires and as having submitted memorandums and representations to the commission.

68. E. Krishna Narayana and M. Ramaiah of the Vahnikula Kshatriyas, T. V. Thimmegowda of the Agnikula Kshatriyas, and V. Ramaswamy and M. Muniram of the Shambukula Kshatriyas were among them.

69. The organization has four subcommittees. The education subcommittee aims at providing measures that raise educational skills within the community—for instance, through scholarships. The land reforms subcommittee has been the most effective through the prevention of land acquisition in about fifty to sixty villages in the 1970s. The health subcommittee tries to provide free medical facilities and some financial assistance. The employment subcommittee has been active in a number of areas—for instance, in trying to provide alternative means of employment to the Tigalas as well as loans to vendors.

70. The Tigala community seems to have followed the dual process outlined by Rudolph and Rudolph 1967 for other such paracommunities—for instance, the

Vanniyars of Tamil Nadu—such as the adoption of a twice-born "Kshatriya" status and making demands to the state regarding representation in political, administrative, and educational arenas. The Vanniyars of Tamil Nadu, a group earlier called the "Palli" and concentrated in the four northern districts of the state, were referred to as the Vanniya Kula Kshatriyas by 1931 due to their organized efforts a decade earlier.

71. Interview with S. Srinivas, February 14, 1997.

72. Among the more active committees were the education subcommittee, which disbursed thirty-eight scholarships ranging from 50 to 100 rupees per month, and the employment subcommittee. The latter ran a number of coaching classes for Tigalas to train them to take government examinations for various posts, ranging from telecommunications apprentices to police subinspectors and clerks, in public-sector industries, and for positions as engineers and doctors.

73. For instance, Mr. Perumal, a minister in Karnataka, won political support from Tigalas, but the Vahnikula Kshatriyas characterize him as a Vanniya (the main fire-born caste in Tamil Nadu), not a Tigala.

74. The special invitees included a former chief minister, Ramakrishna Hegde; Janata Dal Party leaders S. R. Bommai and H. D. Deve Gowda; representatives from the Bharatiya Janata Party; and members of legislature.

75. These were such castes as the Malis in Andhra Pradesh and the Pallis and Kuruvans in Tamil Nadu.

76. This meeting was called the "Karnataka Rajyada Tigala Janangada Bruhat Samavesha."

77. This is called the "Akhila Karnataka Vahnikula Kshatriya (Tigala) Jagruti Sangha."

78. Interview with E. Krishna Narayana, December 30, 1996.

79. The ministers included the deputy chief minister, Mr. Siddaramaiah; the transport minister, P. G. R. Scindia; the minister for urban development, Mr. Bachchegowda; the horticulture minister, D. T. Jayakumar; and the textiles minister, R. L. Jalappa.

80. For instance, the Kurubas in Karnataka, the Dharmaraja Kapus in Andhra Pradesh, or the Tillas in Kerala. According to Lakshmana, the word "Tigala" itself is derived from the word "Triganaru"; this word refers to the members of the three "sects" in south India—the Shaivas, the Vaishnava, and the Madhwas.

81. See also Lakshmana (1999, 23–27, 39–44) for a detailed discussion and set of claims about the origin of and relationship between these three groups. He states that Tigala origins can be traced ultimately to the Ganga Dynasty in Karnataka, although there were waves of migration of other fire-born groups later.

82. Interview with K. Lakshmana, December 18, 1996.

5. The Primal Goddess, the Polyandrous Spouse, and Celibate Warriors

1. For example, the Ramlila of Banaras cited by Schechner 1985.

2. For example, the cult of Pattini cited by Obeyesekere 1984.

3. In the 1940s and 1950s, the Karaga bearer was Chinna Bodappa (Family I). In the 1950s, the Karaga bearer was Chinnappa (Family I). In the 1960s and early 1970s, the Karaga bearer was Munibalappa (Family III). In 1974–84, the Karaga bearer was Shiv Shankar (Family II). In 1984–90, the role of the Karaga bearers rotated be-

tween Shiv Shankar (Family II) and Adiseshaiah (Family I). In 1991–93, the Karaga bearer was Shiv Shankar (Family II). In 1994, the Karaga bearer was Abhimanyu (Family III). In 1995, the Karaga bearer was Shiv Shankar (Family II). In 1996–97, the Karaga bearer was Abhimanyu (Family III).

4. See Beck 1981; Fuller 1979; Kapadia 1996; Tapper 1979.

5. "Malurina Karaga Vaibhava" 1983, 41–42.

6. These insignia are known as *shanka, chakra, trishula, gada,* and *damaru,* respectively.

7. These are known as *baku* and *mantrabetta,* respectively.

8. Mahalingam 1975, 68–70.

9. Zarrilli 1994, 10–51.

10. This is celebrated on the first day of the lunar month of "Sravana."

11. This story told by Abhimanyu is similar in its main framework to the *Mahabharata* episode "The Death of Baka" performed by Terukkuttu players in Tamil Nadu; see Hiltebeitel (1988a, 169–82) for a detailed discussion of this play and its relationship to the Sanskrit and Tamil epic renderings.

12. These are Annaiappa's gymnasium, which is visited on the sixth day of the festival; Kunjanna's gymnasium, visited on the day of the Karaga's birth (the seventh day of the festival); and Venkatdasappa's gymnasium, visited on the eighth day of the festivities.

13. Venkatarayappa 1957 states that gymnasiums were scattered all over the city in the 1950s. One of the most important ones was found near Shivaji talkies. Every week gymnasiums held wrestling matches conducted in the evenings that were attended by large crowds. Venkatarayappa (ibid., 89) reports: "Doddamma hall and the newly formed stage near Bharat talkies are very famous for these wrestling matches.... The winners are carried on the shoulders in a procession with shouts of victory."

14. The *Karnataka State Bangalore District Gazetteer* (1990, 200–201) states that an amateur wrestling association was formed in 1968 in Bangalore, and in 1978 the Karnataka Amateur Wrestling Association was formed.

15. The *Karnataka State Bangalore District Gazetteer* (1990, 933) claims that the temple appears to be an eighteenth-century creation in the Mysore style, with Vijayanagara features dominating it. It adds that features outside the sanctum, chiefly the pillared hall, were probably added in the nineteenth century.

16. *Krishnaswami padala Govinda!*
    Dharmarajaswami padala Govinda!
    Panchapandavara padala Govinda!
    Adi shakti padala Govinda!
    Panchali padala Govinda!

17. There was apparently also a community narrative about origins in the form of a written text, but this has been lost. Jois 1988 cites a written *Vanhi Purana,* but claims that this was lost as a result of Muslim raids (it is unclear which raids these were and when they occurred).

18. It is also said that this site earlier housed a cobra that was seven "coils" long and that the area was named after the cobra. As Hiltebeitel (1991a, 429–30) points out, the seven-ringed forts are usually associated with demons and enemies. Forts can be associated with the Pandavas's palace and Draupadi temples and specifically with Draupadi as Kali. See Hiltebeitel (1991a, chapter 13) for an extensive dis-

cussion of the place of fort-destruction and -entry rituals in the Draupadi cult in Tamil Nadu. In the Karaga *jatre,* the "Seven-Circled Fort" of Elusuttinakote seems to be the home of the Primal Goddess, the Seven Mothers, and Potha Raja. As I will show in the course of this chapter and the next, the tale of the association between these personages is recited outside this temple while the goat sacrifice is performed within the Dharmaraja Temple, converting the latter into the arena of a prewar sacrifice.

19. This was called the "Vahnikula Kshatriya Virakumara Sangha."

20. These flank the image of the Primal Goddess clockwise: Maheshwari, Koumari, Vaishnavi, Varahi, Indrani, Chamundeshwari, and Chaturmukhi Brahmi.

21. See especially Hiltebeitel (1988a, 333–93) for an extensive discussion of "Pottu Raja" in the Draupadi cult in Tamil Nadu. I reserve the discussion of some aspects of his argument to the next chapter.

22. See Elmore 1915; Whitehead 1921.

23. White (1996, 1–14) states that these concepts were available at least from the second century BCE and are found in the Vedic corpus (especially the *Atharva Veda*). Tantric practices, Indian medical traditions like Ayurveda, and alchemical and yogic traditions were heirs to these themes. Following various tenth- and eleventh-century reconfigurations, these were aestheticized and internalized in various ways, although they continue in the practices of various Siddhas who were considered to be alchemists and masters of yoga.

24. White 1996, 16.

25. Ibid., 20–26.

26. Ibid., 27–28.

27. Vermilion and turmeric, red, white, and yellow have various significations during the festival. The red vermilion, like the white jasmine, appears to not only signify "a hot state," but also to stand in contrast to the cooler turmeric and yellow colors. Thus the Karaga priest primarily wears yellow-colored clothes during the period of the festival to signify the singular and unmarried state of the goddess although he carries the red icon. The hero-sons similarly tie on their wrists woolen threads wrapped around turmeric roots signifying their allegiance to this hot goddess whose "children" they are.

28. According to one Gante Pujari, these are called the *virachati, arshana pettige, shelambu, gante, pampai,* and *belli bhandara,* respectively. T. M. Manoharan, a community leader, gave another interpretation of these *sacra,* which he said consisted of five objects: a drum *(damarga)* and two types of bells *(gante),* which provided sound *(shabda* or *nadya);* a whip *(chati),* which provided wakefulness *(echchara);* and a turmeric container *(arshana bhandara),* which provided peace *(shanti).*

29. Merry 1982 points out that in south India, as in other parts of the subcontinent, religious festivals are timed primarily in relation to lunar months, a month corresponding to a synodic revolution of the moon. A lunar month comprised of thirty lunar phases is reckoned between successive new moons. The fifteenth phase of the bright fortnight is reckoned as the full moon. The solar year is sidereal, which means that the revolution around the sun is calculated with reference to fixed stars. The year lasts a little more than 365 days, with twelve solar months that correspond to the twelve signs of the zodiac. The point at which the sun leaves one zodiac sign and enters another is called a *samkranti.* The name of the solar month begins with the name of the zodiac sign into which it moves on a *samkranti.* Since the solar year

is 365–66 days in duration, whereas the lunar year has fewer days, the two are synchronized by various rules. While the solar year begins with the movement of the sun into Aries, the luni-solar year in most areas begins with the preceding new moon in the lunar month of Chaitra. This rule, which is largely followed in Karnataka, ensures that the lunar months roughly correspond to the same solar months every year. The discrepancies between the two are corrected by deleting or adding some lunar time phases. Although the luni-solar calendar is common in Karnataka and the new year begins on the new moon of Chaitra, in Tamil Nadu a completely solar sidereal year prevails, although the names of the months are derived from the names of lunar months. This makes the new year in Tamil Nadu begin when the sun enters the zodiac sign of Aries, which occurs some days after the new moon and the beginning of the luni-solar year in Chaitra. The luni-solar month and the solar month roughly correspond to the Gregorian month of March-April. Although the Indian national calendar is based on the Gregorian one, for most Hindu festivals it is not used.

30. See Hiltebeitel (1988a, 135–46) for a discussion of the "three performative modes" of the Draupadi cult festival in Tamil Nadu: the recitation of the *Mahabharata* epic in Tamil by a reciter, the street drama, and a local ritual enactment. Neither the recitation of the epic nor the street drama is found in the City Karaga *jatre*, although there are themes in the plays of the street drama that strike resonances with the oral epic recited during the Karaga performance. The ritual enactment is discussed by Hiltebeitel 1991a and presents some similarities to the Karaga *jatre*.

31. Hiltebeitel 1991a carried out a detailed study of Draupadi cult rituals in Tamil Nadu. His main focus is on two ritual sites, the ritual battlefield and the firepit, although he pays attention to the rituals related to the Draupadi Temple and street drama. To summarize the hypothesis of his extremely rich account and analysis: "If there is one principle that has emerged here, it is that the most singular and durable features of Draupadi cult ritual are those that tie in not with the classical story as such, though it is hardly ignored in the ritual, but with figures and episodes from the Draupadi cult folk tradition" (3). He goes on to say that the rituals of this folk cult actually take us beyond folk traditions to the wider world of Vedic sacrifice, the Hindu temple cult, and other aspects of Hindu ritual. The ritual cycle outline he gives (36–39), which is the basis of the book's chapter scheme, involves eighteen days of rituals spread out in a larger time frame from June 2 to August 18, 1981. Of the rituals he describes, only those associated with festival opening and closing rites, including flag hoisting and lowering, the tying of the wristband, and leave-taking with turmeric water, are found in the Karaga *jatre*.

32. In 1997, there was also a ceremony that involved the initiation of the Ganachari (the man who is considered the ritual head of the community for the Karaga performance) and his wife. This man, Gopi, was replacing his brother; the latter had been the Ganachari for eight years, but had left for Australia. Gopi's wife, wearing white, also sat with him for the rituals, her presence and participation necessary for the proper acquittal of duties by her husband. By the end of the rite, she seemed to be in a trance.

33. These areas are chiefly Tigalarapet, Siddapura, Mavalli, Akkitimmanahalli, and the neighborhood of the Annamma Temple near Kempe Gowda Road (Lakshmana 1999, 65–66).

34. Moreno and Marriott 1989 also cite a similar case for a Murukan shrine in Tamil Nadu: a left-handed "cold" caste, the Natukottai Cettiyars, offer hot substances to the cooled deity at Tai Pucam, whereas the right-handed "hot" caste of the Konkuvellala Kavuntars offer cool substances during Pankuni Uttirain.

35. The Gante Pujari, Ganachari, and others blessed this priest-designate (Lakshmisha) and his wife (he was married about five months before the Karaga *jatre* in 1997). Lakshmisha had been accompanying the current priest, Abhimanyu, in all activities as an apprentice preparing for his role.

36. This tale forms part of a cycle called the *kuravanci* cycle. See also Hiltebeitel (1988a, 301–9) for an account of the transitional role of Draupadi in the play "Draupadi the Gypsy," revealing the liminal attributes that she has assumed in the forest and her heroic or cosmic aspects.

37. This is called *onge mara* locally.

38. As Hiltebeitel 1988b states, especially in shorter festivals that last ten days or less in the Draupadi cult, the nine grains *(navadhanya)* are connected to opening ceremonies such as flag hoisting and the tying of the protective amulets or wristbands on the chief officiants at the festival. Sometimes they also indicate a connection with Potha Raja, because his icon also has an amulet tied around it. In longer festivals, the nine grains are sown in the context of Draupadi's wedding. See also Hiltebeitel's account of the drama "Draupadi the Gypsy," which links the nine grain ceremonies to the story where Draupadi and Arjuna are handed roasted grains that sprout amazingly through Krishna's intervention into nine different types (Hiltebeitel 1988b, 85–86).

39. See Hiltebeitel 1985 for an analysis of Potha Raja's role in the buffalo and goat sacrifices in Serur, North Karnataka, and Gingee, Tamil Nadu. He states that the etymology of Potha Raja's name is "buffalo king," and this figure seems to be the form that the buffalo victim of the goddess takes when he is slain by her. His buffalo form removed, he becomes her devotee and handles the impure, violent, and bloody aspects of sacrifice (193).

40. This is the interpretation that T. M. Manoharan, a community leader, gave me in an interview conducted on September 30, 1999.

41. The pamphlet advertising the City Karaga *jatre* shows Krishna and Arjuna at the top of the pamphlet, with Krishna delivering the *Bhagavad Gita* sermon to Arjuna. Framing the ritual calendar on either side are depictions of the ten incarnations of Vishnu; at the bottom of the pamphlet is a depiction of the Pandava brothers and Draupadi. The framing of events is thus largely based on Vishnu's incarnations. This is not necessarily true of other sites where the performance may emphasize various goddesses.

42. This Karaga is called "Sri Muthyallamma Deviya Huvina Karaga"; the invitation pamphlet shows the goddess Muthyallamma in the center as a Primal Goddess, Ganesha on her right, and the trio of Rama, Lakshmana, and Sita (the main characters in the *Ramayana* epic) on her left.

43. Two other shrines were added around 1985: one houses the images of Arjuna, Krishna, and Dharmaraja, whereas the other houses a Ganesha image.

44. These are Maramma, Gangamma, Chowdeshpuriamma, Bhuvaneshwariamma, and Maheshwari.

45. *Mysore Gazetteer* 1930, vol. 5, 29–31.

292 • Notes to Chapter 66

46. See Lakshmana 1999, 64.

47. The first drainage system began from the Shivajinagar area and flowed past the localities of Cox Town and others in the Cantonment area to the Ulsoor Tank. This then continued past the locality now known as Damlur to reach Challaghatta Tank (an area that adjoins a golf course near the airport) southeast of the City. The second system included drains from the City Market area, Majestic, and Shantinagar to the Koramangala Tank (the site of a sports complex construction) and on into the Bellandur Tank in the south. The third system began in the localities of Malleswaram and Rajajinagar and flowed to a tank in Kengeri (a satellite town of Bangalore) on the southwest side of the City. The fourth system went northeast, flowing from the city toward the Hebbal Tank and then on to the Yellammallappa Tank near another satellite town, Krishnarajapuram.

48. *Karnataka State Gazetteer Bangalore District* 1990, 150. Around 1925, it is said that the Wodeyar rulers recognized a ritual head of the Lingayat community as a "world-guru" *(jagadguru)*, in addition to the guru of the Sringeri Monastery with whom the kings were associated, a recognition of the significance of this community in Mysore state (I am grateful to K. V. Narendra and S. Manjunath for this insight).

49. See the *Karnataka State Bangalore District Gazetteer* (1990, 932–35) for a description of some of the main shrines on this route as well as the communities connected with them. It states that most of these temples were created in the nineteenth century and renovated later.

50. *Mysore Gazetteer* 1930, vol. 5, 29–31, 257, 398–99, 592–93, 901–2, 1091–92, 1221, 1375.

51. The theme of dismemberment is common to many narratives in eighteenth-century warrior kingdoms (see Bayly 1989, 48–55).

52. Buchanan 1870, vol.1, 134–166, 165–183.

53. Ibid., 252–53, 266–68.

54. See Bakhtin 1990; Gardiner 1992.

6. Cities and Forests

1. This concept has echoes with M. M. Bakhtin's idea of the chronotope, although the chronotope was mainly applied to textual rather than oral materials. Bakhtin, the Russian philosopher of language, used the concept of the chronotope most exhaustively in his essay "Forms of Time and of the Chronotope in the Novel," which was an attempt to construct a "historical poetics" (Bakhtin 1981). The chronotope (literally, time-space) is a category he uses to refer to "the intrinsic connectedness of temporal and spatial relationships that are artistically expressed in literature" (84). "Time, as it were, thickens, takes on flesh, becomes artistically visible; likewise, space becomes charged and responsive to the movements of time, plot and history" (84). As the editor of his translated work points out, the importance of this concept lies in the fact that neither time nor space is privileged; rather, they are interdependent in forming an "optic" with which to view the cultural forces at work in a text (425–26). Elsewhere Bakhtin seemed to suggest that although chronotopes define genres and generic distinctions, they emerge from the space and time of the world to achieve representation in created works (Bakhtin 1986, 36–42, 134).

2. The theory of five landscapes in ancient Tamil literature is another referent for the Karaga *jatre*. The mountain landscape is related to bamboo but it is the

second landscape, the forest, that provides hints of the Karaga that is decorated with jasmine (*mallige* in Kannada, *mullai* in Tamil) from which this landscape also derives its name (see Sontheimer 1993, 12).

3. See, for instance, Das 1968. However, Lakshmana (1999, 15–16, 18), a Vahnikula Kshatriya writer, claims that the *Vahni Purana* is one of the eighteen Sanskrit *purana* and occurs after the *Skanda Purana*. He also states that the Vahni lineage is mentioned in the *Bhagvata Purana*.

4. Shulman 1980, 40–47.

5. The Sanskrit *Mahabharata* is usually dated between 500 BCE and 400 CE; the oldest extant texts of the *Mahabharata* belong to the medieval period in two versions: a northern and southern. By 1000, it also existed in Kannada and Tamil, for instance. The classical Sanskrit epic is narrated in eighteen books: the first is the *Adi Parvan*, which tells of the origin of the Lunar Dynasty and the marriage of the Pandava heroes to Draupadi; the second book, *Sabha Parvan*, tells of the dice match that results in the loss of the Pandavas' kingdom to their cousins. The third book, *Aranyaka Parvan*, tells of the exile of the Pandavas and Draupadi for twelve years in the forest. These are the three books that appear to be of relevance to the *Karaga Purana*. See also Bruin 1994; Frasca 1984; and Hiltebeitel 1988a and 1991a.

6. Alf Hiltebeitel's corpus of work on the Draupadi cult is crucial for this chapter. I am indebted to Alf for reading this chapter, discussing ways in which there were intersections between the *Karaga Purana* and the Draupadi cult, and offering extensive comments. Although this is not exhaustive, an interested reader may look for the following themes in his works that have a bearing on this chapter. See Hiltebeitel 1999 for an exploration of the relationship between the Draupadi cult *Mahabharata*, South Asian regional martial epics, and classical epics. See Hiltebeitel 1988a on the relationship between Potha Raja (or Pottu Raja-Pormannan), and Telugu and Tamil mythologies that connect him with other goddesses (347–67); on the genealogical history of Potha Raja/Pormannan (339); on Potha Raja/Pormannan and "Sivanandapuri," a city that has seven forts that Parvati drew on the ground with a piece of wood and Shiva brought to life, predicting that it would also be destroyed by wood (336–40); on Potha Raja's father's beheading (343–47); and on Bhima's entry into the fort of Potha Raja (340–41). Specifically with respect to Draupadi, see Hiltebeitel on the relationship between Draupadi and Krishna and the fact that Arjuna's many wives are seen as Krishna's sisters in the Tamil Draupadi cult (1988a: 10, 219); on the invocation to Draupadi (4–5); on cult implements in the Draupadi cult in Tamil Nadu (382–93); on the role of the forest Draupadi (7, 74–75, 287–309); on Draupadi giving birth nongenitally in her forest aspect (292–94); on Draupadi and Kali (132, 291, 294, 307, 434); on Draupadi's cosmic form (85, 291, 293); on Draupadi's marriage to the five Pandavas and her second birth (Hiltebeitel 1991a, 483–89); and on Draupadi temple personnel (22–34).

7. See Venkatesha Acharya 1981.

8. The war occurs after the fifth book of the classical Sanskrit epic and for six more books.

9. The persona of Pampa's patron, Arikesari II of the Rashtrakutas, is superimposed onto the character of Arjuna in his version.

10. See Venkatesha Acharya 1981.

11. See especially Coburn 1984, 1991, and 1996.

12. The "Devi: The Great Goddess" exhibition at the Sackler Gallery of the Smithsonian, June–September 1999, had some of these exhibits, especially in two sections, "Cosmic Force" and "Local Protectors." The exhibition publication is Dehejia 1999.

13. Pampa, who belongs to the classical tradition of Kannada literature, wrote a Kannada *Mahabharata* called *Vikramarjunavijaya* in the tenth century in a style known as *champu*, which interspersed prose and poetry. For Tamil literature, Perundevanar, who composed a *Mahabharata* in the ninth century, also used a similar form of composition. It has been speculated that after the tenth century, these compositions became very popular in south India and that it may have been Jain poets, who cultivated Kannada in the early days of its history, who were the originators of this form (Mugali [1946] 1990, 154–55).

14. See Eco (1979, 21), for instance, on the idea of "intertextual knowledge."

15. See also Jois 1988, Lakshmana 1999, Nanjundayya and Iyer (1931, vol. 4, 609–20), and Rao 1978, for a description of the roles of some of these players.

16. Interview with Y. Vasudev and S. Tyagaraja, July 23, 1996.

17. Biardeau 1989b deals extensively with Potha Raja, but in this chapter I refer mostly to Hiltebeitel's interpretation of Potha Raja, whenever appropriate, in the context of the Draupadi cult.

18. The translation and transcription of the *Karaga Purana* from a 1996 recording is given hereafter. The information presented in square brackets is my gloss of the words used in the narrative. The epic is presented here in the order in which the prose and song sections were presented during the recitation. I am deeply indebted to Mrs. Nirmala Sarma, who translated and transcribed these sections of the *Karaga Purana* from a recording that I made of the narration in 1996. One change that I have made in the text of the recitation is in Potha Raja's name. He was referred to in the original recitation as Pothu Raju, the way that he is generally referred to in the Telugu of the recitation. However, I have used "Potha Raja," the way in which he was otherwise referred to, to prevent confusion.

19. This invocation of Rama's name is a suggestion of the connections of this community with both Vaishnavism and Shaivism. It also makes the link, in this specific context, between Draupadi, who was lost with the kingdom in the game of dice, her humiliation at the hands of the Kauravas, and her saving by Krishna, whose "sister" she is seen as in the south Indian context. As avatars of Vishnu, Rama and Krishna can be identified.

20. I can only speculate that "Utdanda" is a combination of *uttara* (northern) and *danda* (rod of authority), suggesting that Potha Raja was an authority of the northern region.

21. This is known as *rangoli* in Kannada or *kolam* in Tamil.

22. In the *Epic of Palnadu* (Roghair 1982), Shiva has also ruled a fort called Sivanandi in the distant past, and it comes to be associated with Potha Raja, who guards it. He then becomes a sort of caretaker of two children, a boy and a girl, in the fort who leave various articles of cult worship behind when they escape from pursuers who lay siege to the fort. They also leave behind infant twins, a boy and a girl.

23. In the *Karaga Purana*, they were described as "Lambanis," a nomadic group in this part of south India.

24. These were the *aralingam, gurulingam, trishulam, dabargam,* and *viragombe,* respectively.

25. The "leaf from which milk trickled" suggests a tree's latex and could be identified with the Sanskrit *sami* (fire) tree—the Tamil *vanni* tree—which is said to give both milk and fire, by providing a horizontal stick associated with Vedic sacrifice; the *vanni* tree is also significant in Vanniyar marriages (see Hiltebeitel 1988a, 35–36). Potha Raja's handling of this "leaf" portends both sacrifice and marriage.

26. See Lakshmana (1999, 52–54), where a similar story is cited. Here it is Parvati who goes to Brahma for help and asks for Shiva, who is destroying the world, five times. Brahma grants her wish, but since it was fivefold, he states that either she may have her one husband in five lives or all five parts of her husband in one life. She opts for the latter, and as Draupadi in her next life is married to five men.

27. In the *Devi Mahatmya,* the "mothers" appear from seven gods in the third story: from Brahma, Brahmani; from Shiva, Maheshwari; from Skanda, Kaumari; from Vishnu, Vaishnavi; from Varaha (Vishnu's boar incarnation), Varahi; from Narasimha (Vishnu's man-lion incarnation), Narasimhi; and from Indira, Indrani or Aindri (Coburn 1984, 314–15).

28. Coburn 1984, 108.

29. This is found in chapter 88 of the *Devi Mahatmya;* see Coburn 1984, 109–10.

30. The name "Suvarnagiri" ("golden mountain") for one of them is an immediately recognizable reference to the golden mountain, Meru, where Shiva and Parvati were thought to reside.

31. Kinsley 1997, 81.

32. Alternately, another interpretation is that the headdress is basically of the kind worn by brides of the community.

33. Kinsley 1997, 81.

34. Tamil myths (see Shulman 1980) sometimes insist on the presence of milk with blood at the same moment that a sacred site is discovered or founded, and this may be represented in the form of certain colors, white and red for instance. Often blood and milk can be combined in one image—for instance, the breast. In the case of the Karaga, the red color of the icon is combined with the white of jasmine flowers.

35. The central element of the Tamil myths, according to Shulman 1980, is the marriage of the goddess to the god; this is important for the cult, as it is the central event of the shrine, and also as a prototype for human marriage. The male deity usually joins the goddess at her shrine: The latter is earthbound and linked to dark soil and the womb. Therefore, to merge with the goddess is to merge with the life-giving but dark world of the goddess. In the Tamil country and much of south India, the woman is conceived of mythically as a concentration of dangerous erotic power that is sometimes represented as residing in her breasts. Therefore, women must be controlled, and a major form of this control is chastity. A chaste woman safeguards the life and prosperity of her male relatives, and the lack of chastity is life-threatening for men. The virgin goddess is a focus of "violent eroticism": she is at her most powerful as long as she is a virgin; the god marrying her is exposed to danger, because he is wedded to an incarnation of violent power, a lustful but murderous bride. This sometimes leads to a bifurcation of the goddess into a dark and a light

image so that the god marries the light bride after the sacrifice, whereas the dark one is confined to the edges of the shrine or the city. In other versions, the wedding is postponed to the end of time or the other gods prevent the marriage; she has to be kept a virgin to fight enemies, because the power accumulated through virginity cannot be squandered or dissipated. Yet virgin motherhood is important; children are conceived asexually and miraculously. Therefore, the goddess is split into at least three forms, sometimes coexistent in the same narrative: a virgin mother without a husband; a chaste wife devoted to her husband; and a divine being united with the devotee, a form of marriage (Shulman 1980, 138–50; 155–58). Draupadi does not seem particularly lustful in the *Karaga Purana,* but self-procreative motherhood seems important.

36. In the context of the Gangamma *jatre* in Tirupati in south India where a number of men embody the goddess in public spheres, Handelman 1995 argues that part of this process is the shaping of the deity's self-identity and that of the devotees. The deity acquires increasing self-awareness as she changes her guise and each one of these guises is revealed to be not her true self. At the same time, gender is shown to be a continuum of cultural imaginings to men who appear in the city as women.

37. In Mysore, the royal goddess Chamundeshwari, whose temple is on the hill outside the city, is identified with the Mahisasura myth. In many villages in Karnataka, buffalo sacrifice (although banned by the government) is still offered to village goddesses; the male god in Andhra Pradesh is sometimes a buffalo king (called Pothu Raja).

38. Mohini, in the classics, embodies the power of illusion that is connected with Vishnu when he sleeps during the night, and he projects this power as an enchanter to seduce demons. It also reminds us of other cult performances in Tamil Nadu in which Krishna appears as a woman, Mohini, and marries the son of Arjuna, Aravan, before his sacrifice on the battlefield (see Hiltebeitel 1988a, 317–32, and Hiltebeitel 1998).

39. Sontheimer 1993, 56.

40. Dravidian systems of kinship make a distinction between cross-cousins (children of opposite-sex siblings) and parallel cousins (children of same-sex siblings). They frame this within a rule of approximately this form: one shall marry a cross-cousin or a relative of one's generation who is not related as a sibling (siblings and parallel cousins are classified together). Cross-cousin marriage can occur in three varieties: bilateral, matrilateral, or patrilateral. The rule for the bilateral variety, for instance, states that a man shall marry his mother's brother's daughter or his father's sister's daughter. Because this rule does not prefer one cross-cousin to another, it requires a minimum of two intermarrying groups to establish a self-sufficient exchange. In other words, it assumes that in the beginning of the cycle two sisters are exchanged between two men (Trautman 1981, especially 200–202).

41. Most, if not all, marriages occur within the Vahnikula Kshatriya community; alliances are struck between different families, or "houses" as they are called. A system of exogamous clans within the community that is found among some groups does not appear to be present. Rather, a continuous system of receiving and giving brides between a few families from one generation to another in exchange for the giving or receiving of a bride between generations appears to be the norm. There-

fore, in the larger endogamous group of the Vahnikula Kshatriyas, there appear to be smaller circuits of endogamy that involve a few families. This exchange system is typified by the exchange between Potha Raja and Dharmaraja in the *Karaga Purana.*

42. In a large number of castes in south India, the first preference is given to a man choosing his elder sister's daughter as a bride. Another type of preferred marriage is a man's marriage with his father's sister's daughter. The third type of preferential mating is that of a man with his mother's brother's daughter (Karve 1965, 211–64).

43. The fortune-teller is an important figure in folk literature who describes a heroine's love, often for a local god. This figure was inherited by the "gypsy poetry," a late genre that inherited the soothsayer/fortune-teller of earliest Tamil love poetry (first century BCE). The fortune-teller can be a suitor-god in disguise who dresses as a woman and pretends to read signs in order to achieve union with his beloved (Shulman 1980, 289).

44. Hiltebeitel (1988a, 295–98) suggests that the role of Draupadi between her forest aspect and her role in the classical *Mahabharata* is her role as flower stringer in the kingdom of Virata, in exile, where she appears as a hairdresser to the king's wife. The collaboration between Bhima and Draupadi leads to the death of the queen's brother (with Bhima in disguise as Draupadi); it also evokes the transvestitism in Bhima and Arjuna's role.

45. There is a very strong connection here between Potha Raja and Kuttantavar—the Aravan of the Draupadi cult (son of the Pandava Arjuna and a snake princess) who is sacrificed for success in battle—analyzed by Hiltebeitel 1998. Hiltebeitel points out that at Arvan's main ritual center in South Arcot there are all kinds of "hairy" associations.

46. This son is called Abhimanyu; he dies in the battle and is succeeded by his son Parikshit. In fact, during the vow-taking by the Virakumaras, they are initiated into classes that bear the names of Abhimanyu, Parikshit, Krishna, Potha Raja, Dharmaraja, and Draupadi (the last is reserved for the two or three households that bear the Karaga by turns).

47. For an account of urban paradigms with respect to Ayodhya, the capital city of the epic hero of the *Ramayana,* see Lutgendorf 1997, which seems to describe a north Indian urban landscape.

48. See the *Karnataka State Gazetteer Bangalore District* 1990 for a detailed account of the historical periods before Bangalore's founding.

49. See Heitzman (1997a, 82–120) on "temple urbanism" in south India.

Conclusion

1. See also Srinivas 1999a.

2. Amitabh Bacchan, one of India's most popular film stars in the post-1960 era of Indian (Hindi) cinema, ran the ABCL.

3. These included two fly-overs (at Sirsi Circle and Richmond Circle), three grade separators (at Hudson Circle, Mekhri Circle, and Trinity Church Circle), one park (in Yeshwantpura), one pedestrian subway (near Sangam Theater), one crematorium (in Banashankari), the vertical expansion of Madiwala Market, and the improvement of Tavarekere Park (Gowda 1998).

4. Venkatachalam 1998.

5. *Bangalore Metropolitan Region (BMR) Draft Structure Plan* 1998, 1. This was prepared by GHK International, United Kingdom, the Tata Institute of Social Sciences, and Tata Economics Consultancy Services, India.

6. As it happened, the Congress Party, historically more centrist, won the state elections. Among the Backward Classes, the Vahnikula Kshatriyas in Bangalore had hoped to be offered two seats in the election by either the Bharatiya Janata Party or the Congress Party for their leaders, but were disappointed in receiving none. According to many people, their vote was therefore divided between the two parties.

Glossary

adi shakti: a term designating the Primal Goddess.

agni: the Sanskrit word for fire; the god of fire.

Agnikula Kshatriyas: a subgroup of a larger community called the Tigala; Kannada speakers considered indigenous to the Karnataka region.

Ambasura: a demon in the oral epic of the Karaga performance.

Amma: literally, mother; a term also used to refer to a goddess.

Anjaneya: the monkey hero and deity associated chiefly with the *Ramayana* epic as the loyal companion and devotee of the epic hero Rama; also known as Hanuman in north India.

Annamma: a local goddess whose temple is on the north side of the old Bangalore settlement.

Arati Dipa: the festival of lights during the Karaga performance, taking place on the twelfth day of the first luni-solar month, Chaitra.

Arjuna: one of the five Pandava brothers, hero of the *Mahabharata* epic.

Arokiamariamma: a local term describing Our Lady of Health at St. Mary's basilica in the Bangalore Cantonment; also known as Aarokkiya Maataa, Annai Arockiamarie, Aarogiamaate, Kanika Maata, and so on.

Bhima: one of the five Pandava brothers, hero of the *Mahabharata* epic.

Brahmin: a term designating a caste group in India that is considered ritually superior to other castes in the social hierarchy.

Cantonment: a term designating the British Civil and Military Station founded in 1809 on the eastern side of contemporary Bangalore.

Chaitra: the first luni-solar month of the Hindu calendar in Karnataka.

Chamundeshwari: a goddess believed to have felled the demon Mahisasura; associated with the dynasty of the Wodeyars in Mysore as the royal goddess.

Chola: a dynasty in south India that ruled from the ninth to the thirteenth centuries.

City: a term referring to the old settlement and market of Bangalore, founded in 1537 on the western side of the contemporary metropolis.

Dakkini Muslims: Muslims from the Deccan region of south India.

Damlur: a settlement in Bangalore near a tank by the same name, now called Domlur.

Dassera: the nine-day autumn harvest festival.

Devi Mahatmya: the most famous of all texts devoted to goddess worship, probably written about the fifth or sixth century.

Dharmambudi: a central tank in Bangalore, now extinct.

Dharmaraja: the eldest brother among the five heroes of the *Mahabharata* epic, after whom the temple associated with the Karaga performance is named; also known as Dharmaraya, Yudhishthira, Dharmananda, etc.

Dhrishtadyumna: the brother of Draupadi.

Diwans: ministers who were chief administrators under the Wodeyar rulers of Mysore.

Draupadi: the heroine of the *Mahabharata* epic who was married to the five Pandava brothers; born from fire and also known as Krishnaa, Panchali, and so on.

Dukanhalli: a settlement in Bangalore, now called Doopanahalli.

Elusuttinakote: the "Seven-Circled Fort," a temple associated with the Primal Goddess in the City area of Bangalore.

Gadagamma: a local goddess whose temple is on the east side of contemporary Bangalore, also called Gadadamma.

Ganachari: the spiritual instructor of the Karaga priest, also considered to be the "chieftain" of the lineage of the Vahnikula Kshatriyas.

Ganesha: a male deity with an elephant head, considered the son of the god Shiva and his consort Parvati.

Gante Pujari: a term referring to an individual who recites the oral epic during the Karaga performance or sing hymns that invoke Draupadi; the chief Gante Pujari is the Durga Pujari.

Govinda: another name for the male deity Krishna.

Gowda: a headman of the Vahnikula Kshatriyas in a specific area.

Haider Ali: the ruler of the kingdom of Mysore in the eighteenth century.

Haider Shah Jilani: a saint of the Qadiriya order of Sufism, who lies buried in a shrine in the Bangalore Cantonment.

Halsur: a settlement in Bangalore close to a tank by the same name, often spelled Ulsoor.

Hasi Karaga: the seventh day of the Karaga performance, when the sacred icon manifests itself.

jatre: a periodic festival in honor of a deity, usually involving the movement of a chariot carrying the image of the deity; related to *yatra,* or pilgrimage; an interlocal festival between settlements.

Kali: a fierce goddess who appears in the *Devi Mahatmya* and defeats two demons, Canda and Munda.

Kalyani Devi: the wife of the ruler of the fort city of Kalyanapuri or Shivananda Pattana in the oral epic of the *Karaga Purana*.

Kannada: the language of the southern state of Karnataka.

Karaga: a sacred pot embodying the goddess's power.

Karaga Purana: the oral epic associated with the Karaga performance, also known as the *Vahni Purana*.

Karnataka: the state in southern India of which Bangalore is the capital city.

Kempambudi: a central tank in Bangalore.

Kempe Gowda: the military chief who "founded" Bangalore in 1537.

kere: a tank, or large, artificially constructed body of water.

kote: a fort.

Krishna: the scion of the Yadavas; a male deity whose sister, Subhadra, is married to Arjuna, one of the Pandava brothers in the *Mahabharata* epic; also known as an incarnation of the deity Vishnu.

Kutchi Memons: Muslim merchants from Kutch in Gujarat state; important retailers in the Bangalore Cantonment.

Lalbagh: a botanical garden in Bangalore founded by the ruler Haider Ali in the second half of the eighteenth century.

Lingayats: one of the two dominant landed communities at the village level in Karnataka; influential in state-level politics, worshipers of Shiva.

Mahabharata: a pan-Indian epic found in Sanskrit (usually dated between 500 BCE and 400 CE), as well as in other languages in both oral and written forms; the oldest extant texts have been found in two versions, northern and southern.

Mahisasura: a buffalo-demon vanquished in myth by the goddess Chamundeshwari.

Mariamma: a local goddess usually petitioned by those with afflictions associated with the pox.

Munivenkatappa, S. M.: a prominent Vahnikula Kshatriya leader of the twentieth century.

Muthyallamma: a local goddess whose temple is on the northeast side of Bangalore near Ulsoor Tank.

Mysore: a city southwest of Bangalore; also, an older name for the region and kingdom that later constituted the state of Karnataka.

Nagalamuddamma: the sister of Potha Raja in the oral epic of the *Karaga Purana*.

Nayaka: a title for a local ruler with military powers from the fourteenth to the eighteenth centuries in south India.

Palegara: a title for a local ruler with military powers from the fourteenth to the eighteenth centuries in south India.

Pandavas: one of the two main families and protagonists (along with the Kauravas) in the *Mahabharata* epic.

Parvati: a female deity, also regarded as the consort of Shiva.

Patalamma: a local goddess whose temple is on the south side of contemporary Bangalore.

pete: a term for a settlement and market.

Pete Karaga: the night of the full moon of the Karaga performance when there is a procession through Bangalore City.

Potha Raja: the ruler of the fort city of Shivananda Pattana who is linked to the heroes of the *Mahabharata* epic through sister exchange.

pujari: a priest.

purana: a genre of literature dealing with creation, genealogies, cycles of time, histories of dynasties, local cults, sects, and origins of castes or places.

Raja Rajeshwari: a goddess revered by the religious leader Tiruchi Swamigal, whose temple lies on the southwestern outskirts of Bangalore City.

Rama: a male deity, hero of the *Ramayana* epic; also known as an incarnation of the deity Vishnu.

Sampangi: a central tank in Bangalore, now extinct.

Sampangihalli: a settlement near Sampangi Tank, now called Sampangiramnagar.

Shaiva: pertaining to the deity Shiva; devotee of Shiva.

shakti: the female principle of divinity and power.

Shambukula Kshatriyas: a subgroup of a larger community called the Tigala, traditionally Tamil speakers who migrated to Bangalore, largely in the mid-nineteenth and early twentieth centuries.

Shankavalli: the sister of the Pandava heroes in the oral epic of the *Karaga Purana.*

Shiva: a male deity usually revered in his forms as an erect phallus *(linga),* an ascetic, or a fierce destroyer, whose consort is Parvati.

Shivalinga Raju: the ruler of the fort city of Kalyanapuri or Shivananda Pattana in the oral epic of the *Karaga Purana.*

smarana: memory, recollection, reminiscence.

smriti: memory, recollection, reminiscence.

Sufi: a person following the path of Islamic mysticism; a holy man.

Tamil: the language of the southern state of Tamil Nadu.

Tawakkul Mastan Baba: a Sufi whose shrine lies in the Bangalore City area.

Telugu: the language of the southern state of Andhra Pradesh.

Terukkuttu: a Tamil theater form largely based on the Tamil *Mahabharata.*

Tigalas: a Backward Class community found chiefly in Bangalore, Kolar, and Tumkur districts; mainly Tamil speakers held to have migrated from Tamil Nadu in the past few centuries; includes subgroups such as the Tamil-speaking

Vahnikula Kshatriyas and Shambukula Kshatriyas and the Kannada-speaking Agnikula Kshatriyas.

Timirasura: a demon in the oral epic of the Karaga performance.

Tippu Sultan: a ruler of the kingdom of Mysore in the eighteenth century.

Tiruchi Swamigal: a religious teacher originally from the state of Tamil Nadu, now based in Bangalore.

Upnirinakunte: literally, "saltwater pond"; a sacred site associated with the "birth" of the Karaga icon in Bangalore's Cubbon Park.

Vahni Purana: the oral epic associated with the Karaga performance, also known as the *Karaga Purana.*

Vahnikula Kshatriyas: a subgroup of a larger community called the Tigala, traditionally gardeners by occupation and Tamil speakers.

Vaishakha: the second luni-solar month of the Hindu calendar in Karnataka.

Vaishnava: pertaining to the deity Vishnu; devotee of Vishnu.

vanni: Tamil word for fire.

Vijayanagar: an empire in south India that was dominant from the twelfth to the sixteenth centuries, with its main capital at Vijayanagara.

Virakumaras: "hero-sons" who accompany the Karaga icon as protectors.

Vokkaliga: one of the two dominant landed communities at the village level in Karnataka that is influential in state-level politics.

Vokkuta Samsthe: the "Unity Organization" of the Karnataka Tigala community, including the Vahnikula, Shambukula, and Agnikula Kshatriyas.

Wodeyars: rulers associated with the kingdom of Mysore between the sixteenth and twentieth centuries.

Yakshagana: a traditional theater form in Karnataka.

Yellamma: a local goddess associated with the pox and petitioned for healing.

Bibliography

Abu-Lughod, Janet. 1989. *Before European Hegemony: The World System A.D. 1250–1350.* New York: Oxford University Press.

Agarwal, Anil, and Sunita Narain, eds. 1997. *Dying Wisdom: Rise, Fall and Potential of India's Traditional Water Harvesting Systems. State of India's Environment 4. A Citizen's Report.* New Delhi: Centre for Science and Environment.

Aiyangar, Krishnaswami S. 1910–11. "Fire-walking Ceremony at the Dharmaraja Festival." *Quarterly Journal of the Mythic Society* 2 (2): 29–31.

Allchin, F. R. 1995. *The Archaeology of Early Historic South Asia: The Emergence of Cities and States.* Cambridge: Cambridge University Press.

Alter, Joseph S. 1992. *The Wrestler's Body: Identity and Ideology in North India.* Berkeley and Los Angeles: University of California Press.

————. 1995. "The Celibate Wrestler: Sexual Chaos, Embodied Balance and Competitive Politics in North India." *Contributions to Indian Sociology,* n.s., 29 (1–2): 109–31.

Amstrong, Warwick, and T. G. McGee. 1985. *Theatres of Accumulation: Studies in Asian and Latin American Urbanization.* London: Metheun.

Appadurai, Arjun, and Carol Breckenridge. 1976. "The South Indian Temple: Authority, Honour and Redistribution." *Contributions to Indian Sociology,* n.s., 10 (2): 187–211.

Appadurai, Arjun, Frank J. Korom, and Margaret A. Mills, eds. 1994. *Gender, Genre and Power in South Asian Expressive Traditions.* Delhi: Motilal Banarsidass.

Arendt, Hannah. 1958. *The Human Condition.* Chicago: University of Chicago Press.

Ashton, Martha Bush, and Bruce Christie. 1977. *Yaksagana: Dance Drama of India.* New Delhi: Abhinav Publications.

Assayag, Jackie. 1993. "The Goddess and the Saint: Acculturation and Hindu-Muslim Communalism in a Place of Worship in South India (Karnataka)." *Studies in History,* n.s., 9 (2): 220–45.

Babb, Lawrence. 1974. *Walking on Flowers: A Hindu Festival Cycle.* Working Paper No. 27, Department of Sociology, University of Singapore, Singapore.

Baker, Christopher John. 1984. *An Indian Rural Economy 1880–1955: The Tamilnad Countryside.* Delhi: Oxford University Press.

Bakhtin, M. M. 1981. *The Dialogic Imagination.* Austin: University of Texas Press.
———. 1986. *Speech Genres and Other Late Essays.* Austin: University of Texas Press.
———. 1990. *Art and Answerability: Early Philosophical Essays by M. M. Bakhtin.* Austin: University of Texas Press.
Bakker, Hans. 1986. *Ayodhya.* Groningen: E. Forsten.
Banga, Indu, ed. 1991. *The City in Indian History: Urban Demography, Society and Politics.* Delhi: Manohar Publications.
Bangalore Development Authority. 1984. *Comprehensive Development Plan Report.* Bangalore: Bangalore Development Authority.
———. 1995. *Comprehensive Development Plan (Revised) Bangalore Report.* Bangalore: Bangalore Development Authority.
Bangalore Metropolitan Region (BMR) Draft Structure Plan. 1998. Executive Summary. Document prepared by GHK International, United Kingdom, and the Tata Institute of Social Sciences and Tata Economics Consultancy Services, India, for the Karnataka Urban Infrastructure Development and Finance Corporation Ltd., July.
Bapat, Meera. 1981. *Shanty Town and City: The Case of Poona.* Oxford and Elmsford, N.Y.: Pergamon Press.
Bateson, Gregory. [1936] 1958. *Naven: A Survey of Problems Suggested by a Comparative Picture of the Culture of a New Guinea Tribe Drawn from Three Points of View.* Rev. ed. Stanford: Stanford University Press.
Bauman, Richard. 1986. *Story, Performance and Event: Contextual Studies of Oral Narrative.* Cambridge: Cambridge University Press.
Bayly, C. A. [1983] 1988. *Rulers, Townsmen, and Bazaars: North Indian Society in the Age of British Expansion, 1770–1870.* Cambridge: Cambridge University Press.
Bayly, Susan. 1989. *Saints, Goddesses and Kings: Muslims and Christians in South Indian Society 1700–1900.* Cambridge: Cambridge University Press.
Beals, Alan R. 1964. "Conflict and Interlocal Festivals in a South Indian Region." *Journal of Asian Studies* 23: 99–114.
Beck, Brenda E. F. 1981. "The Goddess and the Demon." *Purusartha,* 5: 83–196.
———. 1982. *The Three Twins: The Telling of a South Indian Folk Epic.* Bloomington: Indiana University Press.
Bhandare, Shaila. 1993. *Memory in Indian Epistemology: Its Nature and Status.* Delhi: Sri Satguru Publications.
Bhatnagar, V. S. 1996. *Chandigarh, the City Beautiful: Enviornmental Profile of a Modern Indian City.* New Delhi: A. P. H. Publishing Corporation.
Biardeau, Madeline. 1989a. *Hinduism: The Anthropology of a Civilisation.* Delhi: Oxford University Press.
———. 1989b. *Histoires de Poteaux: Variations Vediques Autour de la Deesse Hindoue.* Paris: Ecole Francaise d'Extreme Orient.
Blackburn, Stuart H. 1988. *Singing of Birth and Death: Texts in Performance.* Philadelphia: University of Pennsylvania Press.
Blackburn, Stuart H., Peter J. Claus, Joyce B. Flueckiger, and Susan S. Wadley, eds. 1989. *Oral Epics in India.* Berkeley: University of California Press.
Blake, Stephen P. 1991. *Shahjahanabad: The Sovereign City of Mughal India, 1639–1739.* New York: Cambridge University Press.
Bodnar, John. 1992. *Remaking America: Public Memory, Commemoration, and Patriotism in the Twentieth Century.* Princeton: Princeton University Press.

Boyer, M. Christine. 1995. "The Great Frame-up: Fantastic Appearances in Contemporary Spatial Politics." In Helen Liggett and David C. Perry, eds. *Spatial Practices: Critical Explorations in Social/Spatial Theory.* Thousand Oaks, Calif.: Sage Publications, 81–109.

———. 1996. *The City of Collective Memory: Its Historical Imagery and Architectural Entertainments.* Cambridge, Mass.: MIT Press.

Broeze, Frank, ed. 1989. *Brides of the Sea: Port Cities of Asia from the Sixteenth–Twentieth Centuries.* Honolulu: University of Hawaii Press.

———, ed. 1997. *Gateways of Asia: Port Cities of Asia in the Sixteenth–Twentieth Centuries.* London: Kegan Paul International.

Bruin, Hanne M. de. 1994. Kattaikkutttu. The Flexibility of a South Indian Theatre Tradition. Ph.D. dissertation, Leiden University.

Buch, Mahesh N. 1987. *Planning the Indian City.* New Delhi: Vikas Publishing House.

Buchanan, Francis. 1870. *A Journey from Madras through the Countries of Mysore, Canara, and Malabar.* 2 volumes. 2nd edition. Madras: Higginbotham and Co.

Calhoun, Craig, ed. 1992. *Habermas and the Public Sphere.* Cambridge, Mass.: MIT Press.

———. 1994. *Neither Gods nor Emperors: Students and the Struggle for Democracy in China.* Berkeley: University of California Press.

Castells, Manuel, ed. 1985. *High Technology, Space and Society.* Beverly Hills: Sage Publications.

———. 1989. *The Informational City: Information Technology, Economic Restructuring and the Urban-Regional Process.* Oxford: Basil Blackwell.

———. 1997. *The Power of Identity: The Information Age. Economy, Society and Culture.* Vol. 2. Malden, Mass.: Blackwell Publishers.

Certeau, Michel de. 1984. *The Practice of Everyday Life.* Berkeley: University of California Press.

Chakrabarti, Dilip K. 1995. *The Archaeology of Ancient Indian Cities.* Delhi: Oxford University Press.

Champakalakshmi, R. 1996. *Trade, Ideology and Urbanization: South India 300 BC to AD 1300.* Delhi: Oxford University Press.

Chandy, Kora. 1983. "Looking Back." *City Tab,* October 16: 9.

Chaudhuri, K. N. 1990. *Asia before Europe. Economy and Civilisation of the Indian Ocean from the Rise of Islam to 1750.* Cambridge: Cambridge University Press.

Chaudhuri, Sukanta, ed. 1990. *Calcutta: The Living City.* 2 volumes. Calcutta: Oxford University Press.

Coburn, Thomas C. 1984. *Devi-Mahatmya: The Crystallization of the Goddess Tradition.* Delhi: Motilal Banarsidass.

———. 1991. *Encountering the Goddess: A Translation of the Devi-Mahatmya and a Study of its Interpretation.* Albany: State University of New York Press.

———. 1996. "Devi: The Great Goddess." In John S. Hawley and Donna M. Wulff, eds. *Devi: Goddesses of India.* Berkeley: University of California Press, 31–48.

Cohen, Lawrence. 1998. *No Aging in India: Alzheimer's, the Bad Family, and Other Modern Things.* Berkeley: University of California Press.

Connerton, Paul. 1989. *How Societies Remember.* Cambridge: Cambridge University Press.

Cutchi Memon Jamath. 1991. *Bangalore Conspectus,* No. 3.

Dadani, Abdul Qadir Moosa. 1971. "A Glimpse into the Past." *Golden Jubilee Souvenir.* Bombay: Cutchi Memon Jamaat.

Dahiwale, S. M. 1988. *Emerging Entrepreneurship among Scheduled Castes of Contemporary India: A Study of Kolhapur City.* New Delhi: Concept Publishing Co.

Das, Veena. 1968. "A Sociological Approach to the Caste Puranas: A Case Study." *Sociological Bulletin* 17 (2): 141–64.

Dasara Cultural Festivities 1981 Souvenir. 1981. Mysore: Government of Karnataka at Government of India Text Book Press.

David, Esther. 1997. *The Walled City.* Madras: East West Books.

Deepak, N. 1993. "Dasara Utsava: Ondu Nenapu." *Janapada* (October). Bangalore: Directorate of Information and Publicity, Government of Karnataka, 6–9.

Dehejia, Vidya. 1999. With contributions by Thomas Coburn and others. *Devi: The Great Goddess. Female Divinity in South Asian Art.* Washington, D.C.: Smithsonian.

De Souza, Alfred, ed. 1978. *The Indian City: Poverty, Ecology, and Urban Development.* New Delhi: Manohar.

Dickey, Sara. 1993. *Cinema and the Urban Poor in South India.* Cambridge: Cambridge University Press.

Dobbin, Christine E. 1972. *Urban Leadership in Western India: Politics and Communities in Bombay City, 1840–1885.* London: Oxford University Press.

D'Souza, Victor S. 1968. *Social Structure of a Planned City, Chandigarh.* Bombay: Orient Longmans.

Dushkin, Lelah. 1974. *The Non-Brahmin Movement in Princely Mysore.* Ph.D. thesis, University of Pennsylvania.

Eaton, R. M. 1978. *Sufis of Bijapur (1300–1700): Social Role of Sufis in Medieval India.* Princeton: Princeton University Press.

Eck, Diana L. 1982. *Banaras, City of Light.* New York: Knopf.

Eco, Umberto. 1979. *Role of the Reader: Explorations in the Semiotics of Texts.* Bloomington: Indiana University Press.

Elmore, W. T. 1915. "Dravidian Gods in Modern Hinduism: A Study of the Local and Village Deities of Southern India." *University Studies* (Nebraska) 15 (1): 1–49.

Engineer, Asgar Ali. 1989. *Muslin Communities of Gujarat: An Exploratory Study of Bohras, Khojas, and Memons.* Delhi: Ajanta Publications.

Fabian, Johannes. 1990. *Power and Performance: Ethnographic Explorations through Proverbial Wisdom and Theater in Shaba, Zaire.* Madison: University of Wisconsin Press.

Favro, Diane. 1996. *The Urban Image of Augustan Rome.* Cambridge: Cambridge University Press.

Fentress, James, and Chris Wickham. 1992. *Social Memory.* Oxford: Blackwell.

Ferguson, Charles A. 1959. "Diglossia." *Word* 15:325–40.

Filliozat, Jean. 1991. *Religion, Philosophy, Yoga.* Delhi: Motilal Banarsidass Publishers, Pvt. Ltd.

Fox, R. G. 1969. *From Zamindar to Ballot Box: Community Change in a North Indian Market Town.* Ithaca, N.Y.: Cornell University Press.

———, ed. 1970. *Urban India: Society, Space and Image.* Monograph and Occasional Papers Series, Monograph No. 10. Program in Comparative Studies on Southern Asia. Durham, N.C.: Duke University.

Frasca, Richard Armand. 1984. *The Terukkuttu: Ritual Theatre of Tamil Nadu.* Ph.D. thesis, University of California.

———. 1994. "Panchali Capatam (The Vow of Draupadi): Images of Ritual and Political Liberation in Tamil Theatre." *Drama Review* 38, 2 (T142), 89–105.

Fritz, John M., George Michell, and M. S. Nagaraja Rao. 1984. *Where Kings and Gods Meet: The Royal Centre at Vijayanagara, India.* Tucson: University of Arizona Press.

Fuller, C. J. 1979. "Gods, Priests and Purity." *Man,* n.s., 14: 459–76.

Gardiner, Michael. 1992. *The Dialogics of Critique: M. M. Bakhtin and the Theory of Ideology.* London: Routledge.

Ghannam, Farha. 1998. "Keeping Him Connected: Labor Migration and the Production of Locality in Cairo." *City and Society,* Annual Review: 65–82.

Ghosh, Amitav. 1995. *The Calcutta Chromosome: A Novel of Fevers, Delirium, and Discovery.* New York: Avon Books.

Gist, Noel P. 1986. "The Ecology of Bangalore, India. An East-West Comparison." In Vinod K. Tewari, Jay A. Weinstein, and V. L. S. Prakasa Rao, eds. *Indian Cities: Ecological Perspectives.* New Delhi: Concept Publishing, 15–32.

Glassberg, David. 1990. *American Historical Pageantry: The Uses of Tradition in the Early Twentieth Century.* Chapel Hill: University of North Carolina Press.

Gollings, John. 1991. *City of Victory, Vijayanagara: The Medieval Hindu Capital of Southern India.* New York: Aperture.

Government of Mysore. 1968. *Outline Development Plan for the Bangalore Metropolitan Region.* Bangalore: Government Press.

Gowda, Rame. 1998. "Infrastructural Projects of Bangalore Mahanagara Palike." Paper presented at the seminar "Status of Infrastructure in Karnataka: A Year After," Bangalore.

Gregory, Steven. 1998. *Black Corona: Race and the Politics of Place in an Urban Community.* Princeton: Princeton University Press.

Gumperz, John, and Dell Hymes, eds. [1972] 1986. *Directions in Sociolinguistics: The Ethnography of Communication.* New York and Oxford: Basil Blackwell.

Gundappa, D. V. 1968. "Bangalore Municipal Presidents." In M. P. Somasekhara Rau, ed. *Growth of Self-Government in Bangalore City.* Bangalore: Gokhale Institute of Public Affairs, 25–34.

Gupta, Narayani. 1991. "Urbanism in South India: Eighteenth and Nineteenth Centuries." In Indu Banga, ed. *The City in Indian History: Urban Demography, Society and Politics.* Delhi: Manohar Publications, 121–47.

Haberman, David L. 1988. *Acting as a Way of Salvation: A Study of Raganuga Bhakti Sadhana.* New York: Oxford University Press.

Habermas, Jürgen. 1991. *The Structural Transformation of the Public Sphere: An Inquiry into a Category of Bourgeois Society.* Cambridge, Mass.: MIT Press.

Halbwachs, Maurice. 1992. *On Collective Memory.* Edited, translated, and with an introduction by Lewis A. Coser. Chicago: University of Chicago Press.

Hancock, Mary. 1999. *Womanhood in the Making: Domestic Ritual and Public Culture in Urban South India.* Boulder: Westview Press.

Handeleman, Don. 1995. "The Guises of the Goddess and the Transformation of the Male: Gangamma's Visit to Tirupati and the Continuum of Gender." In David Shulman, ed. *Syllables of Sky: Studies in South Indian Civilization in Honour of Velcheru Narayana Rao.* Delhi: Oxford University Press, 283–337.

Hannigan, John. 1998. *Fantasy City: Pleasure and Profit in the Postmodern Metropolis.* London: Routledge.

Hanur, Krishnamurthy, ed. 1991. *Encyclopaedia of Folk Culture of Karnataka.* Vol. 1. Thiruvanmiyur, Madras: Institute of Asian Studies.

Harris, Max. 1994. "Muhammed and the Virgin: Folk Dramatizations of the Battles between Moors and Christians in Modern Spain." *Drama Review* 38, 1 (T141), 45–61.

Harris, Nigel. 1978. *Economic Development, Cities and Planning: The Case of Bombay.* Bombay: Oxford University Press.

Harvey, David. 1985. *The Urbanization of Capital: Studies in the History and Theory of Capitalist Urbanization.* Baltimore: Johns Hopkins University Press.

Hasan, M. Fazlul. 1970. *Bangalore through the Centuries.* Bangalore: Historical Publications.

Haynes, Douglas E. 1991. *Rhetoric and Ritual in Colonial India: The Shaping of a Public Culture in Surat City, 1852–1928.* Berkeley: University of California Press.

Heitzman, James. 1992. "Information Systems and Urbanization in South Asia." *Contemporary South Asia* 1 (3): 363–80.

———. 1997a. *Gifts of Power: Lordship in an Early Indian State.* Delhi: Oxford University Press.

———. 1997b. "High Technology Entrepreneurship and Development in Bangalore." *Management Review* 9 (4): 89–97.

———. 1999a. "Corporate Strategy and Planning in the Science City: Bangalore as 'Silicon Valley.'" *Economic and Political Weekly,* January 30: PE2–11.

———. 1999b. "Sports and Conflict in Urban Planning: The Indian National Games in Bangalore." *Journal of Sports and Social Issues* 23 (1): 5–23.

Hiltebeitel, Alf. 1981. "Draupadi's Hair." In Madeline Biardeau, ed. *Autour de la Deesse Hindou, Purusartha,* No. 5: 179–214.

———. 1985. "On the Handling of Meat, and Related Matters, in Two South Indian Buffalo Sacrifices." In Christiano Grottanelli, ed. *Divisione della Carni: Dinamica Sociale e Organizzazione del Cosmo. L Uomo,* No. 9: 171–99.

———. 1988a. *The Cult of Draupadi.* Vol. 1. *Mythologies: From Gingee to Kurukshetra.* Chicago: University of Chicago Press.

———. 1988b. "South Indian Gardens of Adonis Revisited." In Anne-Marie Blondeau and Kristofer Schipper, eds. *Essais sur le Rituel.* Vol. 1. Louvain and Paris: Peeters, 65–91.

———. 1991a. *The Cult of Draupadi.* Vol. 2. *On Hindu Ritual and the Goddess.* Chicago: University of Chicago Press.

———. 1991b. "The Folklore of Draupadi: Saris and Hair." In Arjun Appadurai, Frank J. Korom, and Margaret Mills, eds. *Gender, Genre, and Power in South Asian Expressive Traditions.* Philadelphia: University of Pennsylvania Press, 395–427.

———. 1998. "Hair Like Snakes and Mustached Brides: Crossed Gender in an Indian Folk Cult." In Alf Hiltebeitel and Barabara D. Miller, eds. *Hair: Its Power and Meaning in Asian Cultures.* Albany: State University of New York Press, 143–176.

———. 1999. *Rethinking India's Oral and Classical Epics: Draupadi among Rajputs, Muslims, and Dalits.* Chicago: University of Chicago Press.

Holmstrom, Mark. 1994. *Bangalore as an Industrial District: Flexible Specialisation in a Labour-surplus Economy?* Pondicherry: Institut Francais de Pondicherry.

Holston, James, ed. 1999. *Cities and Citizenship*. Durham, N.C.: Duke University Press.

Huangpu, Chongqing. 1992. "Dixi: Chinese Farmer's Theatre." *Drama Review* 36, 2 (T134), 106–17.

Iyer, L. K. A. 1988. *The Mysore Tribes and Castes*. Vol 4. Delhi: Mittal Publications.

Jacobs, Jane. 1996. *Edge of Empire: Postcolonialism and the City*. London: Routledge.

Jayapal, Maya. 1997. *Bangalore: The Story of a City*. Chennai: Eastwest Books (Madras), Pvt. Ltd.

Jois, B. S. Subramanya. 1988. *Karaga Mahashakti* [The Great Karaga Power]. Bangalore: Vahnikula Kshatriya (Tigalara) Vira Kumarara Sangha.

Joseph, May. 1999. *Nomadic Identities: The Performance of Citizenship*. Minneapolis: University of Minnesota Press.

Joshi, Heather, and Vijay Joshi. 1976. *Surplus Labour and the City: A Study of Bombay*. Delhi: Oxford University Press.

Kalia, Ravi. 1987. *Chandigarh: In Search of an Identity*. Carbondale: Southern Illinois University Press.

———. 1994. *Bhubaneswar: From Temple Town to a Capital City*. Carbondale: Southern Illinois University Press.

Kaliyaramurtti, V. S. 1990. *Tamil Nadu-Karnataka-Pondicherry Region Vanniyakula Kshatriya Social Revolution Volume, 2–10–90*. Kutantai [Kumbakonam] Lesser Circle Vanniyakula Kshatriya Sangam: Kumbakonam.

Kamath, Suryanath U. 1987. "Karnataka's Age-old Festival of Victory: Dasara Celebrations." *March of Karnataka* (September). Bangalore: Directorate of Information and Publicity, Government of Karnataka, 13–18.

Kammen, Michael G. 1991. *Mystic Chords of Memory: The Transformation of Tradition in American Culture*. New York: Knopf.

Kapadia, Karin. 1996. "Dancing the Goddess: Possession and Class in Tamil South India." *Modern Asian Studies* 30 (2): 423–45.

Karashima, Noboru. 1992. *Towards a New Formation: South Indian Society under Vijayanagar Rule*. Delhi: Oxford University Press.

Karnataka Backward Classes Classes Commission Report. 1975. 4 vol. Chairman, L. G. Havanur. Bangalore: Government of Karnataka.

Karnataka State Gazetteer Bangalore District. 1990. Bangalore: Government of Karnataka Publication.

Karnataka State Gazetteer Decennial Supplement (1983–93). 1994. Bangalore: Government of Karnataka Publication.

Karve, Irawati. 1965. *Kinship Organization in India*. Bombay: Asia Publishing House.

Kasson, John F. 1978. *Amusing the Million: Coney Island at the Turn of the Century*. New York: Hill and Wang.

Kersenboom, Saskia. 1995. *Word, Sound, Image: The Life of a Tamil Text*. Oxford and Washington, D.C.: Berg Publishers.

King, Anthony. 1990. *Urbanism, Colonialism and the World Economy: Cultural and Spatial Foundations of the World Economic System*. London: Routledge.

Kinsley, David. 1997. *Tantric Visions of the Divine Feminine: The Ten Mahavidyas*. Berkeley: University of California Press.

Kitazawa, Masakumi. 1992. "Myth, Performance and Politics."*Drama Review* 36, 3 (T135), 160–73.

Koch, Ebba. 1998. "Garden Palaces in the Mughal Garden Tradition." Illustrated lecture delivered as part of the 1998 Hagop Kevorkian Lectures in Near Eastern Art and Civilization, New York University, April 2.

Kondos, Vivienne. 1986. "Images of the Fierce Goddess and Portrayals of Hindu Women." *Contributions to Indian Sociology*, n.s., 20 (2): 173–97.

Kosambi, Meera. 1986. *Bombay in Transition: The Growth and Social Ecology of a Colonial City, 1880–1980*. Stockholm: Almqvist and Wiksell International.

Kuchler, Susanne, and Walter Melion, eds. 1991. *Images of Memory: On Remembering and Representation*. Washington, D.C.: Smithsonian Institution Press.

Kuppuswamy, B. 1978. *Backward Class Movement in Karnataka*. Bangalore: Bangalore University.

Labov, William. 1966. *Social Stratification of English in New York City*. Washington, D.C.: Center for Applied Linguistics.

Lakshmana, K. 1999. *Tigala Janangada Itihasa Mattu Karaga Shaktotsava* [The Tigala People's History and Karaga Shakti Festival]. Bangalore: Rashtrotthana Press.

Lefebvre, Henri. 1991. *The Production of Space*. Translated by Donald Nicholson. Oxford: Blackwell.

Lewandowski, Susan. 1980. *Migration and Ethnicity in Urban India: Kerala Migrants in the City of Madras, 1870–1970*. New Delhi: Manohar.

Llewellyn-Jones, Rosie. 1985. *A Fatal Friendship: The Nawabs, the British, and the City of Lucknow*. Delhi: Oxford University Press.

Ludden, David E. 1985. *Peasant History in South India*. Princeton: Princeton University Press.

Luhrmann, T. M. 1996. *The Good Parsi: The Fate of a Colonial Elite in Postcolonial Society*. Cambridge, Mass.: Harvard University Press.

Lutgendorf, Philip. 1997. "Imagining Ayodhya: Utopia and Its Shadows in a Hindu Landscape." *International Journal of Hindu Studies* 1 (1): 19–54.

Luther, Narendra. 1995. *Hyderabad: Memoirs of a City*. Hyderabad: Orient Longman.

Lynch, Kevin. 1960. *The Image of the City*. Cambridge, Mass.: MIT Press.

Lynch, Owen. 1969. *The Politics of Untouchability: Social Mobility and Social Change in a City of India*. New York: Columbia University Press.

Mahadev, P. D. 1975. *People, Space and Economy of an Indian City: An Urban Morphology of Mysore City*. Mysore: Institute of Development Studies, University of Mysore.

Mahalingam, T. V. 1975. *Administration and Social Life under Vijayanagar: Part 2*. 2nd edition. Madras: University of Madras.

Majumdar, Dhirendra Nath. [1960] 1975. *Social Contours of an Industrial City: Social Survey of Kanpur, 1954–56*. Westport, Conn.: Greenwood Press.

Majumdar, Prasanta S., and Ila Majumdar. 1978. *Rural Migrants in an Urban Setting: A Study of Two Shanty Colonies in the Capital City of India*. Delhi: Hindustan Publishing Corporation.

"Malurina Karaga Vaibhava [The Pomp of Malur's Karaga]." 1983. *Taranga*, May 1: 41–42.

Manor, James. 1977. *Political Change in an Indian State: Mysore, 1917–1955.* Canberra: Australian National University Publications.

———. 1980. "Pragmatic Progressives in Regional Politics: The Case of Dev Raj Urs." *Economic and Political Weekly,* Annual Number, 201–13.

———. 1989. "Karnataka: Caste, Class, Dominance and Politics in a Cohesive Society." In Francine R. Frankel and M. S. A. Rao, eds. *Dominance and State Power in Modern India. Decline of a Social Order.* Vol. 1. Delhi: Oxford University Press.

———. 1993. *Power, Poverty and Poison: Disaster and Response in an Indian City.* Delhi: Sage Publications.

McCarthy, Thomas. 1992. "Practical Discourse: On the Relation of Morality to Politics." In Craig Calhoun, ed. *Habermas and the Public Sphere.* Cambridge, Mass.: MIT Press, 51–72.

Merry, Karen L. 1982. "The Hindu Festival Calendar." In Guy R. Welbon and Glenn E. Yocum, eds. *Religious Festivals in South India and Sri Lanka.* Delhi: Manohar, 1–25.

Michell, George, and Richard Eaton. 1992. *Firuzabad: A Palace City of the Deccan.* London: Oxford University Press.

Mines, Mattison. 1994. *Public Faces, Private Voices: Community and Individuality in South India.* Berkeley: University of California Press.

Misra, Amaresh. 1998. *Lucknow: Fire of Grace. The Story of Its Revolution, Renaissance and the Aftermath.* New Delhi: HarperCollins Publishers India, Pvt. Ltd.

Moreno, Manuel, and McKim Marriot. 1989. "Humoural Transactions in Two Tamil Cults: Murukan and Mariyamman." *Contributions to Indian Sociology* 23 (1): 149–67.

Morrison, Kathleen D. 1993. "Supplying the City: The Role of Reservoirs in an Indian Urban Landscape." *Asian Perspectives* 32 (2): 133–51.

Mugali, R. S. [1946] 1990. *The Heritage of Karnataka.* Mysore: Geetha Book House.

Muir, Edward. 1981. *Civic Ritual in Renaissance Venice.* Princeton: Princeton University Press.

Munivenkatappa, S. M. No date. *Karaga Mahotsava* [The Great Karaga Festival]. Bangalore: Horticultural Press.

———. 1950. *Tarakari Belagalu* [Vegetable Produce]. 2nd ed. Bangalore: Vahnikula and Company.

———. 1957. *Help Tigala Class.* Bangalore: Power Press.

Mysore Gazetteer. 1927–30. 5 volumes. Ed. C. Hayavadana Rao. Bangalore: Government Press.

Naidu, B. N. 1996. *Intellectual History of Colonial India: Mysore 1831–1920.* Jaipur and New Delhi: Rawat Publications.

Nanjundayya. H. V., and L. Krishna Ananthakrishna Iyer. 1928–35. *The Mysore Tribes and Castes.* 4 volumes. Mysore: Mysore University.

Narendra, K. V. 1993. *Lakes of Bangalore: The Current Scenario.* Bangalore: Centre for Science and Technology.

New Catholic Encyclopaedia. 1967. Vol. 7. New York: McGraw Hill Book Co.: 500–501.

Nilekani, Rohini. 1998. *Stillborn: A Medical Thriller.* New Delhi: Penguin Books.

Nora, Pierre. 1989. "Between Memory and History: Les Lieux de Memoire." *Representations* 26 (Spring): 7–25.

Nzegwu, Nkiru. 1996. "Bypassing New York in Re-Presenting Eko: Production of Space in a Nigerian City." In Anthony D. King, ed. *Re-Presenting the City: Ethnicity, Capital and Culture in the Twenty-first-Century Metropolis.* New York: New York University Press, 111–36.

Obeyesekere, Gananath. 1984. *The Cult of the Goddess Pattini.* Chicago: Chicago University Press.

Oldenburg, Philip. 1976. *Big City Government in India: Councilor, Administrator, and Citizen in India.* Tucson: University of Arizona Press.

Olivelle, Patrick. 1998. "Hair and Society: Social Significance of Hair in South Asian Traditions." In Alf Hiltebeitel and Barabara D. Miller, eds. *Hair: Its Power and Meaning in Asian Cultures.* Albany: State University of New York Press, 11–49.

Pani, Narendra. 1983. *Reforms to Pre-empt Change: Land Legislation in Karnataka.* New Delhi: Concept Publishers.

Pantham, Thomas. 1976. *Political Parties and Democratic Census: A Study of Party Organizations in an Indian City.* Delhi: Macmillan Co. of India.

Patel, Sujatha, and Alice Thorner, eds. 1995a. *Bombay: Metaphor for Modern India.* Bombay: Oxford University Press.

———, eds. 1995b. *Bombay: Mosaic of Modern Culture.* Bombay: Oxford University Press.

Perera, Nihal. 1996. "Exploring Colombo: The Relevance of a Knowledge of New York." In Anthony D. King, ed. *Re-Presenting the City: Ethnicity, Capital and Culture in the Twenty-first-Century Metropolis.* New York: New York University Press, 137–57.

Pethe, Vasant P. 1964. *Demographic Profiles of an Urban Population.* Bombay: Popular Prakashan.

Pieper, Jan. 1980. "The Spatial Structure of Suchindram." In Jan Pieper, ed. *Ritual Space in India: Studies in Architectural Anthropology.* Max Mueller Bhavan, Bombay and Art and Archaeology Papers, London, 65–80.

Pillay, K. K. 1975. *A Social History of the Tamils.* Vol. 1. Madras University Historical Series. No. 25. Madras: University of Madras.

Pocock, D. F. 1960. "Sociologies: Urban and Rural." *Contributions to Indian Sociology,* IV: 63–81.

Prakasa, Rao, V. L. S., and Vinod K. Tewari. 1986. "The Ecological Structure of Bangalore." In Vinod K. Tewari, Jay A. Weinstein, and V. L. S. Prakasa Rao, eds. *Indian Cities: Ecological Perspectives.* New Delhi: Concept Publishing Company, 221–42.

Prayer Book of Infant Jesus. 1979. Bangalore: Infant Jesus Church.

Puttaiya, B. 1923. "Kempe Gowda Chiefs." *The Quarterly Journal of the Mythic Society* 13 (4): 723–41.

Rajapurohit, A. R. 1982. "Land Reform and Changing Agrarian Structure in Karnataka." Bangalore: Institute for Social and Economic Change, mimeograph.

Ramanujan, A. K. 1975. *The Inner Landscape: Love Poems from a Classical Tamil Anthology.* Bloomington: Indiana University Press.

Rame Gowda, K. S. 1977. "Bangalore: Planning in Practice." In Allen G. Noble and Ashok K. Dutt, eds. *Indian Urbanization and Planning: Vehicles of Modernization.* New Delhi: Tata McGraw-Hill Publishing Co., Ltd.: 294–312.

Ramu, G. N. 1988. *Family Structure and Fertility: Emerging Patterns in an Indian City.* New Delhi: Sage Publications.

Rao, Hayavadana C. 1924. "Derivation of the Name 'Bangalore.'" *Quarterly Journal of the Mythic Society* 14 (3): 238–40.

Rao, S. K. Ramachandra. 1978. *Bengalurina Karaga* [Bangalore's Karaga]. Bangalore: India Book House.

———. 1994. *Life and Light of Sri Thiruchi Swamigal.* Bangalore: Sri Kailasa Asrama Maha-Samsthana.

Rao, Velcheru Narayana. 1986. "Epics and Indologies: Six Telugu Folk Epics." In S. H. Blackburn and A. K. Ramanujam, eds. *Another Harmony: New Essays on the Folklore of India.* Berkeley: University of California Press, 131–64.

———. 1989. "Tricking the Goddess: Cowherd Katamaraju and the Goddess Ganga in the Telugu Folk Epic." In Alf Hiltebeitel, ed. *Criminal Gods and Demon Devotees.* Albany: State University of New York Press, 105–21.

Rao, Velcheru Narayana, David Shulman, and Sanjay Subrahmanyam. 1992. *Symbols of Substance: Court and State in Nayaka Period Tamilnadu.* Delhi: Oxford University Press.

Ratte, Christopher. 1998. "The Corpse in the City: Intramural Burial and Civic Space in Ancient Greece." Paper presented at the International Center for Advanced Studies, New York University.

Rau, M. P. Somasekhara, ed. 1968. *Growth of Local Self-Government in Bangalore City.* Bangalore: Gokhale Institute of Public Affairs.

Ravindra, A. 1996. *Urban Land Policy: A Metropolitan Perspective.* New Delhi: Concept Publishers.

Ray, Rajat Kanta. 1979. *Urban Roots of Indian Nationalism: Pressure Groups and Conflict of Interests in Calcutta City Politics, 1875–1939.* New Delhi: Vikas.

Richmond, Farley P., Darius L. Swann, and Phillip B. Zarilli, eds. 1991. *Indian Theatre: Traditions of Performance.* Honolulu: University of Hawaaii Press.

Roach, Joseph. 1996. *Cities of the Dead: Circum-Atlantic Performance.* New York: Columbia University Press.

Roghair, Gene H. 1982. *The Epic of Palnadu: A Study and Translation of Palnati Virula Katha, a Telugu Oral Tradition from Andhra Pradesh, India.* Oxford: Clarendon Press.

Rosenthal, Donald B., ed. 1976. *The City in Indian Politics.* Faridabad: Thomson Press.

Rowe, William L. 1973. "Caste, Kinship and Association in Urban India." In Aidan Southall, ed. *Urban Sociology.* New York: Oxford University Press, 211–49.

Rudolph, Lloyd I., and Susanne Hoeber Rudolph. 1967. *The Modernity of Tradition: Political Development in India.* Chicago: University of Chicago Press.

Ryan, Mary. 1997. *Civic Wars: Democracy and Public Life in the American City during the Nineteenth Century.* Berkeley: University of California Press.

Samaj, Bharat Sevak. 1958. *Slums of Old Delhi: Report of the Socio-economic Survey of the Slum Dwellers of Old Delhi City.* Delhi: A. Ram.

Sassen, Saskia. 2000. *Cities in a World Economy.* 2nd edition. Thousand Oaks, Calif.: Pine Forge Press.

Schama, Simon. 1995. *Landscape and Memory.* New York: Knopf.

Seidman, Steven, ed. 1989. *Jürgen Habermas on Society and Politics.* Boston: Beacon Press.

Selvadurai, Shyam. 1998. *Cinnamon Gardens.* New York: Penguin Books.

Sen, Jai. 1975. *The Unintended City: An Essay on the City of the Poor.* Calcutta: Cathedral Social and Relief Services.

Sennet, Richard. 1974. *The Fall of Public Man.* New York: W. W. Norton.

———. 1996. *Flesh and Stone: The Body and the City in Western Civilisation.* New York: W. W. Norton.

Shafi, Sayed S. 1996. "The 'Third Wave' Option." *Seminar* 445 (September): 20–24.

Shulman, David Dean. 1980. *Tamil Temple Myths: Sacrifice and Divine Marriage in the South Indian Saiva Tradition.* Princeton: Princeton University Press.

Simo, Fr. Anthony. No date. *History of the Archdiocese of Bangalore.* Vol. 1. Bangalore: St. Paul's Press.

Singer, Milton. 1972. *When a Great Tradition Modernizes.* Chicago: Chicago University Press.

———. 1991. *Semiotics of Cities, Selves, and Cultures: Explorations in Semiotic Anthropology.* Berlin: Mouton de Gruyter.

Sinopoli, Carla M. 1993. "Defining a Sacred Landscape: Temple Architecture and Divine Images in the Vijayanagara Suburbs." In Adalbert J. Gail and Gerd J. R. Mevissen, eds. *South Asian Archaeology 1991.* Stuttgart: Franz Steiner Verlag, 625–35.

———. 1997. "Nucleated Settlements in the Vijayanagara Metropolitan Region." In Raymond Allchin and Bridget Allchin, eds. *South Asian Archaeology 1995.* New Delhi and Calcutta: Oxford and IBH Publishing Co., Pvt. Ltd., and Science Publishers Inc., U.S.A.

Sinopoli, Carla M., and Kathleen D. Morrison. 1995. "Dimensions of Imperial Control: The Vijayanagara Capital." *American Anthropologist* 97 (1): 83–96.

Smith, Bardwell, and Holly Baker Reynolds, eds. 1987. *The City as a Sacred Center: Essays on Six South Asian Contexts.* Leiden: E. J. Brill.

Sontheimer, Gunther-Deitz. 1993. *Pastoral Deities in Western India.* Delhi: Oxford University Press.

Sorokin, Michael, ed. 1992. *Variations on a Theme Park: The New American City and the End of Public Space.* New York: Hill and Wang.

Souvenir St. Mary's Basilica. 1974. Bangalore: St. Mary's Basilica.

Srinivas, Smriti. 1995. "Cults, Charisma, and Modernity: The Constituency of Faith in South India." Manuscript, Institute for Social and Economic Change, Bangalore.

———. 1997. "Draupadi's Story: Symbolism and Practice in the Karaga Performance." Manuscript, India Foundation for the Arts and Institute for Social and Economic Change, Bangalore.

———. 1998. *The Mouths of People, The Voice of God: Buddhists and Muslims in a Frontier Community of Ladakh.* Delhi: Oxford University Press.

———. 1999a. "Hot Bodies and Cooling Substances: Rituals of Sport in a Science City." *Journal of Sport and Social Issues* 23 (1): 24–40.

———. 1999b. "The Brahmin and the Fakir: Suburban Religiosity in the Cult of Shirdi Sai Baba." *Journal of Contemporary Religion* 14 (2): 245–61.

Stein, Burton. 1989. *Vijayanagara.* Cambridge: Cambridge University Press.

Sundara Rao, B. N. 1985. *Bengalurina Ithihasa* [A History of Bangalore]. Bangalore: Vasanta Sahitya Granthamala.

Tanaka, Masakazu. 1991. *Patrons, Devotees and Goddesses: Ritual and Power among the Tamil Fishermen of Sri Lanka.* Kyoto: Kyoto University Institute for Research in Humanities.

Tapper, Bruce Elliot. 1979. "Widows and Goddesses: Female Roles in Deity Symbolism in a South Indian Village." *Contributions to Indian Sociology,* n.s., 13 (1): 1–31.

Tarn, John Nelson. 1980. "Housing Reform and the Emergence of Town-Planning in Britian Before 1914." In Anthony Sutcliffe, ed. *The Rise of Modern Urban Planning 1800–1914.* London: Mansell Publishing, 71–97.

Taylor, Ian, and Ruth Jamieson. 1997. "'Proper Little Mesters': Nostalgia and Protest Masculinity in De-industrialised Sheffield." In Sallie Westwood and John Williams, eds. *Imagining Cities: Scripts, Signs, Memories.* London: Routledge, 152–78.

Thimmaiah, G. 1993. *Power Politics and Social Justice.* New Delhi: Sage Publications.

Thippaiah, P. 1993. Informal Sector and the Urban Poor in a Metropolitan Area: A Case Study of Bangalore. Ph.D. dissertation, Bangalore University.

Thrift, N. J. 1996. *Spatial Formations.* Thousand Oaks, Calif.: Sage Publications.

Thurston, E. [1909] 1975. *Castes and Tribes of Southern India.* Vol. 7. Delhi: Cosmo Publications.

Tillotson, G. H. R., ed. 1998. *Paradigms of Indian Architecture: Space and Time in Representation and Design.* Richmond, Surrey: Curzon.

Trautmann, Thomas R. 1981. *Dravidian Kinship.* Cambridge: Cambridge University Press.

Uberoi, J. P. S. 1978. *Science and Culture.* New Delhi: Oxford University Press.

Venkatachalam, Lakshmi. 1998. "Outer Ring Road (ORR)." Paper presented at the seminar "Status of Infrastructure in Karnataka: A Year After," Bangalore.

Venkatarayappa, K. N. 1957. *Bangalore (A Socio-Ecological Study).* Sociological Series No. 6, University of Bombay Publications. Bombay: University of Bombay.

Venkataswaminayaka Varma, K. R. 1919. *Vanhivamsha Darpana* [A Mirror of the Vahni Lineage]. Bangalore.

Venkatesa Acharya, Kambaluru. 1981. *Mahabharata and Variations: Perundevanar and Pampa.* Kurnool: Vyasaraja Publications.

Vidyarthi, L. P. 1969. *Cultural Configuration of Ranchi: Survey of an Emerging Industrial City of Tribal India, 1960–62.* Calcutta: J. N. Basu.

Visvanathan, Shiv. 1997. *A Carnival for Science: Essays on Science, Technology and Development.* Delhi: Oxford University Press.

Volosinov, V. N. [1927] 1987. *Freudianism: A Critical Sketch.* Bloomington: Indiana University Press.

———. [1930] 1973. *Marxism and the Philosophy of Language.* New York: Seminar Press.

Vyasulu, Vinod, and Amulya Kumar N. Reddy, convenors. 1985. *Essays on Bangalore.* 4 volumes. Bangalore: Karnataka State Council for Science and Technology, Indian Institute of Science.

Waghorne, Joanne Punzo. 1999. "The Diaspora of the Gods: Hindu Temples in the New World System 1640–1800." *Journal of Asian Studies* 58 (3): 648–86.

Wallace, Mike. 1996. *Mickey Mouse History and Other Essays on American Memory.* Philadelphia: Temple University Press.

Wallerstein, Immanuel. 1974. *The Modern World-System,* Vol. 1: *Capitalist Agriculture and the Origins of the European World-Economy in the Sixteenth Century.* New York: Academic Press.

Watts, Michael. 1996. "Mapping Identities: Place, Space, and Community in an African City." In Patricia Yaeger, ed. *The Geography of Identity.* Ann Arbor: University of Michigan Press, 59–97.

White, David Gordon. 1996. *The Alchemical Body: Siddha Traditions in Medieval India.* Chicago: University of Chicago Press.

Whitehead, H. 1921. *The Village Gods of South India.* Calcutta: Association Press.

Worthern, W. B. 1995. "Disciplines of the Text/Sites of Performance." *Drama Review* 39, 1 (T145), 13–28.

Yaeger, Patricia, ed. 1996. "Introduction: Narrating Space." In Patricia Yaeger, ed. *The Geography of Identity.* Ann Arbor: University of Michigan Press, 1–38.

Yang, Anand. 1999. *Bazaar India: Markets, Society and the Colonial State in Bihan.* Berkeley: University of California Press.

Zarrilli, Phillip B. 1994. "Actualizing Power(s) and Crafting a Self in Kalarippayattu: A South Indian Martial Art and the Yoga and Ayurvedic Paradigms." *Journal of Asian Martial Arts* 3 (3): 10–51.

Index

Abhimanyu, M., 99, 145
Abu-Lughod, Janet, 16
Adam's Peak, 92
Agamudaiyan, 101
Agni Banniraya, 99, 102, 126
Agnikula Kshatriyas, 98, 99, 102–3, 108,
112, 118, 125–26, 136, 283 n.17
Agnikula Kshatriya Sangha, 102–3
Agra, 43
Agri-Horticultural Society, 44
Aiyangar, Krishnaswami S., 110
Akkipet, 3
Albert, Prince of Wales, 47
Ali, Haider. *See* Haider Ali
Alter, Joseph S., 144
Ambalagar, 101
Ambasura, 213, 214–15, 217, 218, 223,
225, 227–29, 231
Amitabh Bacchan Corporation, Ltd.,
238, 297 n.2
Andhra Pradesh, xxv, 21, 69, 93, 117, 129
Anekal, 194, 195, 197, 240
Anekal Gate, 40
Angirasa, 99
Anglo-Mysore wars, 3, 39–40, 44, 237,
279 n.13
Anjaneya (Hanuman), 41, 77–78, 94,
144, 146, 150, 151, 193–94, 278 n.8
Anjaneya Temple, 73
Annaiappa (wrestler), 123, 286 n.64
Annamma, 70, 77, 109

Annamma Temple, 41, 72, 74, 77, 189,
192–94
Aralinga Raju, 211, 218
Arati Dipa, 163–64. *See also* Karaga *jatre*
Arcot district, 23
Arif Shah Bawa. *See* Bawa, Arif Shah
Arjuna: and Draupadi, xviii, 151, 156,
158–59, 162, 173, 175, 246; in *Karaga
Purana*, 206, 207, 211, 219–21, 229,
230, 231–32
Arkavati River, 55
Arokiamariamma, 79–82, 94, 95
Artillery and Cavalry Barracks, 79
Asia, 16
Asian Development Bank, 239
Assayag, Jackie, 83
Aurangazeb, 2
Avenue Road, 192
Ayodhya, 117, 297 n.47
Ayurveda, 144, 156
al-Azam Dastgir, Ghauth, 84

Backward Caste, 131
Backward Classes, 68, 98, 109, 131, 139,
242; commissions, 114–17; move-
ment, 112–18, 284 n.36. *See also* Chin-
nappa Reddy Third Backward Classes
Commission; Havanur Backward
Classes Commission; Nagana Gowda
Committee; Venkataswamy Second
Backward Classes Commission

Smriti Srinivas received a Ph.D. in sociology from the Delhi School of Economics, India, and has taught sociology at the Institute for Social and Economic Change in Bangalore. She is currently assistant professor in the Division of Comparative Studies in the Humanities, Ohio State University. She is author of *The Mouths of People, the Voice of God: Buddhists and Muslims in a Frontier Community of Ladakh,* which focuses on a Himalayan region between India, China, and Pakistan, and of numerous articles on the city and contemporary religious movements and practices.